THE ROMANTIC POETS
BLAKE, WORDSWORTH, AND COLERIDGE

The Romantic Poets
Blake, Wordsworth,
and Coleridge

With an Introduction and
Contemporary Criticism

Edited by JOSEPH PEARCE
and ROBERT ASCH

IGNATIUS PRESS   SAN FRANCISCO

Cover art: "The Cross in the Mountains", 1808, Caspar David Friedrich
Galerie Neue Meister, Dresden, German/© Staatliche
Kunstsammlungen Dresden/Bridgeman Images

Cover design by John Herreid

ISBN 978-1-58617-264-0
Library of Congress Control Number 2014936822
Printed in India ⊗

Dedicated to Stratford and Leonie Caldecott

Tradition is the extension of Democracy through time; it is the proxy of the dead and the enfranchisement of the unborn.

Tradition may be defined as the extension of the franchise. Tradition means giving votes to the most obscure of all classes, our ancestors. It is the democracy of the dead. Tradition refuses to submit to the small and arrogant oligarchy of those who merely happen to be walking about. All democrats object to men being disqualified by the accident of birth; tradition objects to their being disqualified by the accident of death. Democracy tells us not to neglect a good man's opinion, even if he is our groom; tradition asks us not to neglect a good man's opinion, even if he is our father. I, at any rate, cannot separate the two ideas of democracy and tradition.

—G. K. Chesterton

Ignatius Critical Editions—Tradition-Oriented Criticism for a new generation

CONTENTS

Contemporary Criticisms

INTRODUCTION

William Blake (1757–1827), William Wordsworth (1770–1850), and Samuel Taylor Coleridge (1772–1834) are sometimes called the early Romantic poets, in recognition of their pioneering role in English Romanticism and as a means of distinguishing them from the second generation of Romantic poets, of which the most prominent were Lord Byron (1788–1824), Percy Shelley (1792–1822), and John Keats (1795–1821). In order to understand the importance of these hugely influential poets, we need to know something about Romanticism itself. What is Romanticism? Is it right or wrong? Is it right or left? Is it revolutionary or reactionary? What *is* it? Such questions are not academic, nor are they unimportant. On the contrary, they help us to understand the world in which we live.

In the afterword to the third edition of *The Pilgrim's Regress*, C.S. Lewis complained that "romanticism" had acquired so many different meanings that, as a word, it had become meaningless. "I would not now use this word ... to describe anything," he complained, "for I now believe it to be a word of such varying senses that it has become useless and should be banished from our vocabulary."[1] *Pace* Lewis, if we banished words because they have multifarious meanings or because their meanings are abused or debased by maladroit malapropism, we should soon find it impossible to say *anything* at all. Take, for example, the word "love". Few words are more abused, yet few words are more axiomatic to an understanding of ourselves. John Lennon and Jesus Christ do not have the same thing in

[1] C.S. Lewis, afterword to *The Pilgrim's Regress: An Allegorical Apology for Christianity Reason and Romanticism*, third edition (Grand Rapids: William B. Eerdmans, 1992), p. 200.

mind when they speak of love. C. S. Lewis understood this, of course. He understood it so well that he wrote a whole book on the subject. In *The Four Loves* he sought to *define* "love". And what is true of a word such as "love" is equally true of a word like "Romanticism". If we are to advance in understanding, we must abandon the notion of abolishing the word and commence instead with a definition of our terms. Lewis, in spite of his protestations, understood this also, proceeding from his plaintive call for the abolition of the word to the enumerating of various definitions of it, claiming that "we can distinguish at least seven kinds of things which are called 'romantic'."[2] From four loves to seven Romanticisms, Lewis was not about to abandon meaning, or the *mens sana*, to men without minds or chests.

Since Lewis' seven separate definitions of Romanticism are a little unwieldy, it is necessary to hone our definition of Romanticism into an encompassing unity within which the other definitions can be said to subsist. What makes Romanticism distinct, or, to return to our initial question, what *is* it? According to the *Collins Dictionary of Philosophy*, Romanticism is "a style of thinking and looking at the world that dominated 19th century Europe".[3] Arising in early medieval culture, it referred originally to tales in the Romance language about courtly love and other sentimental topics, as distinct from works in classical Latin. From the beginning, therefore, "Romanticism" stood in contradistinction to "classicism". The former referred to an outlook marked by refined and responsive *feelings* and thus could be said to be inward-looking, subjective, "sensitive", and given to noble dreams; the latter is marked by empiricism, governed by science and precise measures, and could be said to be outward-looking.

Having defined our terms, albeit in the broadest and most sweeping sense, we can proceed to a discussion of the ways in which society has oscillated between the two alternative

---

[2] Ibid.
[3] *Collins Dictionary of Philosophy* (London: Collins, 1990).

visions of reality represented by classicism and Romanticism. First, however, we must insist that the oscillation is itself an aberration. It is a product of modernity. In the Middle Ages there was no such oscillation between these two extremes of perception. On the contrary, the medieval world was characterized by, indeed it was defined by, a theological and philosophical unity that transcended the division between Romanticism and classicism. The nexus of philosophy and theology in the Platonic-Augustinian and Aristotelian-Thomistic view of man represented the fusion of *fides et ratio*, the uniting of faith and reason. Take, for example, the use of the figurative or the allegorical in medieval literature, or the use of symbolism in medieval art. The function of the figurative in medieval art and literature was not intended primarily to arouse spontaneous *feelings* in the observer or reader, but to encourage the observer or reader to see the philosophical or theological significance beneath the symbolic configuration. In this sense, medieval art, informed by medieval philosophy and theology, is much more objective and outward-looking than the most "realistic" examples of modern art. The former points to abstract ideas that are the fruits of a philosophical tradition existing independently of either the artist or the observer; the latter derives its "realism" solely from the feelings and emotions of those "experiencing" it. One demands that the artist or the observer reach beyond himself to the transcendent truth that is out there; the other recedes into the transient feelings of subjective experience. The surrender of the transcendental to the transient, the perennial to the ephemeral, is the mark of "post-Christian", and postrational, society. It is also a consequence of the triumph of the subjectivism of a certain type of Romanticism.

The Romantic reaction in England could be said to have had its genesis in 1798 with the publication of *Lyrical Ballads* by Wordsworth and Coleridge. Published only nine years after the French Revolution, the poems in *Lyrical Ballads* represented the poets' recoil from the rationalism that had led to the Reign of Terror. Wordsworth would pass beyond the "serene and blessed mood"[4] of optimistic pantheism displayed in his "Lines composed a few miles above Tintern Abbey" to a full embrace of Anglican Christianity as exhibited in the allegorical depiction of Christ in "Resolution and Independence". Coleridge threw down the allegorical gauntlet of Christianity in "The Rime of the Ancient Mariner", and, in his "Hymn before Sun-Rise, in the Vale of Chamouni", he saw beyond majestic nature ("O sovran BLANC!" [see p. 391, line 3]) to the majesty of the God of nature:

> Who made you glorious as the Gates of Heaven
> Beneath the keen full moon? Who bade the sun
> Clothe you with rainbows? Who, with living flowers
> Of loveliest blue, spread garlands at your feet?—
> GOD! let the torrents, like a shout of nations,
> Answer! and let the ice-plains echo, GOD!
> GOD! sing ye meadow-streams with gladsome voice!
> Ye pine-groves, with your soft and soul-like sounds!
> And they too have a voice, yon piles of snow,
> And in their perilous fall shall thunder, GOD!
>
> (See pp. 393–94, lines 54–63.)

In their reaction against the Enlightenment, Wordsworth and Coleridge had rediscovered the purity and passion of Christianity. In his own quixotically eccentric way, William Blake was also reacting against the Enlightenment, lamenting, in a short poem in his Preface to *Milton*, the "dark Satanic Mills" (see p. 79, line 8) of industrialism. Although he shared the desire of Wordsworth and Coleridge for a purer vision untainted by Enlightenment rationalism, his dabbling in theology was singularly peculiar and ultimately heterodox.

The pattern of reaction initiated by the first wave of Romantic poets would be repeated in the various manifestations

---

[4] William Wordsworth, "Lines composed a few miles above Tintern Abbey, on revisiting the banks of the Wye during a Tour, July 13, 1798", in *The Romantic Poets*, ed. Joseph Pearce and Robert Asch, vol. 1, Ignatius Critical Editions (San Francisco: Ignatius Press, 2014), p. 126, line 41. Subsequent quotations from this edition will be cited in the text.

of neo-medievalism that would follow in its wake and which were a consequence of its influence. The Gothic Revival— heralded by the architect Augustus Pugin in the 1830s, and championed by the art critic John Ruskin twenty years later— sought to discover a purer aesthetic through a return to medieval notions of beauty. The Oxford Movement—spearheaded by John Henry Newman, Edward Pusey, and John Keble— sought a return to a purer Catholic vision for the Church of England, leapfrogging the Reformation in an attempt to graft the Victorian Anglican church onto the Catholic Church of medieval England through the promotion of Catholic liturgy and a Catholic understanding of ecclesiology and the sacraments. The pre-Raphaelite Brotherhood—formed sometime around 1850 by Dante Gabriel Rossetti, John Everett Millais, William Holman Hunt, and others—sought a purer vision of art by leapfrogging the art of the Late Renaissance in pursuit of the clarity of medieval and Early Renaissance painting that existed, so the pre-Raphaelites believed and as their name implied, prior to the innovations of Raphael.

Perhaps the most important poetic voice to emerge from the Romantic reaction is that of Gerard Manley Hopkins, who was received into the Catholic Church by John Henry Newman in 1866, twenty-one years after Newman's own conversion. Influenced by the pre-Reformation figures of Saint Francis of Assisi and Duns Scotus, and by the Counter-Reformation rigor and vigor of Saint Ignatius Loyola, Hopkins wrote poetry filled with the dynamism of religious orthodoxy. Unpublished in his own lifetime, Hopkins was destined to emerge as one of the most influential poets of the twentieth century following the first publication of his verse in 1918, almost thirty years after his death.

Although these manifestations of Romantic neo-medievalism transformed nineteenth-century culture, countering the optimistic and triumphalistic scientism of the Victorian imperial psyche, it would be wrong to imply that Romanticism always led to medievalism. The neo-medieval tendencies of what might be termed light Romanticism were paralleled by a dark

Romanticism, epitomized by the life and work of Byron and Shelley, which tended toward subjectivism and introspective self-indulgence.

If Wordsworth and Coleridge were reacting against the rationalist iconoclasm of the French Revolution, Byron and Shelley seemed to be reacting *against* Wordsworth's and Coleridge's reaction. Greatly influenced by *Lyrical Ballads*, Byron and Shelley were nonetheless uncomfortable at the Christian traditionalism that Wordsworth and Coleridge began to embrace. Byron devoted a great deal of the Preface to *Childe Harold's Pilgrimage* to attacking the "monstrous mummeries of the middle ages",[5] and Shelley, in his "Defense of Poetry", anathematized tradition by insisting that poets were slaves to the zeitgeist and that they were "the mirrors of the gigantic shadows which futurity casts upon the present".[6] Slaves of the spirit of the present, and mirrors of the giant presence of the future, poets were warriors of progress intent on vanquishing the superstitious remnants of tradition. Perhaps these iconoclastic musings could be seen as transient youthful idealism, especially as there appeared to be signs that Byron yearned for something more solid than the inarticulate creedless deism espoused in "The Prayer of Nature", and signs also that Shelley's militant atheism was softening into skylarking pantheism. Their early deaths, and the early death of their confrère, Keats, has preserved them forever as icons of youth whose poetry often attained heights of beauty and perception that transcended the incoherence of their philosophy.

The Byronic aura of the second generation of Romantics crossed the Channel and metamorphosed into the Decadence of Baudelaire, Verlaine, and Huysmans, all of whom plumbed the depths of despair before recoiling in horror into the arms of the Catholic Church. The symbolism of the French Decadence recrossed the Channel under the patronage of Oscar Wilde,

---

[5] George Gordon Byron, *The Poetical Works of Lord Byron*, ed. Henry Frowde (Oxford, 1807), p. 175.

[6] Percy Bysshe Shelley, *The Selected Poetry and Prose of Shelley* (Ware, Hertfordshire, U.K.: Wordsworth Poetry Library, 2002), p. 660.

who was an aficionado of Baudelaire, Verlaine, and Huysmans. From the publication of *Lyrical Ballads* in 1798 to the death of Oscar Wilde in 1900, Romanticism could be seen, in large part, to be a reaction against the rationalism of the Enlightenment. It was, however, schizophrenic. The "light" Romanticism of Wordsworth and Coleridge staggered falteringly in the direction of a revitalized Christianity; the "dark" Romanticism of Byron, Shelley, and Keats led eventually to subjectivism, nihilism, and postmodernism.

Let's conclude by returning to our original questions. What is Romanticism? At its best, it is the generally healthy reaction of the heart to the hardness of the head. Is it right or wrong? It is often brilliantly right and sometimes disastrously wrong, but, in the words of the greatly misunderstood Romantic King Lear, it is perhaps "more sinned against than sinning".[7] Is it right or left? It is neither and defies all efforts to be classified thus. Is it revolutionary or reactionary? It depends, of course, on how we are defining our terms. If, however, we are referring to political revolutions of the ilk of 1789 and 1917, it is counterrevolutionary and reactionary, at least in its English manifestation. What *is* it? It is, at its best, an effort to rediscover what has been lost—a groping in the depths of experience and in the darkness of modernity for the light of truth that tradition preserves. For, as Oscar Wilde reminds us, in his *Lady Windermere's Fan*, "We are all in the gutter but some of us are looking at the stars".

William Blake

Apart from his poetry, Blake is also known as an artist, engraver, and mystic. Born in London on November 28, 1757, his first volume of poetry, *Poetical Sketches*, was published in 1783. Two further collections of verse, *Songs of Innocence* (1789) and *Songs of Experience* (1794), are expressions of loathing for

---

[7] William Shakespeare, *King Lear*, Act 3, scene 2, line 60.

industrialism, rationalism, and materialism. The latter volume also encapsulated the poet's disillusionment with the brutal idealism of the French Revolution and its murderous consequences. In this disillusionment, Blake's reaction parallels that of Wordsworth and Coleridge. Although Blake's poetry predates the publication of Wordsworth and Coleridge's *Lyrical Ballads*, the two younger poets are usually credited with heralding the Romantic age in English poetry because their collaborative volume made an immediate impact, whereas Blake's poetry was not widely read or very influential at the time.

His mystical and prophetical works include the *Book of Thel* (1789), *The Marriage of Heaven and Hell* (1791), and *The Song of Los* (1795). Animated by a quixotically idiosyncratic blend of quasi-Christianity, anticlericalism, antirationalism, and religious dualism, the singularity of Blake's mystical musings brings to mind the quip that mysticism begins in mist and ends in schism. Certainly his mysticism is anything but orthodox.

In *The Marriage of Heaven and Hell*, he wrote that Milton "wrote in fetters when he wrote of Angels & God, and at liberty when of Devils & Hell ... because he was a true Poet and of the Devil's party without knowing it" (see p. 49). This view of *Paradise Lost* was taken up by Percy Shelley in his "Defense of Poetry" and resonates throughout Mary Shelley's *Frankenstein*.

Blake's most important works of art are inspired by Christian literary and biblical themes, such as *The Canterbury Pilgrims*, *Jacob's Dream*, and *The Last Judgment*. In 1826, when he was almost seventy, he published his *Illustrations of the Book of Job*, considered by many to be his finest artistic achievement. At the time of his death, he was working on illustrations to Dante's *Divine Comedy*. He died in London on August 12, 1827.

William Wordsworth

Born in 1770 in Cockermouth, a small town in England's Lake District, William Wordsworth was a student at Cambridge at the time of the French Revolution (1789) and readily imbibed the radical ideas that had inspired it. In the following year, during a walking tour in France, he saw the postrevolutionary nation during the brief honeymoon period before the onslaught of the Great Terror. Inspired by a youthful idealism, his early poetry reflects a passionate adherence to the social creed of the revolution and to the atheist ideas of William Godwin. By 1795, however, he had rejected both the revolution and Godwinism under the benign influence of his sister, Dorothy, and also of his friend and fellow poet Samuel Taylor Coleridge, who had renounced his own revolutionary sympathies.

Opening with Coleridge's "Rime of the Ancient Mariner" and concluding with Wordsworth's "Tintern Abbey", the *Lyrical Ballads* made an immediate impact. Thereafter Wordsworth wrote some of the finest poetry in the English language in which his spiritual progress from pseudo-pantheism to Anglican Christianity is made manifest.

In 1843 he succeeded Robert Southey as poet laureate, a measure of the high esteem in which he was held by his contemporaries. He died at Rydal Mount, his home in the Lake District, on St. George's Day (April 23), 1850. It was indeed appropriate that one of England's finest poets should die on the feast day of England's patron saint and, even more significantly, on the anniversary of Shakespeare's death.

Samuel Taylor Coleridge

Two years younger than Wordsworth, Coleridge was born in 1772, the son of the Anglican vicar of Ottery St. Mary in Devon. Like Wordsworth, Coleridge was educated at Cambridge University and imbibed the same revolutionary ideas. In 1794 he met with Robert Southey in Bristol, and the two poets discussed plans to set up a "pantisocracy", a sort of socialist commune, on the banks of the Susquehanna River in the United States. The utopian scheme came to nothing, not least because Coleridge was becoming disillusioned with radical politics. In "Ode to France", published in his first book of poetry (1796), he recanted his revolutionary views. In religion he had lapsed from the conventional Anglicanism of his youth into a belief in Unitarianism, preaching at Unitarian chapels in Bristol. It was at around this time that he met and befriended Wordsworth, a friendship destined to bear immortal fruit in the collaboration on the above-mentioned *Lyrical Ballads*.

The friendship with Wordsworth and the success of the *Ballads* seemed to bode well for Coleridge's future career as a poet, but his descent into opium addiction heralded a crisis in confidence and a moral torpor that are expressed in his "Dejection: An Ode" (1802), in which he confessed his own failure and distanced himself publicly from the pantheistic tendencies in Wordsworth's verse. Relations between the two men remained strained for the rest of their lives.

Coleridge would never regain the confidence or the inspiration that radiates from his early verse and, apart from these early poems, he is best known to posterity as a philosopher, critic, and defender of Christianity. His conversion to Christian orthodoxy and recantation of Unitarianism would be the major turning point in his life. Thereafter he became an imposing and impassioned apologist for Christianity and an important figure in the Christian revival that would gain momentum in the years following his death in 1834.

WILLIAM BLAKE
1757–1827

From *Poetical Sketches*[1]

Song: "My silks and fine array"

My silks and fine array,[2]
   My smiles and languish'd air,
By love are driv'n away;
   And mournful lean Despair
Brings me yew[3] to deck my grave: 5
Such end true lovers have.

His face is fair as heav'n,
   When springing buds unfold;
O why to him was't giv'n,
   Whose heart is wintry cold?   10
His breast is love's all worship'd tomb,
Where all love's pilgrims come.

Bring me an axe and spade,[4]
   Bring me a winding sheet;[5]
When I my grave have made,   15
   Let winds and tempests beat:
Then down I'll lie, as cold as clay.
True love doth pass away!

---

[1] Blake's first volume, published in 1783; the poems were composed between 1768 and 1777.

[2] *array*: attire.

[3] *mournful lean Despair/Brings me yew*: The yew tree was often planted in churchyards; its branches were an emblem of mourning.

[4] *spade*: shovel.

[5] *winding sheet*: shroud.

To the Muses

Whether on Ida's[6] shady brow,
  Or in the chambers of the East,[7]
The chambers of the sun, that now
  From antient melody have ceas'd;

Whether in Heav'n ye wander fair,   5
  Or the green corners of the earth,
Or the blue regions of the air,
  Where the melodious winds have birth;

Whether on chrystal rocks ye rove,
  Beneath the bosom of the sea[8]   10
Wand'ring in many a coral grove,
  Fair Nine,[9] forsaking Poetry!

How have you left the antient love
  That bards of old enjoy'd in you!
The languid strings do scarcely move!   15
  The sound is forc'd, the notes are few![10]

---

[6] *Ida's*: Ida here may refer either to the mountain near Troy—the site of the Judgement of Paris—or to the Cretan Mount Ida, where the infant Zeus was raised in secrecy.

[7] *East*: The east is a symbol of God for a number of reasons: Jerusalem—the site of the Jewish Temple, and later of the Resurrection of Christ—is to the east of most Christian and Jewish communities, which is why many places of Christian and Jewish worship orient themselves to the east. The sun rising in the east is also a symbol of Christ's Resurrection—itself central to traditional Christian ritual in the Mass.

[8] *Whether in Heav'n ... bosom of the sea*: Blake has just linked the Muses to each of the four elements: "Heav'n" (fire: the stars were originally thought to have been fiery bodies; the imagery of fire is also frequently associated with God and Heaven in both the Old and New Testaments); "the earth"; "the air"; "the sea".

[9] *Fair Nine*: i.e., the Muses: Calliope (Epic Poetry), Clio (History), Erato (Lyric Poetry), Euterpe (Music), Melpomene (Tragedy), Polyhymnia (Choral Poetry), Terpsichore (Dance), Thalia (Comedy), and Urania (Astronomy).

[10] *bards of old ... notes are few*: Of these verses, T. S. Eliot observed, "[Blake's] early poems are technically admirable, and their originality is in an occasional

Song: "Memory, hither come"

Memory, hither come,
　　And tune your merry notes;
And, while upon the wind
　　Your music floats,
I'll pore upon the stream,　　　　　　　　　　　　5
Where sighing lovers dream,
And fish for fancies as they pass
Within the watery glass.

I'll drink of the clear stream,
　　And hear the linnet's song;　　　　　　　　　10
And there I'll lie and dream
　　The day along:
And, when night comes, I'll go
　　To places fit for woe;
Walking along the darken'd valley[11]　　　　　　15
　　With silent Melancholy.[12]

---

rhythm.... But his affection for certain Elizabethans is not so surprising as his affinity with the best work of his own century. He is very like Collins, he is very eighteenth century. The poem *Whether on Ida's Shady Brow* is eighteenth-century work; the movement, the weight of it, the syntax, the choice of words: *The languid strings do scarcely move! The sound is* forc'd, *the notes are few!* this is contemporary with Gray and Collins, it is the poetry of a language which has undergone the discipline of prose. Blake up to twenty is decidedly a traditional" ("William Blake" [1920], in *Selected Essays* [London: Faber and Faber, 1932], p. 318).

[11] *Walking along the darken'd valley*: Cf. Psalm 23:4: "Even though I walk through the valley of the shadow of death, I fear no evil; for you are with me; your rod and your staff, they comfort me." (Scripture quotations are from RSV-2CE, unless otherwise indicated.)

[12] *Melancholy*: Blake had a "lifelong love of Albrecht Dürer, whose *Melancholia* ... was always beside his work-table" (Kathleen Raine, *William Blake* [London: Thames and Hudson, 2000], p. 182).

Song: "How sweet I roam'd"[13]

How sweet I roam'd from field to field,
   And tasted all the summer's pride,
'Till I the prince of love beheld,
   Who in the sunny beams did glide!

He shew'd me lilies for my hair,   5
   And blushing roses for my brow;
He led me through his gardens fair,
   Where all his golden pleasures grow.

With sweet May dews my wings were wet,
   And Phoebus[14] fir'd my vocal rage;[15]   10
He caught me in his silken net,
   And shut me in his golden cage.[16]

He loves to sit and hear me sing,
   Then, laughing, sports and plays with me;
Then stretches out my golden wing,   15
   And mocks my loss of liberty.

The Book of Thel

Published in 1789, *The Book of Thel* is the first of Blake's illuminated Prophetic Books and already features a rudimentary version of his mythology, with a characteristically Blakean blend of biblical imagery (seraphim, shepherds, lamentations, dew, reflections in a glass, shadows, the Dove,

---

[13] The imagery of this poem recalls the myth of Cupid ("the prince of love") and Psyche (the winged soul, the ego of the poem).

[14] *Phoebus:* Apollo—god of the sun, light, poetry, and music.

[15] *vocal rage:* the *furor poeticus,* the inspired frenzy of the poet.

[16] *shut me in his golden cage:* The image of the cage is identified with matrimony in Blake's earlier work. See, for instance, the reference to "Matrimony's Golden Cage" in the song "Hail Matrimony" from chapter 9 of *An Island in the Moon.*

the Voice of God in the Garden, the lily of the valley, grass, Heaven, light, manna, fountains and springs, the Virgin, the Lamb, milk and honey, wine, and so forth) and esoteric themes. The poem is written in unrhymed fourteeners (lines of fourteen syllables, generally of seven feet, in predominantly iambic rhythm).

Interpretations of the poem have varied, though it is clearly concerned with the transition from innocence to experience, both spiritually and sexually (repeated reference is made to virginity, and to Thel's virginity in particular, within a larger context of sexually suggestive imagery).

According to S. Foster Damon, "*The Book of Thel* is best understood a rewriting of Milton's *Comus*."[17] He interprets the Lily as Thel's virginity; the Cloud as impregnation, "the non-moral principle of the fertilizing male"; the Clod as motherhood. "All these characters assure Thel that they have a purpose, even though she may not understand it, and that life consists of self-sacrifice. The poem comes to a climax when Thel hears the voices of her awakening senses, especially sex.... Thel is terrified and flees in revulsion back to the innocent Vales of Har."[18]

For Raine, "the theme of the poem is Neoplatonic, and draws much upon Thomas Taylor's recently published paraphrased translation of Plotinus's *On the Beautiful*, and on the idea of the 'descent' of the soul into generation as described in this and other works of Taylor which appeared about this time."[19]

Pierre Boutang takes a darker view in *William Blake: manichéen et visionnaire*.[20] At the request of George Wyndham,[21]

---

[17] S. Foster Damon, *A Blake Dictionary* (Hanover, N.H.: Brown, 1988), p. 52.
[18] Ibid.
[19] Raine, *William Blake*, p. 52.
[20] Pierre Boutang, *William Blake: manichéen et visionnaire* (Paris: La Différence, 1990).
[21] George Wyndham (1863–1913) was an English aristocrat, soldier, Conservative politician, and literary critic. He was one of the most remarkable men of his time.

there is an interesting paraphrase of *The Book of Thel* written by Fr. John O'Connor (the translator of Paul Claudel's *Satin Slipper* and the inspiration for G. K. Chesterton's Fr. Brown) at the request of George Wyndham:

Essay on The Book of Thel

All the living creatures of the world were busy with their daily life, except the youngest, the Human Soul, the latest thing made on this earth. She gave way to misgivings about the meaning and aim of existence, and allowed herself to be overcome with base self-pity for her doom of death.

But from the lily of the valley she learns the minuteness of its beauty and the constant care of God for its appointed life and course, during which He makes it seem as if all Nature were for its sake. Even when it melts, it nourishes other beauteous things, for the soul of beauty does not die.

Moreover the lily is for the sake of the lamb, the field, the kine, and cheerfully is their minister, smiling in their faces the while.

Yet Thel objects that she is an object of pity, and does not stand alone. She shares the sorrows of the Cloud. Here the lily calls the Cloud to witness that its early death is not a sorrow, and the Cloud affirms that it is but the beginning of its joy, it dies to rise again.

Thel says her life is not like this, and her death is not like the death of the Cloud. The Cloud in its dying is the life of the flowers, but Thel is only food for worms.

Here the Cloud takes up the parable. If so, how great thy usefulness, how good thy fortune! Come forth, Worm of the earth and give earth's queen her lesson!

The worm cannot speak for itself, so Mother-Earth answers for it. The comparison of the worm to a child just born, that only shows life by writhings and cries, is a two-edged sword of poesy. The worm by its writhing, calls to mind the red human thing; the child's cries are heard by Blake as belonging to the worm.

But the Clay, mother of all bodies, makes things clear. "O Beauty of the vales of Har, we live not for ourselves. Even I that of myself can produce nothing wherefor I may live, am by the nuptial grace of God the mother of endless life. This I ponder, though I cannot ponder. Yet, I live and love."

Thel "dries the tears of pity with her white veil." The soul is being converted to see the deep meanings of the least things of creation. But with the white veil of her body she brushes away these tears of sympathy. She grows anxious for the body, that it must leave its shining lot for the cold bed of clay.

So she is admitted to the secrets of the grave, and sees how every human heart is in some measure steadied and orientated by death, has deep anchorage for its tortuous unrest, is made more solicitous about the end and meaning of existence. Death does this—not so much the prospect of our own death, as the death of those we cherish.

Thel witnesses and realizes the sorrow and horror of death in a gross material aspect very different from the sentimental gloom which caused her first questionings. She is stricken dumb. She stood in silence listening to the voices of the ground till to her own grave-plot she came, and there she sat down. But from the hollow pit sorrow driven home to her—real sorrow this time—speaks with a very different voice, asking questions which drive her mind upon one inevitable conclusion.

Why are we tempted through our senses, ears and eyes, helpless as they are to resist what approaches them?

Again, why have our senses such power of expression, attraction, repulsion, so far beyond mere material effects? Note well, "eyelids stored with arrows ready drawn." The eyelashes are compared to weapons of attack. Compare Mrs Meynell's beautiful essay on the eyelid as the greatest organ of expression.

Whence do eye and tongue derive their vast gifts and graces? Why the infinite receptivity of ear and nostril?

ANSWER

There is a soul behind which can reject what the sense cannot refuse.

The eye gives more than itself when it is the almoner of the soul. So does the tongue.

The ear draws in what is endlessly greater than itself, for the soul is not too narrow to contain it all.

The nostril inhales fear because of the spirit that fears—i.e., the nostril widens with fear more than with its natural action of breathing, and the larger draught accelerates the pulse, defending the soul against fear.

In fine, the body is not for its own sake but for something deeper, wider, greater than itself. Its aim and work here, even if it perished without reprieve, would justify its life, and make it worth living.

But: Why a tender curb upon the youthful burning boy? Why a little curtain of flesh on the bed of our desire? Because not even the soul lives for itself, and the body's last expression of the soul's self-giving must be withheld until the soul is ripe for the marriage of true minds, which ought to precede the carnal consummation, and which is the last stage in the soul's growth. Nature says to the body: "Wait for the soul." Here is the body then, dead to its most intimate instinct until the soul's fullness of time. Is this not a parable that the body's complete death is but another "Wait" for a fuller growth of the soul? The brutes obey each impulse implicitly, because they live by a sensitive soul alone, not by a spiritual form which perpetuates, for good or ill the sensitive appetites to which it yields consent.

Thel shrieks with the greatness of the awaking from gentle gloom and irresponsibility, to stern immortality.[22]

[PLATE i]

---

[22] Quoted in Charles T. Gatty, *George Wyndham Recognita* (London: John Murray, 1917), pp. 105–7.

The Book of Thel[23]

THEL'S MOTTO

Does the Eagle know what is in the pit?
Or wilt thou go ask the Mole:[24]
Can Wisdom be put in a silver rod?
Or Love in a golden bowl?[25]

[PLATE 1]

I

The daughters of Mne Seraphim[26] led round their sunny
    flocks,
All but the youngest. She in paleness sought the secret air,

---

[23] The name "Thel" is possibly derived from the Greek for "desire" or "will".

[24] *Does the Eagle ... ask the Mole*: Cf. Blake's *Visions of the Daughters of Albion* (1793): "Does not the eagle scorn the earth & despise the treasures beneath?/But the mole knoweth what is there, & the worm shall tell it thee" (5.39–40); also, cf. John Dryden's *All for Love*: "Men are but children of a larger growth;/Our appetites as apt to change as theirs,/And full as craving too, and full as vain;/And yet the soul, shut up in her dark room,/Viewing so clear abroad, at home sees nothing:/But, like a mole in earth, busy and blind,/Works all her folly up, and casts it outward/To the world's open view: Thus I discovered,/And blamed the love of ruined Antony:/Yet wish that I were he, to be so ruined" (Act 4, scene 1, lines 43–52).

[25] *silver rod?/Or Love in a golden bowl?*: Cf. Ecclesiastes 12:6–8: "[B]efore the silver cord is snapped, or the golden bowl is broken, or the pitcher is broken at the fountain, or the wheel broken at the cistern and the dust returns to the earth as it was and the spirit returns to God who gave it. Vanity of vanities, says the Preacher; all is vanity." The "rod" with which Blake has replaced "cord" is a symbol of authority, also, plausibly, a phallic symbol, which in turn allows the bowl to be seen as a feminine sexual symbol. (Damon, however, sees in the bowl a symbol of the brain; see Damon, *Blake Dictionary*, p. 373.)

[26] *daughters of Mne Seraphim*: In Christian theology, the seraphim (literally, "the burning ones"; see Isaiah 6:1–3) and the cherubim occupy the highest rank in the angelic hierarchy. "Mne Seraphim" is Blake's adaptation or corruption of Cornelius Agrippa's reference to "Bne Seraphim" (the sons of the seraphim) in *Of Occult Philosophy* (1531), bk. 2, pt. 2, chap. 22 (where they correspond to "The Intelligencies of *Venus*").

To fade away like morning beauty from her mortal day:[27]
Down by the river of Adona[28] her soft voice is heard:
And thus her gentle lamentation falls like morning dew: 5

"O life of this our spring! why fades the lotus of the
    water?[29]
Why fade these children of the spring? born but to smile
    & fall.
Ah! Thel is like a watry bow,[30] and like a parting cloud.
Like a reflection in a glass,[31] like shadows in the water,
Like dreams of infants, like a smile upon an infant's face,   10

---

[27] *fade away . . . mortal day*: Cf. Psalm 73:12, 19–20: "Behold, these are the wicked; . . . [who] increase in riches.... How they are destroyed in a moment, swept away utterly by terrors! They are like a dream when one awakes, on waking you despise their phantoms".

[28] *Adona*: "Adona" suggests both "Adonai"—the Hebrew for "Lord/Lords", used to refer to God in the Old Testament—and "Adonis", a figure of Graeco-Roman mystery cults. In Greek mythology, Adonis was a mortal youth of surpassing beauty, raised in the Underworld by Persephone, queen of the dead, and divided as a lover between her and Aphrodite, the goddess of love. When he was killed by a wild boar, the waters of the river Adonis (Nahr Ibrahim, Lebanon) ran red. At Aphrodite's supplication, Zeus granted that Adonis might return to her from the dead during the summer months of every year. Adonis is thought to derive from the death-rebirth cult of the Mesopotamian vegetation god Tammuz; the source of his name is the Semitic *Adon* (Lord). Cf. Milton, *Paradise Lost*: "While smooth Adonis from his native Rock/Ran purple to the Sea, suppos'd with blood/Of Thammuz yearly wounded: the Love-tale/Infected Sions daughters with like heat,/Whose wanton passions in the sacred Porch/Ezekiel saw, when by the Vision led/His eye survay'd dark Idolatries/Of alienated Judah", bk. 1, lines 450–57). Blake was interested and well-read in comparative mythology.

[29] *Down by the river of Adona . . . lotus of the water*: Boutang writes of this passage: "She has chosen the path of Adona, and she descends the length of the river that leads from eternal life to death. She is the *libido moriendi*; she is enthralled by the death that awaits her at the bottom of the valley even though it will not make a woman of her. She is void of *female will*, but her complaint is one of the fairest and falsest in the English language" (Boutang, *William Blake: manichéen*, p. 157).

[30] *watry bow*: rainbow.

[31] *Like a reflection in a glass*: Cf. James 1:23–24: "For if any be a hearer of the word, and not a doer, he is like unto a man beholding his natural face in a glass: For he beholdeth himself, and goeth his way, and straightway forgetteth what manner of man he was" (KJV); also, 1 Corinthians 13:11–12: "When I was a child, I spake as a child, I understood as a child, I thought as a child: but when I

Like the dove's voice, like transient day, like music in
   the air:
Ah! gentle may I lay me down, and gentle rest my head.
And gentle sleep the sleep of death, and gentle hear the
   voice
Of him that walketh in the garden in the evening
   time."[32]

The Lilly of the valley[33] breathing in the humble grass   15
Answer'd the lovely maid and said: "I am a watry weed,
And I am very small, and love to dwell in lowly vales;
So weak, the gilded butterfly scarce perches on my head.
Yet I am visited from heaven and he that smiles on all
Walks in the valley, and each morn over me spreads
   his hand   20
Saying, 'Rejoice thou humble grass, thou new-born lilly
   flower,
Thou gentle maid of silent valleys, and of modest brooks:
For thou shall be clothed in light, and fed with morning
   manna:[34]
Till summer's heat melts thee beside the fountains and
   the springs

---

became a man, I put away childish things. For now we see through a glass, darkly, but then face to face: now I know in part; but then shall I know even as also I am known" (KJV).

[32] *hear the voice . . . in the garden in the evening time*: Cf. the account of the Fall in Genesis 3:6–8: "And when the woman saw that the tree was good for food, and that it was pleasant to the eyes, and a tree to be desired to make one wise, she took of the fruit thereof, and did eat, and gave also unto her husband with her; and he did eat. And the eyes of them both were opened, and they knew that they were naked; and they sewed fig leaves together, and made themselves aprons. And they heard the voice of the LORD God walking in the garden in the cool of the day: and Adam and his wife hid themselves from the presence of the LORD God amongst the trees of the garden" (KJV).

[33] *Lilly of the valley*: Cf. Song of Solomon 2:1: "I am a rose of Sharon, a lily of the valleys." In Blake's works, a lily is a symbol of innocence, virginity, and a love that is pure and free.

[34] *manna*: the food that God miraculously sent to the Israelites during their forty years' sojourn in the desert (see Exodus 16 and Numbers 11:6–9).

To flourish in eternal[35] vales'; then why should Thel
   complain,   25
[PLATE 2]
Why should the mistress of the vales of Har[36] utter
   a sigh?"

She ceasd & smild in tears, then sat down in her silver
   shrine.[37]

Thel answerd, "O thou little virgin of the peaceful valley,
Giving to those that cannot crave, the voiceless, the
   o'ertired.
Thy breath doth nourish the innocent lamb; he smells
   thy milky garments,   5
He crops thy flowers, while thou sittest smiling in his
   face,
Wiping his mild and meekin[38] mouth from all contagious
   taints.
Thy wine doth purify the golden honey; thy perfume,
Which thou dost scatter on every little blade of grass
   that springs
Revives the milked cow, & tames the fire-breathing
   steed.   10
But Thel is like a faint cloud kindled at the rising sun:
I vanish from my pearly throne, and who shall find my
   place?"

[35] *light . . . eternal*: For a similar association of images, see Andrew Marvell's
"On a Drop of Dew".

[36] *Har*: Har is a weak but benevolent father figure to mankind who appears in
Blake's *Tiriel* (1789) and *The Song of Los* (1795). His realm is associated here with
primal innocence and life before birth.

[37] *silver shrine*: In Blake, silver and gold occasionally express a sexual antago-
nism or tension between types of meekness and boldness, respectively.

[38] *meekin*: meek, gentle.

"Queen of the vales," the Lilly answered, "ask the tender
   cloud,
And it shall tell thee why it glitters in the morning sky,
And why it scatters its bright beauty thro' the humid air.   15
Descend O little cloud & hover before the eyes of Thel."

The Cloud descended, and the Lilly bowd her modest
   head:
And went to mind her numerous charge among the
   verdant grass.
[PLATE 3]

II

"O little Cloud," the virgin said, "I charge thee to tell me,
Why thou complainest now when in one hour thou fade
   away:
Then we shall seek thee but not find; ah, Thel is like to
   thee.
I pass away, yet I complain, and no one hears my voice."

The Cloud then shew'd his golden head & his bright
   form emerg'd,   5
Hovering and glittering on the air before the face of
   Thel.[39]

---

[39] *The Cloud then shew'd ... face of Thel:* Thel in her innocence is able to
see what is, for Blake, the true anthropomorphic form of the Cloud. "For Blake,
all is human, since in this world man is central, made in the 'image of God', as
the microcosm.... Man is not 'part of nature', but all natural phenomena have
their existence in consciousness. The human world is the world presented by
human consciousness.... That which Blake and the Florentine painters, Raphael
and Michelangelo in particular, have in common is in reality the Neoplatonic—
and specifically Plotinian—aesthetics, upon which the concept of 'ideal form'
depends; identified by Blake, of course, with his 'divine humanity'" (Raine,
William Blake, pp. 113–14).

"O virgin know'st thou not our steeds drink of the golden
    springs
Where Luvah[40] doth renew his horses:[41] look'st thou on
    my youth,
And fearest thou because I vanish and am seen no more
Nothing remains? O maid I tell thee, when I pass away,   10
It is to tenfold life, to love, to peace, and raptures holy:
Unseen descending, weigh my light wings upon balmy
    flowers:
And court the fair eyed dew, to take me to her shining
    tent;
The weeping virgin, trembling kneels before the
    risen sun,
Till we arise link'd in a golden band,[42] and never part;   15
But walk united, bearing food to all our tender flowers."

"Dost thou O little Cloud? I fear that I am not like thee;
For I walk through the vales of Har, and smell the sweetest
    flowers;
But I feed not the little flowers: I hear the warbling birds,
But I feed not the warbling birds: they fly and seek their
    food.   20
But Thel delights in these no more because I fade away,

---

[40] *Luvah*: one of the four Zoas. The word "Luvah" may be derived from "lover":
Luvah is the Zoa identified with the emotions, from love to hate. The word "Zoa"
is derived from the Greek for the four "beasts" of the Book of Revelation (see
chapters 4 and 5 of KJV), beings also identified with the four "living creatures"
of Ezekiel 1:5. "Blake identified them with the four fundamental aspects of Man:
his body (Tharmas—west); his reason (Urizen—south); his emotions (Luvah—
east); and his imagination (Urthona—north)" (Damon, *Blake Dictionary*, p. 458).
However, when he wrote *The Book of Thel*, Blake's thought on the Zoas was
comparatively undeveloped.

[41] *doth renew his horses*: Helios, the Greek god of the sun—described by Pindar
(ca. 518–438 B.C.) in his Seventh Olympian Ode as "Lord of fire-breathing
horses" (cf. the "fire-breathing steed" of *Thel*, 1.10)—would drive his chariot
across the sky each day, descending into the outermost ocean at dusk.

[42] *golden band*: ring; bond; company of persons in movement; chain; shackle.

And all shall say, 'Without a use this shining woman liv'd,
Or did she only live to be at death the food of worms?' "[43]

The Cloud reclind upon his airy throne and answer'd thus:

"Then if thou art the food of worms, O virgin of the skies,   25
How great thy use, how great thy blessing; every thing
    that lives,
Lives not alone, nor for itself: fear not and I will call
The weak worm from its lowly bed, and thou shalt hear
    its voice.
Come forth worm of the silent valley, to thy pensive
    queen."

The helpless worm[44] arose, and sat upon the Lilly's leaf,   30
And the bright Cloud saild on, to find his partner in the
    vale.
[PLATE 4]

III

Then Thel astonish'd view'd the Worm upon its dewy bed.

"Art thou a Worm? image of weakness, art thou but a
    Worm?
I see thee like an infant wrapped in the Lilly's leaf:

---

[43] *woman liv'd ... at death the food of worms*: The language here is sexually charged, with an association of maiden anxiety, the worm (a phallic symbol), appetite, and death (slang for orgasm). Cf. Mark 9:43–48, Jesus' discourse regarding temptations to sin and his warning of being "thrown into hell, where their worm does not die" (9:47–48).

[44] *worm*: According to Damon, "in *The Book of Thel*, the Worm and the Clod are the baby and its mother" (Damon, *Blake Dictionary*, p. 452). The Worm as depicted in plate 4 bears a striking resemblance to another illustration of Blake's, "the unforgettable first emblem of *The Gates of Paradise* [1793], depicting the caterpillar of the 'natural man' and the dreaming infant soul in its chrysalis of metamorphosis" (Raine, *William Blake*, pp. 35–36).

Ah weep not little voice, thou can'st not speak, but thou
    can'st weep.
Is this a Worm? I see thee lay helpless & naked: weeping,   5
And none to answer, none to cherish thee with mother's
    smiles."

The Clod of Clay[45] heard the Worm's voice, & raisd her
    pitying head;
She bow'd over the weeping infant, and her life exhal'd
In milky fondness; then on Thel she fix'd her humble eyes.

"O beauty of the vales of Har, we live not for ourselves;   10
Thou seest me the meanest[46] thing, and so I am indeed;
My bosom of itself is cold, and of itself is dark,
[PLATE 5]
But he that loves the lowly, pours his oil upon my head,
And kisses me, and binds his nuptial bands around my
    breast.
And says: 'Thou mother of my children, I have loved
    thee.
And I have given thee a crown that none can take
    away.'[47]
But how this is sweet maid, I know not, and I cannot
    know.   5
I ponder, and I cannot ponder; yet I live and love."

The daughter of beauty wip'd her pitying tears with her
    white veil,
And said, "Alas! I knew not this, and therefore did I weep:

[45] *Clay*: flesh; the grave; Mother Earth. See also Blake's "The Clod and the
Pebble" in *Songs of Experience*.
    [46] *meanest*: commonest; occupying the lowest rung.
    [47] *crown that none can take away*: Cf. 1 Peter 5:4: "And when the chief Shep-
herd is manifested you will obtain the unfading crown of glory"; also, cf. Rev-
elation 3:11: "I am coming soon; hold fast what you have, so that no one may
seize your crown."

That God would love a Worm I knew, and punish the
   evil foot
That wilful, bruis'd its helpless form:[48] but that he
   cherish'd it   10
With milk and oil, I never knew; and therefore did I
   weep,
And I complaind in the mild air, because I fade away,
And lay me down in thy cold bed, and leave my
   shining lot."

"Queen of the vales," the matron Clay answered; "I heard
   thy sighs.
And all thy moans flew o'er my roof, but I have call'd
   them down: 15
Wilt thou O Queen enter my house? 'Tis given thee to
   enter,
And to return; fear nothing, enter with thy virgin feet."[49]
[PLATE 6]

---

[48] *punish the evil foot . . . bruis'd its helpless form:* Cf. Genesis 3:15–16, where God said, "'I will put enmity between you [the serpent] and the woman, and between your seed and her seed; he shall bruise your head, and you shall bruise his heel.' To the woman he said, 'I will greatly multiply your pain in childbearing; in pain you shall bring forth children, yet your desire shall be for your husband, and he shall rule over you'"; also, cf. Blake's "The Fly" in *Songs of Experience.*

[49] *virgin feet:* "The feet, for Blake, always represent visionary stance; here an irony, as only Thel's feet will cease to be virgin, in her brief encounter with Experience" (Harold Bloom, *The Oxford Anthology of English Literature*, vol. 4, *Romantic Poetry and Prose* [New York: Oxford University Press, 1973], p. 32).

IV

The eternal gates' terrific[50] porter[51] lifted the
   northern bar;[52]
Thel enter'd in & saw the secrets of the land unknown:
She saw the couches of the dead, & where the fibrous
   roots
Of every heart on earth infixes deep its restless twists:[53]
A land of sorrows & of tears where never smile was seen.   5

She wandered in the land of clouds thro' valleys dark,
   listning
Dolours & lamentations; waiting oft beside a dewy grave
She stood in silence, listning to the voices of the ground,

[50] *terrific*: terrifying; very severe.

[51] *porter*: Blake's porter reminds us of the guardian genius of Edmund Spenser's Neoplatonic Garden of Adonis, with its cycle of human regeneration (see *Faerie Queene*, bk. 3, canto 6). His terrifying appearance (he bears some resemblance to the doorkeepers in Kafka's "Before the Law") may owe something to the Kabbalistic tradition of angels guarding the gates of the Seven Heavens. See *Hekhalot Rabbati: The Greater Treatise concerning the Palaces of Heaven*, trans. Morton Smith, chapter 15 [206]: "Said Rabbi Ishmael: Thus did Rabbi Nehunya ben Hakkanah say to me: Totrosi'ai the Lord God of Israel of Hosts sitteth within seven palaces, one within another. And at the entrance to each palace are eight door-keepers.... And at the door of the seventh palace stand angry all the heroes, warlike, strong, harsh, fearful, terrific, taller than mountains and sharper than peaks. Their bows are strung and stand before them; their swords are sharpened in their hands. And lightnings flow and issue forth from the balls of their eyes". The Gates of Hades were guarded by the terrible three-headed giant dog Cerberus, while Sin and Death guard the Gates of Hell in Milton's *Paradise Lost*. In Blake's later Prophetic Book *Milton* (1804), the porter is identified with the Zoa Los— "Los is Poetry, the expression in this world of the Creative Imagination. He is the manifestation in space and time of Urthona, the deepest Zoa, who is the center of each individual" (Damon, *Blake Dictionary*, pp. 246–47).

[52] *northern bar*: The "northern bar" refers to the two entrances to the Cave of the Naiads (sea nymphs) in book 13 of Homer's *Odyssey*: the southern one for gods, the northern for men. Blake knew the Neoplatonist interpretation of this as an allegory of the soul's "descent" into generation, and he indeed illustrated it (1821) for Thomas Taylor's translation of Porphyry's *De Antro Nympharum*.

[53] *fibrous roots ... twists*: Cf. "The Human Abstract" in *Songs of Experience*; cf. also, Edward Young (1681–1765), *Night Thoughts*, 5.1063–64: "O the soft commerce! O the tender ties,/Close twisted with the fibres of the heart!" (Blake illustrated *Night Thoughts* in 1797.)

Till to her own grave plot she came, & there she sat down,
And heard this voice of sorrow breathed from the
   hollow pit: 10

"Why cannot the Ear be closed to its own destruction?
Or the glistening Eye to the poison of a smile?
Why are Eyelids[54] stord with arrows ready drawn,
Where a thousand fighting men in ambush lie?
Or an Eye of gifts & graces, show'ring fruits & coinèd
   gold!   15
Why a Tongue impress'd with honey from every wind?
Why an Ear a whirlpool fierce to draw creations in?
Why a Nostril wide inhaling terror, trembling, & affright?
Why a tender curb upon the youthful burning boy?
Why a little curtain of flesh on the bed of our desire?"[55]   20

The Virgin started from her seat, & with a shriek
Fled back unhinderd till she came into the vales of Har.
The End

From *Songs of Innocence and of Experience*[56]

In the full title to *Songs of Innocence and of Experience* (1794),
Blake refers to innocence and experience as "the two contrary
states of the human soul". They do not correspond to the sim-
ple process of living and learning through life in this world,
but to spiritual attitudes, akin to the unfallen state of origi-
nal harmonious bliss, on the one hand, and the fallen state of

[54] *Eyelids*: Eyelids recur with significance in the poetry of Blake's disciple Yeats
(see, for example, Yeats' "News for the Delphic Oracle").

[55] *Why cannot the Ear ... bed of our desire*: Each of the senses is referred to in
this speech, touch, characteristically for Blake, being identified with sex. "The
symbol of the death of the four Senses and the cursing of the fifth runs through
Blake's works from *Tiriel* to the *Illustrations of the Book of Job*" (Damon, *Blake
Dictionary*, p. 408).

[56] The full title is *Songs of Innocence and of Experience: Showing the Two Contrary
States of the Human Soul*, which contains two collections of poems: *Songs of
Innocence* and *Songs of Experience*; *Songs of Innocence* was first published in 1789.

misery and disharmony with oneself, with the divine and with nature, on the other—although for Blake, this change occurs during the lifetime of every man, rather than before conception. Innocence is the native state of man and creation, full of physical, spiritual, and imaginative joy and vigor. Experience is a more complex term, implying a subjugation to the false values and repressive rules of corrupt human society.

According to Blake it is possible, though rare, for men to learn and suffer without loss of innocence—and indeed the experience of many things that a traditional Christian society would consider immoral (such as sexual encounters driven by desire, without regards to marital bonds) Blake believed to be incorruptibly natural and innocent. Certain other traditional virtues such as meekness, he held to be evils, portrayed disingenuously as good by stupid or manipulative authorities. Innocence and experience must not be mistaken for ignorance and knowledge, which are very different in Blake's understanding: while "Aged-Ignorance" (depicted in his *Gates of Paradise* clipping the wings of youth) is the symbol of experience that maims or destroys innocence; knowledge, especially that gained through a spiritually awakened observance of the world (as opposed to what is drilled in schools), was paramount to Blake—the creed he developed (and which he believed to be a true and inspired vision of the universe) was a "gnostic" one. Blake came to believe that the imposition of rules, moral codes, and irrelevant learning upon freeborn individuals represses the sacred life force within them, corrupts their minds, and suppresses the development of their native gifts, while their happiness is lost in secret or public bitterness as they strive to fit into a system which constrains them by such means as politics, formal education, and religion.

Blake believed in the Old Testament as the most powerful work of truth-conveying symbolic literature, and in Jesus Christ as a divine savior whose sacrifice had changed the nature of heroism, and whose life was the ultimate paradigm; he also identified Jesus with the divine and salvific power of the imagination. "He is 'Jesus, the Imagination', the 'supreme state' of humanity which transcends, and releases from, all the states of good and evil through which human souls pass. The presence of Jesus the Imagination is with every man at all times present, born with every birth, accompanying every soul throughout life as the 'saviour' who releases the man from his present state. It is Satan, the Selfhood, who identifies the man with his present state; and who therefore is the Accuser who condemns."[57] But although he called himself a Christian, he scorned Christianity as an oppressive and false systematic corruption of these truths. Christian images appear as part of both *Innocence* and *Experience*, along with many mythical symbols of classical origin, and of his own inspiration.

Blake's conception of the universe is dynamic and contrapuntal. "Good" and "evil" are both necessary and perhaps of equal value (though the meaning he assigns these terms is not what is generally understood by them). Although the vast majority of poems in *Experience* describe a tortured, decayed state of mental or physical being, there are some that suggest hope—a hope that lies in passing through this suffering, rather than in turning back, which is impossible. Equally, some of the poems in *Innocence* are imbued with a sense of foreboding and hint that the state of delight they describe is threatened. The possibility of perceiving or even participating in one state while in the other—the precariousness of an innocent existence in the world as man has made it, and yet the natural striving toward such a state out of the darkness—is made especially clear in several ambiguous poems which Blake moved from one book to another. "To Tirzah", the final poem, was added some years after the two books had been written and published as a collection, and is generally thought to summarize the whole.

The poems in each book, especially *Songs of Innocence*, are deceptively simple—reminiscent of eighteenth-century

---

[57] Kathleen Raine, *Golgonooza, City of Imagination: Last Studies in William Blake* (Hudson, N.Y.: Lindisfarne, 1991), p. 154; see also Blake's "On Another's Sorrow", line 30, below in this section.

children's verses (though various other genres are also played upon). It is crucial to note that Blake's figures and designs, both in the illustrations that surround the original plates, and in the stanzas themselves, are archetypal and deeply symbolic, while the simple language and rhythm seems to embody the uncomplicated, open state of soul he is describing through various characters. Many of the poems in both sections deal with children and their relations with adults: in *Innocence*, their situation is generally happy, but when danger threatens, they are able to trust in the nearby presence of guardians; In *Experience*, they discover that this trust is betrayed by domineering or irresponsible figures of authority. These scenarios are both literal and symbolic illustrations of the two states; they also have a monitory purpose, as Blake witnessed the misery of many young and innocent beings in a harsh world. Nature in its many forms furnishes most other characters, but is imbued with spirits which are at once separate and inspiring entities, and a projection of the imaginations and spirits of mortals. The key symbols in each book are contrasting embodiments of the different elements of creation, existing in their flourishing and harmonious, or perverted and disproportionate forms.

From *Songs of Innocence*

Introduction

Piping down the valleys wild
Piping songs of pleasant glee
On a cloud I saw a child,
And he laughing said to me:

"Pipe a song about a Lamb!"[58]   5
So I piped with merry chear.

---

[58] *Lamb*: above all, Jesus, "the Lamb of God" (John 1:29), associated with both innocence and suffering.

"Piper pipe that song again—"
So I piped, he wept to hear.[59]

"Drop thy pipe thy happy pipe,
Sing thy songs of happy chear." 10
So I sung the same again
While he wept with joy to hear.

"Piper sit thee down and write
In a book that all may read—"
So he vanish'd from my sight. 15
And I pluck'd a hollow reed,

And I made a rural pen,
And I stain'd the water clear,
And I wrote my happy songs
Every child may joy to hear. 20

The Ecchoing Green[60]

The Sun does arise,
And make happy the skies.
The merry bells ring
To welcome the Spring.
The sky-lark and thrush, 5
The birds of the bush,
Sing louder around,
To the bells chearful sound.
While our sports[61] shall be seen
On the Ecchoing Green. 10

---

[59] *merry chear . . . wept to hear*: Cf. "Proverbs of Hell" in *The Marriage of Heaven and Hell*: "Excess of sorrow laughs. Excess of joy weeps" (line 26).

[60] *Green*: "A piece of grassy land situated in or near a town or village" (*Oxford English Dictionary*, s.v. "green"). In this context it also suggests the Garden of Eden.

[61] *sports*: frolicking, games.

Old John, with white hair
Does laugh away care,
Sitting under the oak,
Among the old folk.
They laugh at our play,   15
And soon they all say,
"Such, such were the joys
When we all girls & boys,
In our youth-time were seen,
On the Ecchoing Green."   20

Till the little ones weary
No more can be merry.
The sun does descend,
And our sports have an end:
Round the laps of their mothers,   25
Many sisters and brothers,
Like birds in their nest,
Are ready for rest;
And sport no more seen,
On the darkening Green.   30

The Lamb[62]

Little Lamb, who made thee?
  Dost thou know who made thee?
Gave thee life & bid thee feed
By the stream & o'er the mead;
Gave thee clothing of delight,   5
Softest clothing wooly bright;
Gave thee such a tender voice,
Making all the vales rejoice:

---

[62] The contrary to this poem in *Songs of Experience* is "The Tyger". See also
Songs of Innocence, "Introduction", line 5.

Little Lamb who made thee?
Dost thou know who made thee?   10

Little Lamb I'll tell thee,
Little Lamb I'll tell thee:
He is called by thy name,
For he calls himself a Lamb:
He is meek & he is mild,   15
He became a little child:
I a child & thou a lamb,
We are callèd by his name.
Little Lamb God bless thee.
Little Lamb God bless thee.   20

The Little Black Boy

Blake detested slavery. The British movement to abolish slavery had begun in earnest in the 1780s; Quaker activism (leading to the presentation to Parliament of the first slave petition in 1783) and the work of William Wilberforce (1759–1833), assisted by his friend the prime minister William Pitt (1759–1806), ultimately led to the Slave Trade Act of 1807, abolishing the slave trade within the British Empire, and the Slavery Abolition Act of 1833, abolishing slavery itself. The imagery of this poem is also consistent with the biblical theme of the bondage of the fallen life, and the liberation (prefigured in the Exodus) brought by Christ; see Galatians 5:1: "Stand fast therefore in the liberty wherewith Christ hath made us free, and be not entangled again with the yoke of bondage" (KJV).

The Little Black Boy

My mother bore me in the southern wild,
And I am black, but O! my soul is white;
White as an angel is the English child:[63]
But I am black as if bereav'd of light.

My mother taught me underneath a tree   5
And sitting down before the heat of day,
She took me on her lap and kissèd me,
And pointing to the east[64] began to say:

"Look on the rising sun: there God does live
And gives his light and gives his heat away.   10
And flowers and trees and beasts and men receive
Comfort in morning, joy in the noon day.

And we are put on earth a little space,
That we may learn to bear the beams of love,
And these black bodies and this sun-burnt face   15
Is but a cloud, and like a shady grove.

For when our souls have learn'd the heat to bear
The cloud will vanish; we shall hear his voice,

[63] *White as an angel ... English child*: Cf. Saint Gregory the Great on pagan English slaves in Rome in the late sixth century: "Alas, quoth he, it is a piteous case, that the author of darkness should possess such a bright-beautied people, and men of so fair a face should inwardly bear so foul a soul. Then enquired he another thing further, what was the name of that nation, or people? And when answer was given, that they were called *Angles* [Angli], or English. Truely not without cause, quoth he, they be called *Angles*, for they have an *Angels' face* [Anglicam faciem]. And it is meet such men were partakers and inheritors with the Angels in heaven" (Saint Bede the Venerable, *Ecclesiastical History of the English People*, trans. Thomas Stapleton, ed. Philip Hereford [1565; repr., London: Burns, Oates and Washbourne, 1935], bk. 2, chap. 2, pp. 69–70).

[64] *east*: See "To the Muses", line 2, note 7.

Saying: 'Come out from the grove, my love & care,
And round my golden tent[65] like lambs rejoice.'"   20

Thus did my mother say and kissèd me,
And thus I say to little English boy.
When I from black and he from white cloud free,
And round the tent of God like lambs we joy:

I'll shade him from the heat till he can bear   25
To lean in joy upon our father's knee.
And then I'll stand and stroke his silver hair,
And be like him, and he will then love me.

The Chimney Sweeper[66]

When my mother died I was very young,
And my father sold me while yet my tongue
Could scarcely cry weep weep weep weep.[67]
So your chimneys I sweep & in soot I sleep.

---

[65] *cloud will vanish ... round my golden tent*: Cf. Matthew 17:1–5 (the Transfiguration): "Jesus took with him Peter and James and John his brother, and led them up a high mountain apart. And he was transfigured before them, and his face shone like the sun, and his garments became white as light.... And behold, there appeared to them Moses and Elijah, talking with him. And Peter said to Jesus, 'Lord, ... I will make three booths here, one for you and one for Moses and one for Elijah.' He was still speaking, when behold, a bright cloud overshadowed them, and a voice from the cloud said, 'This is my beloved Son, with whom I am well pleased'".

[66] The contrary to this poem in *Songs of Experience* has the same title: "The Chimney Sweeper". Children were often employed as apprentice chimney sweeps. It was dangerous and unhygienic work, and in 1788 an Act for the Better Regulation of Chimney Sweepers and Their Apprentices was passed, limiting their working hours, the number of their apprentices, and prohibiting their employment before the age of eight. It proved difficult to enforce the Act, however.

[67] *weep weep weep weep*: reference to the sweeps' cry of "Sweep! Sweep! Sweep! Sweep!"

There's little Tom Dacre, who cried when his head   5
That curl'd like a lamb's back, was shav'd, so I said,
"Hush Tom never mind it, for when your head's bare,
You know that the soot cannot spoil your white hair."⁶⁸

And so he was quiet, & that very night,
As Tom was a sleeping he had such a sight,⁶⁹   10
That thousands of sweepers Dick, Joe, Ned & Jack
Were all of them lock'd up in coffins of black.

And by came an Angel who had a bright key,
And he open'd the coffins & set them all free.⁷⁰
Then down a green plain leaping laughing they run,   15
And wash in a river⁷¹ and shine in the Sun.⁷²

Then naked⁷³ & white,⁷⁴ all their bags⁷⁵ left behind,
They rise upon clouds, and sport in the wind.

---

⁶⁸ *white hair*: This could equally designate very fair hair.

⁶⁹ *sleeping he had such a sight*: Cf. John Bunyan, "As I walk'd through the wilderness of this world, I lighted on a certain place, where was a Den; and I laid me down in that place to sleep: and as I slept I dreamed a Dream. I dreamed, and behold *I saw a man clothed with Rags, standing in a certain place, with his face from his own House, a Book in his hand, and a great burden upon his back*" (John Bunyan, *The Pilgrim's Progress* [Oxford: Clarendon, 1879], p. 11).

⁷⁰ *by came an Angel ... set them all free*: Cf. Acts 12:6–7: "Peter was sleeping between two soldiers, bound with two chains, and sentries before the door were guarding the prison; and behold, an angel of the Lord appeared, and a light shone in the cell; and he struck Peter on the side and woke him, saying, 'Get up quickly.' And the chains fell off his hands."

⁷¹ *wash in a river*: symbol of baptism; crossing the river is also a symbol of death prominent in both classical literature (Charon ferries the dead across the rivers Styx and Acheron to the Underworld; see Virgil, *Aeneid*, bk. 6, lines 298–301) and in Bunyan's Christian allegory, *The Pilgrim's Progress*, illustrated by Blake in 1824.

⁷² *Sun*: The sun is often a symbol of Christ (also involving a pun on "Son"). See the note to line 98 of Samuel Taylor Coleridge's "The Rime of the Ancient Mariner".

⁷³ *naked*: i.e., naked like Adam and Eve before the Fall; see Genesis 2:25: "And the man and his wife were both naked, and were not ashamed."

⁷⁴ *white*: Cf. Revelation 7:9: "[A] great multitude [was] standing before the throne and before the Lamb, clothed with white robes".

⁷⁵ *bags*: i.e., bags to be used to clean soot from the chimneys; also, "burdens", as in the burden left behind by Bunyan's pilgrim when he dies.

And the Angel told Tom if he'd be a good boy,
He'd have God for his father & never want[76] joy.   20

And so Tom awoke and we rose in the dark[77]
And got with our bags & our brushes to work.
Tho' the morning was cold, Tom was happy & warm,
So if all do their duty, they need not fear harm.

The Divine Image

The starting point for "The Divine Image" is familiarity with
the Bible's teaching that God created man in his image.[78]
R.B. Kennedy also sees Christian theosophist Emanuel
Swedenborg's (1688–1772) influence:

> One of Swedenborg's central teachings is that there is a cor-
> respondence between natural and spiritual things, as between
> effects and causes; in particular, Man is made in the image
> of God in the sense that Man's true nature is divine. Blake
> accepted this as one of his own basic beliefs, and *The Divine
> Image* presents an aspect of it: mercy, pity, peace, and love
> would be mere abstractions if they were not incarnated in
> human beings. Blake expressed his sense of this "correspon-
> dence" in one of his annotations to Swedenborg's *Divine Love
> and Divine Wisdom* (Erdman and Bloom, *The Poetry and Prose
> of William Blake*, p. 593): "Think of a white cloud as being holy,
> you cannot love it; but think of a holy man within the cloud,

[76] *want*: i.e., want for.

[77] *awoke and we rose in the dark*: The sweeps began work early in the morning:
at five in the winter, seven in the summer.

[78] See Genesis 1:26–27: "God said, 'Let us make man in our image, after our
likeness'.... So God created man in his own image, in the image of God he cre-
ated him; male and female he created them." Further, see Matthew 25:37–40:
"Then the righteous will answer him, 'Lord, when did we see you hungry and
feed you, or thirsty and give you drink ... a stranger and welcome you, or naked
and clothe you ... [and] sick or in prison and visit you?' And the King will answer
them, 'Truly, I say to you, as you did it to one of the least of these my brethren,
you did it to me.'"

love springs up in your thoughts, for to think of holiness distinct from man is impossible to the affections."[79]

The Divine Image[80]

To Mercy Pity Peace and Love,
All pray in their distress:
And to these virtues of delight
Return their thankfulness.

For Mercy Pity Peace and Love   5
Is God our father dear:
And Mercy Pity Peace and Love
Is Man his child and care.

For Mercy has a human heart
Pity, a human face: 10
And Love,[81] the human form divine,
And Peace, the human dress.

Then every man of every clime,
That prays in his distress,
Prays to the human form divine   15
Love Mercy Pity Peace.

And all must love the human form,
In heathen, turk,[82] or jew.
Where Mercy, Love & Pity dwell
There God is dwelling too.   20

---

[79] William Blake, *Songs of Innocence and of Experience and Other Works*, ed. R. B. Kennedy (London: Macdonald and Evans, 1975), pp. 151–52.

[80] There are two contraries to this poem in *Songs of Experience*: "A Divine Image" and "The Human Abstract".

[81] *Love*: Cf. 1 John 4:7–8: "Beloved, let us love one another; for love is of God, and he who loves is born of God and knows God. He who does not love does not know God; for God is love."

[82] *heathen, turk*: After centuries of Muslim aggression and Christian crusades, the Turks (the dominant Islamic power from the fifteenth century) had become a synonym of the aggressive heathen.

On Another's Sorrow

Can I see another's woe,
And not be in sorrow too?
Can I see another's grief,
And not seek for kind relief?

Can I see a falling tear,   5
And not feel my sorrow's share?
Can a father see his child
Weep, nor be with sorrow filled?

Can a mother sit and hear
An infant groan, an infant fear?   10
No no never can it be.
Never never can it be.

And can he who smiles on all
Hear the wren[83] with sorrows small,
Hear the small bird's grief & care   15
Hear the woes that infants bear—

And not sit beside the nest
Pouring pity in their breast,
And not sit the cradle near
Weeping tear[84] on infant's tear?   20

---

[83] *Hear the wren*: Cf. Luke 12:6–7: "Are not five sparrows sold for two pennies? And not one of them is forgotten before God. Why, even the hairs of your head are all numbered. Fear not; you are of more value than many sparrows."

[84] *Weeping tear*: Cf. John 11:32–35, the death and raising of Lazarus: "Then Mary, when she came where Jesus was and saw him, fell at his feet, saying to him, 'Lord, if you had been here, my brother would not have died.' When Jesus saw her weeping, and the Jews who came with her also weeping, he was deeply moved in spirit and troubled; and he said, 'Where have you laid him?' They said to him, 'Lord, come and see.' Jesus wept."

And not sit both night & day,
Wiping all our tears away?[85]
O! no never can it be.
Never never can it be.

He doth give his joy to all.   25
He becomes an infant small.[86]
He becomes a man of woe.[87]
He doth feel the sorrow too.

Think not, thou canst sigh a sigh,
And thy maker[88] is not by.   30
Think not, thou canst weep a tear,
And thy maker is not near.

---

[85] *Wiping all our tears away*: Cf. Revelation 21:4: And God "will wipe away every tear from their eyes, and death shall be no more, neither shall there be mourning nor crying nor pain any more, for the former things have passed away."

[86] *He becomes an infant small*: Cf. Luke 2:11–12: "[F]or to you is born this day in the city of David a Savior, who is Christ the Lord. And this will be a sign for you; you will find a baby wrapped in swaddling cloths and lying in a manger."

[87] *He becomes a man of woe*: Cf. the Passion of Christ (see Matthew 26:30—27:66, Mark 14:26—15:47, Luke 22:39—23:56, and John 18:1—19:42), as well as its prophecy in Isaiah 53:3: "He was despised and rejected by men; a man of sorrows, and acquainted with grief; and as one from whom men hide their faces he was despised, and we esteemed him not."

[88] *maker*: The word "poet" is derived from the Greek ποιητής, which means both "poet" and "maker" (as in the Scots *makar*: "poet" and "maker"). For Blake, Jesus is the supreme artist/creator:

> On his engraving, made late in life, of the Laocoön Group Blake inscribed his *credo* of the religion of the Imagination: "The Eternal Body of Man is the Imagination, that is, God himself.... It manifests itself in his Works of Art (In Eternity All is Vision)." Blake is not the originator of the concept of the Imagination as the second Person of the Trinity: according to his own spiritual Master, Boehme [1575–1624], the Creation is "the Imagination of God". For Blake, therefore, the God within is "Jesus, the Imagination", the Divine Humanity, present in all and to all men. "The religion of Jesus", as Blake understood it, is the life of the Imagination; Jesus and his apostles were "all artists". (Raine, *Golgonooza*, pp. 5–6. See also the introductory text to *Songs of Innocence and of Experience* above, pp. 19–22.)

O! he gives to us his joy,
That our grief he may destroy;
Till our grief is fled & gone   35
He doth sit by us and moan.

From *Songs of Experience*

Introduction

Hear the voice of the Bard![89]
Who Present, Past, & Future sees
Whose ears have heard,
The Holy Word,[90]
That walk'd among the ancient trees.[91]   5

Calling the lapsèd Soul
And weeping[92] in the evening dew:
That might controll
The starry pole:[93]
And fallen fallen light renew!   10

---

[89] *Bard*: Celtic poet-musicians, reputedly gifted with prophetic powers. See, in this regard, Thomas Gray's poem "The Bard", illustrated by Blake (ca. 1797). Here, "the Bard" is Blake himself.

[90] *Holy Word*: i.e., the Second Person of the Holy Trinity, God the Son, Jesus Christ. See John 1:1: "In the beginning was the Word, and the Word was with God, and the Word was God."

[91] *That walk'd among the ancient trees*: Cf. Genesis 3:8: "And they heard the sound of the LORD God walking in the garden in the cool of the day, and the man and his wife hid themselves from the presence of the LORD God among the trees of the garden." In identifying God the Son with this episode, Blake is following Milton rather than Genesis (see *Paradise Lost*, bk. 10, lines 71–108).

[92] *weeping*: This refers to the Holy Word.

[93] *starry pole*: the pivot or axis about which the heavens appear to revolve. Cf. *Paradise Lost* where the devils are cast into a Hell "as far removed from God and light of Heaven / As from the center thrice to the utmost pole" (bk. 1, lines 72–73).

"O Earth O Earth return! [94]
Arise from out the dewy grass;
Night is worn,
And the morn
Rises from the slumberous mass.   15

"Turn away no more:
Why wilt thou turn away
The starry floor
The watry shore
Is giv'n thee till the break of day."   20

The Clod and the Pebble

"Love seeketh not Itself to please,[95]
Nor for itself hath any care;
But for another gives its ease,
And builds a Heaven in Hell's despair."

   So sang a little Clod of Clay   5
   Trodden with the cattle's feet:
   But a Pebble of the brook,
   Warbled out these metres meet:

"Love seeketh only Self to please,
To bind another to its delight;   10
Joys in another's loss of ease,
And builds a Hell in Heaven's despite."

---

[94] *O Earth O Earth return!*: Cf. Jeremiah 22:29: "O earth, earth, earth, hear the word of the LORD" (KJV), and, particularly, Song of Songs: 6:2–13: "My beloved is gone down into his garden.... I am my beloved's, and my beloved is mine.... Thou art beautiful, O my love, as Tirzah, comely as Jerusalem.... Return, return, O Shulamite; return, return, that we may look upon thee" (KJV).

[95] *Love seeketh not Itself to please*: The Clod echoes a celebrated passage in Saint Paul's First Epistle to the Corinthians: "Charity ... seeketh not her own" (13:4–5 [KJV]; see esp. the entire chapter of I Corinthians 13).

The Sick Rose[96]

O Rose thou art sick.
The invisible worm[97]
That flies in the night,[98]
In the howling storm:

Has found out thy bed   5
Of crimson joy:[99]
And his dark secret love
Does thy life destroy.

The Fly[100]

Little Fly,
Thy summer's play
My thoughtless hand
Has brush'd away.

Am not I   5
A fly like thee?[101]

---

[96] The contrary to this poem in *Songs of Innocence* is "The Blossom". The rose is a symbol of love, here, under the aspect of experience, an unhealthy, sentimental form, unreconciled to sexuality.

[97] *worm*: See *Book of Thel*, 2.23. Here, however, Blake also means the caterpillar, "always for Blake, as in the Bible and Shakespeare, a 'piller' or pillager, the chief enemy of the Rose.... 'As the catterpiller chooses the fairest leaves to lay her eggs on, so the priest lays his curse on the fairest joys' [see *The Marriage of Heaven and Hell*, "Proverbs of Hell", plate 9, line 16, p. 52 below]" (Damon, *Blake Dictionary*, p. 74).

[98] *flies in the night*: Cf. Psalm 91:5: "You will not fear the terror of the night, nor the arrow that flies by day".

[99] *Of crimson joy*: Cf. Isaiah 1:18: "Come now, let us reason together, says the LORD: though your sins are like scarlet, they shall be as white as snow; though they are red like crimson, they shall become like wool."

[100] *Fly*: i.e., the butterfly, which is also the Greek symbol of the soul (and often so used by Blake).

[101] *Am not I/A fly like thee?*: Cf. Thomas Gray's (1716–1771) "Ode on the Spring": "Yet hark, how thro' the peopled air/The busy murmur glows!/The

Or art not thou
A man like me?

For I dance
And drink & sing;   10
Till some blind hand
Shall brush my wing.

If thought is life
And strength & breath;
And the want   15
Of thought is death;

Then am I
A happy fly,
If I live,
Or if I die.   20

The Tyger

The symbolism of the central figure in "The Tyger", perhaps Blake's most famous poem, has been much debated. T. S. Eliot refers to "Christ the tiger" in "Gerontion" (line 20), a reference derived in part from Lancelot Andrewes's Nativity Sermon of 1622; in part, as seems likely, from the panther—"the friend of every beast but the dragon"[102]—identified with Christ in medieval bestiaries, and also, perhaps, from this poem of Blake's. Kennedy is persuasive:

---

insect youth are on the wing.... To Contemplation's sober eye/Such is the race of man ... Brush'd by the hand of rough Mischance.... Methinks I hear in accents low/The sportive kind reply:/Poor moralist! and what art thou?/A solitary fly!" Blake admired Gray and illustrated his poems without a view to publication. Cf. also *King Lear*: "As flies to wanton boys are we to the gods;/They kill us for their sport" (Act 4, scene 1, lines 36–37).

[102] St. Isidore of Seville (ca. 560–636), *Etymologies* 12.2.8.

It is a marvel that God made both [the tiger and the lamb], but not seriously doubted. The God of wrath who created the tiger and also Lucifer (Satan), chief of the fallen angels, also created the lamb of Innocence; in fact Christ is symbolized by both lamb and tiger: in his person equilibrium is achieved.[103]

The Tyger[104]

Tyger, Tyger, burning bright,
In the forests[105] of the night:
What immortal hand or eye,
Could frame thy fearful symmetry?

In what distant deeps or skies   5
Burnt the fire of thine eyes?
On what wings dare he aspire?
What the hand, dare sieze the fire?[106]

And what shoulder, & what art,
Could twist the sinews of thy heart?   10
And when thy heart began to beat,
What dread hand? & what dread feet?

What the hammer? what the chain?
In what furnace was thy brain?
What the anvil? what dread grasp,   15
Dare its deadly terrors clasp?

---

[103] Kennedy, *Songs of Innocence and of Experience*, p. 174.

[104] The contrary to this poem in *Songs of Innocence* is "The Lamb".

[105] *forests*: These forests are psycho-sexual realities and resemble the symbolic forests at the beginning of Dante's *Divine Comedy*, Milton's *Comus*, and near the beginning of Spenser's *Faerie Queene*.

[106] *On what wings ... sieze the fire*: These lines evoke Classical images of transgression: the myths of Icarus flown too close to the sun on wings of wax, and Prometheus, who stole fire from the gods and gave it to man.

When the stars threw down their spears
And water'd heaven with their tears:[107]
Did he smile his work to see?[108]
Did he who made the Lamb[109] make thee?　　　　　　　20

Tyger, Tyger burning bright,
In the forests of the night:
What immortal hand or eye,
Dare frame thy fearful symmetry?

My Pretty Rose Tree[110]

A flower was offerd to me;
Such a flower as May never bore.
But I said, "I've a Pretty Rose-tree."
And I passed the sweet flower o'er.

Then I went to my Pretty Rose-tree,　　　　　　　5
To tend her by day and by night.
But my Rose turn'd away with jealousy:
And her thorns were my only delight.

[107] *When the stars . . . water'd heaven with their tears*: See Blake's *The Four Zoas* (1797), where Urizen (the Zoa identified, among other things, with the Lawgiver and the avenging conscience, but also, when fallen, with Satan) speaks of his fall: "I hid myself in black clouds of my wrath./I calld the stars around my feet in the night of councils dark./The stars threw down their spears & fled naked away./We fell" (64.25–28).

[108] *Did he smile his work to see*: Cf. Genesis 1:25: "And God made the beasts of the earth according to their kinds and the cattle according to their kinds, and everything that creeps upon the ground according to its kind. And God saw that it was good."

[109] *Lamb*: See "The Lamb" in *Songs of Innocence.* Cf. Isaiah 11:6: "The wolf shall dwell with the lamb, and the leopard shall lie down with the kid, and the calf and the lion and the fatling together, and a little child shall lead them."

[110] *My pretty rose tree*: here, a symbol of the jealous wife.

Ah! Sun-Flower[111]

Ah Sun-flower! weary of time,
Who countest the steps of the Sun:
Seeking after that sweet golden clime
Where the traveller's journey is done.[112]

Where the Youth pined away with desire,   5
And the pale Virgin shrouded in snow:
Arise from their graves, and aspire,
Where my Sun-flower wishes to go.

The Lilly[113]

The modest Rose puts forth a thorn:
The humble Sheep, a threat'ning horn:
While the Lilly white, shall in Love delight,
Nor a thorn nor a threat stain her beauty bright.

The Garden of Love

The "Garden of Love" evokes both the Garden of Eden and
Milton's account of Adam and Eve's lustful intercourse imme-
diately following the Fall[114]—an association (disordered

---

[111] In this poem, Blake alludes to the myth of the nymph Clytie's spurning by
the sun (Sol/Helios). Definitively abandoned, she sat following the sun's course
with her eyes, feeding on nothing but tears and dew for nine days until, rooted
to the ground and face ever turned to the Sun, she turned into a heliotrope (see
Ovid, *Metamorphoses* 4.190–273). For Blake, the sunflower involves a spiritual
straining against the limits of life in the body.

[112] *Where the traveller's journey is done*: i.e., the West, identified both with
America, the land of liberty, and with the going down of the sun, death.

[113] In Blake, the Lily is the complement or opposite of the Rose: the Lily is pure
because it delights openly in Love, as opposed to the Rose, with its false modesty,
secret lusts, and thorns.

[114] See *Paradise Lost*, bk. 9, lines 780–1131.

sexuality and the Fall) that Blake repudiated. "Love" also evokes the specifically Christian dimension of revelation and the tension between the Letter of the Law (associated with the Old Testament) and its Spirit (associated with the New Testament); see 2 Corinthians 3:6: God "hath made us able ministers of the new testament; not of the letter, but of the spirit: for the letter killeth, but the spirit giveth life" (KJV).

The Garden of Love

I went to the Garden of Love,
And saw what I never had seen:
A Chapel was built in the midst,
Where I used to play on the green.

And the gates of this Chapel were shut,[115]   5
And Thou shalt not writ over the door;[116]
So I turn'd to the Garden of Love,
That so many sweet flowers bore.

And I saw it was filled with graves,
And tomb-stones where flowers should be: 10
And Priests in black gowns, were walking their rounds,
And binding with briars, my joys & desires.[117]

[115] *gates of this Chapel were shut*: In Blake's time, the poor often found it difficult to secure seating in London churches, and sometimes even found themselves denied entry altogether.

[116] *And Thou shalt not writ over the door*: Cf. Deuteronomy 6:5–18 (KJV), a combination of positive and negative commandments: "[T]hou shalt love the LORD thy God with all thine heart, and with all thy soul, and with all thy might. And these words, which I command thee this day, shall be in thine heart ...: And thou shalt write them upon the posts of thy house, and on thy gates.... Thou shalt fear the LORD thy God, and serve him, and shalt swear by his name. Ye shall not go after other gods, of the gods of the people which are round about you; (For the LORD thy God is a jealous God among you) lest the anger of the LORD thy God be kindled against thee, and destroy thee from off the face of the earth.... Ye shall diligently keep the commandments of the LORD your God".

[117] *binding with briars, my joys & desires*: Blake held that "the most harmful error of Rome lay in its debasement of sex" (Damon, *Blake Dictionary*, p. 83). That said, the priests in this poem are not primarily Catholic, and

London

I wander thro' each charter'd[118] street,
Near where the charter'd Thames does flow.
And mark in every face I meet
Marks[119] of weakness, marks of woe.

In every cry of every Man,   5
In every Infant's cry of fear,

---

the vengeful morality which appalled [Blake] in Dante is that of the rational Deism of his own England.... Gilchrist [Alexander Gilchrist, 1828–1861, Blake's biographer] reluctantly admitted the admiration Blake in later years evidently felt, not only for Gothic art, or certain Catholic mystics (especially St. Teresa of Avila), but for the Catholic religion: "If it *must* be told, that he did not go to church, it should also be told that he was no scoffer at sacred mysteries; and, although thus isolated from the communion of the faithful, ever professed his preference of the Church to any sort of sectarianism. On one occasion he expressed the uneasiness he should have felt (had he been a parent) at a child of his dying unbaptized. One day, rather in an opposing mood, I think, he declared that the Romish Church was the only one which taught forgiveness of sins." (Raine, *William Blake*, pp. 197–98)

[118] *charter'd*: This word involves a multiplicity of references. In the first place, London was fast becoming the largest city and port in the world, as well as its financial capital. Thus, while "charter'd" might apply to the physical definition of the river and to the transportation for hire there, the Thames was above all the principal avenue of trade in a city bristling with banks and chartered companies. Further, it connotes the multiplying corporate charters that Blake saw as extending monopolies at the expense of the poor and dispossessed. Finally, what Burke called "the chartered rights of Englishmen" ("Speech on Fox's East India Bill" [December 1, 1783]) were suppressed (in Blake's opinion) when pressures and anxieties connected to the war with revolutionary France led William Pitt's government to suspend the Habeas Corpus Act—whose foundations were established by the Magna Carta (or Great Charter) in 1215—from 1794 to 1801.

[119] *Marks*: For marks of the blessed and banned, see Revelation 7:2–3 (the seal of the elect): "I saw another angel ... with the seal of the living God, and he called with a loud voice to the four angels ... saying, 'Do not harm the earth ... till we have sealed the servants of our God upon their foreheads'"; Genesis 4:10–11, 15 (the mark of Cain): "The LORD said, ... '[Y]ou are cursed from the ground, which has opened its mouth to receive your brother's blood from your hand.' ... And the LORD put a mark on Cain"; and Revelation 13:16–17; 14:8–10 (the mark of the beast): "[I]t causes all ... to be marked on the right hand or the forehead.... If any one worships the beast and its image, and receives a mark on his forehead or on his hand, he shall drink the wine of God's wrath".

In every voice, in every ban,[120]
The mind-forg'd manacles I hear:

How the Chimney-sweeper's cry
Every black'ning Church appalls,[121]   10
And the hapless Soldier's sigh,
Runs in blood down Palace walls.[122]

But most thro' midnight streets I hear
How the youthful Harlot's curse
Blasts[123] the new-born Infant's tear   15
And blights with plagues the Marriage hearse.

[120] *ban*: summons to arms; proclamation of marriage; formal church denunciation; prohibition; curse.

[121] *appalls*: to dismay; to make pale; to cover with a pall, a "cloth spread over a coffin, hearse or tomb ... a dark or gloomy covering that extends over a thing or region" (*Oxford English Dictionary*, s.v. "pall").

[122] *Soldier's sigh, / Runs in blood down Palace walls*: France declared war on Great Britain on February 1, 1793, and—aside from the brief interlude of the Treaty of Amiens (March 25, 1802, through May 18, 1803)—the two powers remained at war until Napoleon's defeat (1814–1815). Blake was a radical, initially sympathetic to the French Revolution, though later he grew completely disillusioned with politics. Through his publisher, Joseph Johnson, he was introduced to a radical circle that included such influential figures as Thomas Paine, William Godwin, Mary Wollstonecraft, Henry Fuseli, and Joseph Priestley.

[123] *Blasts*: "to blow or breathe on, to blight" (*Oxford English Dictionary*, s.v. "blast"); to curse; to infect. Venereal diseases such as syphilis and gonorrhea were a cause of blindness in newborn babies.

The Human Abstract[124]

Pity would be no more,
If we did not make somebody Poor:
And Mercy no more could be,
If all were as happy as we;[125]

And mutual fear brings peace;   5
Till the selfish loves increase.
Then Cruelty knits a snare,
And spreads his baits with care.

He sits down with holy fears,
And waters the ground with tears: 10
Then Humility takes its root
Underneath his foot.[126]

Soon spreads the dismal shade
Of Mystery over his head;[127]

---

[124] The contrary to this poem in *Songs of Innocence* is "The Divine Image". "In Blake's writings, 'abstract' usually can be translated 'non-human.' It is 'opposed to the Visions of Imagination' (*Jerusalem* 74:26)" (Damon, *Blake Dictionary*, p. 4). Blake identified "abstract" with logical systems and exoteric religion.

[125] *Pity would be no more ... If all were as happy as we*: This is a parody of the complacent tone sometimes found in the English hymnody of the period (e.g., Isaac Watts' *Divine Songs for Children*: "Whene'er I take my walks abroad,/How many poor I see?/What shall I render to my God/For all his gifts to me?" ["Praise for Mercies Spiritual and Temporal"]; "How do I pity those that dwell/Where ignorance and darkness reigns" ["Praise for Birth and Education in a Christian Land"]).

[126] *waters the ground ... his foot*: Cf. *Book of Thel*, 4.1–5.

[127] *shade/Of Mystery over his head*: the first appearance in Blake of the Tree of Mystery. Blake identified it with the Garden of Eden's Tree of the Knowledge of Good and Evil (see Genesis 2:8—3:24). As such, it is the tree of spiritual death, identified by Blake (as are mystery, morality, and abstraction) with "false religion"—as opposed to the Tree of Life, which Blake identified with enlightenment through sex. For Blake, the Tree of Mystery is the same as the Cross on which Jesus was crucified; and he seems to have derived it, in part, from the Javanese upas tree (reputed to poison anything in its vicinity); the banyan tree—

And the Catterpiller[128] and Fly,[129]   15
Feed on the Mystery.

And it bears the fruit of Deceit,
Ruddy and sweet to eat;
And the Raven[130] his nest has made
In its thickest shade.   20

The Gods of the earth and sea
Sought thro' Nature to find this Tree,
But their search was all in vain:
There grows one in the Human Brain.

Infant Sorrow[131]

My mother groand! my father wept.
Into the dangerous world I leapt:
Helpless, naked, piping loud:
Like a fiend hid in a cloud.

Struggling in my father's hands: 5
Striving against my swadling bands:
Bound and weary I thought best
To sulk upon my mother's breast.

---

a Tree of Knowledge or Immortality in Hindu tradition; and Yggdrasil, the World
Tree in Norse mythology, whose roots extend to the Underworld and whose
branches extend into the heavens.

[128] *Catterpiller*: See "The Sick Rose", line 2, note 97.

[129] *Fly*: i.e., butterfly; see "The Fly", note 101.

[130] *Raven*: fear of death, emphasized by "institutional Christianity".

[131] The contrary to this poem in *Songs of Innocence* is "Infant Joy".

A Poison Tree[132]

I was angry with my friend:
I told my wrath, my wrath did end.
I was angry with my foe:
I told it not, my wrath did grow.

And I waterd it in fears,   5
Night & morning with my tears:
And I sunnèd it with smiles.
And with soft deceitful wiles.

And it grew both day and night.
Till it bore an apple bright.   10
And my foe beheld it shine.
And he knew that it was mine.

And into my garden stole.
When the night had veild the pole;[133]
In the morning glad I see   15
My foe outstretchd beneath the tree.

[132] See "The Human Abstract", line 14, note 127.
[133] *When the night had veild the pole*: See *Songs of Experience*, "Introduction", line 9, note 93.

To Tirzah[134]

Whate'er is Born of Mortal Birth,
Must be consumèd with the Earth
To rise from Generation free;
Then what have I to do with thee?[135]

The Sexes sprung from Shame & Pride[136]   5
Blow'd[137] in the morn: in evening died.
But Mercy changed Death into Sleep;
The Sexes rose to work & weep.

Thou Mother of my Mortal part
With cruelty didst mould my Heart,   10
And with false self-decieving tears,
Didst bind my Nostrils, Eyes & Ears.

---

[134] *Tirzah*: Tirzah was the capital of Israel (the Northern Kingdom), later conquered and enslaved by Babylon—the opposite, for Blake, of his symbol of the true religion, Jerusalem, the capital of Judah (the Southern Kingdom). In Blake's poetry, Tirzah is also a figure of withheld, manipulative sex; the mother of the physical body; and of death. See Song of Solomon 6:4: "You are beautiful as Tirzah, my love, comely as Jerusalem"; also, see *Songs of Experience*, "Introduction", line 11, note 94.

[135] *Then what have I to do with thee?* Cf. John 2:1–4 (KJV): "And the third day there was a marriage in Cana of Galilee; and the mother of Jesus was there: And both Jesus was called, and his disciples, to the marriage. And when they wanted wine, the mother of Jesus saith unto him, They have no wine. Jesus saith unto her, Woman, what have I to do with thee? mine hour is not yet come." Jesus' response to his Mother's request to provide more wine at the marriage at Cana is a standard anti-Catholic (because ostensibly anti-Marian) Scripture reference for Protestants. "Blake renounced completely any worship of the Virgin. He scoffed at Mary's virginity" (Damon, *Blake Dictionary*, p. 83), not only because he hated consecrated virginity and held sex to be a gate to Eternity, the "Birthplace of the Lamb of God incomprehensible" (*Jerusalem*, 7.67), but also because traditional Marian doctrine guaranteed the unity of Christ's Godhead with his human body, through his Passion and Resurrection, the redemption and glorification of the body, and, by extension and association, of matter itself.

[136] *Sexes sprung from Shame & Pride*: For Blake, sexual differentiation comes with the Fall; Blake's Albion (roughly consistent with the Adam Kadmon of Kabbalism and theosophy's Eternal Man) is androgynous (see From *Jerusalem* section, note 256).

[137] *Blow'd*: i.e., bloomed.

Didst close my Tongue in senseless clay,[138]
And me to Mortal Life betray:
The Death of Jesus set me free;   15
Then what have I to do with thee?

From *The Marriage of Heaven and Hell*[139]

In spite of being identified by some critics as Blake's manifesto, *The Marriage of Heaven and Hell*'s millenarianism distinguishes it from Blake's later, and most elaborately developed, Prophetic Books. "By 'marriage' Blake means that the contraries are to be reconciled, but are not to absorb or subsume one another."[140] The title is a reference to Emanuel Swedenborg's *Treatise Concerning Heaven and Hell*, of which it is in some respects a satire. Blake was influenced by Swedenborg (1688–1772), whose visionary theosophy he greatly admired; nevertheless, Blake considered Swedenborg's greatest failing his inability to resolve the "problem" of "Christian dualism", and, consequently, his acceptance of "conventional" moral categories.

Although published in 1793, *The Marriage of Heaven and Hell* was written between 1790 and 1792, before the execution of Louis XVI (January 21, 1793) and France's declaration of war on Great Britain (February 1, 1793), and largely, if not entirely, before France's declaration of war on Austria (April 20, 1792). These and ensuing events, such as the Reign of Terror (June 1793–July 1794) and the invasion of Switzerland (February 1798), undermined most of whatever support the revolutionary movement in France had hitherto enjoyed in Britain. "The progress of the Revolution disillusioned Blake

---

[138] *Didst bind my Nostrils, Eyes & Ears / Didst close my Tongue in senseless clay*: Cf. Luke 7:22: "And he [Jesus] answered them, 'Go and tell John [the Baptist] what you have seen and heard: the blind receive their sight, the lame walk, lepers are cleansed, and the deaf hear, the dead are raised up'". See also Mark 7:32–37 and John 9:1–7.

[139] Illuminated Prophetic Book, published in 1793.

[140] Bloom, *Oxford Anthology*, p. 34.

no less than the other Romantics. The mood of the earlier Prophetic Books gradually changes from rapturous hope in a new dawn to an atmosphere of apocalyptic terror and gloom, culminating in the *Song of Los* with its grim frontispiece showing a headless figure brooding over a desolate landscape."[141]

The subject and title of this book are the *points de départ* of C. S. Lewis' *The Great Divorce*.

THE VOICE OF THE DEVIL[142]

All Bibles or sacred codes have been the causes of the following Errors:

1. That Man has two real existing principles, Viz: a Body & a Soul.

2. That Energy, calld Evil, is alone from the Body; & that Reason, calld Good, is alone from the Soul.

3. That God will torment Man in Eternity for following his Energies.

But the following Contraries to these are True:

1. Man has no Body distinct from his Soul, for that calld Body is a portion of Soul discernd by the five Senses, the chief inlets of Soul in this age.

2. Energy is the only life and is from the Body and Reason is the bound or outward circumference of Energy.

3. Energy is Eternal Delight.

[PLATE 5]

Those who restrain desire, do so because theirs is weak enough to be restrained; and the restrainer or reason usurps its place & governs the unwilling.

And being restraind it by degrees becomes passive till it is only the shadow of desire.

---

[141] Christopher Dawson, *The Gods of Revolution* (London: Sidgwick and Jackson, 1972), p. 143.

[142] In *The Marriage of Heaven and Hell*, devils are geniuses—the inspired, original, and unconventional, as well as identified, like Hell, with energy—while angels and Heaven are identified with reason, uniformity, and conformity. This symbolism is not universal in Blake.

The history of this is written in Paradise Lost, & the Governor or Reason is call'd Messiah.

And the original Archangel, or possessor of the command of the heavenly host, is calld the Devil or Satan, and his children are call'd Sin & Death.[143]

But in the Book of Job Milton's Messiah is call'd Satan.[144]

For this history has been adopted by both parties.

It indeed appear'd to Reason as if Desire was cast out, but the Devil's account is, that the Messiah fell, & formed a heaven of what he stole from the Abyss.

[PLATE 6]

This is shewn in the Gospel, where he prays to the Father to send the comforter[145] or Desire that Reason may have Ideas to build on, the Jehovah of the Bible being no other than he who dwells in flaming fire.

Know that after Christ's death, he became Jehovah.

But in Milton, the Father is Destiny, the Son, a Ratio[146] of the five senses, & the Holy-ghost, Vacuum![147]

Note. The reason Milton wrote in fetters when he wrote of Angels & God, and at liberty when of Devils & Hell, is because he was a true Poet and of the Devil's party without knowing it.

---

[143] *Satan . . . his children are call'd Sin & Death*: Cf. *Paradise Lost* bk. 2, lines 648ff.

[144] *Satan*: "accuser" or "adversary" in Hebrew, and it is thus he appears in the Book of Job, contesting the substance of Job's piety and being permitted by God to put Job to the test by visiting him with every manner of affliction. In book 10 of *Paradise Lost*, Milton has God send the Son to judge and punish Satan, Adam, and Eve after the Fall.

[145] *shewn in the Gospel, . . . send the comforter*: See John 14:15–16: "If ye love me, keep my commandments. And I will pray the Father, and he shall give you another Comforter, that he may abide with you for ever" (KJV).

[146] *Ratio*: i.e., the sum total; also, what the reason organizes out of sensory data. This involves a dig at Locke's theory that knowledge is entirely determined by experience deriving from sense perception. "Blake would have agreed with de Maistre in his view that 'contempt of Locke is the beginning of wisdom', and both assailed the philosophy of Bacon with the same animosity, as in Blake's epitaph on Bacon: O reader behold the Philosopher's grave: He was born quite a Fool and he died quite a Knave" (Dawson, *Gods of Revolution*, p. 142).

[147] *Holy-ghost, Vacuum*: It is a commonplace of Milton criticism that the Holy Spirit appears to play a negligible role in *Paradise Lost*; this has sometimes been attributed to Milton's unorthodox Trinitarian theology.

PROVERBS OF HELL[148]

In seed time learn, in harvest teach, in winter enjoy.

Drive your cart and your plow over the bones of the dead.

The road of excess leads to the palace of wisdom.

Prudence is a rich ugly old maid courted by Incapacity.

He who desires but acts not, breeds pestilence.

The cut worm forgives the plow.

Dip him in the river who loves water.

A fool sees not the same tree that a wise man sees.

He whose face gives no light, shall never become a star.

Eternity is in love with the productions of time.

The busy bee has no time for sorrow.

The hours of folly are measur'd by the clock, but of wisdom:
   no clock can measure.

All wholsom food is caught without a net or a trap.

Bring out number, weight, & measure in a year of dearth.

No bird soars too high, if he soars with his own wings.

A dead body revenges not injuries.

The most sublime act is to set another before you.

If the fool would persist in his folly he would become wise.

Folly is the cloke of knavery.

Shame is Pride's cloke.

[PLATE 8]

Prisons are built with stones of Law, Brothels with bricks of
   Religion.

The pride of the peacock is the glory of God.

The lust of the goat is the bounty of God.

The wrath of the lion is the wisdom of God.

---

[148] "So strikingly the heralds of Nietzsche" (Pierre Boutang, *Apocalypse du désir* [Paris: Grasset, 1979], p. 410, n. 29). Cf. also Oscar Wilde's preface to *The Picture of Dorian Gray*, "A Few Maxims for the Instruction of the Over-Educated", and "Phrases and Philosophies for the Use of the Young". The form here imitates the biblical Book of Proverbs—to which it is a sort of "contrary"—as well as such collections as the *Maxims* of La Rochefoucauld, the *Reflections and Maxims* of Vauvenargues, and Lavater's *Aphorisms on Man*.

The nakedness of woman is the work of God.

Excess of sorrow laughs. Excess of joy weeps.

The roaring of lions, the howling of wolves, the raging of
the stormy sea, and the destructive sword, are portions
of eternity too great for the eye of man.

The fox condemns the trap, not himself.

Joys impregnate. Sorrows bring forth.

Let man wear the fell[149] of the lion, woman the fleece of
the sheep.

The bird a nest, the spider a web, man friendship.

The selfish, smiling fool & the sullen frowning fool shall be
both thought wise, that they may be a rod.

What is now proved was once only imagin'd.

The rat, the mouse, the fox, the rabbet watch the roots; the
lion, the tyger, the horse, the elephant, watch the fruits.

The cistern contains; the fountain overflows.

One thought fills immensity.

Always be ready to speak your mind, and a base man will
avoid you.

Every thing possible to be believ'd is an image of truth.

The eagle never lost so much time as when he submitted to
learn of the crow.

[PLATE 9]

The fox provides for himself, but God provides for the lion.

Think in the morning, Act in the noon, Eat in the evening,
Sleep in the night.

He who has sufferd you to impose on him knows you.

As the plow follows words, so God rewards prayers.

The tygers of wrath are wiser than the horses of instruction.

Expect poison from the standing water.

You never know what is enough unless you know what is
more than enough.

Listen to the fool's reproach! it is a kingly title!

---

[149] *fell*: hide, skin.

The eyes of fire, the nostrils of air, the mouth of water, the
    beard of earth.

The weak in courage is strong in cunning.

The apple tree never asks the beech how he shall grow, nor
    the lion the horse how he shall take his prey.

The thankful receiver bears a plentiful harvest.

If others had not been foolish, we should be so.

The soul of sweet delight can never be defil'd,

When thou seest an Eagle, thou seest a portion of Genius; lift
    up thy head!

As the catterpiller[150] chooses the fairest leaves to lay her eggs
    on, so the priest lays his curse on the fairest joys.

To create a little flower is the labour of ages.

Damn braces:[151] Bless relaxes.[152]

The best wine is the oldest, the best water the newest.

Prayers plow not! Praises reap not!

Joys laugh not! Sorrows weep not!

[PLATE 10]

The head Sublime, the heart Pathos, the genitals Beauty,
    the hands & feet Proportion.

As the air to a bird or the sea to a fish, so is contempt to
    the contemptible.

The crow wish'd every thing was black, the owl, that every
    thing was white.

Exuberance is Beauty.

If the lion was advis'd by the fox, he would be cunning.

Improvement makes strait roads, but the crooked roads
    without

Improvement are roads of Genius.

Sooner murder an infant in its cradle than nurse unacted
    desires.

Where man is not nature is barren.

---

[150] *catterpiller*: See "The Sick Rose", line 2, note 97.

[151] *Damn braces*: i.e., hatred is a tonic.

[152] *Bless relaxes*: i.e., kindness weakens.

Truth can never be told so as to be understood, and not be believ'd.

Enough! or Too much.

A Song of Liberty

1. The Eternal Female[153] groand! it was heard over all the Earth:

2. Albion's[154] coast is sick silent; the American meadows faint!

3. Shadows of Prophecy shiver along by the lakes and the rivers and mutter across the ocean. France, rend down thy dungeon;[155]

4. Golden Spain, burst the barriers of old Rome;[156]

5. Cast thy keys,[157] O Rome, into the deep down falling, even to eternity down falling,

6. And weep.

7. In her trembling hands she took the new born terror[158] howling:

8. On those infinite mountains of light, now barr'd out by the atlantic sea,[159] the new born fire stood before the starry king![160]

---

[153] *Eternal Female*: identified with Enitharmon, the Emanation (feminine portion) of Los (see *Book of Thel*, 4.1), his twin, consort, and inspiration. She is Spiritual Beauty, the Great Mother, the weaver of bodies, the Moon to Los' Sun.

[154] *Albion's*: i.e., Britain's.

[155] *France, rend down thy dungeon*: The Bastille, identified by revolutionaries and fellow travelers as a symbol of royal tyranny, was stormed on July 14, 1789, and demolished by the end of the year.

[156] *Golden Spain, burst the barriers of old Rome*: A reference both to Spain's Roman Catholicism and ancient Roman cultural and historical ties.

[157] *keys*: The keys are the symbol of papal authority; see Matthew 16:18–19: "And I tell you, you are Peter, and on this rock I will build my church, and the gates of Hades shall not prevail against it. I will give you the keys of the kingdom of heaven, and whatever you bind on earth shall be bound in heaven, and whatever you loose on earth shall be loosed in heaven."

[158] *new born terror*: This is Orc—the spirit of revolution, the energy of life, the revolt of suppressed desire; he is also identified with the tempter-serpent in Eden.

[159] *atlantic sea*: the legendary Atlantis.

[160] *starry king*: Urizen, "the southern Zoa, who symbolizes Reason. But he is much more than we commonly understand by 'reason': he is the limiter of Energy, the law-maker, and the avenging conscience. He is a plowman, a builder, and

9. Flag'd[161] with grey brow'd snows and thunderous visages, the jealous wings wav'd over the deep.

10. The speary hand burned aloft, unbuckled was the shield; forth went the hand of jealousy among the flaming hair, and hurl'd the new born wonder thro' the starry night.

11. The fire, the fire, is falling![162]

12. Look up! look up! O citizen of London, enlarge thy countenance! O Jew, leave counting gold! return to thy oil and wine. O African! black African! (go, winged thought, widen his forehead.)

13. The fiery limbs, the flaming hair, shot like the sinking sun into the western sea.

14. Wak'd from his eternal sleep, the hoary element[163] roaring fled away:

15. Down rushd, beating his wings in vain, the jealous king; his grey brow'd councellors, thunderous warriors, curl'd veterans, among helms, and shields, and chariots, horses, elephants: banners, castles, slings and rocks,

16. Falling, rushing, ruining! buried in the ruins, on Urthona's[164] dens.

17. All night beneath the ruins; then, their sullen flames faded, emerge round the gloomy king.

18. With thunder and fire, leading his starry hosts thro' the waste wilderness, he promulgates his ten commands, glancing his beamy eyelids over the deep in dark dismay,

19. Where the son of fire in his eastern cloud, while the morning plumes her golden breast,

---

driver of the sun-chariot. His art is architecture, his sense is Sight, his metal is Gold, his element is Air. His Emanation [feminine portion] is Ahania (pleasure); his Contrary, in the north, is Urthona (the Imagination)" (Damon, *Blake Dictionary*, p. 419).

[161] *Flag'd*: either "clogged" or "paved as with flagstones".

[162] *fire, is falling*: Cf. Luke 10:18: "And he said to them, 'I saw Satan fall like lightning from heaven.'"

[163] *hoary element*: the ocean. Cf. Revelation 21:1: "Then I saw a new heaven and a new earth; for the first heaven and the first earth had passed away, and the sea was no more."

[164] *Urthona's*: Urthona is the northern Zoa, identified with the imagination of the individual (as opposed to Jesus, the Universal Imagination).

20. Spurning the clouds written with curses, stamps the stony law[165] to dust, loosing the eternal horses[166] from the dens of night, crying

"Empire is no more! and now the lion & wolf shall cease."

From *America: A Prophecy*[167]

[PLATE 7]

In thunders ends the voice. Then Albion's Angel wrathful
   burnt
Beside the Stone of Night;[168] and like the Eternal
   Lion's howl
In famine & war, reply'd, "Art thou not Orc;[169] who
   serpent-form'd
Stands at the gate of Enitharmon[170] to devour her
   children?

---

[165] *stony law*: the Ten Commandments. See Exodus 31:18: "And he gave to Moses, when he had made an end of speaking with him upon Mount Sinai, two tables of the covenant, tables of stone, written with the finger of God."

[166] *loosing the eternal horses*: Cf. Revelation 6:1–8: "Now I saw when the Lamb opened one of the seven seals, and I heard one of the four living creatures say, as with a voice of thunder, 'Come!' And I saw, and behold, a white horse, and its rider had a bow; ... and he went out conquering.... When he opened the second seal, I heard the second living creature say, 'Come!' And out came another horse, bright red; its rider was permitted to take peace from the earth.... When he opened the third seal, I heard the third living creature say, 'Come!' And I saw, and behold, a black horse, and its rider had a balance in his hand.... When he opened the fourth seal, I heard the voice of the fourth living creature say, 'Come!' And I saw, and behold, a pale horse, and its rider's name was Death, and Hades followed him; and they were given power over a fourth part of the earth, to kill with sword and with famine and with pestilence and by wild beasts of the earth."

[167] Illuminated Prophetic Book, published in 1793.

[168] *wrathful burnt/Beside the Stone of Night*: the "druidic" doctrine of revenge. The "Stone" derives from Stonehenge; Blake associated stone circles and other megalithic sites with druidic human sacrifice.

[169] *Orc*: See *The Marriage of Heaven and Hell*, "A Song of Liberty", number 7, note 158.

[170] *Enitharmon*: See *The Marriage of Heaven and Hell*, "A Song of Liberty", number 1, note 153.

Blasphemous Demon, Antichrist,[171] hater of Dignities;   5
Lover of wild rebellion, and transgresser of God's Law;
Why dost thou come to Angels' eyes in this terrific form?"

[PLATE 8]
The terror answerd: "I am Orc, wreath'd round the accursed
    tree:[172]
The times are ended; shadows pass the morning 'gins to
    break;
The fiery joy, that Urizen[173] perverted to ten commands,
What night he led the starry hosts thro' the wide
    wilderness:
That stony law I stamp to dust: and scatter religion abroad   5
To the four winds as a torn book, & none shall gather
    the leaves;
But they shall rot on desart sands, & consume in bottom-
    less deeps,
To make the desarts blossom, & the deeps shrink to their
    fountains,
And to renew the fiery joy, and burst the stony roof,
That pale religious letchery, seeking Virginity,   10
May find it in a harlot, and in coarse-clad honesty
The undefil'd, tho' ravish'd in her cradle night and morn:
For every thing that lives is holy, life delights in life;
Because the soul of sweet delight can never be defil'd.

[171] *to devour her children? / Blasphemous Demon, Antichrist*: Cf. Revelation
12:1–4: "And a great sign appeared in heaven, a woman clothed with the sun....
[S]he was with child and she cried out in her pangs of birth, in anguish for deliv-
ery. And another sign appeared in heaven; behold, a great red dragon.... And
the dragon stood before the woman who was about to bear a child, that he might
devour her child when she brought it forth".

[172] *accursed tree*: the Tree of Mystery. See *Songs of Experience*, "The Human
Abstract", line 14, note 127. Blake's language recalls Michelangelo's depiction of
Satan tempting Adam and Eve, in the Sistine Chapel.

[173] *Urizen*: See *The Marriage of Heaven and Hell*, "A Song of Liberty", num-
ber 8, note 160.

Fires inwrap the earthly globe, yet man is not consumd;[174]   15
Amidst the lustful fires he walks: his feet become like
   brass,
His knees and thighs like silver, & his breast and head
   like gold."[175]

From "The Rossetti Manuscript"[176]

The Question Answered

What is it men in women do require?
The lineaments of Gratified Desire.
What is it women do in men require?
The lineaments of Gratified Desire.

[174] *Fires inwrap the earthly globe, yet man is not consumd:* Cf. Daniel 3 in which
the Jews Shadrach, Meshach, and Abednego—thrown into a furnace by the
Babylonian King Nebuchadnezzar for refusing to worship an idol of gold he had
erected—survive uscathed through God's protection: "But I see four men loose,
walking in the midst of the fire, and they are not hurt" (3:25).

[175] *like brass . . . like silver, & . . . like gold:* See Daniel 2:31–45 for Daniel's inter-
pretation of Nebuchadnezzar's dream of successive dominant kingdoms, figured
as a great statue, destroyed by the initially insignificant Kingdom of the Messiah,
figured as a small stone that grows into a mountain: "This image's head was of
fine gold, his breast and his arms of silver, his belly and his thighs of brass, His
legs of iron, his feet part of iron and part of clay.... [A] stone was cut out without
hands, which smote the image upon his feet that were of iron and clay, and brake
them to pieces. Then was the iron, the clay, the brass, the silver, and the gold,
broken to pieces together ... and the stone that smote the image became a great
mountain, and filled the whole earth" (KJV). The image Orc presents doesn't
have feet of clay.

[176] Blake's Notebook, so-called because it was purchased by Dante Gabriel
Rossetti (1828–1882) in 1847. Blake appears to have inherited it from his
brother, Robert, who died in 1787; Blake continued to use it until 1818.

"Mock on Mock on Voltaire Rousseau"[177]

Mock on Mock on Voltaire Rousseau
Mock on Mock on tis all in vain
You throw the sand against the wind
And the wind blows it back again.

And every sand becomes a Gem,   5
Reflected in the beams divine
Blown back they blind the mocking Eye[178]
But still in Israel's paths they shine

The Atoms of Democritus[179]
And Newton's Particles of light[180]   10
Are sands upon the Red sea[181] shore
Where Israel's tents do shine so bright[182]

[177] Voltaire (François-Marie Arouet, 1694–1778) was a French satirist, dramatist, and poet; Jean-Jacques Rousseau (1712–1778) was a Swiss philosopher, man of letters, and composer. In many ways diametrically opposed, Voltaire and Rousseau were probably the two greatest influences on the sensibilities of the French revolutionaries. Blake admired Voltaire for his hostility to hypocrisy and "organized religion", and Rousseau as a herald of revolution; but he would not forgive Voltaire his Rationalism, Rousseau his theory of aboriginal virtue, nor either of them their Deism.

[178] *Eye*: Blake identified the Eye with Urizen (see *The Marriage of Heaven and Hell*, "A Song of Liberty", number 8), and looking *with* it, rather than *through* it, as typical of Rationalism—cf. "Auguries of Innocence", line 126. Cf. also Matthew 7:1, 3: "Judge not, that you be not judged.... And why do you see the speck that is in your brother's eye, but do not notice the log that is in your own eye?"

[179] *Atoms of Democritus*: Democritus was a Greek materialist philosopher (ca. 460–ca. 370 B.C.); he was a determinist who believed everything to be composed of indestructible atoms of different shapes and sizes in perpetual movement.

[180] *Newton's Particles of light*: Sir Isaac Newton (1643–1727), the great physicist and mathematician. The "particles of light" refer to Newton's theory of the refraction of light (see *Opticks*, bk. 2). "The universe of Newtonian science Blake condemned as a universe of abstractions and formulae, not of experience. Man's earth is what he perceives; and, as such, 'though it appears without, it is within/In your Imagination [*Jerusalem*, 71.17]'" (Raine, *William Blake*, p. 114).

[181] *Red sea*: i.e., the Red Sea, which God parted to let the children of Israel escape from Egyptian slavery, and which he closed again upon Pharaoh's pursuing chariots (see Exodus 14).

[182] *Israel's tents ... so bright*: Cf. Numbers 24:5: "How fair are your tents, O Jacob, your encampments, O Israel!"

From "The Pickering Manuscript"[183]

The Smile

There is a Smile of Love,
And there is a Smile of Deceit,
And there is a Smile of Smiles
In which these two Smiles meet.

And there is a Frown of Hate,   5
And there is a Frown of disdain,
And there is a Frown of Frowns
Which you strive to forget in vain,

For it sticks in the Heart's deep Core[184]
And it sticks in the deep Back bone;   10
And no Smile that ever was smild,
But only one Smile alone,

That betwixt the Cradle & Grave
It only once Smild can be;
But, when it once is Smild   15
There's an end to all Misery.

---

[183] Named for its owner at the time of the publication of its contents in 1863, B.M. Pickering. The poems appear to have been written around 1803.

[184] *Heart's deep Core*: Cf. two followers of Blake: D.G. Rossetti, translation of Cavalcanti's sonnet to Dante, "He reports, in a feigned Vision, the successful Issue of Lapo Gianni's Love", line 1: "Dante, a sigh that rose from the heart's core"; W.B. Yeats, "The Lake Isle of Innisfree", line 12: "I hear it in the deep heart's core."

The Golden Net[185]

Three Virgins at the break of day:
"Whither, young Man, whither away?
Alas for woe! Alas for woe!"
They cry, & tears for ever flow.
The one was Clothd in flames of fire,   5
The other Clothd in iron wire,[186]
The other Clothd in tears & sighs
Dazling bright before my Eyes.
They bore a Net of golden twine
To hang upon the Branches fine.   10
Pitying I wept to see the woe
That Love & Beauty undergo,
To be consumd in burning Fires
And in ungratified desires,
And in tears clothd Night & day   15
Melted all my Soul away.
When they saw my Tears, a Smile
That did Heaven itself beguile,
Bore the Golden Net aloft
As on downy Pinions soft   20
Over the Morning of my day.
Underneath the Net I stray:
Now intreating Burning Fire,
Now intreating Iron Wire,
Now intreating Tears & Sighs.   25
O when will the morning rise?

---

[185] The Net symbolizes the snares of sex. Cf. Blake's "How sweet I roam'd".
[186] *Clothd in iron wire*: a symbol of restraint.

The Mental Traveller

"The Mental Traveller" is one of Blake's most important, and difficult, poems. According to Bloom,

> The poem may be described, briefly, as a report upon a grotesque planet given by a being alien to it, who cannot quite understand the horrors he sees. He describes two cycles moving in opposite directions, and out of phase with one another. The natural cycle (symbolized by the female) is moving backward, the human (symbolized by the male) forward. There are only two personages in the poem, but they move through several phases, and phantoms of earlier phases sometimes linger. The human cycle moves between an infant Orc and an aged, beggared Urizen, and then back again. The natural sequence is Tirzah (Nature-as-Necessity), Vala (Nature-as-Temptress), and Rahab (Nature-as-Destroyer), and then back again.[187]

For Damon it presents "the formula of the history of the idea of Liberty, showing how it is born, how it triumphs, how in its age its opposite is born, how it is cast out, how it then rejuvenates, until it becomes a babe again, and the cycle recurs".[188] F. W. Bateson has offered the following interpretation: "The male cycle—baby, youth, husband, old man, lover, baby—seems to symbolize mankind's progress from barbarism to civilization and then, with the decadence of civilization, a return to barbarism. The female cycle—old woman, virgin, baby, maiden, old woman—represents Nature's reactions to human progress."[189]

[187] *Oxford Anthology*, p. 65.
[188] *Blake Dictionary*, p. 268.
[189] *Selected Poems of William Blake*, ed. F. W. Bateson (London: Heinemann, 1957), p. 137.

The Mental Traveller

I traveld thro' a Land of Men,
A Land of Men and Women too,
And heard & saw such dreadful things
As cold Earth wanderers never knew.

For there the Babe is born in joy   5
That was begotten in dire woe;
Just as we Reap in joy the fruit
Which we in bitter tears did sow.[190]

And if the Babe is born a Boy
He's given to a Woman Old,[191]   10
Who nails him down upon a rock,
Catches his shrieks in cups of gold.[192]

She binds iron thorns around his head,
She pierces both his hands & feet,
She cuts his heart out at his side[193]   15
To make it feel both cold & heat.

Her fingers number every Nerve,
Just as a Miser counts his gold;

[190] *we in bitter tears did sow*: Cf. Psalm 126:5:"May those who sow in tears reap with shouts of joy!" The woe of sexual intercourse and joy of childbirth indicate a fallen existence.

[191] *given to a Woman Old*: possibly a symbol of society.

[192] *nails him down upon a rock,/Catches his shrieks in cups of gold*: possible echo of Norse mythology; for his part in the murder of Balder, Loki was bound by the entrails of his son to three great rocks and exposed to the maws of an enormous serpent, dripping poison on his face. The poison is caught by his wife, Sigyn, in a wooden bowl. When she is obliged to empty the bowl, the agonizing poison drips into his face and eyes.

[193] *binds iron thorns around his head ... pierces both his hands & feet ... cuts his heart out at his side*: There are echoes here and above of both the birth, Passion, and Crucifixion of Christ, and of the punishment meted out to Prometheus; for stealing fire from the gods and giving it to man he was bound to a rock where a great eagle came daily to devour his immortal liver.

She lives upon his shrieks & cries,
And she grows young as he grows old.   20

Till he becomes a bleeding youth,
And she becomes a Virgin bright;
Then he rends up his Manacles
And binds her down for his delight.

He plants himself in all her Nerves,   25
Just as a Husbandman his mould;[194]
And she becomes his dwelling-place
And Garden fruitful seventy fold.[195]

An agèd Shadow, soon he fades,
Wandring round an Earthly Cot,[196]   30
Full fillèd all with gems & gold
Which he by industry had got.

And these are the gems of the Human Soul,
The rubies & pearls of a lovesick eye,
The countless gold of the akeing heart,   35
The martyr's groan & the lover's sigh.

They are his meat, they are his drink;
He feeds the Beggar & the Poor
And the wayfaring Traveller:
For ever open is his door.   40

[194] *mould*: loose, rich soil.
[195] *seventy fold*: Cf. Matthew 18:21–22: "Then Peter came up and said to him, 'Lord, how often shall my brother sin against me, and I forgive him? As many as seven times?' Jesus said to him, 'I do not say to you seven times, but seventy times seven.'" "Seventy" also recalls the Babylonian Captivity; the Jews were held captive in Babylon for seventy years (see Jeremiah 29:10: "For thus says the LORD: When seventy years are completed for Babylon, I will visit you"); and "Babylonian Captivity" was applied by Luther and his followers to the decadence of the late medieval Church.
[196] *Earthly Cot*: cottage.

His grief is their eternal joy;
They make the roofs & walls to ring;
Till from the fire on the hearth
A little Female Babe[197] does spring.

And she is all of solid fire   45
And gems & gold, that none his hand
Dares stretch to touch her Baby form,
Or wrap her in his swaddling-band.

But She comes to the Man she loves,
If young or old, or rich or poor;   50
They soon drive out the agèd Host,
A Beggar at another's door.

He wanders weeping far away,
Until some other take him in;
Oft blind & age-bent, sore distrest,   55
Until he can a Maiden win.

And to allay his freezing Age
The Poor Man takes her in his arms;[198]
The Cottage fades before his sight,
The Garden & its lovely Charms.   60

The Guests are scattered thro' the land,
For the Eye altering alters all;
The Senses roll themselves in fear,
And the flat Earth becomes a Ball.[199]

---

[197] *little Female Babe*: the whore Rahab (see Joshua 2), whom Blake identifies with the Whore of Babylon (Revelation 17:5) and the false church.

[198] *he can a Maiden win . . . his freezing Age / The Poor Man takes her in his arms*: Cf. 1 Kings 1:1–2: "Now king David was old and advanced in years; and although they covered him with clothes, he could not get warm. Therefore his servants said to him, 'Let a young maiden be sought for my lord the king, and let her wait upon the king, and be his nurse; let her lie in your bosom, that my lord the king may be warm.'"

[199] *flat Earth becomes a Ball*: Blake believed that the Earth only appeared spherical "to the weak traveller confin'd beneath the moony shade"; "the traveller thro' Eternity" recognizes it as "one infinite plane" (see *Milton*, 15.21–35).

The Stars, Sun, Moon, all shrink away:
A desart vast without a bound,
And nothing left to eat or drink,
And a dark desart all around.

The honey of her Infant lips,
The bread & wine of her sweet smile, 70
The wild game of her roving Eye,
Does him to Infancy beguile.

For as he eats & drinks he grows
Younger & younger every day;
And on the desart wild they both 75
Wander in terror & dismay.

Like the wild Stag[200] she flees away,
Her fear plants many a thicket wild;
While he pursues her night & day,
By various arts of Love beguild, 80

By various arts of Love and Hate,
Till the wide desart planted o'er
With Labyrinths of wayward Love,
Where roams the Lion, Wolf & Boar;

Till he becomes a wayward Babe, 85
And she a weeping Woman Old.
Then many a Lover wanders here;
The Sun and Stars are nearer rolld.

The trees bring forth sweet Extacy
To all who in the desart roam; 90
Till many a City there is Built,
And many a pleasant Shepherd's home.

---

[200] *Like the wild Stag*: Cf. Psalm 42:1: "As a deer longs for flowing streams, so longs my soul for you, O God."

But when they find the frowning Babe,
Terror strikes thro' the region wide:
They cry "The Babe! the Babe is Born!" 95
And flee away on Every side.

For who dare touch the frowning form,
His arm is wither'd to its root;
Lions, Boars, Wolves, all howling flee,
And every Tree does shed its fruit. 100

And none can touch that frowning form,
Except it be a Woman Old;
She nails him down upon the Rock,
And all is done as I have told.

The Land of Dreams

"Awake, awake my little Boy!
Thou wast thy Mother's only joy;
Why dost thou weep in thy gentle sleep?
Awake! thy Father does thee keep."

"O, what Land is the Land of Dreams? 5
What are its Mountains & what are its Streams?
O Father, I saw my Mother there,
Among the Lillies by waters fair.

"Among the Lambs, clothed in white,
She walk'd with her Thomas in sweet delight. 10
I wept for joy, like a dove I mourn;
O! when shall I again return?"

"Dear Child, I also by pleasant Streams
Have wander'd all Night in the Land of Dreams;

But tho calm & warm the waters wide,   15
I could not get to the other side."[201]

"Father, O Father! what do we here
In this Land of unbelief & fear?
The Land of Dreams is better far,
Above the light of the Morning Star."   20

The Crystal Cabinet[202]

"The Crystal Cabinet" is a poem about the limitations of sexual enlightenment—essentially, the limitations of what Blake calls Beulah. Beulah is the moonlit world midway between Eternity and Ulro (the material world). It is the source of dreams and poetic inspiration. "Here the Humanity is divided from his Emanation [feminine portion], but is joined in the perfect marriage.... Seen from above, Beulah is a descent into division and dreams; but seen from below, it is an ascent into an ideal, which opens the way into Eternity."[203] The striking consistencies between "The Crystal Cabinet" and the very early "How sweet I roam'd" (see above) are a good illustration of the continuity of Blake's thought.

The Crystal Cabinet

The Maiden caught me in the Wild,
Where I was dancing merrily;
She put me into her Cabinet
And Lock'd me up with a golden Key.

---

[201] *I could not . . . other side*: See "The Chimney Sweeper", line 16.
[202] The theme of this poem and some of its handling are similar to Keats' "La Belle Dame Sans Merci".
[203] Damon, *Blake Dictionary*, p. 367.

This Cabinet is formd of Gold 5
And Pearl & Crystal shining bright,
And within it opens into a World[204]
And a little lovely Moony Night.

Another England there I saw,
Another London with its Tower, 10
Another Thames & other Hills,
And another pleasant Surrey[205] Bower.

Another Maiden like herself,
Translucent, lovely, shining clear;
Threefold each in the other closd— 15
O, what a pleasant trembling fear!

O, what a smile! a threefold Smile
Filld me, that like a flame I burnd:
I bent to Kiss the lovely Maid,
And found a Threefold Kiss returnd. 20

I strove to sieze the inmost Form,
With ardor fierce & hands of flame,
But burst the Crystal Cabinet,
And like a Weeping Babe became—

A weeping Babe upon the wild, 25
And Weeping Woman pale reclind;
And in the outward air again
I filld with woes the passing Wind.

[204] *golden Key . . . opens into a World*: Cf. George MacDonald (1824–1905), *The Golden Key* and *Phantastes*. MacDonald was much influenced by both Blake and Swedenborg.

[205] *Surrey*: a county in South East England. Lambeth—where Blake spent some of his happiest and most creatively fruitful years—was in Surrey (it has since been absorbed into Greater London).

The Grey Monk

"I die, I die!" the Mother said,
"My Children die for lack of Bread.
What more has the merciless Tyrant said?"
The Monk sat down on the Stony Bed.

The blood red ran from the Grey Monk's side, 5
His hands & feet were wounded wide,[206]
His Body bent, his arms & knees
Like to the roots of ancient trees.

His eye was dry, no tear could flow;
A hollow groan first spoke his woe. 10
He trembled & shudder'd upon the Bed;
At length with a feeble cry he said:

"When God commanded this hand to write
In the studious hours of deep midnight,
He told me the writing I wrote should prove 15
The bane of all that on Earth I lovd.

"My Brother starvd between two Walls,
His Children's Cry my Soul appalls;[207]
I mockd at the wrack[208] & griding[209] chain,
My bent body mocks their torturing pain. 20

"Thy Father drew his sword in the North,
With his thousands strong he marchèd forth;
Thy Brother has arm'd himself in Steel
To avenge the wrongs thy Children feel.

[206] *hands & feet were wounded wide*: His wounds recall those of the crucified Christ.
[207] *appalls*: See "London", line 10.
[208] *wrack*: rack.
[209] *griding*: scraping; grating; cutting.

"But vain the Sword & vain the Bow,   25
They never can work War's overthrow.
The Hermit's Prayer[210] & the Widow's tear
Alone can free the World from fear.

"For a Tear is an Intellectual[211] Thing,
And a Sigh is the Sword of an Angel King,   30
And the bitter groan of the Martyr's woe
Is an Arrow from the Almightie's Bow.

"The hand of Vengeance found the Bed
To which the Purple[212] Tyrant fled;
The iron hand crushd the Tyrant's head   35
And became a Tyrant in his stead."[213]

Auguries of Innocence[214]

To see a World in a Grain of Sand
And a Heaven in a Wild Flower:
Hold Infinity in the palm of your hand
And Eternity in an hour.

[210] *Hermit's Prayer*: For the Romantics, the hermit was a figure of peculiar spiritual authority. See Coleridge, "The Rime of the Ancient Mariner" and von Weber's opera *Der Freischütz*.

[211] *Intellectual*: In Blake the intellect (as opposed to reason) is of central importance; it is the fountain of ideas.

[212] *Purple*: the color of blood and royalty.

[213] *iron hand crushd the Tyrant's head . . . became a Tyrant in his stead*: plainly— though not merely—an expression of disillusionment in the French Revolution.

[214] This poem is a quatrain followed by a series of apophthegmatic couplets; in it Blake expounds his conviction that "true innocence can be recovered at any given moment: it simply depends on how you look at it—'it' being the simplest object in the world around you, a grain of sand or a wild flower. The world, Heaven, infinity, and eternity are not to be comprehended by enormous sweeps of intellect, or even of imagination, but by attending to 'minute particulars'" (Kennedy, *Songs of Innocence and of Experience*, p. 245). See Pre-Raphaelitism in this regard, and particularly the poetry of D. G. Rossetti (e.g., "The Woodspurge", "My Sister's Sleep", "Silent Noon", etc.).

A Robin Red breast[215] in a Cage 5
Puts all Heaven in a Rage.
A dove house filld with doves & Pigeons
Shudders Hell thro all its regions.
A dog starvd at his Master's Gate
Predicts the ruin of the State. 10
A Horse misusd upon the Road
Calls to Heaven for Human blood.[216]
Each outcry of the hunted Hare
A fibre from the Brain does tear.
A Skylark wounded in the wing, 15
A Cherubim[217] does cease to sing.
The Game Cock[218] clipd & armd for fight
Does the Rising Sun affright.
Every Wolf's & Lion's howl
Raises from Hell a Human Soul. 20
The wild deer, wandring here & there
Keeps the Human Soul from Care.
The Lamb misusd breeds Public strife
And yet forgives the Butcher's Knife.
The Bat that flits at close of Eve 25
Has left the Brain that won't Believe.
The Owl that calls upon the Night

---

[215] *Robin Red breast*: This is the English Robin (*Erithacus rubecula melophilus*), a subspecies of the European Robin (*Erithacus rubecula*), a charming little red-orange-throated passerine bird; it is not closely related to the American Robin (*Turdus migratorius*), a type of thrush rarely found (*pace* Mary Poppins) in Britain.

[216] *Calls to Heaven for Human blood*: Cf. Genesis 4:9–10: "Then the LORD said to Cain, 'Where is Abel your brother?' He said, 'I do not know; am I my brother's keeper?' And the LORD said, 'What have you done? The voice of your brother's blood is crying to me from the ground.'" Curiously, Nietzsche's mental breakdown appears to have followed his attempt to protect a horse that was being whipped in a public square in Turin.

[217] *A Cherubim*: Technically, "cherubim" is plural (Hebrew: "the near ones/familiars/bodyguards/courtiers"; see *Book of Thel*, 1.1); the singular should be "cherub".

[218] *Game Cock*: roosters specially bred for cockfighting. Cockfighting was not banned in England and Wales until the Cruelty to Animals Act of 1835.

Speaks the Unbeliever's fright.
He who shall hurt the little Wren
Shall never be belov'd by Men.   30
He who the Ox to wrath has movd
Shall never be by Woman lovd.
The wanton Boy that kills the Fly
Shall feel the Spider's enmity.
He who torments the Chafer's[219] sprite[220]   35
Weaves a Bower in endless Night.
The Catterpiller on the Leaf[221]
Repeats to thee thy Mother's grief.
Kill not the Moth nor Butterfly,
For the Last Judgment draweth nigh   40
He who shall train the Horse to War
Shall never pass the Polar Bar.[222]
The Begger's Dog & Widow's Cat:
Feed them & thou wilt grow fat.
The Gnat that sings his Summer's song   45
Poison gets from Slander's tongue.
The poison of the Snake & Newt
Is the sweat of Envy's Foot.
The Poison of the Honey Bee
Is the Artist's Jealousy.   50
The Prince's Robes & Beggar's Rags
Are Toadstools on the Miser's Bags.
A truth that's told with bad intent
Beats all the Lies you can invent.
It is right it should be so: 55
Man was made for Joy & Woe,
And when this we rightly know
Thro the World we safely go.
Joy & Woe are woven fine,

---

[219] *Chafer's*: i.e., a cockchafer, a beetle of the genus *Melolontha*.
[220] *sprite*: Spirit.
[221] *Catterpiller on the Leaf*: See "The Sick Rose", line 2, note 97, and also *The Marriage of Heaven and Hell*, "Proverbs of Hell", plate 9.
[222] *Polar Bar*: See *Songs of Experience*, "Introduction", line 9, note 93.

A Clothing for the Soul divine;   60
Under every grief & pine
Runs a joy with silken twine.
The Babe is more than swadling Bands;
Throughout all these Human Lands.
Tools were made, & Born were hands,   65
Every Farmer Understands.
Every Tear from Every Eye
Becomes a Babe in Eternity;
This is caught by Females bright
And returnd to its own delight.   70
The Bleat, the Bark, Bellow & Roar,
Are Waves that Beat on Heaven's Shore.
The Babe that weeps the Rod beneath
Writes Revenge in realms of death.
The Beggar's Rags, fluttering in Air,   75
Does to Rags the Heavens tear.
The Soldier, armd with Sword & Gun,
Palsied[223] strikes the Summer's Sun.
The poor Man's Farthing is worth more
Than all the Gold on Afric's Shore.   80
One Mite wrung from the Labrer's hands
Shall buy & sell the Miser's Lands,
Or if protected from on high
Does that whole Nation sell & buy.
He who mocks the Infant's Faith   85
Shall be mock'd in Age & Death.
He who shall teach the Child to Doubt
The rotting Grave shall ne'er get out.
He who respects the Infant's faith
Triumphs over Hell & Death.   90
The Child's Toys & the Old Man's Reasons
Are the Fruits of the Two seasons.
The Questioner who sits so sly
Shall never know how to Reply;

---

[223] *Palsied*: crippled with involuntary tremors.

He who replies to words of Doubt 95
Doth put the Light of Knowledge out.
The Strongest Poison ever known
Came from Caesar's Laurel Crown.
Nought can deform the Human Race
Like to the Armour's iron brace. 100
When Gold & Gems adorn the Plow
To peaceful Arts shall Envy Bow.
A Riddle or the Cricket's Cry
Is to Doubt a fit Reply.
The Emmet's[224] Inch & Eagle's Mile 105
Make Lame Philosophy to smile.
He who Doubts from what he sees
Will ne'er Believe, do what you Please.
If the Sun & Moon should doubt,
They'd immediately Go out. 110
To be in a Passion you Good may do,
But no Good if a Passion is in you.
The Whore & Gambler, by the State
Licenc'd, build that Nation's Fate.
The Harlot's cry from Street to Street 115
Shall weave Old England's winding Sheet.[225]
The Winner's Shout, the Loser's Curse,[226]
Dance before dead England's Hearse.
Every Night & every Morn
Some to Misery are Born. 120
Every Morn & every Night
Some are Born to sweet delight.
Some are Born to sweet delight,
Some are Born to Endless Night.
We are led to Believe a Lie 125
When we see not Thro the Eye,[227]

---

[224] *Emmet's*: i.e., ant's.

[225] *winding Sheet*: shroud.

[226] *Winner's Shout, the Loser's Curse*: The reference here is to gambling.

[227] *we see not Thro the Eye*: See "Mock on Mock on Voltaire Rousseau", line 7, note 178.

Which was Born in a Night to perish in a Night,[228]
When the Soul Slept in Beams of Light.
God Appears & God is Light
To those poor Souls who dwell in Night,   130
But does a Human Form Display
To those who Dwell in Realms of day.

Long John Brown and Little Mary Bell

Little Mary Bell had a Fairy[229] in a Nut;
Long John Brown had the Devil[230] in his Gut.
Long John Brown lovd Little Mary Bell,
And the Fairy drew the Devil into the Nut-shell.

Her Fairy Skipd out & her Fairy Skipd in;   5
He laughd at the Devil saying "Love is a Sin."
The Devil he raged & the Devil he was wroth,
And the Devil enterd into the Young Man's broth.

He was soon in the Gut of the loving Young Swain,
For John eat & drank to drive away Love's pain;   10
But all he could do he grew thinner & thinner,
Tho he eat & drank as much as ten Men for his dinner.

Some said he had a Wolf in his stomach[231] day & night,
Some said he had the Devil & they guessed right;

---

[228] *Born in a Night to perish in a Night*: Cf. Jonah 4:9–10, where God reproves Jonah: "But God said to Jonah, 'Do you do well to be angry for the plant?' And he said, 'I do well to be angry, angry enough to die.' And the LORD said, 'You pity the plant, for which you did not labor, nor did you make it grow, which came up into being in a night, and perished in a night.'"

[229] *Fairy*: Blake had a theosophical view of fairies as natural spirits or elementals (see the note to line 132 of Coleridge's "The Rime of the Ancient Mariner"). He associated fairies with sexual delight.

[230] *Devil*: i.e., sexual desire.

[231] *Wolf in his stomach*: Cf. Shakespeare, *Troilus and Cressida*, Act I, scene 3, line 121: "And appetite, an universal wolf".

The fairy skipd about in his Glory, Joy & Pride,   15
And he laughd at the Devil till poor John Brown died.

Then the Fairy skipd out of the old Nut shell,
And woe & alack for Pretty Mary Bell!
For the Devil crept in when the Fairy skipd out,
And there goes Miss Bell with her fusty[232] old Nut.   20

William Bond

I wonder whether the Girls are mad,[233]
And I wonder whether they mean to kill,
And I wonder if William Bond will die,
For assuredly he is very ill.

He went to Church in a May morning,   5
Attended by Fairies,[234] one, two, & three;
But the Angels of Providence[235] drove them away,
And he returnd home in Misery.

He went not out to the Field nor Fold,
He went not out to the Village nor Town,   10
But he came home in a black, black cloud,
And took to his Bed & there lay down.

And an Angel of Providence at his Feet,
And an Angel of Providence at his Head,
And in the midst a Black, Black Cloud,   15
And in the midst the Sick Man on his Bed.

---

[232] *fusty*: stale; dry with age; moldy-smelling; peevish. Cf. Shakespeare, *Troilus and Cressida*, Act 2, scene 1, line 103: "as good crack a fusty nut with no kernel".
[233] *mad*: insane.
[234] *Attended by Fairies*: See "Long John Brown and Little Mary Bell", line 1.
[235] *Angels of Providence*: spirits of "conventional" morality.

And on his Right hand was Mary Green,
And on his Left hand was his Sister Jane,
And their tears fell thro the black, black Cloud,
To drive away the sick man's pain.   20

"O William, if thou dost another Love,
Dost another Love better than poor Mary,
Go & take that other to be thy Wife,
And Mary Green shall her Servant be."

"Yes, Mary, I do another Love,   25
Another I Love far better than thee,
And Another I will have for my Wife;
Then what have I to do with thee?[236]

"For thou art Melancholy, Pale,
And on thy Head is the cold Moon's shine,   30
But she is ruddy & bright as day,
And the sun beams dazzle from her eyne."

Mary trembled & Mary chilld
And Mary fell down on the right-hand floor,
That William Bond & his Sister Jane   35
Scarce could recover Mary more.

When Mary woke & found her laid
On the Right hand of her William dear—
On the Right hand of his loved Bed,
And saw her William Bond so near—   40

The Fairies that fled from William Bond
Danced around her Shining Head;
They danced over the Pillow White,
And the Angels of Providence left the Bed.

[236] *Then what have I to do with thee?*: See "To Tirzah", line 4.

I thought Love livd in the hot sun shine,   45
But O, he lives in the Moony light!
I thought to find Love in the heat of day,
But sweet Love is the Comforter of Night.

Seek Love in the Pity of others'
Woe, In the gentle relief of another's care,   50
In the darkness of night & the winter's snow,
In the naked & outcast, Seek Love there.

From Milton[237]

"And did those feet in ancient time"[238]

And did those feet in ancient time
Walk upon England's mountains green:[239]
And was the holy Lamb of God,
On England's pleasant pastures seen!

And did the Countenance Divine,   5
Shine forth upon our clouded hills?

---

[237] Illuminated Prophetic Book, 1804–1815. In it, Milton returns from Heaven, and enters into Blake in order to grapple with his (Milton's) own theological errors and redeem the world. The poem involves an extended consideration of Milton's spirituality, "errors", and relationship to Blake, as well as the very writing of the poem.

[238] Also known as the hymn "Jerusalem", famously set to music by Sir Hubert Parry (1848–1918).

[239] *did those feet in ancient time/Walk upon England's mountains green*: Some legends relate that the boy Jesus traveled to Britain with Saint Joseph of Arimathea—a figure important to Blake (he is equated with Los in *The Four Zoas*), and further identified in legend as the bearer of the Holy Grail to Britain and a founder of Glastonbury Abbey. It was Saint Joseph of Arimathea who provided the tomb for Christ's body after the Crucifixion (see Mark 15:43–46).

And was Jerusalem[240] builded here,
Among these dark Satanic Mills?[241]

Bring me my Bow of burning gold:
Bring me my Arrows of desire: 10
Bring me my Spear: O clouds unfold!
Bring me my Chariot of fire![242]

I will not cease from Mental Fight,[243]
Nor shall my Sword sleep in my hand:
Till we have built Jerusalem,   15
In England's green & pleasant Land.[244]

Would to God that all the Lord's people were Prophets.

Numbers, xi. ch. 29 v.

[240] *Jerusalem*: the Divine Vision, the City of Peace, Liberty, the Emanation (feminine portion) of Albion, the Bride of the Lamb.

[241] *dark Satanic Mills*: According to Raine,

> For Blake, outward events and circumstances were the *expressions* of states of mind, ideologies, mentalities, and not, as for the determinist-materialist ideologies of the modern world, their causes. Blake's "dark Satanic Mills", so often invoked in the name of social reform, prove ... to be the mechanistic "laws" of Bacon, Newton and Locke, of which the industrial landscape was a reflection and expression. Man has made his machines in the image of his ideology.... Only a change of the heart and mind of the nation can create a new society and new cities less hideous than those created by an atheist and mechanistic rationalism. (Raine, *William Blake*, pp. 73–74)

[242] *O clouds unfold ... Chariot of fire*: Cf. 2 Kings 2:11: "And as they [Elisha and Elijah] still went on and talked, behold, a chariot of fire and horses of fire separated the two of them. And Elijah went up by a whirlwind into heaven."

[243] *I will not cease from Mental Fight*: Cf. Ephesians 6:11–12: "Put on the whole armor of God, that you may be able to stand against the wiles of the devil. For we are not contending against flesh and blood, but against the principalities, against the powers, against the world rulers of this present darkness".

[244] *built Jerusalem, / In England's green & pleasant Land*: To what it means to "build Jerusalem in England's green and pleasant land" Owen Barfield replies,

> And what *can* it mean except this, which is not the concern of England alone, but of all humanity, to rise from the Consciousness Soul to the Imaginative Soul?—The other Jerusalem—the visible one—can only arise as the outward form of this invisible City of the mind. The "Satanic Mills", which have arisen over England since Blake's time, will never be thrust

The following is from book 2, 40.28–41.28.

But turning toward Ololon[245] in terrible majesty Milton
Replied, "Obey thou the Words of the Inspired Man!
All that can be annihilated must be annihilated,   30
That the Children of Jerusalem may be saved from slavery.
There is a Negation, & there is a Contrary:
The Negation must be destroyd to redeem the Contraries.
The Negation is the Spectre, the Reasoning Power
    in Man.
This is a false Body: an Incrustation over my Immortal   35
Spirit: a Selfhood, which must be put off & annihilated
    alway.[246]
To cleanse the Face of my Spirit by Self-examination,

[PLATE 41]
To bathe in the Waters of Life, to wash off the Not Human,
I come in Self-annihilation & the grandeur of Inspiration!
To cast off Rational Demonstration by Faith in the
    Saviour,
To cast off the rotten rags of Memory by Inspiration,
To cast off Bacon, Locke,[247] & Newton[248] from Albion's[249]
    covering,   5

---

down from their hideous tyranny, until those of which he actually sang—
the dead thinking of Newton, Locke, and Hobbes—have been burst asun-
der from within. (Owen Barfield, *Romanticism Comes of Age* [San Rafael,
Calif.: Barfield Press, 2006], p. 83)

[245] *Ololon*: the sixfold Emanation (feminine portion) of Milton.
[246] *alway*: i.e., throughout all time.
[247] *Bacon, Locke*: Sir Francis Bacon (1561–1626) was an English empiricist phi-
losopher, scientist, statesman, and man of letters. For Locke (and Bacon), see *The
Marriage of Heaven and Hell*, "The Voice of the Devil", plate 6, note on "Ratio".
[248] *Newton*: See "Mock on Mock on Voltaire Rousseau", line 10.
[249] *Albion's*: i.e., Britain's.

To take off his filthy garments, & clothe him with
   Imagination!
To cast aside from Poetry all that is not Inspiration,
That it no longer shall dare to mock with the aspersion
   of Madness
Cast on the Inspired by the tame high finisher of paltry
   Blots
Indefinite, or paltry Rhymes; or paltry Harmonies;   10
Who creeps into State Government like a catterpiller[250]
   to destroy!
To cast off the idiot Questioner who is always questioning.
But never capable of answering; who sits with a sly grin
Silent plotting when to question, like a thief in a cave;
Who publishes doubt & calls it knowledge; whose
   Science is Despair,   15
Whose pretence to knowledge is Envy: whose whole
   Science is
To destroy the wisdom of ages to gratify ravenous Envy,
That rages round him like a Wolf day & night without
   rest.
He smiles with condescension; he talks of Benevolence
   & Virtue,
And those who act with Benevolence & Virtue, they
   murder time on time: 20
These are the destroyers of Jerusalem,[251] these are the
   murderers
Of Jesus, who deny the Faith & mock at Eternal Life:
Who pretend to Poetry, that they may destroy
   Imagination:[252]
By imitation of Nature's Images drawn from Remembrance.

---

[250] *like a catterpiller*: See "The Sick Rose", line 2.

[251] *These are the destroyers of Jerusalem*: See "And did those feet in ancient time", line 7.

[252] *Of Jesus . . . Imagination*: On Jesus, the Imagination, see the introductory text to *Songs of Innocence and of Experience*, pp. 20–21.

These are the Sexual Garments,[253] the Abomination of
   Desolation[254]   25
Hiding the Human Lineaments as with an Ark &
   Curtains
Which Jesus rent:[255] & now shall wholly purge away
   with Fire
Till Generation is swallowd up in Regeneration."

From *Jerusalem:*
The Emanation of the Giant Albion[256]

The following is from chapter 2, plate 44, lines 21–40.

And Los prayed and said, "O Divine Saviour arise
Upon the Mountains of Albion as in ancient time.
   Behold!
The Cities of Albion seek thy face, London groans
   in pain
From Hill to Hill & the Thames laments along the Valleys
The little Villages of Middlesex[257] & Surrey[258] hunger &
   thirst   25
The Twenty-eight Cities of Albion stretch their hands
   to thee:

[253] *Sexual Garments*: the flesh.

[254] *Abomination of Desolation*: Cf. Matthew 24:15–16: "When ye therefore shall see the abomination of desolation, spoken of by Daniel the prophet, stand in the holy place, (whoso readeth, let him understand) Then let them which be in Judaea flee into the mountains" (KJV). Jesus is referring to Daniel 9:26–27.

[255] *Ark & Curtains/Which Jesus rent*: the events immediately following Jesus' death on the Cross; see Matthew 27:50–51: "Jesus cried again with a loud voice and yielded up his spirit. And behold, the curtain of the temple was torn in two, from top to bottom; and the earth shook, and the rocks were split".

[256] Illuminated Prophetic Book, 1804–1820—Blake's longest, most ambitious work. It is the story of the fall of Albion (Britain/Cosmic Man) from union with Jesus; his banishment of his Emanation (feminine portion), Jerusalem; his seduction by Vala, the goddess of nature; his eventual reunion through the efforts of Los (poetry/the creative impulse/Blake himself).

[257] *Middlesex*: county in South East England. In Blake's day, Middlesex contained much of London.

[258] *Surrey*: See "The Crystal Cabinet", line 12.

Because of the Opressors of Albion in every City &
   Village:
They mock at the Labourer's limbs! they mock at his
   starvd Children!
They buy his Daughters that they may have power to
   sell his Sons:
They compel the Poor to live upon a crust of bread by
   soft mild arts: 30
They reduce the Man to want: then give with pomp &
   ceremony.
The praise of Jehovah is chaunted from lips of hunger &
   thirst:

"Humanity knows not of Sex: wherefore are Sexes in
   Beulah?[259]
In Beulah the Female lets down her beautiful Tabernacle;
Which the Male enters magnificent between her
   Cherubim:[260]   35
And becomes One with her, mingling, condensing in
   Self-love
The Rocky Law of Condemnation[261] & double Generation,
   & Death.
Albion hath enterd the Loins, the place of the Last
   Judgment:[262]

[259] *Humanity knows not of Sex . . . Sexes in Beulah*: See introductory text to "The
Crystal Cabinet", p. 67.

[260] *Tabernacle . . . between her Cherubim*: The Tabernacle is the portable sanc-
tuary of the Divine Presence, housing the Ark of the Covenant in the inner
shrine—the Holy of Holies. See Exodus 25–31. Two cherubim of wrought gold
were placed on the lid of the Ark. Here, the imagery is plainly sexual. See Blake's
sketch of the female genitals as "A chapel all of gold", in Kathleen Raine, *Blake
and Antiquity* (London: Routledge, 2002), illustration 19, p. 130.

[261] *Rocky Law of Condemnation*: See *The Marriage of Heaven and Hell*, "A Song
of Liberty", number 20.

[262] *Last Judgment*: At Christ's Second Coming he will judge the living and the
dead (see Matthew 25:31–46), separating the goats from the sheep, the damned
from the saved. Blake, however, didn't believe in final damnation. By Last
Judgment he means the definitive recognition and casting out of error—either by
the individual or on a larger scale.

And Luvah[263] hath drawn the Curtains around Albion in
    Vala's bosom.
The Dead awake to Generation! Arise O Lord, & rend the
    Veil!"   40

To the Christians

The following is from chapter 3, plate 77.

I give you the end of a golden string,
    Only wind it into a ball:
It will lead you in at Heaven's gate
    Built in Jerusalem's wall.

[263] *Luvah*: See *Book of Thel*, 2.8.

WILLIAM WORDSWORTH

Preface to *Lyrical Ballads*

First published in 1798, the collection *Lyrical Ballads* by William Wordsworth and his friend Samuel Taylor Coleridge was to prove to be an enormously influential volume, to the extent that the birth of the English Romantic movement is conventionally identified with its publication. Although Coleridge's contribution was numerically small (consisting of only four of the twenty-three poems), it included "The Rime of the Ancient Mariner", which was ultimately to prove to be one of the most celebrated long poems in the English language.

Wordsworth's preface was composed for the second edition (1800), and revised and expanded for the third edition (1802); it is this version which is given below. T.S. Eliot asserted that "his critical insight, in this one *Preface* and the *Supplement*, is enough to give him the highest place ... there is, in his poetry and in his Preface, a profound spiritual revival, an inspiration communicated rather to Pusey and Newman, to Ruskin, and to the great humanitarians, than to the accredited poets of the next age."[1]

Following is the preface to *Lyrical Ballads*.

The first Volume of these Poems has already been submitted to general perusal. It was published, as an experiment, which, I hoped, might be of some use to ascertain, how far, by fitting to metrical arrangement a selection of the real language of men in a state of vivid sensation, that sort of pleasure and that quantity of pleasure may be imparted, which a Poet may rationally endeavour to impart.

I had formed no very inaccurate estimate of the probable effect of those Poems: I flattered myself that they who should be pleased with them would read them with more than common

---

[1] T.S. Eliot, *The Use of Poetry and the Use of Criticism* (London: Faber and Faber, 1933), p. 80.

pleasure: and, on the other hand, I was well aware, that by those who should dislike them, they would be read with more than common dislike. The result has differed from my expectation in this only, that a greater number have been pleased than I ventured to hope I should please....

It is supposed, that by the act of writing in verse an Author makes a formal engagement that he will gratify certain known habits of association; that he not only thus apprises the Reader that certain classes of ideas and expressions will be found in his book, but that others will be carefully excluded. This exponent[2] or symbol held forth by metrical language must in different eras of literature have excited very different expectations: for example, in the age of Catullus, Terence, and Lucretius, and that of Statius or Claudian; and in our own country, in the age of Shakespeare and Beaumont and Fletcher, and that of Donne and Cowley, or Dryden, or Pope.[3] I will not take upon

---

[2] In algebra, an exponent is an index, a symbol denoting the power to which a base is raised.

[3] Catullus (ca. 84–ca. 54 B.C.) was a major Roman lyric poet, famous for his impassioned love poetry and invectives. Terence (195 or 185–159 B.C.) was a major Roman author of poetic comedies, renowned for his sensitive character portrayal and a gracious, conversational style. Lucretius (ca. 99–ca. 55 B.C.) was a major Roman epic philosophical (Epicurean) poet and author of *The Nature of Things*. Statius (A.D. ca. 45–ca. 96) was an important Roman epic and lyric poet and author of the *Thebaid*; he features significantly in the closing cantos of Dante's *Purgatory*, joining Dante and Virgil just before the Sixth Terrace and accompanying them as far as the Earthly Paradise. Statius' reputation and influence stood very high in the Middle Ages and Renaissance, but it declined in the nineteenth century. Claudian (A.D. late fourth–early fifth century) was often regarded as the last important poet in the pagan Roman tradition. Catullus, Terence, and Lucretius are usually identified with the early (Republican) Golden Age of Roman literature, Statius with its Silver Age, and Claudian with its decadence or twilight. Francis Beaumont (1584–1616) and John Fletcher (1579–1625), both poets and dramatists, wrote some fifteen plays in collaboration; their standing among the elite of Shakespeare's (1564–1616) contemporaries survived into the early twentieth century. John Donne (1572–1630) was a major metaphysical poet, satirist, and, later in life, clergyman and dean of St. Paul's Cathedral. Although Coleridge (eventually) and, later, Browning admired Donne, his present stature dates from the first third of the twentieth century. Wordsworth described Donne's sonnet "Death, be not proud" as "eminently characteristic of his manner, and at the same time so weighty in the thought, and vigorous in the expression ... though to modern taste it may be repulsive, quaint, and laboured" (Alexander B. Grosart, ed., *The Prose Works of William Wordsworth*, vol. 3 [London, 1876], pp. 332–33).

me to determine the exact import of the promise which, by the act of writing in verse, an Author, in the present day makes to his reader: but it will undoubtedly appear to many persons that I have not fulfilled the terms of an engagement thus voluntarily contracted. They who have been accustomed to the gaudiness and inane phraseology of many modern writers, if they persist in reading this book to its conclusion, will, no doubt, frequently have to struggle with feelings of strangeness and awkwardness: they will look round for poetry, and will be induced to inquire by what species of courtesy these attempts can be permitted to assume that title. I hope therefore the reader will not censure me for attempting to state what I have proposed to myself to perform; and also (as far as the limits of a preface will permit) to explain some of the chief reasons which have determined me in the choice of my purpose: that at least he may be spared any unpleasant feeling of disappointment, and that I myself may be protected from one of the most dishonourable accusations which can be brought against an Author; namely, that of an indolence which prevents him from endeavouring to ascertain what is his duty, or, when his duty is ascertained, prevents him from performing it.

The principal object, then, proposed in these Poems was to choose incidents and situations from common life, and to relate or describe them, throughout, as far as was possible in a selection of language really used by men, and, at the same

---

Abraham Cowley (1618–1667) was an important poet and essayist, and creator of the English "Pindaric" Ode (stanzas of a varying number of rhymed lines of irregular length; among the great achievements in this form are the Odes of Dryden and Wordsworth's own "Intimations of Immortality"). He was the most widely admired poet between Milton and Dryden, but his reputation declined in the nineteenth century, though he is beginning to be rediscovered as a master of familiar and festive verse. Wordsworth was fond of him: "Read all Cowley; he is very valuable to a collector of English sound sense" (ibid., p. 465). John Dryden (1631–1700) was a major poet, satirist, translator, critic, essayist, and dramatist; he was founder of the Augustan style and the greatest literary figure of the Restoration (1660–1689). Alexander Pope (1688–1744) was a major poet, satirist, translator, and the quintessence of the Augustan ideal in poetry and the greatest English poet of the eighteenth century. Wordsworth had a profound aversion to what he saw as "the artifices which have over-run our writings in metre since the days of Dryden and Pope" (ibid., vol. 1, p. 64), though he occasionally expressed considerable admiration for aspects of their poetry.

time, to throw over them a certain colouring of imagination, whereby ordinary things should be presented to the mind in an unusual aspect; and, further, and above all, to make these incidents and situations interesting by tracing in them, truly though not ostentatiously, the primary laws of our nature: chiefly, as far as regards the manner in which we associate ideas in a state of excitement.[4] Humble and rustic life was generally chosen, because, in that condition, the essential passions of the heart find a better soil in which they can attain their maturity,

---

[4] See Derek Roper's excellent summary of Hartley's influence here:

By emphasising the communicative power of poetry Wordsworth raises the question of what it communicates. The traditional formula had been that poetry should both teach and delight; and Wordsworth analyses both processes in terms of the system of psychology set forth by David Hartley (1707–1757) in his *Observations on Man* (1749). Some knowledge of Hartley's doctrines is necessary to a full understanding both of the Preface and of several of Wordsworth's poems. Like modern behaviourists, Hartley taught that character is evolved by continuous and largely automatic processes of conditioning (or "association"), all of which begin with the experience of the senses. From earliest childhood we learn to associate certain sights, sounds, tastes, etc., with pleasant or painful feelings. As more and more associations are formed they build themselves into increasingly complex systems of responses which together make up the whole of our personality, "imagination" being the first faculty thus developed and the "moral sense" the last. Hartley assumed that nature (i.e. the created universe) was rationally organised for a benevolent purpose. From this it followed that the general tendency of nature's conditioning must be to lead men to happiness and virtue. Just as we come to know wholesome food by associating it with pleasure (and bad food by associating it with pain), so by more intricate but essentially similar processes we learn the pleasures of self-approval, sympathy for our fellow-creatures, and the love of God (and the pains of the opposite states). While apparently scientific in character, Hartley's system could be felt to confirm that sense of a living relationship between men and the material universe which it had become increasingly difficult to do in a century dominated by mathematics and Newtonian physics. Coleridge showed his admiration by naming his eldest son "David Hartley" in 1796, and Wordsworth too was strongly influenced by Hartley's ideas during the period when most of the *Lyrical Ballads* were being written. Hartley's optimism may seem shallow to modern readers, but it suited and supported Wordsworth's growing happiness at this time. Furthermore, Hartley's associationist psychology showed Wordsworth the importance of unconscious processes in our mental and emotional life and gave him terms to describe them. (*Lyrical Ballads 1805*, ed. Derek Roper [London: Macdonald and Evans, 1979], pp. 274–75)

are less under restraint, and speak a plainer and more emphatic language; because in that condition of life our elementary feelings coexist in a state of greater simplicity, and, consequently, may be more accurately contemplated, and more forcibly communicated; because the manners of rural life germinate from those elementary feelings, and, from the necessary character of rural occupations, are more easily comprehended, and are more durable; and, lastly, because in that condition the passions of men are incorporated with the beautiful and permanent forms of nature. The language, too, of these men has been adopted (purified indeed from what appear to be its real defects, from all lasting and rational causes of dislike or disgust) because such men hourly communicate with the best objects from which the best part of language is originally derived; and because, from their rank in society and the sameness and narrow circle of their intercourse, being less under the influence of social vanity, they convey their feelings and notions in simple and unelaborated expressions. Accordingly, such a language, arising out of repeated experience and regular feelings, is a more permanent, and a far more philosophical language, than that which is frequently substituted for it by Poets, who think that they are conferring honour upon themselves and their art, in proportion as they separate themselves from the sympathies of men, and indulge in arbitrary and capricious habits of expression, in order to furnish food for fickle tastes, and fickle appetites, of their own creation.[5]

I cannot, however, be insensible to the present outcry against the triviality and meanness, both of thought and language, which some of my contemporaries have occasionally introduced into their metrical compositions; and I acknowledge that this defect, where it exists, is more dishonourable to the Writer's own character than false refinement or arbitrary innovation, though I should contend at the same time, that it is far less pernicious in the sum of its consequences. From such verses the Poems in these volumes will be found distinguished at least by one mark of difference, that each of them

---

[5] "It is worth while here to observe that the affecting parts of Chaucer are almost always expressed in language pure and universally intelligible to this day" (Wordsworth's note, 1800, though in Coleridge's handwriting in the manuscript).

has a worthy *purpose*. Not that I always began to write with a distinct purpose formerly conceived; but habits of meditation have, I trust, so prompted and regulated my feelings, that my descriptions of such objects as strongly excite those feelings, will be found to carry along with them a *purpose*. If this opinion be erroneous, I can have little right to the name of a Poet. For all good poetry is the spontaneous overflow of powerful feelings: and though this be true, Poems to which any value can be attached were never produced on any variety of subjects but by a man who, being possessed of more than usual organic sensibility, had also thought long and deeply. For our continued influxes of feeling are modified and directed by our thoughts, which are indeed the representatives of all our past feelings; and, as by contemplating the relation of these general representatives to each other, we discover what is really important to men, so, by the repetition and continuance of this act, our feelings will be connected with important subjects, till at length, if we be originally possessed of much sensibility, such habits of mind will be produced, that, by obeying blindly and mechanically the impulses of those habits, we shall describe objects, and utter sentiments, of such a nature, and in such connexion with each other, that the understanding of the Reader must necessarily be in some degree enlightened, and his affections strengthened and purified.[6]

It has been said that each of these poems has a purpose. Another circumstance must be mentioned which distinguishes these Poems from the popular Poetry of the day; it is this, that the feeling therein developed gives importance to the action and situation, and not the action and situation to the feeling.

A sense of false modesty shall not prevent me from asserting, that the Reader's attention is pointed to this mark of

[6] According to Roper,

The latter part of this passage describes in Hartleian terms the process by which a poet acquires what we should now call "values" and communicates them to others. Wordsworth sees that this process need not be a matter of explicit moralising but of the poet's unconsciously ("blindly and mechanically") expressing his own habits of mind. Thus the poet "teaches" whenever he gives himself fully to the theme he is engaged on—though it be only the story of an old man cutting wood. What is "taught" depends on the quality of his response to this theme. (*Lyrical Ballads*, p. 276)

distinction, far less for the sake of these particular Poems than from the general importance of the subject. The subject is indeed important! For the human mind is capable of being excited without the application of gross and violent stimulants; and he must have a very faint perception of its beauty and dignity who does not know this, and who does not further know, that one being is elevated above another, in proportion as he possesses this capability. It has therefore appeared to me, that to endeavour to produce or enlarge this capability is one of the best services in which, at any period, a Writer can be engaged; but this service, excellent at all times, is especially so at the present day. For a multitude of causes, unknown to former times, are now acting with a combined force to blunt the discriminating[7] powers of the mind, and, unfitting it for all voluntary exertion, to reduce it to a state of almost savage torpor. The most effective of these causes are the great national events which are daily taking place, and the increasing accumulation of men in cities, where the uniformity of their occupations produces a craving for extraordinary incident, which the rapid communication of intelligence[8] hourly gratifies. To this tendency of life and manners the literature and theatrical exhibitions of the country have conformed themselves. The invaluable works of our elder writers, I had almost said the works of Shakespeare and Milton, are driven into neglect by frantic novels, sickly and stupid German Tragedies, and deluges of idle and extravagant stories in verse.—When I think upon this degrading thirst after outrageous stimulation, I am almost ashamed to have spoken of the feeble endeavour made in these volumes to counteract it; and, reflecting upon the magnitude of the general evil, I should be oppressed with no dishonourable melancholy, had I not a deep impression of certain inherent and indestructible qualities of the human mind, and likewise of certain powers in the great and permanent objects that act upon it, which are equally inherent and indestructible; and were there not added to this impression a belief, that the time is approaching when the evil will be systematically opposed, by men of greater powers, and with far more distinguished success.

---

[7] *discriminating*: able to make or recognize distinctions.
[8] *communication of intelligence*: information, news.

Having dwelt thus long on the subjects and aim of these
Poems, I shall request the Reader's permission to apprise him
of a few circumstances relating to their *style*, in order, among
other reasons, that he may not censure me for not having per-
formed what I never attempted. The Reader will find that per-
sonifications of abstract ideas rarely occur in these volumes; and
are utterly rejected, as an ordinary device to elevate the style,
and raise it above prose. My purpose was to imitate, and, as far
as is possible, to adopt the very language of men; and assuredly
such personifications do not make any natural or regular part of
that language. They are, indeed, a figure of speech occasionally
prompted by passion, and I have made use of them as such;
but have endeavoured utterly to reject them as a mechanical
device of style, or as a family language which Writers in metre
seem to lay claim to by prescription. I have wished to keep the
Reader in the company of flesh and blood, persuaded that by
so doing I shall interest him. Others who pursue a different
track will interest him likewise; I do not interfere with their
claim, but wish to prefer a claim of my own. There will also be
found in these volumes little of what is usually called poetic
diction; as much pains has been taken to avoid it as is ordi-
narily taken to produce it; this has been done for the reason
already alleged, to bring my language near to the language of
men; and further, because the pleasure which I have proposed
to myself to impart, is of a kind very different from that which
is supposed by many persons to be the proper object of poetry.
Without being culpably particular, I do not know how to give
my Reader a more exact notion of the style in which it was
my wish and intention to write, than by informing him that I
have at all times endeavoured to look steadily at my subject;
consequently, there is I hope in these Poems little falsehood
of description, and my ideas are expressed in language fitted
to their respective importance. Something must have been
gained by this practice, as it is friendly to one property of all
good poetry, namely, good sense: but it has necessarily cut me
off from a large portion of phrases and figures of speech which
from father to son have long been regarded as the common
inheritance of Poets. I have also thought it expedient to restrict
myself still further, having abstained from the use of many
expressions, in themselves proper and beautiful, but which

have been foolishly repeated by bad Poets, till such feelings of disgust are connected with them as it is scarcely possible by any art of association to overpower.

If in a poem there should be found a series of lines, or even a single line, in which the language, though naturally arranged, and according to the strict laws of metre, does not differ from that of prose, there is a numerous class of critics, who, when they stumble upon these prosaisms, as they call them, imagine that they have made a notable discovery, and exult over the Poet as over a man ignorant of his own profession. Now these men would establish a canon of criticism which the Reader will conclude he must utterly reject, if he wishes to be pleased with these volumes. And it would be a most easy task to prove to him, that not only the language of a large portion of every good poem, even of the most elevated character, must necessarily, except with reference to the metre, in no respect differ from that of good prose, but likewise that some of the most interesting parts of the best poems will be found to be strictly the language of prose when prose is well written. The truth of this assertion might be demonstrated by innumerable passages from almost all the poetical writings, even of Milton[9] himself. To illustrate the subject in a general manner, I will here adduce a short composition of Gray,[10] who was at the head of those who, by their reasonings, have attempted to widen the space of separation betwixt Prose and Metrical composition, and was more than any other man curiously elaborate in the structure of his own poetic diction.

[9] John Milton (1608–1674) was an icon to the English Romantics, as a poet and a man (see, for instance, Wordsworth's "London, 1802"); his language is highly idiosyncratic, and Dr. Johnson had written of him in 1779, "Through all his greater works there prevails an uniform peculiarity of diction, a mode and cast of expression which bears little resemblance to that of any former writer; and which is so far removed from common use, that an unlearned reader, when he first opens his book, finds himself surprised by a new language" ("Life of Milton", in *Lives of the Most Eminent English Poets* [Warne, 1885], p. 76).

[10] Thomas Gray (1716–1771) was a major eighteenth-century lyric poet and scholar. Gray's reputation survived Wordsworth's assault (and Samuel Johnson's before it), and to the Victorians he was, in Arnold's words, "our poetical classic of that literature and age" ("The Study of Poetry", in *Essays in Criticism*, 2nd series [London: Macmillan, 1958], p. 25).

"In vain to me the smiling mornings shine,
And reddening Phœbus[11] lifts his golden fire:
The birds in vain their amorous descant[12] join,
Or cheerful fields resume their green attire.
These ears, alas! for other notes repine;[13]
A different object do these eyes require;
My lonely anguish melts no heart but mine;
And in my breast the imperfect joys expire;
Yet morning smiles the busy race to cheer,
And new-born pleasure brings to happier men;
The fields to all their wonted tribute bear;
To warm their little loves the birds complain.
I fruitless mourn to him that cannot hear,
And weep the more because I weep in vain."[14]

It will easily be perceived, that the only part of this Sonnet which is of any value is the lines printed in Italics; it is equally obvious, that, except in the rhyme, and in the use of the single word "fruitless" for fruitlessly, which is so far a defect, the language of these lines does in no respect differ from that of prose.

By the foregoing quotation it has been shown that the language of Prose may yet be well adapted to Poetry; and it was previously asserted, that a large portion of the language of every good poem can in no respect differ from that of good Prose. We will go further. It may be safely affirmed, that there neither is, nor can be, any *essential* difference between the language of prose and metrical composition. We are fond of tracing the resemblance between Poetry and Painting, and, accordingly, we call them Sisters: but where shall we find bonds of

[11] *Phœbus*: Apollo—god of the sun, light, poetry, and music.

[12] *descant*: a melodious accompaniment to plainchant, sung or played above it; the highest part of a score in part-singing; a melodious tune; harmony. Cf. Milton, *Paradise Lost*, bk. 4, line 603: "all but the wakeful nightingale/She all night long her amorous descant sung." Here, there is also perhaps a suggestion of the sung psalms and canticles of Anglican Morning Prayer.

[13] *repine*: "long discontentedly for" (*Oxford English Dictionary*, s.v. "repine").

[14] *In vain to me ... weep in vain*: Gray's "Sonnet on the Death of Mr. Richard West"; it was to West (1716–1742) that Gray had written that "the language of the age is never the language of poetry" (letter, April 8, 1742, in *The Letters of Thomas Gray*, ed. Duncan C. Tovey (London: George Bell and Sons, 1900), p. 97.

connexion sufficiently strict to typify the affinity betwixt metrical and prose composition? They both speak by and to the same organs; the bodies in which both of them are clothed may be said to be of the same substance, their affections are kindred, and almost identical, not necessarily differing even in degree; Poetry[15] sheds no tears "such as Angels weep," but natural and human tears; she can boast of no celestial ichor[16] that distinguishes her vital juices from those of prose; the same human blood circulates through the veins of them both.

If it be affirmed that rhyme and metrical arrangement of themselves constitute a distinction which overturns what has just been said on the strict affinity of metrical language with that of prose, and paves the way for other artificial distinctions which the mind voluntarily admits, I answer that the language of such Poetry as is here recommended is, as far as is possible, a selection of the language really spoken by men; that this selection, wherever it is made with true taste and feeling, will of itself form a distinction far greater than would at first be imagined, and will entirely separate the composition from the vulgarity and meanness of ordinary life; and, if metre be superadded thereto, I believe that a dissimilitude will be produced altogether sufficient for the gratification of a rational mind. What other distinction would we have? Whence is it to come? and where is it to exist? Not, surely, where the Poet speaks through the mouths of his characters: it cannot be necessary here, either for elevation of style, or any of its supposed ornaments: for, if the Poet's subject be judiciously chosen, it will naturally, and upon fit occasion, lead him to passions the

---

[15]*Poetry:* "I here use the word *poetry* (though against my own judgment) as opposed to the word *prose*, and synonymous with metrical composition. But much confusion has been introduced into criticism by this contradistinction of poetry and prose, instead of the more philosophical one of poetry and matter of fact, or science. The only strict antithesis to prose is metre; nor is this in truth a *strict* antithesis, because lines and passages of metre so naturally occur in writing prose that it would be scarcely possible to avoid them, even were it desirable" (William Wordsworth, "Preface to the Lyrical Ballads, Additions of 1802", in *Wordsworth and Coleridge, Lyrical Ballads,* eds. R. L. Brett and A. R. Jones, 2nd ed. (London and New York, 1991), p. 254.

[16]*ichor:* "the ethereal fluid, not blood, supposed to flow in the veins of the gods" (*Oxford English Dictionary,* s.v. "ichor").

language of which, if selected truly and judiciously, must nec-
essarily be dignified and variegated, and alive with metaphors
and figures. I forbear to speak of an incongruity which would
shock the intelligent Reader, should the Poet interweave any
foreign splendour of his own with that which the passion natu-
rally suggests: it is sufficient to say that such addition is unnec-
essary. And, surely, it is more probable that those passages,
which with propriety abound with metaphors and figures, will
have their due effect, if, upon other occasions where the pas-
sions are of a milder character, the style also be subdued and
temperate.

But, as the pleasure which I hope to give by the Poems now
presented to the Reader must depend entirely on just notions
upon this subject, and, as it is in itself of high importance to
our taste and moral feelings, I cannot content myself with these
detached remarks. And if, in what I am about to say, it shall
appear to some that my labour is unnecessary, and that I am like
a man fighting a battle without enemies, such persons may be
reminded, that, whatever be the language outwardly holden[17]
by men, a practical faith in the opinions which I am wishing to
establish is almost unknown. If my conclusions are admitted,
and carried as far as they must be carried if admitted at all, our
judgements concerning the works of the greatest Poets both
ancient and modern will be far different from what they are at
present, both when we praise, and when we censure: and our
moral feelings influencing and influenced by these judgements
will, I believe, be corrected and purified.

Taking up the subject, then, upon general grounds, let
me ask, what is meant by the word Poet? What is a Poet? To
whom does he address himself? And what language is to be
expected from him?—He is a man speaking to men: a man, it
is true, endowed with more lively sensibility, more enthusiasm
and tenderness, who has a greater knowledge of human nature,
and a more comprehensive soul, than are supposed to be com-
mon among mankind; a man pleased with his own passions
and volitions, and who rejoices more than other men in the
spirit of life that is in him; delighting to contemplate similar

---

[17] *holden*: in constant or habitual use.

volitions and passions as manifested in the goings-on of the Universe, and habitually impelled to create them where he does not find them. To these qualities he has added a disposition to be affected more than other men by absent things as if they were present; an ability of conjuring up in himself passions, which are indeed far from being the same as those produced by real events, yet (especially in those parts of the general sympathy which are pleasing and delightful) do more nearly resemble the passions produced by real events, than anything which, from the motions of their own minds merely, other men are accustomed to feel in themselves:—whence, and from practice, he has acquired a greater readiness and power in expressing what he thinks and feels, and especially those thoughts and feelings which, by his own choice, or from the structure of his own mind, arise in him without immediate external excitement.

But whatever portion of this faculty we may suppose even the greatest Poet to possess, there cannot be a doubt that the language which it will suggest to him, must often, in liveliness and truth, fall short of that which is uttered by men in real life, under the actual pressure of those passions, certain shadows of which the Poet thus produces, or feels to be produced, in himself.

However exalted a notion we would wish to cherish of the character of a Poet, it is obvious, that while he describes and imitates passions, his employment is in some degree mechanical, compared with the freedom and power of real and substantial action and suffering. So that it will be the wish of the Poet to bring his feelings near to those of the persons whose feelings he describes, nay, for short spaces of time, perhaps, to let himself slip into an entire delusion, and even confound and identify his own feelings with theirs; modifying only the language which is thus suggested to him by a consideration that he describes for a particular purpose, that of giving pleasure. Here, then, he will apply the principle of selection which has been already insisted upon. He will depend upon this for removing what would otherwise be painful or disgusting in the passion; he will feel that there is no necessity to trick out or to elevate nature: and, the more industriously he applies this principle, the deeper will be his faith that no words, which *his* fancy or imagination can suggest, will be to be compared with those which are the emanations of reality and truth.

But it may be said by those who do not object to the general spirit of these remarks, that, as it is impossible for the Poet to produce upon all occasions language as exquisitely fitted for the passion as that which the real passion itself suggests, it is proper that he should consider himself as in the situation of a translator, who does not scruple to substitute excellencies of another kind for those which are unattainable by him; and endeavours occasionally to surpass his original, in order to make some amends for the general inferiority to which he feels that he must submit. But this would be to encourage idleness and unmanly despair. Further, it is the language of men who speak of what they do not understand; who talk of Poetry as of a matter of amusement and idle pleasure; who will converse with us as gravely about a *taste* for Poetry, as they express it, as if it were a thing as indifferent as a taste for rope-dancing,[18] or Frontiniac[19] or Sherry. Aristotle, I have been told, has said, that Poetry is the most philosophic of all writing: it is so: its object is truth, not individual and local, but general, and operative; not standing upon external testimony, but carried alive into the heart by passion; truth which is its own testimony, which gives competence and confidence to the tribunal to which it appeals, and receives them from the same tribunal. Poetry is the image of man and nature. The obstacles which stand in the way of the fidelity of the Biographer and Historian, and of their consequent utility, are incalculably greater than those which are to be encountered by the Poet who comprehends the dignity of his art. The Poet writes under one restriction only, namely, the necessity of giving immediate pleasure to a human Being possessed of that information which may be expected from him, not as a lawyer, a physician, a mariner, an astronomer, or a natural philosopher, but as a Man. Except this one restriction, there is no object standing between the Poet and the image of things; between this, and the Biographer and Historian, there are a thousand.

[18] *rope-dancing:* tightrope walking.
[19] *Frontiniac:* a sweet French muscat wine.

Nor let this necessity of producing immediate pleasure be considered as a degradation of the Poet's art. It is far otherwise. It is an acknowledgement of the beauty of the universe, an acknowledgement the more sincere, because not formal, but indirect; it is a task light and easy to him who looks at the world in the spirit of love: further, it is a homage paid to the native and naked dignity of man, to the grand elementary principle of pleasure, by which he knows, and feels, and lives, and moves. We have no sympathy but what is propagated by pleasure: I would not be misunderstood; but wherever we sympathize with pain, it will be found that the sympathy is produced and carried on by subtle combinations with pleasure. We have no knowledge, that is, no general principles drawn from the contemplation of particular facts, but what has been built up by pleasure, and exists in us by pleasure alone. The Man of science, the Chemist and Mathematician, whatever difficulties and disgusts[20] they may have had to struggle with, know and feel this. However painful may be the objects with which the Anatomist's knowledge is connected, he feels that his knowledge is pleasure; and where he has no pleasure he has no knowledge. What then does the Poet? He considers man and the objects that surround him as acting and re-acting upon each other, so as to produce an infinite complexity of pain and pleasure; he considers man in his own nature and in his ordinary life as contemplating this with a certain quantity of immediate knowledge, with certain convictions, intuitions, and deductions, which from habit acquire the quality of intuitions; he considers him as looking upon this complex scene of ideas and sensations, and finding everywhere objects that immediately excite in him sympathies which, from the necessities of his nature, are accompanied by an overbalance of enjoyment.

To this knowledge which all men carry about with them, and to these sympathies in which, without any other discipline than that of our daily life, we are fitted to take delight, the Poet principally directs his attention. He considers man and nature as essentially adapted to each other, and the mind of man as naturally the mirror of the fairest and most interesting properties of nature. And thus the Poet, prompted by this feeling of

[20] *disgusts*: something loathsome; profound dissatisfaction; annoyance.

pleasure, which accompanies him through the whole course of his studies, converses with general nature, with affections akin to those, which, through labour and length of time, the Man of science has raised up in himself, by conversing with those particular parts of nature which are the objects of his studies. The knowledge both of the Poet and the Man of science is pleasure; but the knowledge of the one cleaves to us as a necessary part of our existence, our natural and unalienable inheritance; the other is a personal and individual acquisition, slow to come to us, and by no habitual and direct sympathy connecting us with our fellow-beings. The Man of science seeks truth as a remote and unknown benefactor; he cherishes and loves it in his solitude: the Poet, singing a song in which all human beings join with him, rejoices in the presence of truth as our visible friend and hourly companion. Poetry is the breath and finer spirit of all knowledge; it is the impassioned expression which is in the countenance of all Science. Emphatically may it be said of the Poet, as Shakespeare hath said of man, "that he looks before and after."[21] He is the rock of defence for human nature; an upholder and preserver, carrying everywhere with him relationship and love. In spite of difference of soil and climate, of language and manners, of laws and customs: in spite of things silently gone out of mind, and things violently destroyed; the Poet binds together by passion and knowledge the vast empire of human society, as it is spread over the whole earth, and over all time. The objects of the Poet's thoughts are every where; though the eyes and senses of man are, it is true, his favourite guides, yet he will follow wheresoever he can find an atmosphere of sensation in which to move his wings. Poetry is the first and last of all knowledge—it is as immortal as the heart of man. If the labours of Men of science should ever create any material revolution, direct or indirect, in our condition, and in the impressions which we habitually receive, the Poet will sleep then no more than at present; he will be ready to follow the steps of the Man of science, not only in those general indirect effects, but he will be at his side, carrying sensation into the midst of the objects of the science itself. The remotest discoveries of the Chemist, the Botanist, or Mineralogist, will

---

[21] *that he looks before and after*: paraphrase of *Hamlet*, Act 4, scene 4, line 37.

be as proper objects of the Poet's art as any upon which it can be employed, if the time should ever come when these things shall be familiar to us, and the relations under which they are contemplated by the followers of these respective sciences shall be manifestly and palpably material to us as enjoying and suffering beings. If the time should ever come when what is now called science, thus familiarized to men, shall be ready to put on, as it were, a form of flesh and blood, the Poet will lend his divine spirit to aid the transfiguration, and will welcome the Being thus produced, as a dear and genuine inmate of the household of man.—It is not, then, to be supposed that any one, who holds that sublime notion of Poetry which I have attempted to convey, will break in upon the sanctity and truth of his pictures by transitory and accidental ornaments, and endeavour to excite admiration of himself by arts, the necessity of which must manifestly depend upon the assumed meanness of his subject.

What has been thus far said applies to Poetry in general; but especially to those parts of composition where the Poet speaks through the mouths of his characters; and upon this point it appears to authorize the conclusion that there are few persons of good sense, who would not allow that the dramatic parts of composition are defective, in proportion as they deviate from the real language of nature, and are coloured by a diction of the Poet's own, either peculiar to him as an individual Poet or belonging simply to Poets in general; to a body of men who, from the circumstance of their compositions being in metre, it is expected will employ a particular language.

It is not, then, in the dramatic parts of composition that we look for this distinction of language; but still it may be proper and necessary where the Poet speaks to us in his own person and character. To this I answer by referring the Reader to the description before given of a Poet. Among the qualities there enumerated as principally conducing to form a Poet, is implied nothing differing in kind from other men, but only in degree. The sum of what was said is, that the Poet is chiefly distinguished from other men by a greater promptness to think and feel without immediate external excitement, and a greater power in expressing such thoughts and feelings as are produced in him in that manner. But these passions and thoughts and feelings are the general passions and thoughts and feelings of men. And with what are they connected? Undoubtedly with our moral sentiments and animal sensations, and with the causes which excite these; with the operations of the elements, and the appearances of the visible universe; with storm and sunshine, with the revolutions[22] of the seasons, with cold and heat, with loss of friends and kindred, with injuries and resentments, gratitude and hope, with fear and sorrow. These, and the like, are the sensations and objects which the Poet describes, as they are the sensations of other men, and the objects which interest them. The Poet thinks and feels in the spirit of human passions. How, then, can his language differ in any material degree from that of all other men who feel vividly and see clearly? It might be *proved* that it is impossible. But supposing that this were not the case, the Poet might then be allowed to use a peculiar language when expressing his feelings for his own gratification, or that of men like himself. But Poets do not write for Poets alone, but for men. Unless therefore we are advocates for that admiration which subsists upon ignorance, and that pleasure which arises from hearing what we do not understand, the Poet must descend from this supposed height; and, in order to excite rational sympathy, he must express himself as other men express themselves. To this it may be added, that while he is only selecting from the real language of men, or, which amounts to the same thing, composing accurately in the spirit of such selection, he is treading upon safe ground, and we know what we are to expect from him. Our feelings are the same with respect to metre; for, as it may be proper to remind the Reader, the distinction of metre is regular and uniform, and not, like that which is produced by what is usually called POETIC DICTION, arbitrary, and subject to infinite caprices upon which no calculation whatever can be made. In the one case, the Reader is utterly at the mercy of the Poet, respecting what imagery or diction he may choose to connect with the passion; whereas, in the other, the metre obeys certain laws, to which the Poet and Reader both willingly submit because they are certain, and because no interference is made by them with the passion, but such as the concurring testimony of ages has

[22] *revolutions*: cyclic change.

shown to heighten and improve the pleasure which co-exists with it.

It will now be proper to answer an obvious question, namely, Why, professing these opinions, have I written in verse? To this, in addition to such answer as is included in what has been already said, I reply, in the first place, Because, however I may have restricted myself, there is still left open to me what confessedly constitutes the most valuable object of all writing, whether in prose or verse; the great and universal passions of men, the most general and interesting of their occupations, and the entire world of nature before me—to supply endless combinations of forms and imagery. Now, supposing for a moment that whatever is interesting in these objects may be as vividly described in prose, why should I be condemned for attempting to superadd to such description, the charm which, by the consent of all nations, is acknowledged to exist in metrical language? To this, by such as are yet unconvinced, it may be answered that a very small part of the pleasure given by Poetry depends upon the metre, and that it is injudicious to write in metre, unless it be accompanied with the other artificial distinctions of style with which metre is usually accompanied, and that, by such deviation, more will be lost from the shock which will thereby be given to the Reader's associations than will be counterbalanced by any pleasure which he can derive from the general power of numbers. In answer to those who still contend for the necessity of accompanying metre with certain appropriate colours of style in order to the accomplishment of its appropriate end, and who also, in my opinion, greatly under-rate the power of metre in itself, it might, perhaps, as far as relates to these Volumes, have been almost sufficient to observe, that poems are extant, written upon more humble subjects, and in a still more naked and simple style, which have continued to give pleasure from generation to generation. Now, if nakedness and simplicity be a defect, the fact here mentioned affords a strong presumption that poems somewhat less naked and simple are capable of affording pleasure at the present day; and, what I wish *chiefly* to attempt, at present, was to justify myself for having written under the impression of this belief.

But various causes might be pointed out why, when the style is manly, and the subject of some importance, words metrically arranged will long continue to impart such a pleasure to mankind as he who proves the extent of that pleasure will be desirous to impart. The end of Poetry is to produce excitement in co-existence with an overbalance of pleasure; but, by the supposition, excitement is an unusual and irregular state of the mind; ideas and feelings do not, in that state, succeed each other in accustomed order. If the words, however, by which this excitement is produced be in themselves powerful, or the images and feelings have an undue proportion of pain connected with them, there is some danger that the excitement may be carried beyond its proper bounds. Now the co-presence of something regular, something to which the mind has been accustomed in various moods and in a less excited state, cannot but have great efficacy in tempering and restraining the passion by an intertexture of ordinary feeling, and of feeling not strictly and necessarily connected with the passion. This is unquestionably true; and hence, though the opinion will at first appear paradoxical, from the tendency of metre to divest language, in a certain degree, of its reality, and thus to throw a sort of half-consciousness of unsubstantial existence over the whole composition, there can be little doubt but that more pathetic[23] situations and sentiments, that is, those which have a greater proportion of pain connected with them, may be endured in metrical composition, especially in rhyme, than in prose. The metre of the old ballads is very artless;[24] yet they contain many passages which would illustrate this opinion; and, I hope, if the following Poems be attentively perused, similar instances will be found in them. This opinion may be further illustrated by appealing to the Reader's own experience of the reluctance with which he comes to the re-perusal of the distressful parts of *Clarissa Harlowe*,[25] or *The Gamester*;[26] while Shakespeare's writings, in the most pathetic scenes, never act upon us, as

[23] *pathetic*: moving; exciting or arising from pity, sadness, strong emotion.

[24] *artless*: clumsy; unartificial; natural.

[25] Clarissa Harlowe: *Clarissa, or The History of a Young Lady*, by Samuel Richardson (1689–1761), one of the greatest, darkest, and most harrowing novels in the English language.

[26] The Gamester: popular and acclaimed domestic tragedy by Edward Moore (1712–1757), adapted from a rather dark comedy by James Shirley (1596–1666).

pathetic, beyond the bounds of pleasure[27]—an effect which, in a much greater degree than might at first be imagined, is to be ascribed to small, but continual and regular impulses of pleasurable surprise from the metrical arrangement. On the other hand (what it must be allowed will much more frequently happen) if the Poet's words should be incommensurate with the passion, and inadequate to raise the Reader to a height of desirable excitement, then, (unless the Poet's choice of his metre has been grossly injudicious) in the feelings of pleasure which the Reader has been accustomed to connect with metre in general, and in the feeling, whether cheerful or melancholy, which he has been accustomed to connect with that particular movement of metre, there will be found something which will greatly contribute to impart passion to the words, and to effect the complex end which the Poet proposes to himself.

If I had undertaken a SYSTEMATIC defence of the theory here maintained, it would have been my duty to develop the various causes upon which the pleasure received from metrical language depends. Among the chief of these causes is to be reckoned a principle which must be well known to those who have made any of the Arts the object of accurate reflection; namely, the pleasure which the mind derives from the perception of similitude in dissimilitude. This principle is the great spring of the activity of our minds, and their chief feeder. From this principle the direction of the sexual appetite, and all the passions connected with it, take their origin: it is the life of our ordinary conversation; and upon the accuracy with which similitude in dissimilitude, and dissimilitude in similitude are perceived, depend our taste and our moral feelings. It would not be a useless employment to apply this principle to the consideration of metre, and to show that metre is hence enabled to afford much

---

[27]Cf. Dr. Samuel Johnson (1709–1784), English essayist, lexicographer, moralist, biographer, poet, conversationalist, and editor, and perhaps the greatest critic of the eighteenth century, as well as one of the towering figures of English literature: "I was many years ago so shocked by Cordelia's death, that I know not whether I ever endured to read again the last scenes of the play till I undertook to revise them as an editor" ("Concluding Notes" to *The Plays of William Shakespeare*, in *Samuel Johnson: The Major Works*, ed. Donald Greene [Oxford: Oxford University Press, 2008], p. 465).

pleasure, and to point out in what manner that pleasure is produced. But my limits will not permit me to enter upon this subject, and I must content myself with a general summary.

I have said that poetry is the spontaneous overflow of powerful feelings: it takes its origin from emotion recollected in tranquillity: the emotion is contemplated till, by a species of reaction, the tranquillity gradually disappears, and an emotion, kindred to that which was before the subject of contemplation, is gradually produced, and does itself actually exist in the mind. In this mood successful composition generally begins, and in a mood similar to this it is carried on; but the emotion, of whatever kind, and in whatever degree, from various causes, is qualified by various pleasures, so that in describing any passions whatsoever, which are voluntarily described, the mind will, upon the whole, be in a state of enjoyment. If Nature be thus cautious to preserve in a state of enjoyment a being so employed, the Poet ought to profit by the lesson held forth to him, and ought especially to take care, that, whatever passions he communicates to his Reader, those passions, if his Reader's mind be sound and vigorous, should always be accompanied with an overbalance of pleasure. Now the music of harmonious metrical language, the sense of difficulty overcome, and the blind association of pleasure which has been previously received from works of rhyme or metre of the same or similar construction, an indistinct perception perpetually renewed of language closely resembling that of real life, and yet, in the circumstance of metre, differing from it so widely—all these imperceptibly make up a complex feeling of delight, which is of the most important use in tempering the painful feeling always found intermingled with powerful descriptions of the deeper passions. This effect is always produced in pathetic and impassioned poetry; while, in lighter compositions, the ease and gracefulness with which the Poet manages his numbers are themselves confessedly a principal source of the gratification of the Reader. All that it is *necessary* to say, however, upon this subject, may be effected by affirming, what few persons will deny, that, of two descriptions, either of passions, manners, or characters, each of them equally well executed, the one in prose and the other in verse, the verse will be read a hundred times where the prose is read once.

Having thus explained a few of my reasons for writing in verse, and why I have chosen subjects from common life, and endeavoured to bring my language near to the real language of men, if I have been too minute in pleading my own cause, I have at the same time been treating a subject of general interest; and for this reason a few words shall be added with reference solely to these particular poems, and to some defects which will probably be found in them. I am sensible that my associations must have sometimes been particular instead of general, and that, consequently, giving to things a false importance, I may have sometimes written upon unworthy subjects; but I am less apprehensive on this account, than that my language may frequently have suffered from those arbitrary connexions of feelings and ideas with particular words and phrases, from which no man can altogether protect himself. Hence I have no doubt, that, in some instances, feelings, even of the ludicrous, may be given to my Readers by expressions which appeared to me tender and pathetic. Such faulty expressions, were I convinced they were faulty at present, and that they must necessarily continue to be so, I would willingly take all reasonable pains to correct. But it is dangerous to make these alterations on the simple authority of a few individuals, or even of certain classes of men; for where the understanding of an Author is not convinced, or his feelings altered, this cannot be done without great injury to himself: for his own feelings are his stay and support; and, if he set them aside in one instance, he may be induced to repeat this act till his mind shall lose all confidence in itself, and become utterly debilitated. To this it may be added, that the critic ought never to forget that he is himself exposed to the same errors as the Poet, and, perhaps, in a much greater degree: for there can be no presumption in saying of most readers, that it is not probable they will be so well acquainted with the various stages of meaning through which words have passed, or with the fickleness or stability of the relations of particular ideas to each other; and, above all, since they are so much less interested in the subject, they may decide lightly and carelessly.

Long as the Reader has been detained, I hope he will permit me to caution him against a mode of false criticism which has been applied to Poetry, in which the language closely resembles that of life and nature. Such verses have been triumphed over in parodies, of which Dr. Johnson's[28] stanza is a fair specimen:—

> "I put my hat upon my head
> And walked into the Strand,[29]
> And there I met another man
> Whose hat was in his hand."

Immediately under these lines let us place one of the most justly admired stanzas of the "*Babes in the Wood.*"[30]

> "These pretty Babes with hand in hand
> Went wandering up and down;
> But never more they saw the Man
> Approaching from the Town."

In both these stanzas the words, and the order of the words, in no respect differ from the most unimpassioned conversation. There are words in both, for example, "the Strand," and "the Town," connected with none but the most familiar ideas; yet the one stanza we admit as admirable, and the other as a fair example of the superlatively contemptible. Whence arises this difference? Not from the metre, not from the language, not from the order of the words; but the *matter* expressed in Dr. Johnson's stanza is contemptible. The proper method of treating trivial and simple verses, to which Dr. Johnson's stanza would be a fair parallelism, is not to say, this is a bad kind of poetry, or, this is not poetry; but, this wants sense; it is neither interesting in itself, nor can *lead* to anything interesting;

[28] *Dr. Johnson's*: i.e., Dr. Samuel Johnson's. Johnson was not, in fact, parodying the "artless" old ballads per se; "in fact, Johnson spent two months with Thomas Percy helping to prepare the *Reliques of Ancient English Poetry* for publication (and to find a publisher for it), provided it with a dedication, and gave it considerable publicity in his notes to Shakespeare's plays. But when Percy sought to profit from the publicity by composing a feeble pseudo-ballad of his own, Johnson thought little of it. These quatrains are the result" (ibid., p. 797).

[29] *Strand*: a busy and important street in central London, running near the banks of the Thames (hence its name) from Trafalgar Square to the city, where it turns into Fleet Street at Temple Bar. Dr. Johnson lived within a couple of minutes of the Strand.

[30] "*Babes in the Wood*": an old ballad, first published in Norwich in 1595. It tells of a little orphaned brother and sister who die abandoned and lost in the woods; the robins take pity on them and cover their bodies with leaves.

the images neither originate in that sane state of feeling which arises out of thought, nor can excite thought or feeling in the Reader. This is the only sensible manner of dealing with such verses. Why trouble yourself about the species till you have previously decided upon the genus? Why take pains to prove that an ape is not a Newton, when it is self-evident that he is not a man?

One request I must make of my reader, which is, that in judging these Poems he would decide by his own feelings genuinely, and not by reflection upon what will probably be the judgement of others. How common is it to hear a person say, I myself do not object to this style of composition, or this or that expression, but, to such and such classes of people it will appear mean or ludicrous! This mode of criticism, so destructive of all sound unadulterated judgement, is almost universal: let the Reader then abide, independently, by his own feelings, and, if he finds himself affected, let him not suffer such conjectures to interfere with his pleasure.

If an Author, by any single composition, has impressed us with respect for his talents, it is useful to consider this as affording a presumption, that on other occasions where we have been displeased, he, nevertheless, may not have written ill or absurdly; and further, to give him so much credit for this one composition as may induce us to review what has displeased us, with more care than we should otherwise have bestowed upon it. This is not only an act of justice, but, in our decisions upon poetry especially, may conduce, in a high degree, to the improvement of our own taste; for an *accurate* taste in poetry, and in all the other arts, as Sir Joshua Reynolds[31] has observed, is an *acquired* talent, which can only be produced by thought and a long-continued intercourse with the best models of composition. This is mentioned, not with so ridiculous a purpose

---

[31] *Sir Joshua Reynolds:* Sir Joshua Reynolds (1723–1792) was one of the greatest of British painters—particularly of portraits—the first president of the Royal Academy, and, as author of the *Discourses*, an important prose writer and major art critic; also, he was the dedicatee of Boswell's *Life of Samuel Johnson* (1791). At the time he delivered the last of his *Discourses* to the Royal Academy, in 1790, he was "perhaps the most universally respected figure in any field of British culture" (Pat Rogers, introduction to Sir Joshua Reynolds, *Discourses* [London: Penguin, 1992] p. 51). For the context of Wordsworth's reference, see Discourse 7 (on "The reality of a standard of taste"), especially pp. 193 and 202 in *Discourses*.

as to prevent the most inexperienced Reader from judging for himself, (I have already said that I wish him to judge for himself;) but merely to temper the rashness of decision, and to suggest, that, if Poetry be a subject on which much time has not been bestowed, the judgement may be erroneous; and that, in many cases, it necessarily will be so.

Nothing would, I know, have so effectually contributed to further the end which I have in view, as to have shown of what kind the pleasure is, and how that pleasure is produced, which is confessedly produced by metrical composition essentially different from that which I have here endeavoured to recommend: for the Reader will say that he has been pleased by such composition; and what more can be done for him? The power of any art is limited; and he will suspect, that, if it be proposed to furnish him with new friends, that can be only upon condition of his abandoning his old friends. Besides, as I have said, the Reader is himself conscious of the pleasure which he has received from such composition, composition to which he has peculiarly attached the endearing name of Poetry; and all men feel an habitual gratitude, and something of an honourable bigotry,[32] for the objects which have long continued to please them: we not only wish to be pleased, but to be pleased in that particular way in which we have been accustomed to be pleased. There is in these feelings enough to resist a host of arguments; and I should be the less able to combat them successfully, as I am willing to allow, that, in order entirely to enjoy the Poetry which I am recommending, it would be necessary to give up much of what is ordinarily enjoyed. But, would my limits have permitted me to point out how this pleasure is produced, many obstacles might have been removed, and the Reader assisted in perceiving that the powers of language are not so limited as he may suppose; and that it is possible for poetry to give other enjoyments, of a purer, more lasting, and more exquisite nature. This part of the subject has not been altogether neglected, but it has not been so much my present aim to prove, that the interest excited by some other kinds of poetry is less vivid, and less worthy of the nobler powers of the mind, as to offer reasons for presuming, that if my purpose

---

[32] *bigotry*: state of being obstinate and nonrational.

were fulfilled, a species of poetry would be produced, which is genuine poetry; in its nature well adapted to interest mankind permanently, and likewise important in the multiplicity and quality of its moral relations.

From what has been said, and from a perusal of the Poems, the Reader will be able clearly to perceive the object which I had in view: he will determine how far it has been attained; and, what is a much more important question, whether it be worth attaining: and upon the decision of these two questions will rest my claim to the approbation of the Public.

The Thorn[33]

I

There is a thorn; it looks so old,
In truth, you'd find it hard to say,
How it could ever have been young,
It looks so old and grey.
Not higher than a two-years' child,   5
It stands erect, this aged thorn;
No leaves it has, no thorny points;
It is a mass of knotted joints,
A wretched thing forlorn.
It stands erect, and like a stone   10
With lichens is it overgrown.

[33] Published in *Lyrical Ballads*, 1798. In a note introduced in the 1800 edition (and which has divided critics ever since), Wordsworth drew attention to the superstitious character of his narrator and encouraged readers to interpret the poem as a psychological study. "Arose out of my observing, on the ridge of Quantock Hill, on a stormy day, a thorn which I had often past in calm and bright weather without noticing it. I said to myself, 'Cannot I by some invention do as much to make this thorn permanently an impressive object, as the storm has made it to my eyes at this moment?' I began the poem accordingly, and composed it with great rapidity" (William Wordsworth, *The Fenwick Notes*, ed. Jared Curtis (London: Bristol Classical Press, 1993), p. 14.

II

Like rock or stone, it is o'ergrown
With lichens to the very top,
And hung with heavy tufts of moss,
A melancholy crop: 15
Up from the earth these mosses creep,
And this poor thorn they clasp it round
So close, you'd say that they were bent
With plain and manifest intent,
To drag it to the ground;   20
And all had joined in one endeavour
To bury this poor thorn for ever.

III

High on a mountain's highest ridge,
Where oft the stormy winter gale
Cuts like a scythe, while through the clouds   25
It sweeps from vale to vale;
Not five yards from the mountain-path,
This thorn you on your left espy;
And to the left, three yards beyond,
You see a little muddy pond   30
Of water, never dry;
I've measured it from side to side:
'Tis three feet long, and two feet wide.[34]

IV

And close beside this aged thorn,
There is a fresh and lovely sight,
A beauteous heap, a hill of moss,   35

---

[34] *I've measured it . . . wide*: My selection of this earlier version of "The Thorn" over the later revision was determined partly by these lines, probably the most famous bad lines ever written by a major English poet—and partly in deference to the many critics who insist that Wordsworth's later revisions are invariably inferior.

Just half a foot in height.
All lovely colours there you see,
All colours that were ever seen,
And mossy network too is there,   40
As if by hand of lady fair
The work had woven been,
And cups, the darlings of the eye,
So deep is their vermilion dye.

V

Ah me! what lovely tints are there!   45
Of olive-green and scarlet bright,
In spikes, in branches, and in stars,
Green, red, and pearly white.
This heap of earth o'ergrown with moss,
Which close beside the thorn you see,   50
So fresh in all its beauteous dyes,
Is like an infant's grave in size
As like as like can be:
But never, never any where,
An infant's grave was half so fair.   55

VI

Now would you see this aged thorn,
This pond and beauteous hill of moss,
You must take care and choose your time
The mountain when to cross.
For oft there sits, between the heap   60
That's like an infant's grave in size,
And that same pond of which I spoke,
A woman in a scarlet cloak,
And to herself she cries,
"Oh misery! oh misery!   65
Oh woe is me! oh misery!"

VII

At all times of the day and night
This wretched woman thither goes,
And she is known to every star,
And every wind that blows;   70
And there beside the thorn she sits
When the blue day-light's in the skies,
And when the whirlwind's on the hill,
Or frosty air is keen and still,
And to herself she cries,   75
"Oh misery! oh misery!
Oh woe is me! oh misery!"

VIII

"Now wherefore thus, by day and night,
In rain, in tempest, and in snow,
Thus to the dreary mountain-top   80
Does this poor woman go?
And why sits she beside the thorn
When the blue day-light's in the sky,
Or when the whirlwind's on the hill,
Or frosty air is keen and still,   85
And wherefore does she cry?—
Oh wherefore? wherefore? tell me why
Does she repeat that doleful cry?"

IX

I cannot tell; I wish I could;
For the true reason no one knows,   90
But if you'd gladly view the spot,
The spot to which she goes;
The heap that's like an infant's grave,
The pond—and thorn, so old and grey,
Pass by her door—'tis seldom shut—   95
And if you see her in her hut,

Then to the spot away!—
I never heard of such as dare
Approach the spot when she is there.

X

"But wherefore to the mountain-top   100
Can this unhappy woman go,
Whatever star is in the skies,
Whatever wind may blow?"
Nay rack your brain—'tis all in vain,
I'll tell you every thing I know;   105
But to the thorn, and to the pond
Which is a little step beyond,
I wish that you would go:
Perhaps, when you are at the place
You something of her tale may trace.   110

XI

I'll give you the best help I can:
Before you up the mountain go,
Up to the dreary mountain-top,
I'll tell you all I know.
'Tis now some two-and-twenty years,   115
Since she (her name is Martha Ray)
Gave with a maiden's true good will
Her company to Stephen Hill;
And she was blithe and gay,
And she was happy, happy still   120
Whene'er she thought of Stephen Hill.

XII

And they had fixed the wedding-day,
The morning that must wed them both;
But Stephen to another maid
Had sworn another oath;   125

And with this other maid to church
Unthinking Stephen went—
Poor Martha! on that woful day
A cruel, cruel fire, they say,
Into her bones was sent: 130
It dried her body like a cinder,
And almost turned her brain to tinder.

XIII

They say, full six months after this,
While yet the summer-leaves were green,
She to the mountain-top would go,   135
And there was often seen.
'Tis said, a child was in her womb,
As now to any eye was plain;
She was with child, and she was mad,
Yet often she was sober sad   140
From her exceeding pain.
Oh me! ten thousand times I'd rather
That he had died, that cruel father!

XIV

Sad case for such a brain to hold
Communion with a stirring child!   145
Sad case, as you may think, for one
Who had a brain so wild!
Last Christmas when we talked of this,
Old Farmer Simpson did maintain,
That in her womb the infant wrought   150
About its mother's heart, and brought
Her senses back again:
And when at last her time drew near,
Her looks were calm, her senses clear.

XV

No more I know, I wish I did,   155
And I would tell it all to you;
For what became of this poor child
There's none that ever knew:
And if a child was born or no,
There's no one that could ever tell;   160
And if 'twas born alive or dead,
There's no one knows, as I have said,
But some remember well,
That Martha Ray about this time
Would up the mountain often climb.   165

XVI

And all that winter, when at night
The wind blew from the mountain-peak,
'Twas worth your while, though in the dark,
The church-yard path to seek:
For many a time and oft were heard   170
Cries coming from the mountain-head,
Some plainly living voices were,
And others, I've heard many swear,
Were voices of the dead:
I cannot think, whate'er they say,   175
They had to do with Martha Ray.

XVII

But that she goes to this old thorn,
The thorn which I've described to you,
And there sits in a scarlet cloak,
I will be sworn is true.   180
For one day with my telescope,
To view the ocean wide and bright,
When to this country first I came,
Ere I had heard of Martha's name,

I climbed the mountain's height: 185
A storm came on, and I could see
No object higher than my knee.

XVIII

'Twas mist and rain, and storm and rain,
No screen, no fence could I discover,
And then the wind! in faith, it was   190
A wind full ten times over.
I looked around, I thought I saw
A jutting crag, and off I ran,
Head-foremost, through the driving rain,
The shelter of the crag to gain,   195
And, as I am a man,
Instead of jutting crag, I found
A woman seated on the ground.

XIX

I did not speak—I saw her face,
Her face it was enough for me;   200
I turned about and heard her cry,
"Oh misery! oh misery!"
And there she sits, until the moon
Through half the clear blue sky will go,
And when the little breezes make   205
The waters of the pond to shake,
As all the country know,
She shudders and you hear her cry,
"Oh misery! oh misery!"

XX

"But what's the thorn? and what's the pond?   210
And what's the hill of moss to her?
And what's the creeping breeze that comes

The little pond to stir?"
I cannot tell; but some will say
She hanged her baby on the tree, 215
Some say she drowned it in the pond,
Which is a little step beyond,
But all and each agree,
The little babe was buried there,
Beneath that hill of moss so fair. 220

XXI

I've heard the scarlet moss is red
With drops of that poor infant's blood;
But kill a new-born infant thus!
I do not think she could.
Some say, if to the pond you go, 225
And fix on it a steady view,
The shadow of a babe you trace,
A baby and a baby's face,
And that it looks at you;
Whene'er you look on it, 'tis plain 230
The baby looks at you again.

XXII

And some had sworn an oath that she
Should be to public justice brought;
And for the little infant's bones
With spades they would have sought. 235
But then the beauteous hill of moss
Before their eyes began to stir;
And for full fifty yards around,
The grass it shook upon the ground;
But all do still aver 240
The little babe is buried there,
Beneath that hill of moss so fair.

XXIII

I cannot tell how this may be,
But plain it is, the thorn is bound
With heavy tufts of moss, that strive   245
To drag it to the ground.
And this I know, full many a time,
When she was on the mountain high,
By day, and in the silent night,
When all the stars shone clear and bright,   250
That I have heard her cry,
"Oh misery! oh misery!
Oh woe is me! oh misery!"

We Are Seven[35]

A simple child, dear brother Jim,
That lightly draws its breath,
And feels its life in every limb,
What should it know of death?

I met a little cottage girl,   5
She was eight years old, she said;
Her hair was thick with many a curl
That clustered round her head.

She had a rustic, woodland air,
And she was wildly clad;   10

[35] Published in *Lyrical Ballads*, 1798. "Written at Alfoxden in the spring of 1798, under circumstances somewhat remarkable. The little girl who is the heroine, I met within the area of Goodrich Castle in the year 1793.... [W]hile walking to and fro I composed the last stanza first, having begun with the last line. When it was all but finished, I came in and recited it to Mr. Coleridge and my sister, and said, 'A prefatory stanza must be added, and I should sit down to our little tea-meal with greater pleasure if my task was finished.' I mentioned in substance what I wished to be expressed, and Coleridge immediately threw off the stanza" (Wordsworth, *The Fenwick Notes*, p. 3).

Her eyes were fair, and very fair,
—Her beauty made me glad.

"Sisters and brothers, little maid,
How many may you be?"
"How many? seven in all," she said,   15
And wondering looked at me.

"And where are they, I pray you tell?"
She answered, "Seven are we,
And two of us at Conway[36] dwell,
And two are gone to sea.   20

"Two of us in the church-yard lie,
My sister and my brother,
And in the church-yard cottage, I
Dwell near them with my mother."

"You say that two at Conway dwell,   25
And two are gone to sea,
Yet you are seven; I pray you tell
Sweet Maid, how this may be?"

Then did the little Maid reply,
"Seven boys and girls are we;   30
Two of us in the church-yard lie,
Beneath the church-yard tree."

"You run about, my little maid,
Your limbs they are alive;
If two are in the church-yard laid,   35
Then ye are only five."

"Their graves are green, they may be seen,"
The little Maid replied,

---

[36] *Conway*: Conwy, North Wales.

"Twelve steps or more from my mother's door,
And they are side by side.   40

"My stockings there I often knit,
 My 'kerchief there I hem;
 And there upon the ground I sit—
I sit and sing to them.

"And often after sunset, Sir,   45
When it is light and fair,
I take my little porringer,[37]
And eat my supper there.

"The first that died was little Jane;
In bed she moaning lay,   50
Till God released her of her pain,
And then she went away.

"So in the church-yard she was laid,
And all the summer dry,
Together round her grave we played,   55
My brother John and I.

"And when the ground was white with snow,
And I could run and slide,
My brother John was forced to go,
And he lies by her side."   60

"How many are you, then," said I,
"If they two are in heaven?"
The little Maiden did reply,
"O Master! we are seven."

---

[37] *porringer*: "a small bowl, often with a handle, for soup, broth, porridge, etc."
(*Oxford English Dictionary*, s.v. "porringer").

"But they are dead; those two are dead! 65
Their spirits are in heaven!"
'Twas throwing words away; for still
The little Maid would have her will,
And said, "Nay, we are seven!"

Lines composed a few miles above
Tintern Abbey, on revisiting the banks of
the Wye during a Tour, July 13, 1798[38]

Tintern Abbey is a ruined Cistercian abbey on the Welsh bank
of the river Wye in Monmouthshire (the river forms part of the
border between England and Wales). The Abbey's community
was dissolved in 1536 by Henry VIII during his suppression of
the monasteries, and its buildings soon fell into disrepair. The
ruins are among the most impressive of their kind in Britain.

> No poem of mine was composed under circumstances more
> pleasant for me to remember than this. I began it upon leaving
> Tintern, after crossing the Wye, and concluded it just as I was
> entering Bristol in the evening, after a ramble of four or five
> days, with my Sister. Not a line of it was altered, and not any
> part of it written down till I reached Bristol.[39]

In some respects, "Tintern Abbey" resembles an ode: "I have
not ventured to call this Poem an Ode; but it was written with
a hope that in the transitions, and the impassioned music of
the versification, would be found the principal requisites of
that species of composition"[40]. Indeed, some of the poem's
themes are resumed in the "Ode: Intimations of Immortality",
in particular, certain elements of Platonism (see lines 46, 140),
and the analysis of the stages of individual psycho-spiritual
development, and their relationship to nature. Wordsworth

[38] Published in *Lyrical Ballads*, 1798.
[39] Wordsworth, *The Fenwick Notes*, p. 15.
[40] Ibid., p. 113.

identifies three such stages in "Tintern Abbey": the animal spirits of childhood (lines 74–75); the romantic, emotion-dominated world of youth (lines 68–86); and the philosophical reflection available to maturity (lines 86–103).

Finally, something needs to be said of the element of doubt that runs like a dark thread through the poem's fabric. The poet's ultimately confident triumph over frankly acknowledged incertitude (e.g., lines 50–51) involves its assimilation, as a kind of antitoxin. "Tintern Abbey" comes across as a particularly honest poem—of hope, real but hard-won, rather than shallow optimism. And this made an enduring impression on Victorians:

> [O]ne may go so far as to say that besides his Bible and his classical authors, the early Victorian intellectual was most conspicuously influenced by five literary works which did more to form his ideas, quicken his emotions and inspire his motives than any other influence of a cultural or philosophic kind. The five works were Butler's *Analogy*, Wordsworth's poems, Sir Walter Scott's novels, Coleridge's *Aids to Reflection* and Keble's *The Christian Year*.[41]

Tintern Abbey

Five years have past; five summers, with the length
Of five long winters![42] and again I hear
These waters, rolling from their mountain-springs
With a soft inland murmur.—Once again

[41] David Newsome, *Godliness and Good Learning* (London: John Murray, 1961), p. 12.

[42] This brings us back to the summer of 1793 and the early weeks of Britain's involvement in the French Revolutionary Wars. Wordsworth had visited France on his walking tour of the Alps, July–October 1790, and returned in November of 1791, staying on till December 1792. The euphoric impression made on him by the nascent Republican movement is recorded in *The Prelude*, and its influence is apparent in much of his best early work. A relationship with a young Frenchwoman, Annette Vallon (1766–1841), produced an illegitimate daughter, Caroline (1792–1862), born December 15, 1792. Britain's hostility to the

Do I behold these steep and lofty cliffs, 5
That on a wild secluded scene impress
Thoughts of more deep seclusion; and connect
The landscape with the quiet of the sky.
The day is come when I again repose
Here, under this dark sycamore, and view 10
These plots of cottage-ground, these orchard-tufts,
Which, at this season, with their unripe fruits,
Among the woods and copses lose themselves,
Nor, with their green and simple hue, disturb
The wild green landscape. Once again I see 15
These hedge-rows, hardly hedge-rows, little lines
Of sportive wood run wild; these pastoral farms
Green to the very door; and wreaths of smoke
Sent up, in silence, from among the trees,[43]
With some uncertain notice, as might seem,
Of vagrant dwellers in the houseless woods, 20
Or of some Hermit's[44] cave, where by his fire
The Hermit sits alone.

        Though absent long,
These forms of beauty have not been to me,
As is a landscape to a blind man's eye: 25
But oft, in lonely rooms, and mid the din
Of towns and cities, I have owed to them,
In hours of weariness, sensations sweet,
Felt in the blood, and felt along the heart,
And passing even into my purer mind 30

Revolutionary movement, the descent into war (February 1793), and his inability to return to France to see Annette and Caroline had provoked a moral, intellectual, and emotional crisis in Wordsworth's life, which was complicated by the Reign of Terror (June 1793–July 1794) and the invasion of Switzerland (February 1798). Thus these five years—and particularly their summer and winter months—shook Wordsworth to his foundations and were of decisive, permanent importance in the evolution of his interpretation of experience.

[43] *wreaths of smoke . . . among the trees*: This is a reference to charcoal burning.

[44] *Hermit's*: For the Romantics, the hermit was a figure of peculiar spiritual authority. See Coleridge, "The Rime of the Ancient Mariner" and von Weber's opera *Der Freischütz*. Cf. line 27 of Blake's "The Grey Monk".

With tranquil restoration:—feelings too
Of unremembered pleasure; such, perhaps,
As may have had no trivial influence
On that best portion of a good man's life;
His little, nameless, unremembered acts   35
Of kindness and of love. Nor less, I trust,
To them I may have owed another gift,
Of aspect more sublime; that blessed mood,
In which the burthen[45] of the mystery,
In which the heavy and the weary weight   40
Of all this unintelligible world
Is lightened:—that serene and blessed mood,
In which the affections gently lead us on,
Until, the breath of this corporeal frame,
And even the motion of our human blood   45
Almost suspended, we are laid asleep
In body, and become a living soul:[46]
While with an eye made quiet by the power
Of harmony, and the deep power of joy,
We see into the life of things.

                       If this   50
Be but a vain belief,[47] yet, oh! how oft,
In darkness, and amid the many shapes
Of joyless day-light; when the fretful stir
Unprofitable, and the fever of the world,[48]
Have hung upon the beatings of my heart,   55
How oft, in spirit, have I turned to thee

---

[45] *burthen*: burden.

[46] *living soul*: Cf. Genesis 2:7: "[T]he LORD God formed man of dust from the ground, and breathed into his nostrils the breath of life; and man became a living soul." Within the context of the poem, this also appears to express a Platonic view of the soul's sentience (i.e., that its acquisition of knowledge is not dependent on the senses).

[47] *If this / Be but a vain belief*: Cf. *Prelude*, bk. 2, lines 419ff.

[48] *Unprofitable, and the fever of the world*: Cf. Wordsworth's "The world is too much with us" (below), and Shakespeare, *Hamlet*, Act 1, scene 2, lines 133–37: "How weary, stale, flat and unprofitable, / Seem to me all the uses of this world! / Fie on't! ah fie! 'tis an unweeded garden, / That grows to seed; things rank and gross in nature / Possess it merely."

O sylvan Wye! thou wanderer through the woods,
How often has my spirit turned to thee!

    And now, with gleams of half-extinguished thought,
With many recognitions dim and faint, 60
And somewhat of a sad perplexity,
The picture of the mind revives again:
While here I stand, not only with the sense
Of present pleasure, but with pleasing thoughts
That in this moment there is life and food 65
For future years. And so I dare to hope
Though changed, no doubt, from what I was, when first
I came among these hills; when like a roe
I bounded o'er the mountains, by the sides
Of the deep rivers, and the lonely streams, 70
Wherever nature led; more like a man
Flying from something that he dreads, than one
Who sought the thing he loved. For nature then
(The coarser pleasures of my boyish days,
And their glad animal movements all gone by,) 75
To me was all in all.—I cannot paint
What then I was. The sounding cataract
Haunted me like a passion: the tall rock,
The mountain, and the deep and gloomy wood,
Their colours and their forms, were then to me 80
An appetite: a feeling and a love,
That had no need of a remoter charm,
By thought supplied, nor any interest
Unborrowed from the eye.—That time is past,
And all its aching joys are now no more, 85
And all its dizzy raptures. Not for this
Faint I, nor mourn nor murmur: other gifts
Have followed, for such loss, I would believe,
Abundant recompense. For I have learned
To look on nature, not as in the hour 90
Of thoughtless youth, but hearing oftentimes
The still, sad music of humanity,
Nor harsh nor grating, though of ample power

To chasten and subdue. And I have felt
A presence that disturbs me with the joy   95
Of elevated thoughts; a sense sublime
Of something far more deeply interfused,
Whose dwelling is the light of setting suns,[49]
And the round ocean, and the living air,
And the blue sky, and in the mind of man,   100
A motion and a spirit, that impels
All thinking things, all objects of all thought,
And rolls through all things. Therefore am I still
A lover of the meadows and the woods,
And mountains; and of all that we behold   105
From this green earth; of all the mighty world
Of eye and ear, both what they half create,[50]
And what perceive; well pleased to recognize
In nature and the language of the sense,
The anchor of my purest thoughts, the nurse,   110
The guide, the guardian of my heart, and soul
Of all my moral being.
                    Nor, perchance,
If I were not thus taught, should I the more
Suffer[51] my genial[52] spirits to decay:
For thou art with me, here, upon the banks   115

[49] *Whose dwelling is the light of setting suns*: Tennyson described this line as "almost the grandest in the English language, giving the sense of the abiding in the transient" (Hallam Tennyson, *Alfred Lord Tennyson: A Memoir*, vol. 2 [London: Macmillan, 1897], p. 288).

[50] *both what they half create*: "This line has a close resemblance to an admirable line of Young, the exact expression of which I cannot recollect" (Wordsworth's note, 1800). Cf. Edward Young, *Night Thoughts*, 6.417–30: "Seek in thy naked self, and find it there; / ... Sky-born, sky-guided, sky-returning race! / ... In senses, which inherit earth, and heav'ns; / ... Take in, at once, the landscape of the world / ... And half-create the wondrous world they see. / Our senses, as our reason, are divine. / But for the magic organ's powerful charm, / Earth were a rude, uncolour'd chaos still."

[51] *Suffer*: also, to suffer with the sense of "allow".

[52] *genial*: sympathetically cheerful; marked by genius; cf. Milton, *Samson Agonistes*, lines 594–95: "So much I feel my genial spirits droop / My hopes all flat".

Of this fair river; thou my dearest Friend,[53]
My dear, dear Friend, and in thy voice I catch
The language of my former heart, and read
My former pleasures in the shooting lights
Of thy wild eyes. Oh! yet a little while   120
May I behold in thee what I was once,
My dear, dear Sister! and this prayer I make,
Knowing that Nature never did betray
The heart that loved her; 'tis her privilege,
Through all the years of this our life, to lead   125
From joy to joy: for she can so inform
The mind that is within us, so impress
With quietness and beauty, and so feed
With lofty thoughts, that neither evil tongues,[54]
Rash judgments, nor the sneers of selfish men,   130
Nor greetings where no kindness is, nor all
The dreary intercourse of daily life,
Shall e'er prevail against us, or disturb
Our cheerful faith that all which we behold
Is full of blessings. Therefore let the moon   135
Shine on thee in thy solitary walk;
And let the misty mountain winds be free
To blow against thee: and in after years,
When these wild ecstasies shall be matured

---

[53] *thou my dearest Friend*: the poet's sister, Dorothy Wordsworth (1771–1855), important diarist. She and William were extremely close, and she continued to live with him after his marriage to Mary Hutchinson (1802). It is now generally acknowledged that she exerted an indirect influence on the Romantic movement in general through her considerable personal influence on Wordsworth and Coleridge.

[54] *evil tongues*: Cf. Milton, *Paradise Lost*, bk. 7, lines 24–26: "More safe I sing with mortal voice, unchanged/To hoarse or mute, though fallen on evil days,/On evil days though fallen, and evil tongues". Milton's position as a Republican (and attaché to what had been a regicide government) was dangerous after the restoration of the monarchy in 1660. Both Wordsworth and Coleridge had felt similar insecurities following their support of early Republican developments in France and their criticism of Britain's stance. See, for example, *Prelude*, books 6–11; "London, 1802"; "Great Men have been among us"; and Coleridge's "Fears in Solitude".

Into a sober pleasure, when thy mind   140
Shall be a mansion[55] for all lovely forms,
Thy memory be as a dwelling-place
For all sweet sounds and harmonies; Oh! then,
If solitude, or fear, or pain, or grief,
Should be thy portion, with what healing thoughts   145
Of tender joy wilt thou remember me,
And these my exhortations! Nor, perchance,
If I should be, where I no more can hear
Thy voice, nor catch from thy wild eyes these gleams[56]
Of past existence, wilt thou then forget   150
That on the banks of this delightful stream
We stood together; and that I, so long
A worshipper of Nature, hither came,
Unwearied in that service: rather say
With warmer love, oh! with far deeper zeal   155
Of holier love. Nor wilt thou then forget,
That after many wanderings, many years
Of absence, these steep woods and lofty cliffs,
And this green pastoral landscape, were to me
More dear, both for themselves, and for thy sake.   160

[55] *mansion*: abiding place; apartment (in a large house); house; "the chief residence of a lord", hence, "a large and stately residence" (*Oxford English Dictionary*, s.v. "mansion"). Cf. John 14:1–2 (KJV): "Let not your heart be troubled: ye believe in God, believe also in me. In my Father's house are many mansions: if it were not so, I would have told you. I go to prepare a place for you."

[56] *gleams*: Cf. "Intimations of Immortality", line 56; *Prelude*, bk. 2, line 368, bk. 11, line 322; "Elegiac Stanzas", line 14.

Nutting[57]

——It seems a day
(I speak of one from many singled out),
One of those heavenly days which cannot die,
When forth I sallied from our cottage-door,[58]
And with a wallet[59] o'er my shoulders slung,   5
A nutting crook[60] in hand, I turned my steps
Towards the distant woods, a Figure quaint,
Tricked out[61] in proud disguise of Beggar's weeds[62]
Put on for the occasion, by advice
And exhortation of my frugal Dame.[63]   10
Motley accoutrements![64] of power to smile
At thorns, and brakes,[65] and brambles, and, in truth,
More ragged than need was. Among the woods,
And o'er the pathless rocks, I forced my way
Until, at length, I came to one dear nook   15
Unvisited, where not a broken bough
Drooped with its withered leaves, ungracious sign
Of devastation, but the hazels rose
Tall and erect, with milk-white clusters hung,

---

[57] Published in *Lyrical Ballads*, 1800. Originally intended for *The Prelude* "but struck out as not being wanted there" (Wordsworth, *The Fenwick Notes*, p. 13). The poem contains a striking epiphany (see lines 19–21) within the context of a remarkable passage that moves from erotic temptation, through indulgence, to imagery suggestive of rape (see lines 42–52).

[58] *our cottage-door*: "The house at which I was boarded during the time I was at School" (Wordsworth's note, *Lyrical Ballads*, 1800. Cf. *The Prelude*, bk. 1).

[59] *wallet*: a bag or knapsack for carrying food, clothes, etc., especially on a journey.

[60] *nutting crook*: a long stick with a hooked end for culling nuts from trees.

[61] *Tricked out*: decorated, adorned.

[62] *weeds*: clothes.

[63] *my frugal Dame*: Mrs. Ann Tyson. Wordsworth and his brothers lodged with her when they were sent to school at Hawkshead, Lancashire, following the death of their mother in 1778.

[64] *Motley accoutrements*: many-colored outfits.

[65] *brakes*: "a clump of bushes, brushwood, or briers; a thicket" (*Oxford English Dictionary*, s.v. "brakes").

A virgin scene!—A little while I stood,   20
Breathing with such suppression of the heart
As joy delights in; and with wise restraint
Voluptuous, fearless of a rival, eyed
The banquet, or beneath the trees I sate
Among the flowers, and with the flowers I played;   25
A temper known to those, who, after long
And weary expectation, have been blest
With sudden happiness beyond all hope.
Perhaps it was a bower beneath whose leaves
The violets of five seasons re-appear   30
And fade, unseen by any human eye,
Where fairy water-breaks[66] do murmur on
For ever,[67] and I saw the sparkling foam,[68]
And with my cheek on one of those green stones
That, fleeced with moss, beneath the shady trees,   35
Lay round me scattered like a flock of sheep,
I heard the murmur and the murmuring sound,
In that sweet mood when pleasure loves to pay
Tribute to ease, and, of its joy secure
The heart luxuriates with indifferent things,   40
Wasting its kindliness on stocks[69] and stones,
And on the vacant air. Then up I rose,
And dragged to earth both branch and bough, with crash
And merciless ravage; and the shady nook
Of hazels, and the green and mossy bower,   45
Deformed and sullied, patiently gave up
Their quiet being: and unless I now
Confound my present feelings with the past,
Even then, when from the bower I turned away,

[66] *water-breaks*: patches of rippled or choppy water.

[67] *murmur on/For ever*: Cf. Tennyson, "The Brook", lines 21–24: "I chatter over stony ways,/In little sharps and trebles,/For men may come and men may go,/But I go on for ever."

[68] *sparkling foam*: Cf. Keats, "Ode to a Nightingale", lines 69–70: "magic casements, opening on the foam/Of perilous seas, in faery lands forlorn."

[69] *stocks*: logs; blocks of wood.

Exulting, rich beyond the wealth of kings   50
I felt a sense of pain when I beheld
The silent trees and the intruding sky.—

Then, dearest Maiden![70] move along these shades
In gentleness of heart; with gentle hand
Touch,—for there is a spirit in the woods.   55

The Lucy Poems

"Strange fits of passion have I known"[71]

"Strange fits of passion have I known" together with "She dwelt among th' untrodden ways", "A slumber did my spirit seal", "Three years she grew in sun and shower", and "I travelled among unknown men" comprise a group known as the "Lucy poems" (the ballad "Lucy Gray" is not generally included among them). Although Wordsworth himself never identified them as a group or series, they were written in the same period (the first four between October 1798 and April 1799; the last, "I travelled", early in 1801, and associated by Wordsworth with "She dwelt") and are each concerned with the relationship between personal identity, nature, and death—in particular, the death of the speaker's love and muse, recollected at some distance in time. This young woman is referred to as "Lucy" in four of the poems. No "original" of Lucy has ever been convincingly identified. Both William Collins (1721–1759) and Samuel Rogers (1763–1855) composed poems certainly known to Wordsworth, featuring rural loves named Lucy and containing similar themes or imagery to his own "Lucy poems", for example, Collins' "Song: The Sentiments borrowed from

[70] *dearest Maiden*: originally identified as "Lucy" in an introductory passage, which Wordsworth deleted before publication. It has been suggested that the "dearest Maiden" is Dorothy Wordsworth, but it is possible that, as in the "Lucy poems", no "real" person is being referred to.

[71] Published in *Lyrical Ballads*, 1800.

Shakespeare": "Each maid was woe—but Lucy chief,/Her grief o'er all was tried;/Within his grave she dropp'd in grief,/And o'er her loved one died"; and Rogers' "A Wish": "Around my ivy'd porch shall spring/Each fragrant flower that drinks the dew;/And Lucy, at her wheel, shall sing/In russet gown and apron blue."

"Strange fits of passion have I known"

Strange fits[72] of passion have I known,
And I will dare to tell,
But in the lover's ear alone,
What once to me befell.

When she I loved, was strong and gay   5
And like a rose in June,[73]
I to her cottage bent my way,
Beneath the evening moon.

Upon the moon I fixed my eye
All over the wide lea;[74]   10
My horse trudged on, and we drew nigh
Those paths so dear to me.

And now we reached the orchard plot,
And, as we climbed the hill,
Towards the roof of Lucy's cot[75]   15
The moon descended still.

[72] *fits*: a sudden seizure; a sudden, transitory state; a (sometimes violently intense) mood; a canto or part of a poem.

[73] *rose in June*: Cf. Robert Burns (1759–1796), "A Red, Red Rose": "O my Luve's like a red, red rose,/That's newly sprung in June:/... And I will luve thee still, my dear,/While the sands o' life shall run./... And I will come again, my Luve,/Tho' it were ten thousand mile!"

[74] *lea*: meadow.

[75] *cot*: cottage.

In one of those sweet dreams I slept,
Kind Nature's gentlest boon![76]
And, all the while, my eyes I kept
On the descending moon.   20

My horse moved on; hoof after hoof
He raised and never stopped:
When down behind the cottage roof
At once the planet dropped.

What fond[77] and wayward thoughts will slide   25
Into a Lover's head—
"O mercy!" to myself I cried,
"If Lucy should be dead!"

"She dwelt among th' untrodden ways"[78]

She dwelt among th' untrodden ways
     Beside the springs of Dove,[79]
A Maid whom there were none to praise
     And very few to love.

A Violet by a mossy stone   5
     Half-hidden from the Eye!
—Fair, as a star when only one
     Is shining in the sky![80]

---

[76] *boon*: blessing; gift; a thing to be thankful for.

[77] *fond*: affectionate; foolishly tender; foolishly credulous.

[78] Published in *Lyrical Ballads*, 1800.

[79] *springs of Dove*: Wordsworth was familiar with rivers named Dove in Yorkshire, Derbyshire, and Westmorland (Cumbria); it is unclear to which this refers.

[80] *Fair, as a star . . . in the sky*: The star is probably Venus, the brightest "star" in the heavens (and as Hesperus, the Evening Star, the first to appear in the evening sky).

She *lived* unknown, and few could know
　　When Lucy ceased to be; 　　　　　　　　　　　　10
But she is in her Grave, And Oh!
　　The difference to me.

"A slumber did my spirit seal"[81]

A slumber did my spirit seal;
　　I had no human fears:
She seemed a thing that could not feel
　　The touch of earthly years.

No motion has she now, no force; 　　　　　　　　5
　　She neither hears nor sees,[82]
Rolled round in earth's diurnal[83] course
　　With rocks and stones and trees.

"Three years she grew in sun and shower"[84]

Three years she grew in sun and shower,
Then Nature said, "A lovelier flower
On earth was never sown;
This Child I to myself will take,
She shall be mine, and I will make 　　　　　　　5
A Lady of my own.

---

[81] Published in *Lyrical Ballads*, 1800. See the introductory section for "Strange fits of passion have I known", pp. 133–34.

[82] *She seemed a thing ... neither hears nor sees*: The dead woman's present existence—and thus, in some measure, her very identity—is being dissociated from contemporary scientific and philosophical discourse: "motion" and "force" are words associated with Newtonian physics, while "hears" and "sees" invoke the language of Empiricism.

[83] *diurnal*: i.e., daily.

[84] Published in *Lyrical Ballads*, 1800. See the introductory section for "Strange fits of passion have I known".

"Myself will to my darling be
Both law and impulse, and with me
The Girl in rock and plain,
In earth and heaven, in glade and bower,   10
Shall feel an overseeing power
To kindle or restrain.

"She shall be sportive as the fawn
That wild with glee across the lawn
Or up the mountain springs,   15
And hers shall be the breathing balm,
And hers the silence and the calm
Of mute insensate things.

"The floating clouds their state shall lend
To her; for her the willow bend,   20
Nor shall she fail to see
Even in the motions of the storm
A beauty that shall mould her form
By silent sympathy.

"The stars of midnight shall be dear   25
To her, and she shall lean her ear
In many a secret place
Where rivulets dance their wayward round,
And beauty born of murmuring sound
Shall pass into her face   30

"And vital feelings of delight
Shall rear her form to stately height,
Her virgin bosom swell,
Such thoughts to Lucy I will give
While she and I together live   35
Here in this happy dell."

Thus Nature spake—The work was done—
How soon my Lucy's race was run!

She died, and left to me
This heath, this calm and quiet scene,   40
The memory of what has been,
And never more will be.

Lucy Gray[85]

Oft I had heard of Lucy Gray,
And when I crossed the Wild,
I chanced to see at break of day
The solitary Child.

No Mate, no comrade Lucy knew;   5
She dwelt on a wide Moor,
The sweetest Thing that ever grew
Beside a human door!

You yet may spy the Fawn at play,
The Hare upon the Green;   10
But the sweet face of Lucy Gray
Will never more be seen.

"To-night will be a stormy night,
You to the Town must go,
And take a lantern, Child, to light   15
Your Mother thro' the snow."

"That, Father! will I gladly do;
'Tis scarcely afternoon—

[85] Published in *Lyrical Ballads*, 1800. See the introductory section for "Strange fits of passion have I known". "It was founded on a circumstance told me by my sister of a little girl who, not far from Halifax in Yorkshire, was bewildered in a snowstorm" (Wordsworth, *The Fenwick Notes*, p. 1).

The Minster-clock[86] has just struck two,
And yonder is the Moon."[87]   20

At this the Father raised his hook
And snapped a faggot-band;[88]
He plied his work, and Lucy took
The lantern in her hand.

Not blither is the mountain roe,   25
With many a wanton stroke
Her feet disperse the powd'ry snow
That rises up like smoke.

The storm came on before its time,
She wandered up and down,   30
And many a hill did Lucy climb
But never reached the Town.

The wretched Parents all that night
Went shouting far and wide;
But there was neither sound nor sight   35
To serve them for a guide.

---

[86] *Minster-clock*: the church clock, by which local time was still regulated: "During the 1840s most of the great railway companies came into being. In 1839 Bradshaw first published his timetable, which immediately caused problems over the continuance of 'local time', still jealously maintained in many parts of the country. Not until the late 1840s did the railway companies succeed in enforcing Greenwich Standard Time for the network; and local time was not officially abolished nationwide until 1880" (David Newsome, *The Victorian World Picture* [London: John Murray, 1997], p. 30).

[87] *Moon*: Crabb Robinson had it from Wordsworth that "his object was to exhibit poetically entire *solitude*, and he represents the child as observing the day-moon, which no town or village girl would even notice" (*Diary, Reminiscences, and Correspondence of Henry Crabb Robinson*, vol. 3, ed. Thomas Sadler [London: Macmillan, 1869], p. 342).

[88] *faggot-band*: band, or withe, for binding a bundle of twigs.

At day-break on a hill they stood
That overlooked the Moor;
And thence they saw the Bridge of Wood
A furlong from their door.   40

And now they homeward turned, and cried
"In Heaven we all shall meet!"
When in the snow the Mother spied
The print of Lucy's feet.

Then downward from the steep hill's edge   45
They tracked the footmarks small;
And through the broken hawthorn-hedge,
And by the long stone-wall;

And then an open field they crossed,
The marks were still the same;   50
They tracked them on, nor ever lost,
And to the Bridge they came.

They followed from the snowy bank
The footmarks, one by one,
Into the middle of the plank,   55
And further there were none.

Yet some maintain that to this day
She is a living Child,
That you may see sweet Lucy Gray
Upon the lonesome Wild.   60

O'er rough and smooth she trips along,
And never looks behind;
And sings a solitary song
That whistles in the wind.

Lines Written with a Slate Pencil upon a Stone, the Largest of a Heap Lying Near a Deserted Quarry, upon One of the Islands at Rydal[89]

Stranger! this hillock of mis-shapen stones
Is not a Ruin spared or made by time,
Nor, as perchance thou rashly deem'st, the Cairn[90]
Of some old British Chief: 'tis nothing more
Than the rude embryo of a little Dome   5
Or Pleasure-house, once destined to be built
Among the birch-trees of this rocky isle.
But, as it chanced, Sir William[91] having learned
That from the shore a full-grown man might wade,
And make himself a freeman of this spot   10
At any hour he chose, the prudent Knight
Desisted, and the quarry and the mound
Are monuments of his unfinished task.
The block on which these lines are traced, perhaps,
Was once selected as the corner-stone[92]   15
Of that intended Pile, which would have been
Some quaint odd plaything of elaborate skill,
So that, I guess, the linnet and the thrush,
And other little builders who dwell here,
Had wondered at the work. But blame him not,   20
For old Sir William was a gentle Knight,
Bred in this vale, to which he appertained
With all his ancestry. Then peace to him,
And for the outrage which he had devised

---

[89] Published in *Lyrical Ballads*, 1800. The poem refers to Rydal Hall, the home of the le Fleming family, on the outskirts of the village of Rydal, Cumbria, in the Lake District; it is opposite Rydal Mount, which was to be Wordsworth's home from 1813 to his death in 1850.

[90] *Cairn*: mound of stones raised as a memorial or tomb.

[91] *Sir William*: Sir William Fleming (1656–1736), 1st Baronet of Rydal.

[92] *corner-stone*: perhaps an ironic echo of Acts 4:11: "This [Christ] is the stone which was rejected by you builders, but which has become the head of the cornerstone."

Entire forgiveness!—But if thou art one   25
On fire with thy impatience to become
An inmate of these mountains,—if, disturbed
By beautiful conceptions, thou hast hewn
Out of the quiet rock the elements
Of thy trim Mansion destined soon to blaze   30
In snow-white splendour,—think again; and, taught
By old Sir William and his quarry, leave
Thy fragments to the bramble and the rose;
There let the vernal slow-worm[93] sun himself,
And let the redbreast[94] hop from stone to stone.   35

"My heart leaps up when I behold"[95]

My heart leaps up when I behold
     A Rainbow in the sky:[96]
So was it when my life began;
So is it now I am a Man;
So be it when I shall grow old,   5
     Or let me die!
The Child is Father of the Man;
And I could wish my days to be
Bound each to each by natural piety.

---

[93] *slow-worm*: legless lizard (*Anguis fragilis*).

[94] *redbreast*: English robin (*Erithacus rubecula melophilus*).

[95] Published in *Poems, in Two Volumes*, 1807.

[96] *Rainbow in the sky*: The rainbow was the sign of the renewed covenant between God, man, and the earth following the Flood; see Genesis 9:12–13: "God said, 'This is the sign of the covenant.... I set my bow in the cloud, and it shall be a sign of the covenant between me and the earth.'"

To the Cuckoo[97]

O blithe New-comer! I have heard,
I hear thee and rejoice:
O Cuckoo! shall I call thee Bird,
Or but a wandering Voice?

While I am lying on the grass,   5
I hear thy restless shout:
From hill to hill it seems to pass,
About, and all about!

To me, no Babbler with a tale[98]
Of sunshine and of flowers,   10
Thou tellest, Cuckoo! in the vale
Of visionary hours.

Thrice welcome, Darling of the Spring!
Even yet thou art to me
No Bird;[99] but an invisible Thing,   15
A voice, a mystery.[100]

The same whom in my School-boy days
I listened to; that Cry
Which made me look a thousand ways;
In bush, and tree, and sky.   20

---

[97] Published in *Poems, in Two Volumes*, 1807. For comparable treatment of the disembodied voice of the symbolic, invisible bird, see John Keats (1795–1821), "Ode to a Nightingale", and Percy Bysshe Shelley (1792–1822), "To a Sky-Lark".

[98] *tale*: story; tally.

[99] *thou art to me/No Bird*: Cf. Shelley, "To a Sky-Lark" (lines 1–2): "Hail to thee, blithe Spirit!/Bird thou never wert".

[100] *invisible Thing/A voice, a mystery*: Cf. Keats, "Ode to a Nightingale" (lines 19–20, 61–64): "That I might drink, and leave the world unseen,/And with thee fade away into the forest dim./...Thou wast not born for death, immortal Bird!/No hungry generations tread thee down;/The voice I hear this passing night was heard/In ancient days by emperor and clown".

To seek thee did I often rove
Through woods and on the green;
And thou wert still a hope, a love;
Still longed for, never seen!

And I can listen to thee yet;   25
Can lie upon the plain
And listen, till I do beget
That golden time again.

O blessed Bird! the earth we pace
Again appears to be   30
An unsubstantial, faery place;
That is fit home for Thee![101]

Resolution and Independence[102]

This old man I met a few hundred yards from my cottage at Town-End, Grasmere; and the account of him is taken from his own mouth. I was in the state of feeling described in the beginning of the poem, while crossing over Barton Fell from Mr Clarkson's, at the foot of Ullswater, towards Askham. The image of the hare I then observed on the ridge of the Fell.[103]

"Resolution and Independence" is written in rhyme royal (seven lines in iambic pentameter, rhyming ababbcc) modified by an

---

[101] *faery place;/That is fit home for Thee*: Cf. ibid., lines 65–70: "Perhaps the self-same song that found a path/Through the sad heart of Ruth, when, sick for home,/She stood in tears amid the alien corn;/The same that oft-times hath/Charmed magic casements, opening on the foam/Of perilous seas, in faery lands forlorn."

[102] Published in *Poems, in Two Volumes*, 1807.

[103] Wordsworth, *The Fenwick Notes*, p. 14. Ullswater is the second-largest lake in the Lake District. Thomas Clarkson (1760–1846) was a leading campaigner for the abolition of slavery; he moved to Ullswater in 1794 and became a friend of the Wordsworths, who admired his work—see Wordsworth's sonnet, "To Thomas Clarkson, On the final passing of the Bill for the Abolition of the Slave Trade, March, 1807".

alexandrine (hexameter) in the seventh line; Wordsworth would have found precedents for this stanza in Chatterton's "An Excelente Balade of Charitie" (often regarded as Chatterton's finest work) and Milton's "On the Morning of Christ's Nativity". Both Chatterton and (implicitly) Milton are referred to in "Resolution and Independence". It is parodied by Lewis Carroll in *Through the Looking-Glass* as "The White Knight's Ballad".

For Charles Williams (1886–1945) the leech-gatherer is a tremendous figure, and one that simultaneously illustrates Wordsworth's powers and limitations:

And greater than beggar or soldier is the Leech-Gatherer. Wordsworth gave that poem a second title—"Resolution and Independence". It is very proper that we should read it as, apparently, he meant us to; it is proper that we should realize what a great and moving poem it is. But it is permissible also that we should derive from it all that it contains; and one of the things it does contain is a sense that the Leech-Gatherer is the impersonated thought of some other state of being, which the acceptance of the noble doctrine it teaches leaves in itself unexplored.... Confronted with this great experience Wordsworth might have done one of two things—in doing the very thing he did do. He asked him, out of the midst of his own bother about his future income—and God, He knows how real and urgent that bother can be; we shall never understand the poets if we pretend that money is not of high importance—he asked him, "How is it that you live, and what is it you do?" And—as if "sent To give me human strength"—the Leech-Gatherer told him, and Wordsworth listened and admired and believed and went away comforted. Nevertheless, that question might have been asked with another meaning—with the desire for some knowledge similar to that which caused Jacob to wrestle with the Angel: "What is thy *name?*" It might have been asked not for strength and comfort, but for discovery and increase of poetic wisdom.

What *is* this apparition—this stone—this sea-beast—this cloud—this dream-like body—this undivided stream of lofty utterance? What is it in itself? Never mind what it means to our lives, what moral or message it has for us, or let that be secondary; "what is thy *name*?" He belongs to that strange world from which the woman came, who bore a pitcher on her head and walked leaning against the wind,[104] and the beggar who wore a label that seemed

> to typify the utmost we can know
> Both of ourselves and of the universe;[105]

and the soldier who was an embodiment of the power of Solitude;[106] and the Highland Reaper[107] who sang "the melancholy song", "the plaintive numbers", of which Wordsworth knew that they might be "of old unhappy far-off things".

Lear on the heath, Satan on Niphates—if these had not been forced by the poets to speak, and speaking, to explain their being, would not they too have seemed to belong to that terrifying world?[108]

Resolution and Independence

I

There was a roaring in the wind all night;
The rain came heavily and fell in floods;
But now the sun is rising calm and bright;
The birds are singing in the distant woods;
Over his own sweet voice the Stock-dove broods;   5
The Jay makes answer as the Magpie chatters;
And all the air is filled with pleasant noise of waters.

II

All things that love the sun are out of doors;
The sky rejoices in the morning's birth;

---

[104] *the woman . . . leaning against the wind*: Prelude, bk. 11 (1805), lines 305ff.
[105] *to typify . . . universe*: Prelude, bk. 7 (1850), lines 645–46, slightly misquoted.
[106] *the soldier . . . Solitude*: Prelude, bk. 4 (1850), lines 384ff.
[107] *Highland Reaper*: "The Solitary Reaper".
[108] Charles Williams, *The English Poetic Mind* (Oxford: Oxford, 1932), pp. 159–61.

The grass is bright with rain-drops; on the moors   10
The Hare is running races in her mirth;
And with her feet she from the plashy earth
Raises a mist; which, glittering in the sun,
Runs with her all the way, wherever she doth run.

III

I was a Traveller then upon the moor;   15
I saw the Hare that raced about with joy;
I heard the woods, and distant waters, roar;
Or heard them not, as happy as a Boy:
The pleasant season did my heart employ:
My old remembrances went from me wholly;   20
And all the ways of men, so vain and melancholy.

IV

But, as it sometimes chanceth, from the might
Of joy in minds that can no farther go,
As high as we have mounted in delight
In our dejection do we sink as low,   25
To me that morning did it happen so;
And fears, and fancies, thick upon me came;
Dim sadness, and blind thoughts I knew not nor could name.

V

I heard the Sky-lark singing in the sky;
And I bethought me[109] of the playful Hare: 30
Even such a happy Child of earth am I;
Even as these blissful Creatures do I fare;
Far from the world[110] I walk, and from all care;
But there may come another day to me,
Solitude, pain of heart, distress, and poverty.   35

---

[109] *bethought me*: recollected, reflected on.
[110] *world*: society, public life. Cf. "The world is too much with us".

VI

My whole life I have lived in pleasant thought,
As if life's business were a summer mood;
As if all needful things would come unsought
To genial faith,[111] still rich in genial good;
But how can He expect that others should   40
Build for him, sow for him, and at his call
Love him, who for himself will take no heed at all?

VII

I thought of Chatterton,[112] the marvellous Boy,
The sleepless Soul that perished in his pride;
Of Him[113] who walked in glory and in joy   45
Behind his plough, upon the mountain-side:
By our own spirits are we deified;
We Poets in our youth begin in gladness;
But thereof comes in the end despondency and madness.

VIII

Now, whether it were by peculiar grace,   50
A leading from above, a something given,
Yet it befel, that, in this lonely place,
When up and down my fancy thus was driven,

---

[111] *needful things . . . genial faith*: See Matthew 6:25–26: "Therefore I [Jesus] tell
you, do not be anxious about your life, what you shall eat or what you shall drink
nor about your body, what you shall put on.... Look at the birds of the air: they
neither sow nor reap ... and yet your heavenly Father feeds them."

[112] *Chatterton*: Thomas Chatterton (1752–1770), one of world literature's
legitimate adolescent geniuses. He wrote pseudo-medieval poetry that he passed
off as genuine. His initial success prompted him to leave his legal apprenticeship
in Bristol to attempt a literary career in London. Meeting with failure and pen-
ury, he committed suicide at the age of seventeen. Chatterton remained a sym-
bol of unrecognized genius throughout much of the nineteenth century. Beyond
Wordsworth, his influence can be seen on Coleridge, Shelley, Keats, Dante
Gabriel Rossetti, Swinburne, and, in France, on Alfred de Vigny.

[113] *Him*: i.e., Robert Burns, the great Scottish poet (and farmer)—much
admired by Wordsworth; he died young, in want, and some social ignominy.

And I with these untoward[114] thoughts had striven,
I saw a Man before me unawares: 55
The oldest Man he seemed that ever wore grey hairs.

IX

My course I stopped as soon as I espied
The Old Man in that naked wilderness:
Close by a Pond, upon the further side,
He stood alone: a minute's space I guess   60
I watched him, he continuing motionless:
To the Pool's further margin then I drew;
He being all the while before me full in view.

X

As a huge Stone is sometimes seen to lie
Couched on the bald top of an eminence;   65
Wonder to all who do the same espy
By what means it could thither come, and whence;
So that it seems a thing endued with sense:
Like a Sea-beast crawled forth, which on a shelf
Of rock or sand reposeth, there to sun itself.   70

XI

Such seemed this Man, not all alive nor dead,
Nor all asleep; in his extreme old age:
His body was bent double, feet and head
Coming together in their pilgrimage;
As if some dire constraint of pain, or rage   75
Of sickness felt by him in times long past,
A more than human weight upon his frame had cast.

[114] *untoward*: unruly (only two syllables here).

XII

Himself he propped, his body, limbs, and face,
Upon a long grey Staff of shaven wood:
And, still as I drew near with gentle pace,   80
Beside the little pond or moorish flood
Motionless as a Cloud the Old Man stood;
That heareth not the loud winds when they call;
And moveth altogether; if it move at all.[115]

XIII

At length, himself unsettling, he the Pond   85
Stirred with his Staff, and fixedly did look
Upon the muddy water, which he conned,[116]
As if he had been reading in a book:
And now such freedom as I could I took;
And, drawing to his side, to him did say,   90
"This morning gives us promise of a glorious day."

XIV

A gentle answer did the Old Man make,
In courteous speech which forth he slowly drew:
And him with further words I thus bespake,
"What kind of work is that which you pursue?   95
This is a lonesome place for one like you."
He answered me with pleasure and surprize;
And there was, while he spake, a fire about his eyes.

XV

His words came feebly, from a feeble chest,
Yet each in solemn order followed each,   100

---

[115] *Old Man ... move at all*: Cf. Sir Richard Steele (1672–1729) in *The Spectator*, no. 6 (March 7, 1711): "I lay it down therefore for a Rule, That the whole Man is to move together."
[116] *conned*: studied.

With something of a lofty utterance drest;
Choice word, and measured phrase; above the reach
Of ordinary men; a stately speech!
Such as grave Livers do in Scotland use,
Religious men, who give to God and Man their dues.   105

XVI

He told me that he to this pond had come
To gather Leeches,[117] being old and poor:
Employment hazardous and wearisome!
And he had many hardships to endure:
From Pond to Pond he roamed, from moor to moor,   110
Housing, with God's good help, by choice or chance:
And in this way he gained an honest maintenance.

XVII

The Old Man still stood talking by my side;
But now his voice to me was like a stream
Scarce heard; nor word from word could I divide;   115
And the whole Body of the man did seem
Like one whom I had met with in a dream;
Or like a Man from some far region sent;
To give me human strength, and strong admonishment.[118]

XVIII

My former thoughts returned: the fear that kills;   120
The hope that is unwilling to be fed;
Cold, pain, and labour, and all fleshy ills;

---

[117] *Leeches*: The medicinal leech (*Hirudo medicinalis*) was still being used for medical purposes well into the twentieth century and indeed is making something of a comeback in microsurgery.

[118] *strong admonishment*: Cf. W. S. Gilbert (1836–1911), *Iolanthe*, Act 2, Private Willis' song: "Though never nurtured in the lap/Of luxury, yet, I admonish you,/I am an intellectual chap./And think of things that would astonish you."

And mighty Poets in their misery dead.[119]
And now, not knowing what the Old Man had said,
My question eagerly did I renew,   125
"How is it that you live, and what is it you do?"

XIX

He with a smile did then his words repeat;
And said, that, gathering Leeches, far and wide
He travelled; stirring thus about his feet
The waters of Ponds where they abide.   130
"Once I could meet with them on every side;
But they have dwindled long by slow decay;
Yet still I persevere, and find them where I may."

XX

While he was talking thus, the lonely place,
The Old Man's shape, and speech, all troubled me: 135
In my mind's eye I seemed to see him pace
About the weary moors continually,
Wandering about alone and silently.
While I these thoughts within myself pursued,
He, having made a pause, the same discourse renewed.   140

XXI

And soon with this he other matter blended,
Cheerfully uttered, with demeanour kind,
But stately in the main; and, when he ended,
I could have laughed myself to scorn, to find
In that decrepit Man so firm a mind.   145
"God", said I, "be my help and stay[120] secure;
I'll think of the Leech-gatherer on the lonely moor."

---

[119] *mighty Poets in their misery dead*: This would include Milton, whose last years—which saw the composition and/or completion of *Paradise Lost, Paradise Regained*, and *Samson Agonistes*—were lived in blindness and political harassment.

[120] *help and stay*: support.

"Nuns fret not at their Convent's narrow room"[121]

Nuns fret not at their Convent's narrow room;
And Hermits[122] are contented with their Cells;
And Students with their pensive Citadels;
Maids at the Wheel,[123] the Weaver at his Loom,
Sit blithe and happy; Bees that soar for bloom,   5
High as the highest Peak of Furness Fells,[124]
Will murmur by the hour in Foxglove bells:
In truth, the prison unto which we doom
Ourselves, no prison is: and hence for me,
In sundry moods, 'twas pastime to be bound   10
Within the Sonnet's scanty plot of ground:
Pleased if some Souls (for such there needs must be)
Who have felt the weight of too much liberty,
Should find brief solace there, as I have found.

Composed upon Westminster Bridge, September 3, 1802[125]

Wordsworth and his sister had taken advantage of the Treaty of Amiens (March 25, 1802–May 18, 1803—ultimately, the only period that Great Britain and France were to be at peace between 1793 and 1814) to go to France to visit his former lover Annette Vallon, and their daughter—now nine years old—Caroline.[126] He left London for Calais on July 31, 1802, and returned on September 3. He had most probably not seen Annette since his departure toward the end of 1792. He was to marry Mary Hutchinson on October 4, 1802.

[121] Published in *Poems, in Two Volumes*, 1807.
[122] *Hermits*: See the note to line 21 of "Tintern Abbey".
[123] *Wheel*: i.e., spinning wheel.
[124] *Peak of Furness Fells*: mountains and hills in the Furness region, Cumbria; most of them lie within the Lake District.
[125] Published in *Poems, in Two Volumes*, 1807.
[126] See the note to line 2 of "Tintern Abbey".

Westminster Bridge is the first of that name, designed by Charles Labelye and completed in 1750 (the present Westminster Bridge was designed by Thomas Page and replaced Labelye's bridge in 1862). It links Lambeth with Westminster; the Palace of Westminster (the Houses of Parliament—though the present buildings date mostly from the 1830s) and Westminster Abbey are immediately to the left as one crosses from Lambeth. The scene as it appeared in Wordsworth's day can be seen in paintings by Canaletto and Turner.

The poet is contemplating the prospect as he looks northwest toward the City of London, with its beautiful cluster of Wren spires and the great dome of St. Paul's Cathedral. By this stage London was well on the way to becoming the largest city—and port—in the world.

Composed upon Westminster Bridge, September 3, 1802

Earth has not anything to shew more fair:
Dull would he be of soul who could pass by
A sight so touching in its majesty:
This City now doth like a garment wear
The beauty of the morning; silent, bare,   5
Ships, towers, domes, theatres, and temples lie
Open unto the fields, and to the sky;
All bright and glittering in the smokeless air.
Never did sun more beautifully steep
In his first splendor valley, rock, or hill;   10
Ne'er saw I, never felt, a calm so deep!
The river[127] glideth at his own sweet will:
Dear God! the very houses seem asleep;
And all that mighty heart is lying still!

---

[127] *river*: Thames River. Cf. Edmund Spenser (1552–1599), "Prothalamion" (refrain): "Sweete Themmes! runne softly, till I end my Song."

"The world is too much with us"[128]

The world is too much with us; late and soon,
Getting and spending, we lay waste our powers:
Little we see in Nature that is ours;
We have given our hearts away, a sordid boon![129]
This Sea that bares her bosom to the moon;   5
The Winds that will be howling at all hours,
And are up-gathered now like sleeping flowers;
For this, for every thing, we are out of tune;[130]
It moves us not.—Great God! I'd rather be
A Pagan suckled in a creed outworn;   10
So might I, standing on this pleasant lea,[131]
Have glimpses that would make me less forlorn;
Have sight of Proteus[132] rising from the sea;
Or hear old Triton[133] blow his wreathèd horn.

[128] Published in *Poems, in Two Volumes*, 1807. "The world" here refers to the superficial affairs of society; the title is ironic: the world that is too much with us is a false image of the real world—Wordsworth is accusing his contemporaries of a species of idolatry. See the note to line 10 of "Written in London, September, 1802".

[129] *boon*: thing to be thankful for.

[130] *out of tune*: Wordsworth is referring to the music of the spheres: the idea (found in Pythagoras, Plato, Saint Augustine, Boethius, Cassiodorus, Dante, Shakespeare, Kepler, and so forth) that the created order (and particularly the celestial bodies) literally involves a sort of harmony. See, for example, Plato, *Republic* 10.

[131] *lea*: meadow. Cf. Spenser, "Colin Clouts Come Home Againe", line 283: "Yet seemed to be a goodly pleasant lea".

[132] *Proteus*: shape-shifting (hence, *protean*) Greek sea god, "The Old Man of the Sea". Cf. *Paradise Lost*, bk. 3, lines 603–4: "Call up unbound/In various shapes old Proteus from the sea".

[133] *Triton*: merman-shaped Greek sea god, the son and herald of Poseidon. He is often depicted (e.g., in Bernini's Fontana del Tritone in Rome) blowing his conch shell—a horn of prodigious power. Cf. Spenser, "Colin Clouts Come Home Againe", line 245: "Is *Triton* blowing loud his wreathèd horne".

"It is a beauteous Evening, calm and free"[134]

It is a beauteous Evening, calm and free,
The holy time is quiet as a Nun
Breathless with adoration; the broad sun
Is sinking down in its tranquillity;
The gentleness of heaven is on the Sea:[135]   5
Listen! the mighty Being is awake
And doth with his eternal motion make
A sound like thunder—everlastingly.
Dear Child! dear Girl![136] that walkest with me here,
If thou appear'st untouched by solemn thought,   10
Thy nature is not therefore less divine:
Thou liest in Abraham's bosom[137] all the year;
And worshipp'st at the Temple's inner shrine,[138]
God being with thee when we know it not.

---

[134] Published in *Poems, in Two Volumes*, 1807.

[135] *gentleness of heaven is on the Sea*: Cf. Genesis 1:1–2: "In the beginning God created the heavens and the earth ... and the Spirit of God was moving over the face of the waters." See "London, 1802", line 10, where the voice of the poet who sang to "justify the ways of God to men" is likened to the voice of the sea.

[136] *Dear Child! dear Girl*: Wordsworth's illegitimate French daughter, Caroline. See the introductory text to "Composed upon Westminster Bridge" and note for line 2 of "Tintern Abbey".

[137] *Thou liest in Abraham's bosom*: the blissful abode of the righteous after death before the Resurrection of Christ unlocked the gates of Heaven to man. The expression is found uniquely in the parable of the rich man and Lazarus, in Luke 16:22–23: "The poor man died and was carried by the angels to Abraham's bosom. The rich man also died and was buried; and in Hades, being in torment, he ... saw Abraham far off and Lazarus in his bosom."

[138] *Temple's inner shrine*: The Tabernacle is the portable sanctuary of the Divine Presence, housing the Ark of the Covenant in the inner shrine—the Holy of Holies. See the note to line 35 of Blake's *Jerusalem*.

To Toussaint L'Ouverture[139]

François-Dominique Toussaint L'Ouverture (1743–1803) was a Haitian freed slave, abolitionist leader of a successful rebellion against French colonial rule, and governor of Haiti. In 1793 he became involved in the local uprisings that followed the French Legislative Assembly's extension of the full rights of citizenship to "free people of colour"; by 1801 he had acquired command of the entire island of Hispaniola and established trade relations with Britain and the United States of America. Napoleon (first consul, but not yet emperor) sent a fleet in December 1801, and, ultimately, some thirty thousand troops to reestablish French control of the colony. Conflict ensued; Toussaint was arrested, deported to France, and imprisoned in the Burgundian fortress of Fort de Joux, where he died of pneumonia. The abolition of slavery in the French colonies was revoked in the law of May 20, 1802, and outrages were committed against Haitian blacks and mulattos in the unsuccessful French attempt to regain full control. Haiti was effectively free by 1804.

To Toussaint L'Ouverture

Toussaint, the most unhappy Man of Men!
Whether the rural Milk-maid by her Cow
Sing in thy hearing, or thou liest now
Alone in some deep dungeon's earless den,
O miserable Chieftain! where and when   5
Wilt thou find patience? Yet die not; do thou
Wear rather in thy bonds a cheerful brow:
Though fallen Thyself, never to rise again,
Live, and take comfort.[140] Thou hast left behind
Powers that will work for thee; air, earth, and skies;   10

---

[139] Published in *Poems, in Two Volumes*, 1807; from the section "Sonnets Dedicated to Liberty".

[140] *Though fallen Thyself . . . Live, and take comfort*: Toussaint L'Ouverture died on April 7, 1803, six months after this sonnet was written.

There's not a breathing of the common wind
That will forget thee; thou hast great allies;
Thy friends are exultations, agonies,
And love, and Man's unconquerable mind.[141]

Written in London, September, 1802[142]

O friend![143] I know not which way I must look
For comfort, being, as I am, opprest,
To think that now our Life is only drest
For show; mean[144] handy-work of craftsman, cook,
Or groom![145]—We must run glittering like a brook   5
In the open sunshine, or we are unblest:
The wealthiest man among us is the best:
No grandeur now in nature or in book

[141] *Man's unconquerable mind*: Cf. Thomas Gray, "The Progress of Poesy", lines 60–65: The Muse "deigns to hear the savage youth repeat / In loose numbers wildly sweet / Their feather-cinctured chiefs, and dusky loves. / Her track, where'er the Goddess roves, / Glory pursue, and generous Shame, / Th' unconquerable Mind, and Freedom's holy flame", and George Gordon, Lord Byron (1788–1824), "Sonnet on Chillon", lines 1–2: "Eternal Spirit of the chainless Mind! / Brightest in dungeons, Liberty! thou art".

[142] Published in *Poems, in Two Volumes*, 1807; from the section "Sonnets Dedicated to Liberty". Wordsworth wrote,

> This was written immediately after my return from France to London, when I could not but be struck, as here described, with the vanity and parade of our own country, especially in great towns and cities, as contrasted with the quiet, and I may say the desolation, that the revolution had produced in France. This must be borne in mind, or else the reader may think that in this and the succeeding Sonnets I have exaggerated the mischief engendered and fostered among us by undisturbed wealth. It would not be easy to conceive with what a depth of feeling I entered into the struggle carried on by the Spaniards for their deliverance from the usurped power of the French. (Wordsworth, *The Fenwick Notes*, p. 28)

[143] *friend*: Coleridge.
[144] *mean*: common; petty.
[145] *groom*: servant who attends to horses.

Delights us. Rapine,[146] avarice, expense,
This is idolatry;[147] and these we adore: 10
Plain living and high thinking are no more:
The homely beauty of the good old cause
Is gone; our peace, our fearful innocence,
And pure religion breathing household laws.

London, 1802[148]

Milton! thou should'st be living at this hour:
England hath need of thee:[149] she is a fen
Of stagnant waters: altar, sword, and pen,
Fireside, the heroic wealth of hall and bower,
Have forfeited their ancient English dower[150] 5
Of inward happiness. We are selfish men;
Oh! raise us up, return to us again;
And give us manners, virtue, freedom, power.
Thy soul was like a Star and dwelt apart:
Thou hadst a voice whose sound was like the sea;[151] 10
Pure as the naked heavens, majestic, free,
So didst thou travel on life's common way,
In cheerful godliness; and yet thy heart
The lowliest duties on herself did lay.

[146] *Rapine*: the seizing of property by force; plunder.

[147] *idolatry*: See the note to "The world is too much with us".

[148] Published in *Poems, in Two Volumes*, 1807; from the section "Sonnets Dedicated to Liberty".

[149] *Milton ... need of thee*: John Milton (1608–1674) was an icon to Wordsworth, both as a poet and public figure; see further the note to line 128 of "Tintern Abbey".

[150] *dower*: endowment; inheritance.

[151] *voice whose sound was like the sea*: This voice most memorably undertook to sing on God's behalf in *Paradise Lost*; see "It is a beauteous Evening, calm and free", line 5, where the sound of the sea is likened to the voice of God.

"It is not to be thought of that the Flood"[152]

A strong current of European Anglophilia developed in the eighteenth century, especially in France (and France's preeminent cultural position at the time meant that the intellectual and the fashionable were quick to follow its lead). Voltaire and Goethe were merely the most prominent foreign luminaries to be impressed by the British development. Fashions aside, of particular value to Anglophiles were Britain's constitutional monarchy, her cultural achievements, the permeability of her social order, and the freedom of her press.

Within Britain, this often translated into the symbols of the Reformation—civil and religious freedom, material prosperity, and cultural glory secured by the Age of Elizabeth: Shakespeare and the Golden Age of English literature; the formation of the Church of England; the founding of the Royal Navy; the destruction of the Spanish Armada; the exploration of the lands beyond the western seas; the development of industry and international trade. Parliamentary authority at the monarch's expense was achieved in the otherwise unsatisfactory Civil War (1642–1651), and finally consolidated by the "Glorious Revolution" of 1688, which banished the last Catholic king and definitively shackled the sovereign's authority. Church and Throne had been retained, but both had been "put in their place".

There was some mythologizing here, to be sure, but it was not wholesale. The movement for the global abolition of slavery was consistently led by Britain and counted Wilberforce, Pitt, Fox, and Grenville among its leaders. The impeachment of Warren Hastings in 1787 (led by Burke and Fox) established that the Empire would be held morally accountable for its government of subject peoples. The Quebec Act of 1774 extended religious liberty to newly conquered Roman Catholic Quebec (and was regarded by the Thirteen Colonies as a major grievance); this was followed by the Papists Act of 1778, which

---

[152] Published in *Poems, in Two Volumes*, 1807; from the section "Sonnets Dedicated to Liberty".

afforded a measure of relief to British Catholics. With the French War at its height, Pitt resigned as Prime Minister in 1801 over the Crown's refusal to follow through with the Irish Catholic emancipation that was to be an integral part of the Act of Union. These measures were remarkable by the standards of the time.

In the world of letters, a host of writers, from Shakespeare to Scott and Byron, were translated and highly influential (for instance, Sterne on Diderot's *Jacques le fataliste*; Handel, Thomson, and Milton on Haydn's oratorios). In political theory, there were Locke, Burke, and radicals such as Priestley, Godwin, and Paine; in music, Handel; in philosophy, Bacon and Hume; in economics, Adam Smith; in history, Gibbon; in jurisprudence, Blackstone. In science, above all, there was the giant figure of Newton. Finally, there were the industrialists, the inventors, and the businessmen: the impact of the Industrial Revolution.

In spite of Wordsworth's anxieties, Britain's prestige was largely enhanced by its role in the French Revolutionary Wars, and showed no signs of faltering until the Second Boer War (1899–1902).

"It is not to be thought of that the Flood"

It is not to be thought of that the Flood[153]
Of British freedom, which to the open Sea
Of the world's praise from dark antiquity
Hath flowed, "with pomp of waters, unwithstood,"[154]
Road by which all might come and go that would,   5
And bear our freights of worth to foreign lands;

---

[153] *Flood*: flowing in of the tide; river; flood. The maritime imagery of this metaphor is deeply connected to historical British identity, experience, and liberty: the sea, island life, the navy, the Spanish Armada of 1588, and the preservation of Anglicanism, exploration, and trade.

[154] *"with pomp of waters, unwithstood,"*: from Samuel Daniel (1562–1619), *The Civil Wars*, bk. 2, stanza 7, line 5.

Which spurns the check of salutary bands,[155]
That this most famous Stream in Bogs and Sands
Should perish; and to evil and to good
Be lost for ever.[156] In our Halls is hung
Armoury of the invincible Knights of old:[157]   10
We must be free or die, who speak the tongue
That Shakspeare spake; the faith and morals hold
Which Milton held. In everything we are sprung
Of Earth's first blood, have titles manifold.

"When I have borne in memory"[158]

When I have borne in memory what has tamed
Great Nations, how ennobling thoughts depart
When men change Swords for Ledgers, and desert
The Student's bower for gold, some fears unnamed
I had, my Country! am I to be blamed?   5
But, when I think of Thee, and what Thou art,
Verily, in the bottom of my heart,
Of those unfilial fears I am ashamed.
For dearly must we prize thee; we who find
In thee a bulwark of the cause of men;   10
And I by my affection was beguiled.
What wonder, if a Poet, now and then,
Among the many movements of his mind,
Felt for thee as a Lover or a Child.

[155] *salutary bands*: shackle; fetter; anything that binds.

[156] *to evil and to good / Be lost for ever*: exemplified for those to the "Left" by Pitt's suspension of habeas corpus between 1794 and 1801 (see the note to line 1 of Blake's "London"), the more so as Pitt had been a great reforming prime minister before the war with France.

[157] *Halls is hung / Armoury of the invincible Knights of old*: This image is redolent of Spenser's *Faerie Queene*, but it also surely evokes the swashbuckling knights of the Elizabethan legend, Sir Walter Raleigh (ca. 1552–1618), Sir Francis Drake (1540–1596), and others who, in the words of "Hey, Jolly Broom Man" "crossed the seas, and back again/ ... and caused the Spanish fleet to quake", many of whose properties ("Halls") and titles date from the Reformation.

[158] Published in *Poems, in Two Volumes*, 1807; from the section "Sonnets Dedicated to Liberty".

"She was a Phantom of delight"[159]

She was a Phantom of delight
When first she gleamed upon my sight;
A lovely Apparition, sent
To be a moment's ornament;
Her eyes as stars of Twilight fair;   5
Like Twilight's, too, her dusky hair;
But all things else about her drawn
From May-time and the cheerful Dawn;
A dancing Shape, an Image gay,
To haunt, to startle, and way-lay.   10

I saw her upon nearer view,
A Spirit, yet a Woman too!
Her household motions light and free,
And steps of virgin liberty;
A countenance in which did meet   15
Sweet records, promises as sweet;
A Creature not too bright or good
For human nature's daily food;
For transient sorrows, simple wiles,
Praise, blame, love, kisses, tears, and smiles.   20

And now I see with eye serene
The very pulse of the machine;[160]
A Being breathing thoughtful breath,
A Traveller betwixt life and death;

---

[159] Published in *Poems, in Two Volumes*, 1807. The subject of the poem is Wordsworth's wife, Mary Hutchinson Wordsworth (1770–1859).

[160] *machine*: body (as a combination of several parts). Wordsworth's use of "machine" for "body" refers, at least implicitly, to the scientist ideology of the Enlightenment; this is the language of Julien Offray de La Mettrie (1709–1751): "Nature had necessarily to employ more art and install more organs to make and maintain a machine that might mark all the throbbings of the heart and mind" (*Man a Machine*, in *Man a Machine and Man a Plant*, trans. Richard A. Watson and Maya Rybalka [Indianapolis: Hackett, 1994], p. 69). Cf. also Shakespeare, *Hamlet*, Act 2, scene 2, line 124: "Thine evermore, most dear lady, whilst this machine is to him".

The reason firm, the temperate will,   25
Endurance, foresight, strength, and skill;
A perfect Woman; nobly planned,
To warn, to comfort, and command;
And yet a Spirit still, and bright
With something of angelic light.   30

Ode to Duty[161]

"Jam non consilio bonus, sed more eò perductus, ut non tan-
tum rectè facere possim, sed nisi rectè facere non possim." (I
am no longer good through deliberate intent, but by long habit
have reached a point where I am not able to do right, but am
unable to do anything but what is right.)[162]

Stern Daughter of the Voice of God![163]
O Duty! if that name thou love
Who art a Light to guide, a Rod
To check the erring, and reprove;
Thou who art victory and law   5
When empty terrors overawe;
From vain temptations dost set free;
And calm'st the weary strife of frail humanity!

---

[161] Published in *Poems, in Two Volumes*, 1807. According to Wordsworth,
"This Ode is on the model of Gray's 'Ode to Adversity', which is copied from
Horace's Ode to Fortune" (IF). The epigraph is from Seneca (4 B.C.–A.D. 65),
Moral Epistles to Lucilius, 120.10: "Now I am good not through conscious decision,
but guided by habit, so that I am not only able to act rightly, but I am not able to
do otherwise." Cf. Newsome, *Godliness and Good Learning*, p. 13: "Indeed, Butler's
view of habit, which Gladstone always regarded as the 'foundation of character',
and which Newman would often recall for the benefit of pupils, might be taken
as one of the most appropriate mottoes of the Victorian moralists: 'Whatever
we do on the call of duty we do easier next time; whatever we fail to do we find
more difficult, that is we are still less disposed to do it. We fall back on the sure
law of habit.'" See also introductory note to "Tintern Abbey" for Newsome on
Wordsworth and the early Victorian intellectuals.
[162] Seneca, Letters, 120.10
[163] *Stern Daughter of the Voice of God*: Cf. Milton, *Paradise Lost*, bk. 9, lines 652–
53: "God so commanded, and left that command/Sole daughter of his voice".

There are who ask not if thine eye
Be on them; who, in love and truth,   10
Where no misgiving is, rely
Upon the genial sense of youth:
Glad Hearts! without reproach or blot;
Who do thy work, and know it not:
O, if through confidence misplaced   15
They fail, thy saving arms, dread Power! around
    them cast.

Serene will be our days and bright,
And happy[164] will our nature be,
When love is an unerring light,
And joy its own security.   20
And they a blissful course may hold
Even now, who, not unwisely bold,
Live in the spirit of this creed;
Yet seek thy firm support, according to their need.

I, loving freedom, and untried;   25
No sport[165] of every random gust,
Yet being to myself a guide,
Too blindly have reposed my trust:
And oft, when in my heart was heard
Thy timely mandate, I deferred   30
The task, in smoother walks to stray;
But thee I now would serve more strictly, if I may.

Through no disturbance of my soul,
Or strong compunction in me wrought,
I supplicate for thy control;   35
But in the quietness of thought.
Me this uncharter'd freedom[166] tires;

[164] *happy*: fortunate.
[165] *sport*: victim of caprice.
[166] *uncharter'd freedom*: See the note to line 1 of Blake's "London".

I feel the weight of chance-desires;
My hopes no more must change their name,
I long for a repose that ever is the same.[167]   40

Yet not the less would I throughout[168]
Still act according to the voice
Of my own wish; and feel past doubt
That my submissiveness was choice:
Not seeking in the school of pride   45
For "precepts over dignified,"[169]
Denial and restraint I prize
No farther than they breed a second Will[170] more wise.

Stern Lawgiver! yet thou dost wear
The Godhead's most benignant grace;   50
Nor know we anything so fair
As is the smile upon thy face:[171]
Flowers laugh before thee on their beds,
And Fragrance in thy footing treads;[172]
Thou dost preserve the Stars from wrong;   55
And the most ancient Heavens, through Thee, are fresh
    and strong.

[167] *long for a repose that ever is the same*: Cf. Dante, *Paradiso*, canto 3, line 85: "and His will is our peace".

[168] This stanza was cancelled in Wordsworth's later collections.

[169] *"precepts over dignified,"*: See Milton, *The Doctrine and Discipline of Divorce* (Preamble): "to set straiter limits to obedience, than God hath set, to enslave the dignity of man, to put a garrison upon his neck of empty and over-dignified precepts".

[170] *Will*: Wordsworth is punning on his name, as Shakespeare does in Sonnet 57, lines 13–14: "So true a fool is love, that in your will,/Though you do anything, he thinks no ill."

[171] *smile upon thy face*: Cf. Thomas Carlyle (1795–1881), *Sartor Resartus*, bk. 2, chap. 2: "Happy he for whom a kind heavenly Sun brightens [Necessity] into a ring of Duty, and plays round it with beautiful prismatic diffractions".

[172] *Flowers laugh . . . Fragrance in thy footing treads*: Cf. Persius (A.D. 34–62), Satire 2, line 38: "wherever he treads may roses appear" and Ben Jonson (1572/1573–1637), *The Sad Shepherd*, Act 1, scene 1, lines 8–9: "And, where she went, the flowers took thickest root,/As she had sowed them with her odorous foot."

To humbler functions, awful[173] Power!
I call thee: I myself commend
Unto thy guidance from this hour;
O, let my weakness have an end!   60
Give unto me, made lowly wise,[174]
The spirit of self-sacrifice;
The confidence of reason give;
And in the light of truth thy Bondman[175] let me live!

Ode: Intimations of Immortality from Recollections of Early Childhood[176]

The Pindaric "Ode: Intimations of Immortality from Recollections of Early Childhood" (stanzas of a varying number of rhymed lines of irregular length) is generally regarded as one of Wordsworth's greatest achievements. The poet summarized its underlying themes in 1815 in a letter to Catherine Clarkson:

> This poem rests entirely upon two recollections of childhood, one that of a splendour in the objects of sense which is passed away, and the other an indisposition to bend to the law of death as applying to our own particular case.

He addressed this at greater length in 1843:

> This was composed during my residence at Town-End, Grasmere. Two years at least passed between the writing of the four first stanzas and the remaining part. To the attentive and competent reader the whole sufficiently explains itself, but

---

[173] *awful*: inspiring awe.

[174] *lowly wise*: Cf. *Paradise Lost*, bk. 8, lines 172–75: "Heaven is for thee too high / To know what passes there; be lowly wise: / Think only what concerns thee and thy being; / Dream not of other worlds".

[175] *Bondman*: serf.

[176] Published in *Poems, in Two Volumes*, 1807. The first four stanzas were composed early in 1802; the rest appears to have been completed by March 1804. Cf. Coleridge's "Dejection: An Ode", which was a response to the first four (1802) stanzas of "Intimations", and see chap. 22 of Coleridge's *Biographia Literaria* for more explicit critical analysis.

there may be no harm in adverting here to particular feelings or *experiences* of my own mind on which the structure of the poem partly rests. Nothing was more difficult for me in childhood than to admit the notion of death as a state applicable to my own being. I have said elsewhere

> "A simple child
> That lightly draws its breath,
> And feels its life in every limb,
> What should it know of death?"[177]

But it was not so much from the source of animal vivacity that my difficulty came as from a sense of the indomitableness of the Spirit within me. I used to brood over the stories of Enoch and Elijah, and almost to persuade myself that, whatever might become of others, I should be translated in something of the same way to heaven. With a feeling congenial to this, I was often unable to think of external things as having external existence, and I communed with all that I saw as something not apart from, but inherent in, my own immaterial nature. Many times while going to school have I grasped at a wall or tree to recall myself from this abyss of idealism to the reality. At that time I was afraid of such processes. In later periods of life I have deplored, as we have all reason to do, a subjugation of an opposite character, and have rejoiced over the remembrances, as is expressed in the lines, "Obstinate questionings," &c. To that dreamlike vividness and splendour which invest objects of sight in childhood, every one, I believe, if he would look back, could bear testimony, and I need not dwell upon it here; but having in the Poem regarded it as presumptive evidence of a prior state of existence, I think it right to protest against a conclusion which has given pain to some good and pious persons, that I meant to inculcate such a belief. It is far too shadowy a notion to be recommended to faith as more than an element in our instincts of immortality. But let us bear in mind that, though the idea is not advanced in Revelation, there is nothing there to contradict it, and the fall of Man presents an analogy in its favour. Accordingly, a pre-existent state has entered into the popular creeds of many nations, and among all persons acquainted with classic literature is known as an ingredient

---

[177] From "We Are Seven", lines 1–4.

in Platonic philosophy. Archimedes said that he could move the world if he had a point whereon to rest his machine. Who has not felt the same aspirations as regards the world of his own mind? Having to wield some of its elements when I was impelled to write this poem on the "Immortality of the Soul," I took hold of the notion of pre-existence as having sufficient foundation in humanity for authorising me to make for my purpose the best use of it I could as a Poet.[178]

> The Child is Father of the Man;
> And I could wish my days to be
> Bound each to each by natural piety.[179]

Ode: Intimations of Immortality from Recollections of Early Childhood

I

There was a time when meadow, grove, and stream,
The earth, and every common sight,
    To me did seem
  Apparelled in celestial light,
The glory and the freshness of a dream.   5
It is not now as it hath been of yore;—
    Turn wheresoe'er I may,
      By night or day,
The things which I have seen I now can see no more.

II

The Rainbow comes and goes,   10
  And lovely is the Rose,
  The Moon doth with delight
Look round her when the heavens are bare,
  Waters on a starry night
  Are beautiful and fair;   15

[178] Wordsworth, *The Fenwick Notes*, p. 62.
[179] *The Child ... natural piety*: From Wordsworth's "My heart leaps up when I behold", lines 7–9. Until 1815 the epigraph had been the first line of Virgil's Fourth Eclogue: "paulò majora canamus" (A little more loftily let us sing).

The sunshine is a glorious birth;
    But yet I know, where'er I go,
That there hath past away a glory from the earth.[180]

III

Now, while the birds thus sing a joyous song,
        And while the young lambs bound   20
            As to the tabor's sound,
To me alone there came a thought of grief:
A timely utterance gave that thought relief,
            And I again am strong:
The cataracts blow their trumpets from the steep;   25
No more shall grief of mine the season wrong;
I hear the Echoes through the mountains throng,
The Winds come to me from the fields of sleep,
        And all the earth is gay,
            Land and sea   30
    Give themselves up to jollity,
        And with the heart of May
    Doth every Beast keep holiday;—
            Thou Child of Joy,
Shout round me, let me hear thy shouts, thou happy
    Shepherd-boy!   35

IV

Ye blessèd Creatures, I have heard the call
    Ye to each other make; I see
The heavens laugh with you in your jubilee;[181]
    My heart is at your festival,
        My head hath its coronal,[182]   40

---

[180] *glory from the earth*: Cf. Thomas à Kempis (1379/1380–1471), *The Imitation of Christ*, bk. 1, chap. 3: "O quam cito transit gloria mundi" (O how swiftly passes the glory of the world).

[181] *jubilee*: exultant joy, jubilation.

[182] *coronal*: coronet; wreath for the head; garland.

The fullness of your bliss, I feel—I feel it all.
  Oh evil day! if I were sullen
  While the Earth herself is adorning,
   This sweet May-morning,
  And the Children are culling   45
   On every side,
  In a thousand valleys far and wide,
  Fresh flowers; while the sun shines warm,
And the babe leaps up on his mother's arm:—
  I hear, I hear, with joy I hear!   50
  —But there's a Tree, of many, one,
A single Field which I have looked upon,
Both of them speak of something that is gone:
  The Pansy at my feet
  Doth the same tale repeat: 55
Whither is fled the visionary gleam?[183]
Where is it now, the glory and the dream?

V

Our birth is but a sleep and a forgetting:[184]
The Soul that rises with us, our life's Star,
  Hath had elsewhere its setting,   60
   And cometh from afar:
  Not in entire forgetfulness,
  And not in utter nakedness,
But trailing clouds of glory do we come
  From God, who is our home: 65
Heaven lies about us in our infancy!

[183] *visionary gleam*: Cf. "Tintern Abbey", line 148; *Prelude*, bk. 2, line 368, bk. 11, line 322; "Elegiac Stanzas", line 14; and Alfred Lord Tennyson (1809–1892), "Merlin and the Gleam": "And, ere it vanishes/Over the margin,/After it, follow it,/Follow The Gleam."

[184] *Our birth . . . forgetting*: Cf. Shakespeare, *The Tempest*, Act 4, scene 1, lines 156–58: "We are such stuff/As dreams are made on; and our little life/Is rounded with a sleep." This passage brings to mind Plato's treatment of metempsychosis, e.g., in the *Phaedo*, and the Myth of Er in *The Republic* (bk. 10).

Shades of the prison-house begin to close
    Upon the growing Boy,
But He beholds the light, and whence it flows,
    He sees it in his joy   70
The Youth, who daily farther from the east[185]
    Must travel, still is Nature's Priest,
    And by the vision splendid
    Is on his way attended;
At length the Man perceives it die away,   75
And fade into the light of common day.

VI

Earth fills her lap with pleasures of her own;
Yearnings she hath in her own natural kind,
And, even with something of a Mother's mind,
    And no unworthy aim,   80
    The homely[186] Nurse[187] doth all she can
To make her Foster-child, her Inmate Man,
    Forget the glories he hath known,
And that imperial palace whence he came.[188]

VII

Behold the Child[189] among his new-born blisses,   85
A six years' Darling of a pigmy size!

---

[185] *east*: symbol of God, the Divine, or spiritual realities; cf. the note to line 2 of Blake's "To the Muses".

[186] *homely*: domestic; belonging to or associated with the home; familiar; simple, plain.

[187] *Nurse*: "a woman employed ... to take charge of a young child or children" (*Oxford English Dictionary*, s.v. "nurse").

[188] *imperial palace whence he came*: That the boys and girls of fallen mankind are in reality princes and princesses in exile is a theme that runs throughout the work of George MacDonald (1824–1905), a writer certainly influenced by Wordsworth and Coleridge; see, for example, *The Princess and the Goblin; The Princess and Curdie*, ed. Roderick McGillis, World's Classics (Oxford: Oxford University Press, 1990), note 5, p. 343.

[189] *Behold the Child*: probably Hartley Coleridge (1796–1849), eldest son of Samuel Taylor Coleridge, and later a very fine poet himself, particularly of sonnets.

See, where 'mid work of his own hand he lies,
Fretted by sallies of his mother's kisses,
With light upon him from his father's eyes!
See, at his feet, some little plan or chart,   90
Some fragment from his dream of human life,
Shaped by himself with newly-learnèd art;
    A wedding or a festival,
    A mourning or a funeral;
        And this hath now his heart,   95
        And unto this he frames his song:
        Then will he fit his tongue
To dialogues of business, love, or strife;
    But it will not be long
    Ere this be thrown aside,   100
    And with new joy and pride
The little actor cons[190] another part;
Filling from time to time his "humorous stage"[191]
With all the Persons, down to palsied Age,[192]
That Life brings with her in her equipage;[193]   105
    As if his whole vocation
    Were endless imitation.

---

[190] *cons*: learns; studies.

[191] *"humorous stage"*: Cf. Samuel Daniel, dedicatory verses to *Musophilus*, lines 1–3: "I do not here upon this hum'rous Stage,/Bring my transformed Verse, apparelled/With others passions, or with others rage". From Hippocrates (fifth century B.C.) till the mid-nineteenth century, the analysis of bodily disorders and temperamental types was based on the relative proportions of the four humors—blood, phlegm, choler, and melancholy (or black bile)—which were supposed the four chief fluids of the human body. They featured prominently in the comedies of the Renaissance stage; Jacques, in *As You Like It*, for instance, is a "melancholic" type.

[192] *all the Persons, down to palsied Age*: Cf. Shakespeare, *As You Like It*, Act 2, scene 7, lines 139–66: "All the world's a stage,/And all the men and women merely players;/They have their exits and their entrances;/And one man in his time plays many parts,/His acts being seven ages. At first the infant,/Mewling and puking in the nurse's arms;/And then the whining schoolboy, with his satchel/And shining morning face, creeping like snail/Unwillingly to school."

[193] *equipage*: train, retinue.

VIII

Thou,[194] whose exterior semblance doth belie
    Thy Soul's immensity;[195]
Thou best Philosopher, who yet dost keep   110
Thy heritage, thou Eye among the blind,
That, deaf and silent, read'st the eternal deep,
Haunted for ever by the eternal mind,—
    Mighty prophet! Seer blest!
    On whom those truths do rest,   115
Which we are toiling all our lives to find,
In darkness lost, the darkness of the grave;
Thou, over whom thy Immortality
Broods like the Day,[196] a Master o'er a Slave,[197]
A Presence which is not to be put by;[198]   120
Thou little Child, yet glorious in the might

[194] *Thou*: the child.

[195] *Thou ... Thy Soul's immensity*: Cf. Léon Bloy (1847–1917), *Letters to His Fiancée*, trans. Barbara Wall (London: Sheed and Ward, 1937), pp. 124–26: "One of the greatest poets of the world, the old Juvenal whom I adore, said that we owe children the *greatest* respect.... [The] childhood [of Christ], says tradition, was perpetually silent and surrounded with silence because the respectful love that was due to such a Child could not express itself in words.... In our absolute ignorance of God's designs on each of His human creatures, it seems to me that the weakest and most tender little child should inspire us with a respectful fear, and sort of boundless veneration.... Well now, in your poem the obsession for the word 'little' is so strong that there is even 'little soul,' which is quite simply monstrous. It is the confusion of which I spoke just now and it hits one in the face— the confusion of the attributes of the flesh with the attributes of the spirit. To say that the soul is *little* because the body is little is a foolery to make the stars recoil."

[196] *Thou, over whom thy Immortality / Broods like the Day*: In glossing MacDonald's "The child is not meant to die" in *The Princess and Curdie*, Roderick McGillis draws our attention to MacDonald's assertion that "Childhood belongs to the divine nature", and to its source, the sermon "The Child in the Midst" (McGillis, *Princess*, note 180, p. 357).

[197] *Master o'er a Slave*: Cf. Coleridge, "Ancient Mariner", lines 414–15: "Still as a slave before his lord, / The ocean hath no blast".

[198] *A Presence which is not to be put by*: Until 1815 this line was originally succeeded by the following: "To whom the grave / Is but a lonely bed without the sense or sight / Of day or the warm light, / A place of thought where we in waiting lie". Wordsworth excised them in response to Coleridge's criticism.

Of heaven-born freedom on thy being's height,
Why with such earnest pains dost thou provoke
The years to bring the inevitable yoke,
Thus blindly with thy blessedness at strife?   125
Full soon thy soul shall have her earthly freight,
And custom lie upon thee with a weight,
Heavy as frost, and deep almost as life![199]

IX

 O joy! that in our embers
 Is something that doth live,   130
 That nature yet remembers
 What was so fugitive!
The thought of our past years in me doth breed
Perpetual benediction: not indeed
For that which is most worthy to be blest;   135
Delight and liberty, the simple creed
Of Childhood, whether busy or at rest,
With new-fledged hope still fluttering in his breast:—
     Not for these I raise
     The song of thanks and praise;   140
  But for those obstinate questionings
  Of sense and outward things,
  Fallings from us, vanishings;
  Blank misgivings of a Creature
Moving about in worlds not realized,   145
High instincts before which our mortal Nature

---

[199] *custom . . . life:* "[The] veneration of habit and custom, incidentally, is one of the chief distinctions between Burke and the Romantics. Romanticism (except for those writers directly influenced, sometimes at the expense of their consistency, by Burke), as Irving Babbitt writes, is 'clearly hostile to habit because it seems to lead to a stereotyped world, a world without vividness and surprise.' Burke dreaded a consuming individualism" (Russell Kirk, *The Conservative Mind* [Chicago: Regnery, 1987], pp. 41–42). Compare this last passage (lines 58–128) with Wordsworth's very different analysis of the stages of human psycho-spiritual development in "Tintern Abbey", lines 74–103.

Did tremble like a guilty Thing surprised:[200]
       But for those first affections,
       Those shadowy recollections,
         Which, be they what they may,   150
Are yet the fountain-light of all our day,
Are yet a master-light of all our seeing;
       Uphold us, cherish, and have power to make
Our noisy years seem moments in the being
Of the eternal Silence: truths that wake,   155
       To perish never:
Which neither listlessness, nor mad endeavour,
       Nor Man nor Boy,
Nor all that is at enmity with joy,
Can utterly abolish or destroy!   160
      Hence in a season of calm weather
       Though inland far we be,
Our Souls have sight of that immortal sea
       Which brought us hither,
        Can in a moment travel thither,   165
And see the Children sport upon the shore,
And hear the mighty waters rolling evermore.

X

Then sing, ye Birds, sing, sing a joyous song!
      And let the young Lambs bound
      As to the tabor's sound!   170
We in thought will join your throng,
      Ye that pipe and ye that play,
      Ye that through your hearts to-day
      Feel the gladness of the May!
What though the radiance which was once so bright   175
Be now for ever taken from my sight,
      Though nothing can bring back the hour

---

[200] *guilty Thing surprised:* Cf. *Hamlet*, Act 1, scene 1, lines 129–30: "And then it started like a guilty thing/Upon a fearful summons."

Of splendour in the grass, of glory in the flower;
>> We will grieve not, rather find
>> Strength in what remains behind; 180
>> In the primal sympathy
>> Which having been must ever be;
>> In the soothing thoughts that spring
>> Out of human suffering;
>> In the faith that looks through death, 185
In years that bring the philosophic mind.

XI

And O ye Fountains,[201] Meadows, Hills, and Groves,
Forebode not any severing of our loves!
Yet in my heart of hearts I feel your might;
I only have relinquished one delight 190
To live beneath your more habitual sway.
I love the Brooks which down their channels fret,[202]
Even more than when I tripped[203] lightly as they;
The innocent brightness of a new-born Day
>> Is lovely yet; 195
The Clouds that gather round the setting sun
Do take a sober colouring from an eye
That hath kept watch o'er man's mortality;
Another race hath been, and other palms are won.[204]
Thanks to the human heart by which we live, 200
Thanks to its tenderness, its joys, and fears,

---

[201] *Fountains*: springs.

[202] *fret*: chafe; move in agitation.

[203] *tripped*: skipped; ran with quick light steps; danced nimbly.

[204] *Another race hath been, and other palms are won*: Cf. 2 Timothy 4:7–8: "I have fought the good fight, I have finished the race, I have kept the faith. From now on there is laid up for me the crown of righteousness"; also, cf. Horace, Epistle 1, lines 49–51: "What wrestler ... / would refuse the great Olympic prize if given the prospect / ... of the palm's glory without the dust?"

To me the meanest[205] flower[206] that blows[207] can give
Thoughts that do often lie too deep for tears.

"I wandered lonely as a Cloud"[208]

I wandered lonely as a Cloud
That floats on high o'er Vales and Hills,
When all at once I saw a crowd
A host[209] of dancing Daffodils;
Along the Lake, beneath the trees,   5
Ten thousand[210] dancing in the breeze.

The waves beside them danced, but they
Outdid the sparkling waves in glee:—[211]
A Poet could not but be gay
In such a laughing company: 10
I gazed—and gazed—but little thought
What wealth the shew[212] to me had brought:

---

[205] *meanest*: least significant.

[206] *meanest flower*: Cf. Thomas Gray, "Ode on the Pleasure Arising from Vicissitude", lines 49–52: "The meanest floweret of the vale,/The simplest note that swells the gale,/The common Sun, the air, and skies,/To him are opening Paradise."

[207] *blows*: blooms.

[208] Published in *Poems, in Two Volumes*, 1807. Wordsworth expressed that "the two best lines in it [lines 15–16] are by Mary [his wife]. The daffodils grew and still grow on the margin of Ulswater, and probably may be seen to this day as beautiful in the month of March nodding their golden heads beside the dancing and foaming waves" (Wordsworth, *The Fenwick Notes*, p. 14).

[209] *host*: an army; a multitude.

[210] *host ... Ten thousand*: Cf. 1 Samuel 18:6–7: "[W]hen David returned from slaying the Philistine, ... the women sang to one another as they made merry, 'Saul has slain his thousands, and David his ten thousands.'"

[211] *waves beside them danced ... waves in glee*: Cf. W. B. Yeats (1865–1939), "The Fiddler of Dooney", lines 1–2: "When I play on my fiddle in Dooney,/Folk dance like a wave of the sea".

[212] *shew*: display.

For oft, when on my couch I lie
In vacant or in pensive mood,
They flash upon that inward eye   15
Which is the bliss of solitude,
And then my heart with pleasure fills,
And dances with the Daffodils.

From *The Prelude*

The Prelude is generally regarded as Wordsworth's central achievement, and one of the greatest long poems in the English language. Never published in his lifetime, nor given a title—Wordsworth referred to it as "the poem to Coleridge", "the poem on the growth of my own mind", "the poem on my own life"—it was finally given a title and subtitle by his widow, Mary, and published in 1850, three months after his death.

The Prelude began as an autobiographical appendix to what was to be a joint project with Coleridge: a philosophical poem of epic length, "containing views of Man, Nature, and Society, and to be entitled *The Recluse*; as having for its principal subject, the sensations and opinions of a poet living in retirement", as he explained in the introductory notes to the 1850 edition. It soon became a personal rather than a dual task, but Coleridge's ancillary role was crucial, and Wordsworth introduced it as "addressed to a dear friend [Coleridge], most distinguished for his knowledge and genius, and to whom the author's intellect is deeply indebted."

Having begun work in 1798–1799 (from which there remains an early version—the 1799 text—consisting in substance of the first two books of the later poem), by 1804 Wordsworth had expanded his original idea and made it a preliminary to the rest of the work. Wordsworth was conscious that it was "a thing unprecedented in literary history that a man should talk so much about himself" (letter to Sir George Beaumont, May 1, 1805), yet the subject of his own development became, through careful self-examination and the prism of poetry, the story of individual experience, in particular the story of the poetic mind, heart, and imagination as worked upon by nature. This prologue, or prelude, was completed in 1805, but Wordsworth refused to publish it without the rest of the larger work it was to introduce. Over the following years he revised and retouched it frequently, on stylistic and philosophical grounds, until about half of the entire piece had been reworked. In 1926, Ernest de Sélincourt (1870–1943) rediscovered and published the 1805 version (in thirteen books, as opposed to the fourteen-book text of 1850). Most critics have expressed preference for the earlier text for being bolder and less polished in style, and also because the final version was carefully sifted of excessively pantheistic expressions or tendencies, in accordance with the poet's later Christian convictions. By the time he was eighty, of the three-part epic, only *The Excursion* had been published (not yet completed, but to universal acclaim) in 1814. Wordsworth did write, however, a poetic *Prospectus* to *The Recluse*, which tells us enough to know that the themes of the larger work had already been prefigured and illustrated in *The Prelude*.

Although *The Prelude* is in many respects reminiscent of the Conversation Poems (see the introductory note to Coleridge's "The Eolian Harp", pp. 275–76), its length and scope are remarkable, describing the poet's encounters with some of Europe's most exalted natural scenery, the sprawling urban phantasmagoria of London, and great historical upheavals such as the French Revolution, and, on an equal footing, many of the small, significant experiences and memories of childhood. Beginning with a walk to the Vale of Grasmere, the poem relates the process of several such journeys on foot, culminating in the ascent of Snowdon. In the course of these, his musings on past and future, on the nature of what he sees and his own responses, give his literal travels the character of a metamorphosis: they are a symbolic journey of the poet's mind and spirit.

In addition to Wordsworth's own interest in poetry and the effects of nature on the imagination, his (and his perception of like-minded people's) experience of—and reaction to—the personal, social, and political crises precipitated by the French Revolution were an integral part of the writing of *The Prelude*, as can be seen in Coleridge's words, written to his friend in September 1799:

> I wish you would write a poem, in blank verse, addressed to those who, in consequence of the complete failure of the French Revolution, have thrown up all hopes of amelioration of mankind, and are sinking into an almost Epicurean self-ishness, disguising the same under the soft titles of domestic attachment and contempt for visionary philosophies. It would do great good.

Both Wordsworth and Coleridge had been enthusiastic supporters of the Revolutionary movement. Wordsworth had spent time in revolutionary France and been strongly moved and influenced by the people he met and saw there, full of fervent ideals and hope. When the Terror came he was greatly disturbed, and later developments only increased his angry disappointment. Turning elsewhere to find a solution to individual misery and cruelty, he was encouraged in his philosophical bent by Coleridge, and urged to express what lay behind his poetic vision for the benefit of others.

Of the many influences on *The Prelude*, the most conspicuous is *Paradise Lost*: the trail Wordsworth and Coleridge were pursuing had been blazed by their icon Milton, for their original intention was that *The Recluse* should surpass his epic poem, in length as in grandeur of conception. The antimonarchical invective in *Paradise Lost* can be felt in some of the more radical passages of *The Prelude*.

Thomas Gray's "Elegy Written in a Country Churchyard" also seems to have had a direct influence on the work. Despite Wordsworth's belief that he was the first to write such a conversational and personal style of poetry, the swain's account of his own life in Gray's poem is similar in form and language, and Gray's "mute inglorious Miltons" return in the mute who is addressed in *The Excursion*—to whom, however, Wordsworth grants the happier fate of being given a voice through the poet.

Another poet whose literary influence is often overlooked is William Cowper (1731–1800). Wordsworth read a copy of Cowper's *The Task* as a schoolboy, and its influence on the conversational style of his poetry, and particularly on "Tintern Abbey" and *The Prelude*, is perceptible. Cowper, disgusted by much of what he saw in polite society's unethical behavior, turned to the living landscape into which he retired, where a vestige of God's order remained, to find a poetic language which would be consistent in morals and beauty—though ultimately his poetry remained dark in its expression of the decay found both in nature and in man. Wordsworth followed him in giving a voice to the trees and other features of nature, which could teach man of higher things—including a patriotic sensibility bound up deeply with a sense of place. Like Cowper, Wordsworth used nature to discuss issues, currently political or existential, pertaining to man, society, and the nation, but in comparison to Cowper's, his own attitude to both the natural and the human world was optimistic, for it did not end by describing the wretched fall of human nature in society, but provided a sense of hope for it, a vision of higher things, to be found in man's own spirit and in the development of the poetic imagination.

Although it is incontestable that Wordsworth's later revisions of his poems were usually inferior, this is not consistently true of *The Prelude*, a text the poet was not sufficiently satisfied with to publish in any form until his death. On the contrary, here I believe we are entitled to suspect the presence of cultural and ideological prejudices in the annoyance many critics have exhibited in their treatment of the 1850 text once a less Christian, "conservative", and Victorian option became available in 1926. (See the note to line 33 of "The Thorn".)

The Prelude's deepest impression and reputation were both made by the 1850 text, which is also the formative or only version known to every major critic and poet between its publication and the 1930s. More than any other poet, Wordsworth—whose profound influence on the following two generations was neither insignificant nor accidental—marks the transition from Romanticism to the Victorian Age. In view of these factors and the highly disputable character of the relative aesthetic merits of 1805 and 1850, I have chosen unfashionably to take my selections from the 1850 text. I have made an exception of the "spots of time" passage from book 11 of *Prelude* (1805), for the sake of comparison and as a concession to the critical majority.

Book First (1850)

INTRODUCTION—CHILDHOOD AND SCHOOL-TIME

O there is blessing in this gentle breeze,[213]
A visitant that while he fans my cheek
Doth seem half-conscious of the joy he brings
From the green fields, and from yon azure sky.
Whate'er his mission, the soft breeze[214] can come   5
To none more grateful than to me; escaped

---

[213] *O there is blessing in this gentle breeze*: This passage, however ambiguous its implications, is unmistakeably suggestive of inspiration through the Holy Spirit; cf. Acts 2:1–2, 4: "When the day of Pentecost had come, they were all together in one place. And suddenly a sound came from heaven like the rush of a mighty wind.... And they were all filled with the Holy Spirit"; also, cf. John 3:8: "The wind blows where it wills, and you hear the sound of it, but you do not know where it comes from or where it goes; so it is with every one who is born of the Spirit." It is no coincidence that Milton invoked the Holy Spirit's aid and patronage at the beginning of *Paradise Lost* (bk. 1, lines 6–23): "Sing, Heavenly Muse .../ I thence invoke thy aid to my adventurous song,/ That with no middle flight intends to soar./... And chiefly thou, O Spirit, that dost prefer/ Before all temples the upright heart and pure,/ Instruct me, for thou know'st; thou from the first/ Wast present, and with mighty wings outspread/ Dove-like sat'st brooding on the vast abyss/ And mad'st it pregnant: what in me is dark/ Illumine". Cf. also Genesis 1:1–2: "In the beginning God created the heavens and the earth.... [A]nd the Spirit of God was moving [brooding] over the face of the waters." Cf. also Cowper, *The Task*, bk. 1, lines 155–56: "we have borne/ The ruffling wind, scarce conscious that it blew".

[214] *O there is blessing ... the soft breeze*: I have given this passage—with its personification of the breeze in lines 2, 3, and 5—as it is found in the printer's copy; the published, posthumous reading of "it ... it ... its" appears to have been an interpolation on the part of Wordsworth's literary executors.

From the vast city,[215] where I long had pined
A discontented sojourner: now free,
Free as a bird to settle where I will.
What dwelling shall receive me? in what vale   10
Shall be my harbour? underneath what grove
Shall I take up my home? and what clear stream
Shall with its murmur lull me into rest?
The earth is all before me.[216] With a heart
Joyous, nor scared at its own liberty,   15
I look about; and should the chosen guide
Be nothing better than a wandering cloud,[217]
I cannot miss my way. I breathe again!
Trances of thought and mountings of the mind
Come fast upon me: it is shaken off,   20
That burthen[218] of my own unnatural self,
The heavy weight of many a weary day
Not mine, and such as were not made for me.
Long months of peace (if such bold word accord
With any promises of human life),[219]   25
Long months of ease and undisturbed delight
Are mine in prospect; whither shall I turn,
By road or pathway, or through trackless field,

---

[215] *city*: Although this "city" is not specific, Wordsworth was doubtless think-ing of his experiences in London, revolutionary Paris, and Goslar, Germany (where Wordsworth and his sister stayed from October 1798 to February 1799, and where he first began to work on *The Prelude*).

[216] *The earth is all before me*: Cf. the last lines of Milton's *Paradise Lost* (bk. 12, lines 645–49) where Adam and Eve have been cast out of Eden into our world: "Some natural tears they dropped, but wiped them soon;/The world was all before them, where to choose/Their place of rest, and Providence their guide./They hand in hand with wandering steps and slow,/Through Eden took their solitary way."

[217] *wandering cloud*: Cf. "I wandered lonely as a Cloud".

[218] *burthen*: burden.

[219] *Long months of peace . . . promises of human life*: France declared war on Great Britain on February 1, 1793, and—aside from the brief interlude of the Treaty of Amiens (March 25, 1802–May 18, 1803)—the two powers remained at war until Napoleon's defeat (1814–1815). See also the introductory note to Wordsworth's sonnet "Composed upon Westminster Bridge, September 3, 1802".

Up hill or down, or shall some floating thing
Upon the river point me out my course?   30

      Dear Liberty! Yet what would it avail
But for a gift that consecrates the joy?
For I, methought, while the sweet breath of heaven
Was blowing on my body, felt within
A correspondent breeze, that gently moved   35
With quickening[220] virtue, but is now become
A tempest, a redundant energy,
Vexing[221] its own creation. Thanks to both,
And their congenial powers, that, while they join
In breaking up a long-continued frost,   40
Bring with them vernal promises, the hope
Of active days urged on by flying hours,—
Days of sweet leisure, taxed with patient thought
Abstruse, nor wanting punctual service high,
Matins[222] and vespers of harmonious verse!   45

      Thus far, O Friend![223] did I, not used to make
A present joy the matter of a song,
Pour forth that day my soul in measured strains
That would not be forgotten, and are here
Recorded: to the open fields I told   50
A prophecy: poetic numbers[224] came
Spontaneously to clothe in priestly robe
A renovated spirit singled out,
Such hope was mine, for holy services.
My own voice cheered me, and, far more, the mind's   55
Internal echo of the imperfect sound;

[220] *quickening*: vivifying.

[221] *Vexing*: troubling, harassing; disturbing physically, tossing about.

[222] *Matins*: also known as Morning Prayer, and Evening Prayer/Evensong—the two daily offices in the Church of England, set out in the Book of Common Prayer.

[223] *Friend*: Coleridge, to whom the entire poem is addressed, and to whom Wordsworth read *The Prelude* in 1807.

[224] *poetic numbers*: poetic harmony or measure; metrics.

To both I listened, drawing from them both
A cheerful confidence[225] in things to come.

Content and not unwilling now to give
A respite to this passion, I paced on   60
With brisk and eager steps; and came, at length,
To a green shady place, where down I sate
Beneath a tree, slackening my thoughts by choice,
And settling into gentler happiness.
'Twas autumn, and a clear and placid day,   65
With warmth, as much as needed, from a sun
Two hours declined towards the west; a day
With silver clouds, and sunshine on the grass,
And in the sheltered and the sheltering grove
A perfect stillness. Many were the thoughts   70
Encouraged and dismissed, till choice was made
Of a known Vale,[226] whither my feet should turn,
Nor rest till they had reached the very door
Of the one cottage[227] which methought I saw.
No picture of mere memory ever looked   75
So fair; and while upon the fancied scene
I gazed with growing love, a higher power
Than Fancy gave assurance of some work
Of glory there forthwith to be begun,
Perhaps too there performed. Thus long I mused,   80
Nor e'er lost sight of what I mused upon,
Save when, amid the stately grove of oaks,
Now here, now there, an acorn, from its cup
Dislodged, through sere leaves rustled, or at once
To the bare earth dropped with a startling sound.   85
From that soft couch I rose not, till the sun
Had almost touched the horizon; casting then

---

[225] *cheerful confidence*: Cf. 1 John 3:21: "Beloved, if our hearts do not condemn us, we have confidence before God".

[226] *known Vale*: Grasmere, in the Lake District (North West England).

[227] *cottage*: Dove Cottage, on the edge of Grasmere.

A backward glance upon the curling cloud
Of city smoke, by distance ruralised;
Keen as a Truant or a Fugitive,   90
But as a Pilgrim resolute, I took,
Even with the chance equipment of that hour,
The road that pointed toward the chosen Vale.
It was a splendid evening, and my soul
Once more made trial of her strength, nor lacked   95
Æolian[228] visitations; but the harp
Was soon defrauded,[229] and the banded host
Of harmony dispersed in straggling sounds,
And lastly utter silence! "Be it so;
Why think of any thing but present good?"   100
So, like a home-bound labourer I pursued
My way beneath the mellowing sun, that shed
Mild influence; nor left in me one wish
Again to bend the Sabbath of that time
To a servile yoke. What need of many words?   105
A pleasant loitering journey, through three days
Continued, brought me to my hermitage.[230]
I spare to tell of what ensued, the life
In common things—the endless store of things,
Rare, or at least so seeming, every day   110
Found all about me in one neighbourhood—
The self-congratulation, and, from morn
To night, unbroken cheerfulness serene.
But speedily an earnest longing rose
To brace myself to some determined aim,   115
Reading or thinking; either to lay up
New stores, or rescue from decay the old

---

[228] *Æolian*: i.e., the soul as an Æolian harp, a musical instrument, named after Æolus, god of the winds; also known as the wind harp. Often it is little more than a simple wooden box with a sounding board and strings stretched across two bridges; it produces sounds when exposed to the wind. Cf. Coleridge, "The Eolian Harp".

[229] *defrauded*: cheated.

[230] *hermitage*: See the note to line 27 of Blake's "The Grey Monk".

By timely interference: and therewith
Came hopes still higher, that with outward life
I might endue some airy phantasies   120
That had been floating loose about for years,
And to such beings temperately deal forth
The many feelings that oppressed my heart.
That hope hath been discouraged; welcome light
Dawns from the east, but dawns to disappear   125
And mock me with a sky that ripens not
Into a steady morning: if my mind,
Remembering the bold promise of the past,
Would gladly grapple with some noble theme,
Vain is her wish; where'er she turns she finds   130
Impediments from day to day renewed.

        And now it would content me to yield up
Those lofty hopes awhile, for present gifts
Of humbler industry. But, oh, dear Friend!
The Poet, gentle creature as he is,   135
Hath, like the Lover, his unruly times;
His fits when he is neither sick nor well,
Though no distress be near him but his own
Unmanageable thoughts: his mind, best pleased
While she as duteous as the mother dove   140
Sits brooding,[231] lives not always to that end,
But like the innocent bird, hath goadings on
That drive her as in trouble through the groves;
With me is now such passion, to be blamed
No otherwise than as it lasts too long.   145

        When, as becomes a man who would prepare
For such an arduous work, I through myself
Make rigorous inquisition, the report
Is often cheering; for I neither seem
To lack that first great gift, the vital soul,   150

---

[231] *brooding*: This once again evokes both the precedent of Milton's *Paradise Lost* and the Holy Spirit; see the note to line 1.

Nor general Truths, which are themselves a sort
Of Elements and Agents, Under-powers,
Subordinate helpers of the living mind:[232]
Nor am I naked of external things,
Forms, images, nor numerous other aids   155
Of less regard, though won perhaps with toil
And needful to build up a Poet's praise.
Time, place, and manners[233] do I seek, and these
Are found in plenteous store, but nowhere such
As may be singled out with steady choice;   160
No little band of yet remembered names
Whom I, in perfect confidence, might hope
To summon back from lonesome banishment,
And make them dwellers in the hearts of men
Now living, or to live in future years.   165
Sometimes the ambitious Power of choice, mistaking
Proud spring-tide swellings for a regular sea,
Will settle on some British theme, some old
Romantic tale by Milton left unsung;[234]
More often turning to some gentle place   170
Within the groves of Chivalry, I pipe
To shepherd swains, or seated harp in hand,
Amid reposing knights by a river side
Or fountain, listen to the grave reports
Of dire enchantments faced and overcome   175
By the strong mind, and tales of warlike feats,
Where spear encountered spear, and sword with sword
Fought, as if conscious of the blazonry[235]
That the shield bore, so glorious was the strife;
Whence inspiration for a song that winds   180
Through ever changing scenes of votive quest[236]

[232] *living mind*: The "living mind" here is the "vital soul" (see line 150) and involves imaginative thought.

[233] *manners*: mores.

[234] *Romantic tale by Milton left unsung*: Before settling on the theme of *Paradise Lost*, Milton had considered writing an Arthurian epic.

[235] *blazonry*: the depiction of heraldic devices, typically found on shields.

[236] *votive quest*: a quest in fulfilment of a religious vow, characteristic of medieval romance.

Wrongs to redress, harmonious tribute paid
To patient courage and unblemished truth,
To firm devotion, zeal unquenchable,
And Christian meekness hallowing faithful loves.[237]   185
Sometimes, more sternly moved, I would relate
How vanquished Mithridates[238] northward passed,
And, hidden in the cloud of years, became
Odin,[239] the Father of a race by whom
Perished the Roman Empire: how the friends   190
And followers of Sertorius,[240] out of Spain

---

[237] *Christian meekness . . . loves:* Cf. Spenser, *The Faerie Queene*, bk. 1, canto 1: "Me, all too meane, the sacred Muse areeds/To blazon broad emongst her learned throng:/Fierce warres and faithful loves shall moralize my song."

[238] *Mithridates:* Mithridates VI—"The Great"—of Pontus (134–63 B.C.), one of Rome's most formidable enemies. He was finally defeated by Pompey in 63 B.C., fled northwest into what is now the Crimea, and, failing in one last attempt to raise an army against Rome, committed suicide.

[239] *Odin:* See Edward Gibbon, *The Decline and Fall of the Roman Empire*, vol. 1 (London, 1776), chap. 10:

> The native and proper habitation of Odin is distinguished by the appellation of As-gard. The unhappy resemblance of that name with As-burg, or As-of, words of a similar signification, has given rise to an historical system of so pleasing a conjecture that we could almost wish to persuade ourselves of its truth. It is supposed that Odin was the chief of a tribe of barbarians which dwelt on the banks of the lake Mæotis, till the fall of Mithridates and the arms of Pompey menaced the north with servitude. That Odin, yielding with indignant fury to a power which he was unable to resist, conducted his tribe from the frontiers of the Asiatic Sarmatia into Sweden with the great design of forming, in that inaccessible retreat of freedom, a religion and a people which, in some remote age, might be, subservient to his immortal revenge; when his invincible Goths, armed with martial fanaticism, should issue in numerous swarms from the neighbourhood of the Polar circle, to chastise the oppressors of mankind.

[240] *Sertorius:* Quintus Sertorius (123–72 B.C.), "a Roman of military genius, one of the champions of the democratic party after the victory of Sulla. He was invited in 80 B.C. to be the leader of the revolted Lusitanians and with the support of a few exiles from Rome he organised the Spanish army, and for eight years maintained a struggle against the senatorial generals (including Pompey), until treacherously murdered by his lieutenant Perpenna" (Paul Harvey, *The Oxford Companion to Classical Literature* [Oxford: Oxford University Press, 1962], p. 391). Legends concerning Sertorius abound, including one that, after his death, his followers took refuge from Roman tyranny in the Fortunate Isles (Canary

Flying, found shelter in the Fortunate Isles,
And left their usages, their arts and laws,
To disappear by a slow gradual death,
To dwindle and to perish one by one,   195
Starved in those narrow bounds: but not the soul
Of Liberty, which fifteen hundred years
Survived, and, when the European came
With skill and power that might not be withstood,
Did, like a pestilence, maintain its hold   200
And wasted down by glorious death that race
Of natural heroes: or I would record
How, in tyrannic times, some high-souled man,
Unnamed among the chronicles of kings,
Suffered in silence for Truth's sake: or tell,   205
How that one Frenchman,[241] through continued force
Of meditation on the inhuman deeds
Of those who conquered first the Indian Isles,
Went single in his ministry across
The Ocean; not to comfort the oppressed,   210
But, like a thirsty wind, to roam about
Withering the Oppressor: how Gustavus[242] sought

Islands), populating them; and it was their descendants who put up a valiant defense against the Spanish invasion of Tenerife in 1493, succumbing ultimately to disease rather than arms. See Plutarch's *Life of Sertorius* and Lionel Johnson's poem "Sertorius".

[241] *that one Frenchman*: i.e., Dominique de Gourgues (1530–1593), French Huguenot nobleman and soldier. De Gourgues is best known for a colonial exploit against the Spanish in the French Wars of Religion (1562–1598); in 1565, Don Pedro Menéndez de Avilés, the first governor of Spanish Florida, and founder of the fort of St. Augustine there, attacked and destroyed the neighboring French Huguenot outpost of Fort Caroline, slaughtering most everyone save the women and children. Outraged by this, de Gourgues raised enough money to pay for three ships, a crew, and an armed force; crossed the Atlantic to Cuba; attacked and took Fort Caroline (now held by the Spanish); and, in an act of revenge, massacred his prisoners. He then returned to France.

[242] *Gustavus*: Gustavus I (1496–1560), king of Sweden, the man most actively responsible for Sweden's break with Rome at the Reformation. He is traditionally depicted as the founder of modern Sweden and its liberator from Danish domination; he has also been characterized as the first autocratic ruler of the kingdom. Captured by the Danes at the Battle of Brännkyrka in 1518, he escaped and

Help at his need in Dalecarlia's mines;
How Wallace[243] fought for Scotland; left the name
Of Wallace to be found, like a wild flower,   215
All over his dear Country; left the deeds
Of Wallace, like a family of Ghosts,
To people the steep rocks and river banks,
Her natural sanctuaries, with a local soul
Of independence and stern liberty.   220
Sometimes it suits me better to invent
A tale from my own heart, more near akin
To my own passions and habitual thoughts;
Some variegated story, in the main
Lofty, but the unsubstantial structure melts   225
Before the very sun that brightens it,
Mist into air dissolving! Then a wish,
My last and favourite aspiration, mounts
With yearning toward some philosophic song
Of Truth that cherishes our daily life;   230
With meditations passionate from deep
Recesses in man's heart, immortal verse
Thoughtfully fitted to the Orphean[244] lyre;
But from this awful burthen[245] I full soon
Take refuge and beguile myself with trust   235
That mellower years will bring a riper mind

---

fled into the province of Dalarna (Dalecarlia). His many adventures there have become the stuff of Swedish legend, and it was among the miners of Dalarna that he found the backbone of support for his national crusade.

[243] *Wallace*: Sir William Wallace (1272–1305), leader of the cause of Scottish independence against the English. He led a heavily outnumbered Scottish army to a famous victory against the English at Stirling Bridge in 1297, but he was defeated at Falkirk in 1298 and went into hiding. He was captured in 1305 and executed for treason. His legendary fame and numerous escapades have led to tales of Wallace being associated with every corner of Scotland.

[244] *Orphean*: Orpheus was a mythical Greek demigod-poet. The genius of his lyre-accompanied song was such that he was able to move rocks and trees to tears and descend into the Underworld unmolested. He was said to be the source of the sacred poems that embodied the esoteric doctrines of the Orphic cults.

[245] *burthen*: burden.

And clearer insight. Thus my days are past
In contradiction; with no skill to part
Vague longing, haply[246] bred by want of power,
From paramount impulse not to be withstood,   240
A timorous capacity from prudence,
From circumspection, infinite delay.
Humility and modest awe themselves
Betray me, serving often for a cloak
To a more subtle selfishness; that now   245
Locks every function up in blank reserve,[247]
Now dupes me, trusting to an anxious eye
That with intrusive restlessness beats off
Simplicity and self-presented truth.
Ah! better far than this, to stray about   250
Voluptuously through fields and rural walks,
And ask no record of the hours, resigned
To vacant musing, unreproved neglect
Of all things, and deliberate holiday.
Far better never to have heard the name   255
Of zeal and just ambition, than to live
Baffled and plagued by a mind that every hour
Turns recreant[248] to her task; takes heart again,
Then feels immediately some hollow thought
Hang like an interdict[249] upon her hopes.   260
This is my lot; for either still I find
Some imperfection in the chosen theme,
Or see of absolute accomplishment
Much wanting, so much wanting, in myself,

[246] haply: perchance.

[247] Locks every function up in blank reserve: Cf. Pope, "The First Epistle of the First Book of Horace Imitated", line 40: "That lock up all the Functions of my soul".

[248] recreant: apostate; false.

[249] interdict: authoritative prohibition; "an authoritative sentence debarring a particular place or person ... from ecclesiastical [particularly sacerdotal] functions and privileges" (Oxford English Dictionary, s.v. "interdict"); Pope Innocent III placed King John and England under an interdict from 1208 to 1213, an episode dealt with in Shakespeare's King John.

That I recoil and droop, and seek repose   265
In listlessness from vain perplexity,
Unprofitably travelling toward the grave,
Like a false steward[250] who hath much received
And renders nothing back.

                    Was it for this
That one, the fairest of all rivers, loved   270
To blend his murmurs with my nurse's song,
And, from his alder shades and rocky falls,
And from his fords and shallows, sent a voice
That flowed along my dreams? For this, didst thou,
O Derwent![251] winding among grassy holms[252]   275
Where I was looking on, a babe in arms,
Make ceaseless music that composed my thoughts
To more than infant softness, giving me
Amid the fretful dwellings of mankind
A foretaste, a dim earnest,[253] of the calm   280
That Nature breathes among the hills and groves.
When he had left the mountains and received
On his smooth breast the shadow of those towers[254]
That yet survive, a shattered monument
Of feudal sway,[255] the bright blue river passed   285
Along the margin of our terrace walk;
A tempting playmate whom we dearly loved.
Oh, many a time have I, a five years' child,
In a small mill-race[256] severed from his stream,
Made one long bathing of a summer's day;   290

[250] *false steward*: For Jesus' parables of bad/false stewards and what they render back, see Matthew 18:21–35; Luke 16:1–8; Matthew 25:14–30; Luke 12:42–48.

[251] *Derwent*: The river Derwent, in the Lake District, flows through Cockermouth, Wordsworth's birthplace.

[252] *grassy holms*: river islands.

[253] *earnest*: pledge.

[254] *those towers*: i.e., Cockermouth Castle—a Norman castle with medieval additions.

[255] *sway*: power, influence.

[256] *mill-race*: a channel for the water flowing to or from a water wheel.

Basked in the sun, and plunged and basked again
Alternate, all a summer's day, or scoured
The sandy fields, leaping through flowery groves
Of yellow ragwort; or, when rock and hill,
The woods, and distant Skiddaw's[257] lofty height,   295
Were bronzed with deepest radiance, stood alone
Beneath the sky, as if I had been born
On Indian plains,[258] and from my mother's hut
Had run abroad in wantonness, to sport
A naked savage, in the thunder shower.   300

    Fair seed-time had my soul, and I grew up
Fostered alike by beauty and by fear:
Much favoured in my birth-place,[259] and no less
In that beloved Vale[260] to which erelong
We were transplanted—there were we let loose   305
For sports of wider range. Ere I had told
Ten birth-days, when among the mountain slopes
Frost, and the breath of frosty wind, had snapped
The last autumnal crocus, 'twas my joy
With store of springes[261] o'er my shoulder hung   310
To range the open heights where woodcocks ran
Along the smooth green turf. Through half the night,
Scudding away from snare to snare, I plied
That anxious visitation;—moon and stars
Were shining o'er my head. I was alone,   315

---

[257] *Skiddaw's*: Skiddaw is a mountain in Cumbria; at 3,054 feet above sea level, it is the fourth highest in England.

[258] *Indian plains*: i.e., in America. Cf. Wordsworth's "The Complaint of a Forsaken Indian Woman", published in *Lyrical Ballads*, 1798.

[259] *birth-place*: Cockermouth, Cumbria, a market town on the fringe of the Lake District in North West England. In the 1805 version of *The Prelude*, this line reads "my 'sweet birthplace'"—a quotation from Coleridge's "Frost at Midnight", line 28.

[260] *that beloved Vale*: i.e., Esthwaite. Hawkshead, where Wordsworth was sent to school in May 1779, is in the Esthwaite Valley.

[261] *springes*: snares for small birds or game. Cf. Shakespeare, *Hamlet*, Act 1, scene 3, line 115: "Ay, springes to catch woodcocks."

And seemed to be a trouble to the peace
That dwelt among them. Sometimes it befel
In these night wanderings, that a strong desire
O'erpowered my better reason, and the bird
Which was the captive of another's toil　　　　　　320
Became my prey; and when the deed was done
I heard among the solitary hills
Low breathings coming after me, and sounds
Of undistinguishable motion, steps
Almost as silent as the turf they trod.　　　　　　325

　　　　Nor less, when spring had warmed the cultured[262]
　　　　　　Vale,
Moved we as plunderers where the mother-bird
Had in high places built her lodge; though mean
Our object and inglorious, yet the end
Was not ignoble. Oh! when I have hung　　　　　　330
Above the raven's nest, by knots of grass
And half-inch fissures in the slippery rock
But ill-sustained, and almost (so it seemed)
Suspended by the blast that blew amain,[263]
Shouldering the naked crag, oh, at that time　　　　335
While on the perilous ridge I hung alone,
With what strange utterance did the loud dry wind
Blow through my ear! the sky seemed not a sky
Of earth—and with what motion moved the clouds!

　　　　Dust as we are, the immortal spirit grows　　　340
Like harmony in music; there is a dark
Inscrutable workmanship that reconciles
Discordant elements, makes them cling together
In one society. How strange that all
The terrors, pains, and early miseries,　　　　　345
Regrets, vexations, lassitudes interfused

---

[262] *cultured*: under cultivation.
[263] *amain*: with full force.

Within my mind, should e'er have borne a part,
And that a needful part, in making up
The calm existence that is mine when I
Am worthy of myself! Praise to the end!   350
Thanks to the means which Nature deigned to employ;
Whether her fearless visitings, or those
That came with soft alarm, like hurtless light
Opening the peaceful clouds; or she would use
Severer interventions, ministry   355
More palpable, as best might suit her aim.

   One summer evening (led by her) I found
A little boat tied to a willow tree
Within a rocky cave, its usual home.
Straight I unloosed her chain, and stepping in   360
Pushed from the shore. It was an act of stealth
And troubled pleasure, nor without the voice
Of mountain-echoes did my boat move on;
Leaving behind her still, on either side,
Small circles glittering idly in the moon,   365
Until they melted all into one track
Of sparkling light.[264] But now, like one who rows,
Proud of his skill, to reach a chosen point
With an unswerving line, I fixed my view
Upon the summit of a craggy ridge,   370
The horizon's utmost boundary; far above
Was nothing but the stars and the grey sky.
She was an elfin pinnace;[265] lustily[266]
I dipped my oars into the silent lake,
And, as I rose upon the stroke, my boat   375
Went heaving through the water like a swan;
When, from behind that craggy steep till then

---

[264] *sparkling light*: Cf. Coleridge, "Ancient Mariner", lines 273–74: "I watched
the water-snakes:/They moved in tracks of shining white".

[265] *elfin pinnace*: small boat.

[266] *lustily*: with appetite and vigor.

The horizon's bound, a huge peak, black and huge,
As if with voluntary power instinct
Upreared its head. I struck and struck again,　　　　380
And growing still in stature the grim shape
Towered up between me and the stars, and still,
For so it seemed, with purpose of its own
And measured motion like a living thing,
Strode after me. With trembling oars I turned,　　　　385
And through the silent water stole my way
Back to the covert of the willow tree;
There in her mooring-place I left my bark,—
And through the meadows homeward went, in grave
And serious mood; but after I had seen　　　　390
That spectacle, for many days, my brain
Worked with a dim and undetermined sense
Of unknown modes of being; o'er my thoughts
There hung a darkness, call it solitude
Or blank desertion. No familiar shapes　　　　395
Remained, no pleasant images of trees,
Of sea or sky, no colours of green fields;
But huge and mighty forms, that do not live
Like living men, moved slowly through the mind
By day, and were a trouble to my dreams.　　　　400

　　　　Wisdom and Spirit of the universe!
Thou Soul that art the eternity of thought,
That givest to forms and images a breath
And everlasting motion,[267] not in vain
By day or star-light thus from my first dawn　　　　405
Of childhood didst thou intertwine for me

---

[267] *Wisdom . . . motion*: This passage appears curiously akin to the Sophiology of such Russian religious thinkers as Vladimir Solovyov (1853–1900), Pavel Florensky (1882–1937), and Sergei Bulgakov (1871–1944). These men were themselves inspired in part by Jakob Böhme (or Behmen, as he was known in England—and well-known, to Blake and Coleridge, among others—1575–1624). For them, Divine Sophia (Wisdom) was the living entity linking God and creation. This is not the only passage in which the "pantheistic" (all *is* God) philosophy of Wordsworth might better be described as panentheistic (all *in* God).

The passions that build up our human soul;
Not with the mean[268] and vulgar[269] works of man,
But with high objects, with enduring things—
With life and nature, purifying thus   410
The elements of feeling and of thought,
And sanctifying, by such discipline,
Both pain and fear, until we recognise
A grandeur in the beatings of the heart.
Nor was this fellowship vouchsafed to me   415
With stinted kindness. In November days,
When vapours rolling down the valley made
A lonely scene more lonesome, among woods,
At noon and 'mid the calm of summer nights,
When, by the margin of the trembling lake,   420
Beneath the gloomy hills homeward I went
In solitude, such intercourse was mine;
Mine was it in the fields both day and night,
And by the waters, all the summer long.

        And in the frosty season, when the sun   425
Was set, and visible for many a mile
The cottage windows blazed through twilight gloom,
I heeded not their summons: happy time
It was indeed for all of us—for me
It was a time of rapture! Clear and loud   430
The village clock tolled six,[270]—I wheeled about,
Proud and exulting like an untired horse
That cares not for his home. All shod with steel,
We hissed along the polished ice[271] in games

---

[268] *mean*: humble; contemptible.

[269] *vulgar*: commonplace.

[270] *clock tolled six*: Cf. the note to line 19 of "Lucy Gray".

[271] *We hissed along the polished ice*: Cf. Erasmus Darwin (doctor, scientist, and poet, as well as grandfather of Charles Darwin and Francis Galton; 1731–1802), *The Botanic Garden*, part 1, canto 3, lines 585–90: "Stout youths and ruddy damsels, sportive train,/Leave the white soil, and rush upon the main;/From isle to isle the moon-bright squadrons stray,/And win in easy curves their graceful way;/On step alternate borne, with balance nice/Hang o'er the gliding steel, and hiss along the ice."

Confederate, imitative of the chase   435
And woodland pleasures,—the resounding horn,
The pack loud chiming, and the hunted hare.
So through the darkness and the cold we flew,
And not a voice was idle; with the din
Smitten, the precipices rang aloud;   440
The leafless trees and every icy crag
Tinkled like iron; while far distant hills
Into the tumult sent an alien sound
Of melancholy not unnoticed, while the stars
Eastward were sparkling clear, and in the west   445
The orange sky of evening died away.
Not seldom from the uproar I retired
Into a silent bay, or sportively
Glanced sideway, leaving the tumultuous throng,
To cut across the reflex[272] of a star   450
That fled, and, flying still before me, gleamed
Upon the glassy plain; and oftentimes,
When we had given our bodies to the wind,
And all the shadowy banks on either side
Came sweeping through the darkness, spinning still   455
The rapid line of motion, then at once
Have I, reclining back upon my heels,
Stopped short; yet still the solitary cliffs
Wheeled by me—even as if the earth had rolled
With visible motion her diurnal[273] round!   460
Behind me did they stretch in solemn train,
Feebler and feebler, and I stood and watched
Till all was tranquil as a dreamless sleep.

      Ye Presences of Nature in the sky
And on the earth! Ye Visions of the hills!   465
And Souls of lonely places! can I think
A vulgar[274] hope was yours when ye employed

---

[272] *reflex*: reflection.
[273] *diurnal*: daily. Cf. Wordworth's "A slumber did my spirit seal".
[274] *vulgar*: common.

Such ministry, when ye through many a year
Haunting me thus among my boyish sports,
On caves and trees, upon the woods and hills,   470
Impressed upon all forms the characters[275]
Of danger or desire; and thus did make
The surface of the universal earth
With triumph and delight, with hope and fear,
Work like a sea?[276]

             Not uselessly employed,   475
Might I pursue this theme through every change
Of exercise and play, to which the year
Did summon us in his delightful round.

        We were a noisy crew; the sun in heaven
Beheld not vales more beautiful than ours;   480
Nor saw a band in happiness and joy
Richer, or worthier of the ground they trod.
I could record with no reluctant voice
The woods of autumn, and their hazel bowers
With milk-white clusters hung;[277] the rod and line,   485
True symbol of hope's foolishness, whose strong
And unreproved enchantment led us on
By rocks and pools shut out from every star,
All the green summer, to forlorn cascades
Among the windings hid of mountain brooks.   490
—Unfading recollections! at this hour
The heart is almost mine with which I felt,
From some hill-top on sunny afternoons,
The paper kite high among fleecy clouds
Pull at her rein like an impetuous courser;[278]   495

[275] *characters*: signs.
[276] *Work like a sea*: Cf. Cowper, *The Task*, bk. 6, lines 734–39: "Six thousand
years of sorrow have well-nigh/Fulfilled their tardy and disastrous course/Over
a sinful world; and what remains/Of this tempestuous state of human things,/Is
merely as the working of a sea/Before a calm, that rocks itself to rest."
[277] *With milk-white clusters hung*: Cf. "Nutting", line 19.
[278] *courser*: stallion.

Or, from the meadows sent on gusty days,
Beheld her breast the wind, then suddenly
Dashed headlong, and rejected by the storm.

      Ye lowly cottages wherein we dwelt,
A ministration of your own was yours;   500
Can I forget you, being as you were
So beautiful among the pleasant fields
In which ye stood? or can I here forget
The plain and seemly countenance with which
Ye dealt out your plain comforts? Yet had ye   505
Delights and exultations of your own.
Eager and never weary we pursued
Our home-amusements by the warm peat-fire
At evening, when with pencil, and smooth slate
In square divisions parcelled out and all   510
With crosses and with cyphers scribbled o'er,[279]
We schemed and puzzled, head opposed to head
In strife too humble to be named in verse:
Or round the naked table, snow-white deal,
Cherry or maple, sate in close array,   515
And to the combat, Loo[280] or Whist, led on
A thick-ribbed army; not, as in the world,
Neglected and ungratefully thrown by
Even for the very service they had wrought,
But husbanded through many a long campaign.   520
Uncouth assemblage was it, where no few
Had changed their functions; some, plebeian cards[281]

---

[279] *crosses and with cyphers scribbled o'er*: i.e., noughts and crosses/tic-tac-toe.

[280] *Loo*: also known as Lanterloo, a trick-taking card game for three to eight players and very popular in eighteenth-century England. The Jack of Clubs ("sooty knave", also called "Pam") is the most valuable card in the game, outranking even the ace of trumps. This scene is modeled on the marvellous mock-epic card game in canto 3 of Alexander Pope's *The Rape of the Lock*, where Pope refers to both Pam and Loo (Lu): "Ev'n mighty *Pam* that Kings and Queens o'erthrew,/And mow'd down Armies in the Fights of *Lu*" (lines 61–62).

[281] *plebeian cards*: Cf. Pope, *Rape of the Lock*, canto 3,, lines 53–54: "Him *Basto* follow'd, but his Fate more hard/Gain'd but one Trump and one *Plebeian* Card."

Which Fate, beyond the promise of their birth,
Had dignified, and called to represent
The persons of departed potentates. 525
Oh, with what echoes on the board they fell!
Ironic diamonds,—clubs, hearts, diamonds, spades,
A congregation piteously akin!
Cheap matter offered they to boyish wit,[282]
Those sooty knaves,[283] precipitated down 530
With scoffs and taunts, like Vulcan[284] out of heaven:
The paramount ace, a moon in her eclipse,
Queens gleaming through their splendour's last decay,
And monarchs surly at the wrongs sustained
By royal visages. Meanwhile abroad 535
Incessant rain was falling, or the frost
Raged bitterly, with keen and silent tooth;[285]
And, interrupting oft that eager game,
From under Esthwaite's[286] splitting fields of ice
The pent-up air, struggling to free itself, 540
Gave out to meadow grounds and hills a loud
Protracted yelling, like the noise of wolves
Howling in troops along the Bothnic Main.[287]

[282] *wit*: invention.

[283] *knaves*: rascals; jacks. Cf. Charles Dickens (1812–1870), *Great Expectations*, chap. 8: "'He calls the knaves, Jacks, this boy!' said Estella with disdain". The Jack of Clubs is the highest ranking card in Loo.

[284] *Vulcan*: Vulcan (Hephæstus), the lame Græco-Roman god of thunder, and blacksmith of the gods. Zeus or Hera—depending on which version one follows—threw him off Mount Olympus, laming him.

[285] *Raged bitterly, with keen and silent tooth*: Cf. Shakespeare, *As You Like It*, Act 2, scene 7, lines 175–80: "Blow, blow, thou winter wind,/Thou art not so unkind/As man's ingratitude./Thy tooth is not so keen,/Because thou art not seen,/Although thy breath be rude"; also Cowper, *The Task*, bk. 4, lines 308–10: "How calm is my recess! and how the frost/Raging abroad, and the rough wind endear/The silence and the warmth enjoyed within!"

[286] *Esthwaite's*: i.e., Esthwaite Water, a smaller lake situated between La Windermere and Coniston Water.

[287] *along the Bothnic Main*: i.e., along the shores of the Baltic Sea.

             Nor, sedulous as I have been to trace
How Nature by extrinsic passion first   545
Peopled the mind with forms sublime or fair,
And made me love them, may I here omit
How other pleasures have been mine, and joys
Of subtler origin; how I have felt,
Not seldom even in that tempestuous time,   550
Those hallowed and pure motions of the sense
Which seem, in their simplicity, to own
An intellectual[288] charm; that calm delight
Which, if I err not, surely must belong
To those first-born[289] affinities that fit   555
Our new existence to existing things,
And, in our dawn of being, constitute
The bond of union between life and joy.

             Yes, I remember when the changeful earth,
And twice five summers on my mind had stamped   560
The faces of the moving year, even then
I held unconscious intercourse with beauty
Old as creation, drinking in a pure
Organic pleasure from the silver wreaths
Of curling mist, or from the level plain   565
Of waters coloured by impending clouds.

        The sands of Westmoreland,[290] the creeks
              and bays
Of Cumbria's[291] rocky limits, they can tell
low, when the Sea threw off his evening shade,

---

lectual: "apprehensible or apprehended only by the intellect; non-
piritual; ideal" (*Oxford English Dictionary*, s.v. "intellectual").
n: already present at birth.
land: formerly a county in North West England; it is now part of

umberland's; Cumberland is formerly a county in North West
a was on its west coast and Scotland on its northern bor-
ighest mountain in England (3,209 ft.), was located there.
f the modern county of Cumbria (created in 1974).

And to the shepherd's hut on distant hills 570
Sent welcome notice of the rising moon,
How I have stood, to fancies such as these
A stranger, linking with the spectacle
No conscious memory of a kindred sight,
And bringing with me no peculiar sense 575
Of quietness or peace; yet have I stood,
Even while mine eye hath moved o'er many a league
Of shining water, gathering as it seemed
Through every hair-breadth in that field of light
New pleasure like a bee among the flowers. 580

Thus oft amid those fits of vulgar[292] joy
Which, through all seasons, on a child's pursuits
Are prompt attendants, 'mid that giddy bliss
Which, like a tempest, works along the blood
And is forgotten; even then I felt 585
Gleams like the flashing of a shield;—the earth
And common face of Nature spake to me
Rememberable things; sometimes, 'tis true,
By chance collisions and quaint accidents
(Like those ill-sorted unions, work supposed 590
Of evil-minded fairies[293]), yet not vain
Nor profitless, if haply[294] they impressed
Collateral objects and appearances,
Albeit lifeless then, and doomed to sleep
Until maturer seasons called them forth 595
To impregnate and to elevate the mind.
—And if the vulgar joy by its own weight
Wearied itself out of the memory,
The scenes which were a witness of that joy
Remained in their substantial lineaments 600
Depicted on the brain, and to the eye

---

[292] *vulgar*: commonplace, ordinary.
[293] *Like those ill-sorted unions ... evil-minded fairies*: as, for example, in
Shakespeare's *A Midsummer Night's Dream*.
[294] *haply*: perchance.

Were visible, a daily sight; and thus
By the impressive discipline of fear,
By pleasure and repeated happiness,
So frequently repeated, and by force   605
Of obscure feelings representative
Of things forgotten, these same scenes so bright,
So beautiful, so majestic in themselves,
Though yet the day was distant, did become
Habitually dear, and all their forms   610
And changeful colours by invisible links
Were fastened to the affections.

                    I began
My story early—not misled, I trust,
By an infirmity of love for days
Disowned by memory—fancying flowers where none,   615
Not even the sweetest, do or can survive,
For him at least whose dawning day they cheered.
Nor will it seem to thee, O Friend! so prompt
In sympathy, that I have lengthened out
With fond and feeble tongue a tedious tale.   620
Meanwhile, my hope has been, that I might fetch
Invigorating thoughts from former years;
Might fix the wavering balance of my mind,
And haply meet reproaches too, whose power
May spur me on, in manhood now mature,   625
To honourable toil. Yet should these hopes
Prove vain, and thus should neither I be taught
To understand myself, nor thou to know
With better knowledge how the heart was framed
Of him thou lovest; need I dread from thee   630
Harsh judgments, if the song be loth to quit
Those recollected hours that have the charm
Of visionary things, those lovely forms
And sweet sensations that throw back our life,
And almost make remotest infancy   635
A visible scene, on which the sun is shining?

One end at least hath been attained; my mind
Hath been revived, and if this genial mood
Desert me not, forthwith shall be brought down
Through later years the story of my life.   640
The road lies plain before me;[295]—'tis a theme
Single and of determined bounds; and hence
I choose it rather at this time, than work
Of ampler or more varied argument,[296]
Where I might be discomfited and lost: 645
And certain hopes are with me, that to thee
This labour will be welcome, honoured Friend!

From *Book Second* (1850)

SCHOOL-TIME—CONTINUED

Sublimer joy; for
I would walk alone,
Under the quiet stars, and at that time
Have felt whate'er there is of power in sound
To breathe an elevated mood, by form   305
Or image unprofaned; and I would stand,
If the night blackened with a coming storm,
Beneath some rock, listening to notes that are
The ghostly language of the ancient earth,
Or make their dim abode in distant winds.   310
Thence did I drink the visionary power;
And deem not profitless those fleeting moods
Of shadowy exultation: not for this,
That they are kindred to our purer mind
And intellectual life; but that the soul,   315
Remembering how she felt, but what she felt
Remembering not, retains an obscure[297] sense

---

[295] *road lies plain before me:* Cf. the note to line 14.
[296] *ampler or more varied argument:* the subject matter or themes of a book.
[297] *obscure:* (emphasis on the first syllable).

Of possible sublimity, whereto
With growing faculties she doth aspire,
With faculties still growing, feeling still   320
That whatsoever point they gain, they yet
Have something to pursue.

                         And not alone
'Mid gloom and tumult, but no less 'mid fair
And tranquil scenes, that universal power
And fitness in the latent qualities   325
And essences of things, by which the mind
Is moved with feelings of delight, to me
Came strengthened with a superadded soul,
A virtue not its own. My morning walks
Were early;—oft before the hours of school   330
I travelled round our little lake, five miles
Of pleasant wandering. Happy time! more dear
For this, that one was by my side, a Friend[298]
Then passionately loved; with heart how full
Would he peruse these lines! For many years   335
Have since flowed in between us, and, our minds
Both silent to each other, at this time
We live as if those hours had never been.
Nor seldom did I lift our cottage latch
Far earlier, ere one smoke-wreath had risen   340
From human dwelling, or the vernal thrush
Was audible; and sate among the woods
Alone upon some jutting eminence,
At the first gleam of dawn-light, when the Vale,
Yet slumbering, lay in utter solitude.   345
How shall I seek the origin? where find
Faith in the marvellous things which then I felt?
Oft in these moments such a holy calm
Would overspread my soul, that bodily eyes
Were utterly forgotten, and what I saw   350

---

[298] *Friend:* "The late Rev. John Fleming, of Rayrigg, Windermere" (note in
Moxon's 1850 edition of *The Prelude*).

Appeared like something in myself, a dream,
A prospect in the mind.

               'Twere long to tell
What spring and autumn, what the winter snows,
And what the summer shade, what day and night,
Evening and morning, sleep and waking, thought   355
From sources inexhaustible, poured forth
To feed the spirit of religious love
In which I walked with Nature. But let this
Be not forgotten, that I still retained
My first creative sensibility;   360
That by the regular action of the world
My soul was unsubdued. A plastic[299] power
Abode with me; a forming hand, at times
Rebellious, acting in a devious mood;
A local spirit of his own, at war   365
With general tendency, but, for the most,
Subservient strictly to external things
With which it communed. An auxiliar light[300]
Came from my mind, which on the setting sun
Bestowed new splendour; the melodious birds,   370
The fluttering breezes, fountains that run on
Murmuring so sweetly in themselves, obeyed
A like dominion, and the midnight storm
Grew darker in the presence of my eye:
Hence my obeisance,[301] my devotion hence,   375
And hence my transport.

[299] *plastic*: shaping. Cf. Coleridge, "Dejection: An Ode", line 86: "My shaping spirit of Imagination", and "The Eolian Harp", lines 44–48: "And what if all of animated nature/Be but organic harps diversely framed,/That tremble into thought, as o'er them sweeps/Plastic and vast, one intellectual breeze,/At once the Soul of each, and God of All?"

[300] *auxiliar light*: Cf. "Tintern Abbey", line 148; "Intimations of Immortality", line 56; *Prelude*, bk. 11, line 322; "Elegiac Stanzas", line 14; and Tennyson's "Merlin and the Gleam".

[301] *obeisance*: submission; prostration in homage or acknowledgement of authority.

　　　　　　　　　Nor should this, perchance,
Pass unrecorded, that I still[302] had loved
The exercise and produce of a toil,
Than analytic industry to me
More pleasing, and whose character I deem　　　　　　380
Is more poetic as resembling more
Creative agency. The song would speak
Of that interminable building reared
By observation of affinities
In objects where no brotherhood exists　　　　　　385
To passive minds.[303] My seventeenth year was come;
And, whether from this habit rooted now
So deeply in my mind; or from excess
In the great social principle of life
Coercing all things into sympathy,　　　　　　390
To unorganic natures were transferred
My own enjoyments; or the power of truth
Coming in revelation, did converse
With things that really are; I, at this time,
Saw blessings spread around me like a sea.　　　　　　395
Thus while the days flew by, and years passed on,
From Nature overflowing on my soul,
I had received so much, that every thought
Was steeped in feeling; I was only then
Contented, when with bliss ineffable　　　　　　400
I felt the sentiment of Being spread
O'er all that moves and all that seemeth still;
O'er all that, lost beyond the reach of thought
And human knowledge, to the human eye
Invisible, yet liveth to the heart;　　　　　　405
O'er all that leaps and runs, and shouts and sings,
Or beats the gladsome air; o'er all that glides
Beneath the wave, yea, in the wave itself,
And mighty depth of waters. Wonder not

---

[302] *still*: ever.
[303] *interminable building . . . passive minds*: Cf. "Tintern Abbey", lines 139–40.

If high the transport, great the joy I felt,   410
Communing in this sort through earth and heaven
With every form of creature, as it looked
Towards the Uncreated with a countenance
Of adoration, with an eye of love.
One song they sang, and it was audible,   415
Most audible, then, when the fleshly ear,
O'ercome by humblest prelude of that strain,[304]
Forgot her functions, and slept undisturbed.

            If this be error, and another faith
Find easier access to the pious mind,   420
Yet were I grossly destitute of all
Those human sentiments that make this earth
So dear, if I should fail with grateful voice
To speak of you, ye mountains, and ye lakes
And sounding cataracts, ye mists and winds   425
That dwell among the hills where I was born.[305]
If in my youth I have been pure in heart,
If, mingling with the world, I am content
With my own modest pleasures, and have lived
With God and Nature communing, removed   430
From little enmities and low desires,
The gift is yours; if in these times of fear,
This melancholy waste of hopes o'erthrown,[306]
If, 'mid indifference and apathy,
And wicked exultation, when good men   435
On every side fall off, we know not how,
To selfishness, disguised in gentle names
Of peace and quiet and domestic love,
Yet mingled not unwillingly with sneers

---

[304] strain: passage; musical sequence; melody.

[305] If this be error . . . born: Cf. "Tintern Abbey", lines 49ff.

[306] This melancholy waste of hopes o'erthrown: particularly his early hopes for
the French Revolution, before they were dashed by civil bloodshed and military
aggression. Cf. the note to line 2 of Wordsworth's "Tintern Abbey", and the note
to line 35 of Blake's "The Grey Monk".

On visionary minds; if, in this time   440
Of dereliction and dismay, I yet
Despair not of our nature, but retain
A more than Roman[307] confidence, a faith
That fails not, in all sorrow my support,
The blessing of my life; the gift is yours,   445
Ye winds and sounding cataracts! 'tis yours,
Ye mountains! thine, O Nature! Thou hast fed
My lofty speculations; and in thee,
For this uneasy heart of ours, I find
A never-failing principle of joy   450
And purest passion.

                    Thou, my Friend! wert reared
In the great city,[308] 'mid far other scenes;
But we, by different roads, at length have gained
The self-same bourne.[309] And for this cause to thee
I speak, unapprehensive of contempt,   455
The insinuated scoff of coward tongues,
And all that silent language which so oft
In conversation between man and man
Blots from the human countenance all trace
Of beauty and of love. For thou hast sought   460
The truth in solitude, and, since the days
That gave thee liberty, full long desired,
To serve in Nature's temple, thou hast been
The most assiduous of her ministers;
In many things my brother, chiefly here   465
In this our deep devotion.

---

[307] *Roman*: The ancient Romans (particularly of the Republican era) were renowned for the courage and self-confidence with which they defended their hearths, their institutions, and their city.

[308] *reared/In the great city*: Although he was born in a small town in Devon, Coleridge was sent to school at Christ's Hospital in the City of London. See the note to line 30 of Coleridge's "This Lime-Tree Bower My Prison"; cf. "Frost at Midnight", lines 52–54.

[309] *bourne*: destination.

Fare thee well!
Health and the quiet of a healthful mind
Attend thee![310] seeking oft the haunts of men,
And yet more often living with thyself,
And for thyself, so haply[311] shall thy days 470
Be many, and a blessing to mankind.

From *Book Fifth* (1850)

BOOKS

One day, when from my lips a like complaint[312] 50
Had fallen in presence of a studious friend,[313]
He with a smile made answer, that in truth
'Twas going far to seek disquietude;
But on the front of his reproof confessed
That he himself had oftentimes given way 55
To kindred hauntings. Whereupon I told,
That once in the stillness of a summer's noon,
While I was seated in a rocky cave
By the sea-side, perusing, so it chanced,
The famous history of the errant knight 60
Recorded by Cervantes,[314] these same thoughts
Beset me, and to height unusual rose,
While listlessly I sate, and, having closed
The book, had turned my eyes toward the wide sea.
On poetry and geometric truth, 65

---

[310] *Health . . . Attend thee*: In the course of his life, Coleridge was troubled with bad health, opium addiction, an unhappy marriage, and thwarted love.

[311] *so haply*: i.e., with fortune.

[312] *complaint*: The "complaint" is that individuals naturally yearn to find immortality either for or in their ideas and dreams; in the midst of an eternal universe they are constantly disappointed to find them ephemeral.

[313] *studious friend*: probably Coleridge.

[314] *Cervantes*: Miguel de Cervantes (1547–1616), Spanish novelist, playwright, and poet, one of the greatest names in Western literature. He is renowned above all for his novel *Don Quixote*, whose eponymous hero is the errant knight referred to above.

And their high privilege of lasting life,
From all internal injury exempt,
I mused, upon these chiefly: and at length,
My senses yielding to the sultry air,
Sleep seized me, and I passed into a dream.[315]   70
I saw before me stretched a boundless plain
Of sandy wilderness, all black and void,
And as I looked around, distress and fear
Came creeping over me, when at my side,
Close at my side, an uncouth shape appeared   75
Upon a dromedary, mounted high.
He seemed an Arab of the Bedouin[316] tribes:
A lance he bore, and underneath one arm
A stone, and in the opposite hand, a shell
Of a surpassing brightness. At the sight   80
Much I rejoiced, not doubting but a guide
Was present, one who with unerring skill
Would through the desert lead me; and while yet
I looked and looked, self-questioned what this freight
Which the new-comer carried through the waste   85
Could mean, the Arab told me that the stone
(To give it in the language of the dream)
Was "Euclid's Elements;"[317] and "This," said he,
"Is something of more worth", and at the word
Stretched forth the shell, so beautiful in shape,   90
In colour so resplendent, with command
That I should hold it to my ear. I did so,
And heard that instant in an unknown tongue,

[315] *Sleep seized me, and I passed into a dream*: This passage is based on a dream of the great French philosopher and mathematician René Descartes (1596–1650), reported in Adrien Baillet's *Vie de Descartes*.

[316] *Bedouin*: a desert-dwelling, nomadic Arab people.

[317] *Euclid's Elements*: Euclid (fourth century B.C.) was a Greek mathematician and "The Father of Geometry". Euclid's *Elements* was the most celebrated and influential mathematical treatise ever written. It remained a standard textbook into the twentieth century. Euclid's geometry is also particularly admired for its logical clarity and beauty; cf. Edna St. Vincent Millay's (1892–1950) "Euclid Alone Has Looked on Beauty Bare".

Which yet I understood, articulate sounds,
A loud prophetic blast of harmony; 95
An Ode, in passion uttered, which foretold
Destruction to the children of the earth
By deluge, now at hand. No sooner ceased
The song, than the Arab with calm look declared
That all would come to pass of which the voice 100
Had given forewarning, and that he himself
Was going then to bury those two books:
The one that held acquaintance with the stars,
And wedded soul to soul in purest bond
Of reason, undisturbed by space or time; 105
The other that was a god, yea many gods,
Had voices more than all the winds, with power
To exhilarate the spirit, and to soothe,
Through every clime, the heart of human kind.
While this was uttering, strange as it may seem, 110
I wondered not, although I plainly saw
The one to be a stone, the other a shell;
Nor doubted once but that they both were books,
Having a perfect faith in all that passed.
Far stronger, now, grew the desire I felt 115
To cleave unto this man; but when I prayed
To share his enterprise, he hurried on
Reckless of me: I followed, not unseen,
For oftentimes he cast a backward look,
Grasping his twofold treasure.—Lance in rest, 120
He rode, I keeping pace with him; and now
He, to my fancy, had become the knight
Whose tale Cervantes tells; yet not the knight,
But was an Arab of the desert too;
Of these was neither, and was both at once.[318] 125
His countenance, meanwhile, grew more disturbed;
And, looking backwards when he looked, mine eyes

[318] *and now . . . both at once*: Cf. Charles Williams on the leech-gatherer in the
introductory note to "Resolution and Independence", pp. 145–46.

Saw, over half the wilderness diffused,
A bed of glittering light: I asked the cause:
"It is," said he, "the waters of the deep   130
Gathering upon us;" quickening then the pace
Of the unwieldy creature he bestrode,
He left me: I called after him aloud;
He heeded not; but, with his twofold charge
Still in his grasp, before me, full in view,   135
Went hurrying o'er the illimitable waste,
With the fleet waters of a drowning world
In chase of him; whereat I waked in terror,
And saw the sea before me, and the book,
In which I had been reading, at my side.   140

From *Book Seventh* (1850)

RESIDENCE IN LONDON[319]

      Yet undetermined to what course of life
I should adhere, and seeming to possess
A little space of intermediate time   60
At full command, to London first I turned,
In no disturbance of excessive hope,
By personal ambition unenslaved,
Frugal as there was need, and, though self-willed,
From dangerous passions free. Three years had flown   65
Since I had felt in heart and soul the shock
Of the huge town's first presence,[320] and had paced
Her endless streets, a transient visitant:

[319] It is remarkable that, in spite of his (at best) equivocal relationship with urban life, it is Wordsworth, the great nature poet, who has provided, in this Seventh Book of *The Prelude*, the poetry of London desired by Arthur Symons (1865–1945), almost a century later (see Symons' "London: A Book of Aspects", in *Cities and Sea-Coasts and Islands*).

[320] *felt in heart and soul the shock . . . first presence:* Cf. *Prelude*, bk. 1, line 7. It made the same impression on Henry James in the 1860s and Karel Čapek in the 1920s.

Now, fixed amid that concourse of mankind[321]
Where Pleasure whirls about incessantly,   70
And life and labour seem but one, I filled
An idler's place; an idler well content
To have a house (what matter for a home?)
That owned him; living cheerfully abroad
With unchecked fancy ever on the stir,   75
And all my young affections out of doors.

    There was a time when whatso'er is feigned
Of airy palaces, and gardens built
By Genii of romance;[322] or hath in grave
Authentic history been set forth of Rome,   80

---

[321] *huge town's first presence ... concourse of mankind*: Charles Lamb to Wordsworth (January 30, 1801) could not but have influenced this part of *The Prelude*:

> I have passed all my days in London, until I have formed as many and intense local attachments as any of you mountaineers can have done with dead nature. The Lighted shops of the Strand and Fleet Street, the innumerable trades, tradesmen, and customers; coaches, wagons, playhouses, all the bustle and wickedness round about Covent Garden, the very women of the town; the Watchmen, drunken scenes, rattles,—life awake, if you awake, at all hours of the night, the impossibility of being dull in Fleet Street, the crowds, the very dirt & mud, the Sun shining upon houses and pavements, the print shops, the old book stalls, parsons cheap'ning books, coffee houses, steams of soups from kitchens, the pantomimes, London itself a pantomime and a masquerade,—all these things work themselves into my mind and feed me, without a power of satiating me. The wonder of these sights impels me into night-walks about her crowded streets, and I often shed tears in the motley Strand from fulness of joy at so much Life.

Cf. also James Boswell (1740–1795) and Johnson on London 1775: "I talked of the cheerfulness of Fleet-street, owing to the constant quick succession of people which we perceive passing through it. JOHNSON. 'Why, Sir, Fleet-street has a very animated appearance; but I think the full tide of human existence is at Charing-cross'" (James Boswell, *Life of Johnson* [Oxford: Oxford University Press, 1989], p. 608).

[322] *Genii of romance*: "Genii" as an English equivalent of the Arabic *Jinn* (or *Jinni*) derives from the *One Thousand and One Nights*—specifically the first English translation (from the French version of Antoine Galland), published as *Arabian Nights' Entertainments* in the first decade of the eighteenth century; it was immediately and enduringly extremely popular and influential.

Alcairo,[323] Babylon,[324] or Persepolis;[325]
Or given upon report by pilgrim friars,
Of golden cities ten months' journey deep
Among Tartarian[326] wilds—fell short, far short,
Of what my fond simplicity believed   85
And thought of London—held me by a chain
Less strong of wonder and obscure delight.
Whether the bolt of childhood's Fancy shot
For me beyond its ordinary mark,
'Twere vain to ask; but in our flock of boys   90
Was One, a cripple from his birth, whom chance
Summoned from school to London; fortunate
And envied traveller! When the Boy returned,
After short absence, curiously I scanned
His mien[327] and person, nor was free, in sooth,[328]   95

[323] *Alcairo*: Memphis, capital of Egypt during the Old Kingdom (third millennium B.C.), near modern Cairo. Cf. *Paradise Lost*, bk. 1, lines 717–19: "Not Babylon,/Nor great Alcairo such magnificence/ Equaled in all their glories".

[324] *Babylon*: Benjamin Disraeli (1804–1881) made a similar association in *Tancred* (1847): "London is a modern Babylon" (chap. 46); "That is most striking in London is its vastness. It is the illimitable feeling that gives it a special character. London is not grand. It possesses only one of the qualifications of a grand city, size; but it wants the equally important one, beauty. It is the union of these two qualities that produced the grand cities, the Romes, the Babylons, the hundred portals of the Pharaohs" (chap. 16).

[325] *Persepolis*: the capital of the ancient Persian Empire, captured and partly destroyed by Alexander the Great in 330 B.C. Cf. Christopher Marlowe (1564–1593), *Tamburlaine, Part I*, Act 2, scene 5, lines 51–54: "Is it not brave to be a king, Techelles?—/Usumcasane and Theridamas,/Is it not passing brave to be a king,/And ride in triumph through Persepolis?"

[326] *Tartarian*: For these golden cities in lands subject to Tartar (and Tamburlaine's/Temir's) domination, see also Milton, *Paradise Lost*, bk. 11, lines 385–96: "His eye might there command wherever stood/City of old or modern fame, the seat/Of mightiest empire, from the destined walls/Of Cambalu, seat of Cathaian Can,/And Samarkand by Oxus, Temir's throne,/To Paquin of Sinaean kings, and thence/To Agra and Lahore of great Mogul,/Down to the golden Chersonese, or where/The Persian in Ecbatan sat, or since/In Hispahan; or where the Russian Ksar/In Moscow, or the Sultan in Bizance,/Turkestan-born". Wordsworth's invocation of the fabled exotic cities of the East establishes an oneiric London, rich and strange, much as O. Henry was to do for late nineteenth-century New York, in his "Bagdad-on-the-Subway".

[327] *mien*: bearing.
[328] *sooth*: truth.

From disappointment, not to find some change
In look and air, from that new region brought,
As if from Fairy-land. Much I questioned him;
And every word he uttered, on my ears
Fell flatter than a caged parrot's note,   100
That answers unexpectedly awry,
And mocks the prompter's listening. Marvelous things
Had vanity (quick Spirit that appears
Almost as deeply seated and as strong
In a Child's heart as fear itself) conceived   105
For my enjoyment. Would that I could now
Recall what then I pictured to myself
Of mitred Prelates,[329] Lords in ermine clad,
The King, and the King's Palace,[330] and, not last,
Nor least, Heaven bless him! the renowned Lord
    Mayor:[331]   110
Dreams not unlike to those which once begot
A change of purpose in young Whittington,[332]
When he, a friendless and a drooping boy,
Sate on a stone, and heard the bells speak out
Articulate music. Above all, one thought   115
Baffled my understanding: how men lived

[329] *mitred Prelates*: the bishops of the Church of England; they sit in the House of Lords as the Lords Spiritual—a practice that predates the Reformation, though its implications have changed.

[330] *King's Palace*: St. James' Palace. Queen Victoria established Buckingham Palace as the main royal residence in London in 1837.

[331] *Lord Mayor*: The lord mayor of London is elected from the aldermen of the City of London at Guildhall on Michaelmas Day (September 29) and sworn in in November. On the following day, a great parade is held, culminating in the lord mayor's oath of allegiance to the Crown.

[332] *Whittington*: One of the most celebrated English fairy tales concerns Dick Whittington, a poor country boy who sets off for London with his cat to make his fortune, having heard that the streets of London were paved with gold. Initially meeting with nothing but adversity, he makes his way out, but stops while climbing Highgate Hill, upon hearing the bells of St. Mary-le-Bow ringing: "Turn again, Dick Whittington, thrice Lord Mayor of London." He returns and, with the aid of his cat, makes his fortune and finds himself indeed at last the lord mayor. The tale is obliquely derived from the career of Sir Richard Whittington, a fourteenth-century merchant and benefactor, three times lord mayor of London.

Even next-door neighbours, as we say, yet still
Strangers, not knowing each the other's name.

     O, wond'rous power of words, by simple faith
Licensed to take the meaning that we love!   120
Vauxhall[333] and Ranelagh![334] I then had heard
Of your green groves, and wilderness of lamps
Dimming the stars, and fireworks magical,
And gorgeous ladies, under splendid domes,
Floating in dance, or warbling high in air   125
The songs of spirits! Nor had Fancy fed
With less delight upon that other class
Of marvels, broad-day wonders permanent:
The River proudly bridged;[335] the dizzy top
And Whispering Gallery of St. Paul's;[336] the tombs   130

---

[333] *Vauxhall*: Major pleasure gardens in South London between the Restoration (1660s) and the early Victorian period (1840s). It was at its peak between the eighteenth century and the Regency (1811–1820). A fragment of it survives as the Spring Gardens in Kennington, near Vauxhall station. It features importantly in Thackeray's *Vanity Fair*.

[334] *Ranelagh*: (pronounced "Ranalee"); important eighteenth-century pleasure gardens in Chelsea, originally featuring a very large (120 ft. diameter) and elaborate rotunda (in which the nine-year-old Mozart performed), a Chinese pavilion, and a Venetian canal. The gardens and rotunda were painted by Canaletto; the gardens survive as part of the grounds of the Royal Hospital Chelsea. Both Vauxhall and Ranelagh provided musical entertainments, masquerades, and fireworks; attracted fashionable society; and were periodically the haunt of prostitutes.

[335] *River proudly bridged*: At the time, the bridges of central London were Old London Bridge and the first versions of Blackfriars Bridge and Westminster Bridge.

[336] *St. Paul's*: St. Paul's is the Anglican cathedral of the bishop of London— third in seniority in the Church of England (as it was before the Reformation), after Canterbury and York. There has been a cathedral in London since Roman times. The building (the present cathedral) to which Wordsworth refers was designed by Sir Christopher Wren (1632–1723) to replace the gothic cathedral destroyed in the Great Fire of London (1666). One of the noblest buildings of Europe, it was also the tallest in London from 1710 to 1962, and, at 365 feet, the top of St. Paul's remains the highest point in the old City. The Whispering Gallery (in the dome, where a whisper to the wall can be heard all round the gallery) and Golden Gallery (with its view from the top) are perennial favorites with visitors to London.

Of Westminster;[337] the Giants of Guildhall;[338]
Bedlam,[339] and those carved maniacs at the gates,
Perpetually recumbent; Statues—man,
And the horse under him—in gilded pomp
Adorning flowery gardens, 'mid vast squares;[340]   135
The Monument,[341] and that Chamber of the Tower
Where England's sovereigns sit in long array,
Their steeds bestriding,—every mimic shape

[337] *Westminster*: Westminster Abbey, a Benedictine abbey until the Reformation, and the coronation site of English monarchs to this day. The first stone abbey was built on the site by St. Edward the Confessor in 1065, and the present structure dates mostly from the second half of the thirteenth century. It houses the tombs of the majority of the English sovereigns from St. Edward the Confessor to George II (many of them in effigy) as well as those of such great figures as Chaucer, Newton, Purcell, Dryden, and Spenser. The abbey made a lasting impression on William Blake, who was sent there during his apprenticeship to draw the sculptures and architecture.

[338] *Guildhall*: The Guildhall is the ceremonial and administrative center of the City of London, the Town Hall. The present building dates in part from the fifteenth century. Gog and Magog were giants of British folklore, traditionally held to be guardians of the City of London. Their carved wooden statues (in various incarnations—the originals were destroyed in the Great Fire of London; their replacements, in turn, in the Blitz) are kept in Guildhall and carried in procession in the Lord Mayor's Parade.

[339] *Bedlam*: Bedlam is the popular name for Bethlem Royal Hospital. Founded in the fourteenth century as a lunatic asylum, it effectively became the world's first mental hospital when it began to refer to the lunatics as "patients" in 1700 and organized "curable" and "incurable" wards some twenty-five years later. It was situated in Bishopsgate, in the City, until 1815. The Danish sculptor Caius Gabriel Cibber (1630–1700) carved two striking statues—"Melancholy" and "Raving Madness"—reclining above the gates. Paid admission to view the patients was available and popular. Cf. Dickens' *A Christmas Carol*: "My clerk, with fifteen shillings a-week, and a wife and family, talking about a merry Christmas. I'll retire to Bedlam."

[340] *Statues . . . vast squares*: such as the equestrian statue of William III in St. James' Square.

[341] *Monument*: 202 ft. Doric column in the City of London, with a viewing platform at the top. Designed by Sir Christopher Wren and the scientist-architect Robert Hooke (1635–1703) to commemorate the Great Fire of London, and built in 1671–1677, it remains the tallest isolated stone column in the world. Until 1831 the inscriptions at the base of the monument slandered the English Catholics with responsibility for the tragedy, stinging the Catholic Alexander Pope to respond, "Where London's column, pointing at the skies/Like a tall bully, lifts the head, and lyes" (*Moral Essays*, Epistle 3, lines 339–40).

Cased in the gleaming mail the monarch wore,
Whether for gorgeous tournament addressed, 140
Or life or death upon the battlefield.[342]
Those bold imaginations in due time
Had vanished, leaving others in their stead:
And now I looked upon the living scene;
Familiarly perused it; oftentimes, 145
In spite of strongest disappointment, pleased
Through courteous self-submission, as a tax
Paid to the object by prescriptive right.

      Rise up, thou monstrous ant-hill on the plain
Of a too busy world! Before me flow, 150
Thou endless stream of men and moving things!
Thy every-day appearance, as it strikes—
With wonder heightened, or sublimed by awe—
On strangers, of all ages; the quick dance
Of colours, lights, and forms; the deafening din; 155
The comers and the goers face to face,
Face after face; the string of dazzling wares,
Shop after shop, with symbols, blazoned names,
And all the tradesman's honours overhead:[343]
Here, fronts of houses, like a title-page, 160
With letters huge inscribed from top to toe;
Stationed above the door, like guardian saints,
There, allegoric shapes, female or male,
Or physiognomies of real men,
Land-warriors, kings, or admirals of the sea, 165
Boyle,[344] Shakespeare, Newton, or the attractive head
Of some quack-doctor, famous in his day.[345]

---

[342] *Chamber of the Tower ... upon the battlefield*: i.e., in the Tower of London.

[343] *symbols ... overhead*: with all the pomp of heraldic symbolism, like the golden grasshopper of the Royal Exchange, or the common pawnbroker's symbol of three suspended spheres.

[344] *Boyle*: Sir Robert Boyle (1627–1691), scientist and inventor.

[345] *quack-doctor, famous in his day*: John Graham (1745–1794), a notorious, and handsome, late eighteenth-century Scottish quack, whose assistants included the young Amy Lyon—later, Emma, Lady Hamilton, Nelson's mistress.

Meanwhile the roar continues, till at length,
Escaped as from an enemy, we turn
Abruptly into some sequestered nook, 170
Still as a sheltered place when winds blow loud!
At leisure, thence, through tracts of thin resort,
And sights and sounds that come at intervals,
We take our way. A raree-show[346] is here,
With children gathered round; another street 175
Presents a company of dancing dogs,
Or dromedary, with an antic[347] pair
Of monkeys on his back; a minstrel band
Of Savoyards;[348] or, single and alone,
An English ballad-singer.[349] Private courts,[350] 180
Gloomy as coffins, and unsightly lanes[351]
Thrilled by some female vendor's scream, belike
The very shrillest of all London cries,[352]
May then entangle our impatient steps;
Conducted through those labyrinths, unawares, 185
To privileged regions and inviolate,
Where from their airy lodges studious lawyers
Look out on waters, walks, and gardens green.[353]

---

[346] *raree-show*: "a show contained or carried about in a box" (*Oxford English Dictionary*, s.v. "raree-show").

[347] *antic*: grotesque; grinning.

[348] *Savoyards*: Savoy has been part of France since 1860. It borders on modern Italy, and in Wordsworth's day it was governed in turn by Sicily and the French revolutionary government.

[349] *English ballad-singer*: effectively, the ancestors of the Music Hall artistes who sprang up in Thackeray's time a generation or so later and remained an influence on British letters through Compton Mackenzie (1883–1972) and T.S. Eliot (1888–1965).

[350] *Private courts*: courtyards.

[351] *Gloomy as coffins, and unsightly lanes*: "Heinrich Heine [1797–1856] was horrified by the poverty—the squalor and starvation—that abounded in the midst of the immense wealth and splendour" (Max Beerbohm, "London Revisited", in *Mainly on the Air* [Toronto: Heinemann, 1946], p. 7).

[352] *London cries*: a familiar aspect of London life till the 1930s, and beyond. See Henry Mayhew, *Mayhew's London* (1851).

[353] *waters, walks, and gardens green*: the Temple—specifically, the Inner Temple and Middle Temple—part of the legal district of London, named for the twelfth-century Round Church built for the Knights Templar, descending

        Thence back into the throng, until we reach,
Following the tide that slackens by degrees,   190
Some half-frequented scene, where wider streets
Bring straggling breezes of suburban air.
Here files of ballads[354] dangle from dead[355] walls;
Advertisements, of giant-size, from high
Press forward, in all colours, on the sight;   195
These, bold in conscious merit, lower down
That,[356] fronted with a most imposing word,
Is, peradventure, one in masquerade.[357]
As on the broadening causeway we advance,
Behold, turned upwards, a face hard and strong   200
In lineaments, and red with over-toil.
'Tis one encountered here and everywhere;
A travelling cripple, by the trunk cut short,
And stumping on his arms.[358] In sailor's garb
Another lies at length, beside a range   205
Of well-formed characters, with chalk inscribed
Upon the smooth flint stones: the Nurse is here,
The Bachelor, that loves to sun himself,
The military Idler, and the Dame,
That field-ward takes her walk with decent steps.   210

---

from Fleet Street to the Thames. Charles Lamb was born and spent his youth in
the Inner Temple, and Shakespeare's *Twelfth Night* was first performed at Middle
Temple Hall. It is still one of the most beautiful nooks in London.

[354] *files of ballads*: The ballads are for sale.

[355] *dead*: windowless.

[356] *These ... That*: Wordsworth is distinguishing different advertisements.

[357] *in masquerade*: i.e., concealing what it is really offering.

[358] *travelling cripple ... his arms*: Samuel Horsey, the "King of Beggars". He
is described by Charles Lamb in "A Complaint of the Decay of Beggars in the
Metropolis", *Essays of Elia* (Moxon, 1823): "These dim eyes have in vain explored
for some months past a well-known figure, or part of the figure, of a man, who
used to glide his comely upper half over the pavements of London, wheeling
along with most ingenious celerity upon a machine of wood.... He was a grand
fragment; as good as an Elgin marble."

Now homeward through the thickening hubbub,
    where
See, among less distinguishable shapes,
The begging scavenger, with hat in hand;
The Italian, as he thrids[359] his way with care,
Steadying, far-seen, a frame of images[360]   215
Upon his head; with basket at his breast
The Jew;[361] the stately and slow-moving Turk,
With freight of slippers piled beneath his arm![362]

    Enough;—the mighty concourse I surveyed
With no unthinking mind, well pleased to note   220
Among the crowd all specimens of man,
Through all the colours which the sun bestows,
And every character of form and face:
The Swede, the Russian; from the genial south,
The Frenchman and the Spaniard; from remote   225
America, the Hunter-Indian; Moors,
Malays, Lascars,[363] the Tartar,[364] the Chinese,
And Negro Ladies in white muslin gowns.

    At leisure, then, I viewed, from day to day,
The spectacles within doors,—birds and beasts   230
Of every nature, and strange plants convened

[359] *thrids*: threads.

[360] *images*: devotional images, with a whiff of idolatrous implication.

[361] *Jew*: The Jews had returned to England in 1657, at Oliver Cromwell's invitation, after having been expelled by Edward I in 1290, and civil disabilities had begun to recede by the end of the eighteenth century (Daniel Mendoza [1764–1836] was the world's heavyweight boxing champion 1794–1795, and, in the following generation, Benjamin Disraeli, who was born a Jew, was twice prime minister [1868, 1874–1880]).

[362] *stately and slow-moving Turk ... beneath his arm*: The unthreatening, and even domesticated, presence of the Turk here symbolizes the extent to which London had become a multicultural metropolis.

[363] *Lascars*: Indian sailors.

[364] *Tartar*: Turkic ethnic group associated historically with the Mongol and Turkish invasions of Europe under Genghis Khan in the early thirteenth century. Cf. line 84.

From every clime; and, next, those sights that ape
The absolute presence of reality,
Expressing, as in mirror, sea and land,
And what earth is, and what she has to shew.   235
I do not here allude to subtlest craft,
By means refined attaining purest ends,
But imitations, fondly made in plain
Confession of man's weakness and his loves.
Whether the Painter, whose ambitious skill   240
Submits to nothing less than taking in
A whole horizon's circuit, do with power,[365]
Like that of angels or commissioned spirits,[366]
Fix us upon some lofty pinnacle,[367]
Or in a ship on waters, with a world   245
Of life, and life-like mockery beneath,
Above, behind, far stretching and before;
Or more mechanic artist represent
By scale exact, in model, wood or clay,
From blended colours also borrowing help,   250
Some miniature of famous spots or things,—
St. Peter's Church; or, more aspiring aim,
In microscopic vision, Rome herself;
Or, haply,[368] some choice rural haunt,—the Falls
Of Tivoli;[369] and, high upon that steep,   255

---

[365] *Painter . . . do with power*: In 1802, the painter Thomas Girtin (1775–1802) produced his celebrated "Eidometropolis", a panorama of London 18 ft. high and over 100 ft. in circumference. Wordsworth was in London when it was on display that year and most likely saw it.

[366] *commissioned spirits*: spirits summoned with authority.

[367] *Fix us upon some lofty pinnacle*: Cf. Matthew 4:1, 5: "Then Jesus was led up by the Spirit . . . to be tempted by the devil. . . . Then the devil took him to the holy city, and set him on the pinnacle of the temple".

[368] *haply*: perchance.

[369] *Tivoli*: ancient Italian (originally Etruscan) town near Rome, known in classical times as Tibur; it was the seat of an important Sybil (oracle) of Apollo, with a temple. Tibur features in Virgil's *Aeneid* and the poetry of Catullus, Statius, and Horace, the last of which had a villa there, as did the emperors Augustus and Hadrian. The sixteenth-century Villa d'Este in Tivoli has one of the most famous, spectacular, and elaborate fountains in the world—celebrated by Franz Liszt (1811–1886) in "Les jeux d'eaux à la Villa d'Este" (*Années de pèlerinage*).

The Sibyl's mouldering Temple! every tree,
Villa, or cottage, lurking among rocks
Throughout the landscape; tuft, stone scratch minute—
All that the traveller sees when he is there.

       Add to these exhibitions, mute and still,   260
Others of wider scope, where living men,
Music, and shifting pantomimic scenes,
Diversified the allurement. Need I fear
To mention by its name, as in degree
Lowest of these and humblest in attempt,   265
Yet richly graced with honours of her own,
Half-rural Sadler's Wells?[370] Though at that time
Intolerant, as is the way of youth
Unless itself be pleased, here more than once
Taking my seat, I saw (nor blush to add,   270
With ample recompense) giants and dwarfs,
Clowns, conjurors, posture-masters, harlequins,[371]
Amid the uproar of the rabblement,
Perform their feats. Nor was it mean delight
To watch crude Nature work in untaught minds;   275
To note the laws and progress of belief;
Though obstinate on this way, yet on that
How willingly we travel, and how far!
To have, for instance, brought upon the scene

[370] *Sadler's Wells*: Famous London theatre in the "half-rural" borough of
Islington, north of the old City. Established in 1683 (and presently in its sixth
building), Saddler's Wells was known in Wordsworth's day for its variety of enter-
tainment, from opera to spectacle, from serious drama featuring artists such as the
great Edmund Kean (1789–1833) to pantomime featuring Grimaldi. The theatre
was also notorious at the time for the riotous drunkenness of its clientele.

[371] *Clowns, conjurors, posture-masters, harlequins*: There can be no doubt that
Wordsworth is describing Joseph Grimaldi (1778–1837), the most famous of
English clowns in a theatrical line that extends through Dan Leno (1860–1904)
to Charlie Chaplin (1889–1977). He was the creator of the modern clown;
he recast the clown as the anarchic center of the *Commedia dell'arte*–derived
Harlequinade; he introduced audience participation and the Pantomime Dame;
he is the key figure linking older theatrical traditions with the development of the
Music Hall. His *Memoirs* (still in print) were edited by Dickens.

The champion, Jack the Giant-killer:[372] Lo!   280
He dons his coat of darkness; on the stage
Walks, and achieves his wonders from the eye
Of living Mortal covert, as the moon
Hid in her "vacant interlunar cave".
Delusion bold! and how can it be wrought?   285
The garb he wears is black as death, the word
"*Invisible*" flames forth upon his chest.

Book Tenth (1850)

RESIDENCE IN FRANCE—CONTINUED

The Tenth Book begins late in October 1792. The import-
ant Battle of Valmy had been fought only a month before,
and Wordsworth has just left his pregnant lover, Annette
Vallon, in Orléans (see the note to line 2 of "Tintern Abbey").
Wordsworth assumes the reader's familiarity with the follow-
ing sequence of political events closely preceding or following
the beginning of the narrative.

On June 21, 1791, King Louis XVI (1754–1793)—de facto
a prisoner in the Tuileries Palace (Paris), denied access to
Catholic confessors, in despair over the political situation and
fearing for his safety and that of his wife and children—fled
with his family in the middle of the night, hoping to reach the
Royalist fortified town of Montmédy in northeastern France,
on the border of the Austrian Netherlands (Belgium). They
narrowly failed; arrested at Varennes, they were brought back
to the Tuileries on June 25 and placed under house arrest.

On August 27, Leopold II of Austria, the Holy Roman
Emperor (Marie Antoinette's brother), and Frederick William
II, king of Prussia, issued the Declaration of Pillnitz (see line

---

[372] *Jack the Giant-killer*: "Jack the Giant-killer" is an English fairy tale set in the
days of King Arthur. The eponymous hero is equipped with a Sword of Sharpness,
Boots of Speed, a Cap of Knowledge, and a Cloak of Darkness (which renders
him invisible).

36), threatening France with serious consequences should Louis and his family be molested. The agitation this provoked led to the declaration of war against the Holy Roman Empire by France's Legislative Assembly (with the imprisoned Louis' reluctant assent) on April 20, 1792. France then unsuccessfully attempted to invade the Austrian Netherlands (Belgium).

Meanwhile, a combined army of Prussians, Austrians, Hessians, and French émigrés (see line 36) was mustering at Koblenz (see line 12), on the Rhine, under the command of Charles William Ferdinand, duke of Brunswick (1735–1806). On July 25, Brunswick issued the Brunswick Manifesto, threatening the citizens of Paris with reprisals should the French royal family be harmed.

This fanned the flames of Republicanism; on August 10, a Parisian mob, backed by the Commune (the revolutionary municipal government of Paris), attempted to storm the Tuileries (see lines 53–54). The king took refuge, with the royal family, in the Legislative Assembly, and subsequently ordered the six hundred loyal Swiss Guards to lay down their arms; they complied and were massacred (see lines 41–43, 55–57). On August 13, the king was arrested (see lines 11–12) and imprisoned in the Temple (a medieval Parisian prison; see lines 51–53).

On August 19, Brunswick's Allied army crossed into French territory, quickly taking Longwy and Verdun. September 2–8, mobs slaughtered over twelve hundred imprisoned people—including children—fewer than one hundred of them aristocrats. These massacres (see lines 41–43, 73) were often of a bestial savagery and included cases of cannibalism. On September 20, Brunswick and his forces were halted by the French at the indecisive Battle of Valmy, and withdrew from France (see lines 12–16, 36). On September 21, the National Assembly abolished the monarchy and declared France a republic (see lines 40–41).

The king was tried in December and condemned to death (by 361 votes to 360) on January 15, 1793. He was executed in the Place de la Révolution (formerly, Place Louis XV; present day, Place de la Concorde).

It was a beautiful and silent day
That overspread the countenance of earth,
Then fading with unusual quietness,—
A day as beautiful as e'er was given
To soothe regret, though deepening what it soothed,   5
When by the gliding Loire[373] I paused, and cast
Upon his rich domains, vineyard and tilth,[374]
Green meadow-ground, and many-coloured woods,
Again, and yet again, a farewell look;
Then from the quiet of that scene passed on,   10
Bound to the fierce Metropolis.[375] From his throne
The King had fallen, and that invading host[376]—
Presumptuous cloud, on whose black front[377] was written
The tender mercies of the dismal wind
That bore it—on the plains of Liberty   15
Had burst innocuous. Say in bolder words,
They—who had come elate as eastern hunters
Banded beneath the Great Mogul,[378] when he

---

[373] *Loire*: the longest river in France, and a major artery of commercial navigation until the coming of the railways. It runs from the Cévennes mountains in south-central France, through Orléans, Tours, and Nantes, reaching the Atlantic at Saint-Nazaire. It forms the northern border of the Vendée. It is famous for its vineyards and beautiful chateaux.

[374] *tilth*: tilled earth.

[375] *fierce Metropolis*: revolutionary Paris.

[376] *host*: army.

[377] *black front*: possibly evoking the dark blue and black uniforms characteristic of the Prussians, and the black eagle of their flag.

[378] *Great Mogul*: the Mughal emperor; the (Muslim) Mughal Empire was the dominant power in the Indian subcontinent between about 1560 and 1710. It went into decline in the eighteenth century, and the last Mughal emperor was deposed by the British in 1857. Cf. the note to line 84 of *Prelude*, bk. 7. The Great Mogul is here perhaps a conflation of Austria, Russia, and Prussia—two of them eastern (European), two of them governed by emperors, two of them at Valmy, all of them monarchies ruled by "potentates" and enemies of revolutionary France.

Erewhile went forth from Agra[379] or Lahore,[380]
Rajahs[381] and Omrahs[382] in his train, intent   20
To drive their prey enclosed within a ring
Wide as a province, but, the signal given,
Before the point of the life-threatening spear
Narrowing itself by moments—they, rash men,
Had seen the anticipated quarry turned   25
Into avengers, from whose wrath they fled
In terror.[383] Disappointment and dismay
Remained for all whose fancies had run wild
With evil expectations; confidence
And perfect triumph for the better cause.   30

    The State, as if to stamp the final seal
On her security, and to the world
Show what she was, a high and fearless soul,
Exulting in defiance, or heart-stung
By sharp resentment, or belike to taunt   35
With spiteful gratitude the baffled League,
That had stirred up her slackening faculties
To a new transition, when the King was crushed,
Spared not the empty throne, and in proud haste
Assumed the body and venerable name   40
Of a Republic. Lamentable crimes,
'Tis true, had gone before this hour, dire work
Of massacre, in which the senseless sword
Was prayed to as a judge; but these were past,
Earth free from them for ever, as was thought,—   45
Ephemeral monsters, to be seen but once;
Things that could only show themselves and die.

---

[379] *Agra*: Indian city; sometime capital of the Mughal emperors. It is the site of the most important fort in India and the Taj Mahal.

[380] *Lahore*: city in Pakistan; sometime capital of the Mughal emperors.

[381] *Rajahs*: Indian kings, princes, noblemen.

[382] *Omrahs*: grandees of the Great Mogul's court.

[383] *They—who had come elate . . . In terror*: The metaphor is of a tiger hunt gone wrong.

Cheered with this hope, to Paris I returned,
And ranged, with ardour heretofore unfelt,
The spacious city,[384] and in progress passed   50
The prison where the unhappy Monarch lay,
Associate with his children and his wife
In bondage; and the palace, lately stormed
With roar of cannon by a furious host.
I crossed the square (an empty area then!)   55
Of the Carrousel,[385] where so late had lain
The dead, upon the dying heaped, and gazed
On this and other spots, as doth a man
Upon a volume whose contents he knows
Are memorable, but from him locked up,   60
Being written in a tongue he cannot read,
So that he questions the mute leaves with pain,
And half upbraids their silence. But that night
I felt most deeply in what world I was,
What ground I trod on, and what air I breathed.   65
High was my room and lonely, near the roof
Of a large mansion or hotel,[386] a lodge
That would have pleased me in more quiet times;
Nor was it wholly without pleasure then.
With unextinguished taper I kept watch,   70
Reading at intervals; the fear gone by
Pressed on me almost like a fear to come.
I thought of those September massacres,
Divided from me by one little month.[387]
Saw them and touched: the rest was conjured up   75
From tragic fictions or true history,
Remembrances and dim admonishments.

---

[384] *spacious city*: Paris was the second-largest city (after London) in the Western world at the time.

[385] *Carrousel*: Place du Carrousel, opposite the Tuileries. The bodies of the Swiss Guards were draped about there following the massacre on August 10, 1792.

[386] *hotel*: "a town mansion" (*Oxford English Dictionary*, s.v. "hotel").

[387] *one little month*: Cf. *Hamlet*, Act 1, scene 2, lines 147–51: "A little month ... O God, a beast that wants discourse of reason / Would have mourned longer!"

The horse is taught his manage,[388] and no star
Of wildest course but treads back his own steps;
For the spent hurricane the air provides   80
As fierce a successor; the tide retreats
But to return out of its hiding-place
In the great deep; all things have second birth;
The earthquake is not satisfied at once;
And in this way I wrought upon myself,   85
Until I seemed to hear a voice that cried,
To the whole city, "Sleep no more."[389] The trance
Fled with the voice to which it had given birth;
But vainly comments of a calmer mind
Promised soft peace and sweet forgetfulness.   90
The place, all hushed and silent as it was,
Appeared unfit for the repose of night,
Defenceless as a wood where tigers roam.

    With early morning towards the Palace-walk
Of Orleans eagerly I turned; as yet   95
The streets were still; not so those long Arcades;[390]
There, 'mid a peal of ill-matched sounds and cries,
That greeted me on entering, I could hear
Shrill voices from the hawkers in the throng,
Bawling, "Denunciation of the Crimes   100
Of Maximilian Robespierre";[391] the hand,

[388] *manage*: paces.

[389] *Sleep no more*: Cf. Shakespeare, *Macbeth*, Act 2, scene 2, lines 33–41:
"Methought I heard a voice cry 'Sleep no more,/Macbeth does murder sleep'—
the innocent sleep,/... Still it cried 'Sleep no more' to all the house,/'Glamis
hath murdered sleep, and therefore Cawdor/Shall sleep no more, Macbeth shall
sleep no more.'"

[390] *Arcades*: of the Palais-Royal; even then the Arcades were full of shops
(including booksellers) and cafés, a favorite resort of writers and intellectuals.

[391] *Maximilian Robespierre*: Maximilien Robespierre (1758–1794) was a law-
yer and Jacobin of the Extreme Left as well as twice president of the National
Convention and from July 27, 1793, was a member (and soon the dominant mem-
ber) of the Committee of Public Safety, which effectively ruled France during
the Terror (June 1793–July 1794). Robespierre was an incorruptible, idealistic,
narrow-minded fanatic, afflicted with hatreds and maniacal political insecurities.

Prompt as the voice, held forth a printed speech,
The same that had been recently pronounced,
When Robespierre, not ignorant for what mark
Some words of indirect reproof had been   105
Intended, rose in hardihood, and dared
The man who had an ill surmise of him
To bring his charge in openness; whereat,
When a dead pause ensued, and no one stirred,
In silence of all present, from his seat   110
Louvet[392] walked single through the avenue,
And took his station in the Tribune, saying,
"I, Robespierre, accuse thee!" Well is known
The inglorious issue of that charge, and how
He, who had launched the startling thunderbolt,   115
The one bold man, whose voice the attack had sounded,
Was left without a follower to discharge
His perilous duty, and retire lamenting
That Heaven's best aid is wasted upon men
Who to themselves are false.

Initially altogether opposed to the death penalty, he came to be virtually identified with the Terror: "Without terror, virtue is impotent. Terror is nothing other than justice, prompt, severe, inflexible; it is therefore an emanation of virtue; it is not so much a special principle as it is a consequence of the general principle of democracy applied to our country's most urgent needs" (Robespierre, Speech to the Convention, February 5, 1794).

[392] *Louvet*: Jean-Baptiste Louvet de Couvrai (1760–1797) was a French novelist, politician (member of the National Convention), and journalist (editor of *La Sentinelle*). He was a Girondin; the Girondins were Liberals, except in the matter of religious toleration. After an initial phase of supporting the idea of a constitutional monarchy, they had turned into firm Republicans, and it was they who had particularly agitated in favor of declaring war against Austria. However, the September massacres shocked them; they were increasingly marginalized as the tone of the National Convention grew more violent; and they lost control of the Jacobin Club to Robespierre in October. Their leaders were mostly guillotined. The exchange Wordsworth records occurred on October 29, 1792. Louvet later claimed that his failure to bring Robespierre and his associates to justice was owing to the poor support he received from fellow Girondists. However that may be, Robespierre turned the attack to his own account and consolidated his position. With the overthrow of the Girondins (May 29–June 2, 1793) Louvet was obliged to flee Paris and go into hiding. He was recalled to the National Convention after the fall of Robespierre (July 27, 1794).

But these are things   120
Of which I speak, only as they were storm
Or sunshine to my individual mind,
No further. Let me then relate that now—
In some sort seeing with my proper eyes
That Liberty, and Life, and Death would soon   125
To the remotest corners of the land
Lie in the arbitrement[393] of those who ruled
The capital City; what was struggled for,
And by what combatants victory must be won;
The indecision on their part whose aim   130
Seemed best, and the straightforward path of those
Who in attack or in defence were strong
Through their impiety—my inmost soul
Was agitated; yea, I could almost
Have prayed that throughout earth upon all men,   135
By patient exercise of reason made
Worthy of liberty, all spirits filled
With zeal expanding in Truth's holy light,
The gift of tongues might fall,[394] and power arrive
From the four quarters of the winds to do   140
For France, what without help she could not do,
A work of honour; think not that to this
I added, work of safety: from all doubts
Or trepidation for the end of things
Far was I, far as angels are from guilt.   145

Yet did I grieve, nor only grieved, but thought
Of opposition and of remedies:
An insignificant stranger and obscure,
And one, moreover, little graced with power
Of eloquence even in my native speech,   150
And all unfit for tumult or intrigue,

[393] *arbitrement*: absolute control.
[394] *gift of tongues might fall*: as it did on the apostles at Pentecost; cf. Acts 2:1, 4:
"When the day of Pentecost had come ... they were all filled with the Holy Spirit
and began to speak in other tongues".

Yet would I at this time with willing heart
Have undertaken for a cause so great
Service however dangerous. I revolved,[395]
How much the destiny of Man had still[396]   155
Hung upon single persons;[397] that there was,
Transcendent to all local patrimony,
One nature, as there is one sun in heaven;
That objects, even as they are great; thereby
Do come within the reach of humblest eyes;   160
That Man is only weak through his mistrust
And want of hope where evidence divine
Proclaims to him that hope should be most sure;
Nor did the inexperience of my youth
Preclude conviction, that a spirit strong   165
In hope, and trained to noble aspirations,
A spirit thoroughly faithful to itself,
Is for Society's unreasoning herd
A domineering instinct, serves at once
For way and guide, a fluent receptacle   170
That gathers up each petty straggling rill
And vein of water, glad to be rolled on
In safe obedience; that a mind, whose rest
Is where it ought to be, in self-restraint,
In circumspection and simplicity,   175
Falls rarely in entire discomfiture
Below its aim, or meets with, from without,
A treachery that foils it or defeats;
And, lastly, if the means on human will,
Frail human will, dependent should betray   180
Him who too boldly trusted them, I felt
That 'mid the loud distractions of the world
A sovereign voice subsists within the soul,

[395] *I revolved*: i.e., turned over in his mind.
[396] *still*: always.
[397] *Hung upon single persons*: one of the Victorian Sage Thomas Carlyle's central convictions; cf. *Heroes and Hero Worship*; also *The French Revolution*.

Arbiter undisturbed of right and wrong,
Of life and death, in majesty severe   185
Enjoining, as may best promote the aims
Of truth and justice, either sacrifice,
From whatsoever region of our cares
Or our infirm affections Nature pleads,
Earnest and blind, against the stern decree.[398]   190

     On the other side, I called to mind those truths
That are the common-places of the schools—
(A theme for boys, too hackneyed for their sires),
Yet, with a revelation's liveliness,
In all their comprehensive bearings known   195
And visible to philosophers of old,
Men who, to business of the world untrained,
Lived in the shade; and to Harmodius known
And his compeer Aristogiton,[399] known
To Brutus[400]—that tyrannic power is weak,   200
Hath neither gratitude, nor faith, nor love,
Nor the support of good or evil men
To trust in; that the godhead which is ours

---

[398] *And, lastly, if the means on human will . . . stern decree*: Cf. John Henry Newman (1801–1890), *Apologia pro Vita Sua*: "I am a Catholic by virtue of my believing in a God; and if I am asked why I believe in a God, I answer that it is because I believe in myself, for I feel it impossible to believe in my own existence (and of that fact I am quite sure) without believing also in the existence of Him, who lives as a Personal, All-seeing, All-judging Being in my conscience", and, "I look out of myself into the world of men, and there I see a sight which fills me with unspeakable distress.... Were it not for this voice, speaking so clearly in my conscience and my heart, I should be an atheist, or a pantheist, or a polytheist when I looked into the world. I am speaking for myself only.... The sight of the world is nothing else than the prophet's scroll, full of 'lamentations, and mourning, and woe.'" ([London: J. M. Dent, 1993], pp. 241, 275–76).

[399] *Harmodius . . . Aristogiton*: Harmodius and Aristogiton were Athenian tyrannicides; they were revered as champions of liberty and democracy for assassinating the tyrant Hipparchus in 514 B.C., for which both were put to death.

[400] *Brutus*: Marcus Junius Brutus (85–42 B.C.), Roman politician. His leading role in the assassination of his friend Julius Caesar in 44 B.C., in a failed effort to preserve the Republic, has made him history's most famous tyrannicide.

Can never utterly be charmed or stilled;
That nothing hath a natural right to last   205
But equity and reason; that all else
Meets foes irreconcilable, and at best
Lives only by variety of disease.

      Well might my wishes be intense, my thoughts
Strong and perturbed, not doubting at that time   210
But that the virtue of one paramount mind
Would have abashed those impious crests[401]—have quelled
Outrage and bloody power, and, in despite
Of what the People long had been and were
Through ignorance and false teaching, sadder proof   215
Of immaturity, and in the teeth
Of desperate opposition from without—
Have cleared a passage for just government,
And left a solid birthright to the State,
Redeemed, according to example given   220
By ancient lawgivers.
                    In this frame of mind,
Dragged by a chain of harsh necessity,
So seemed it,—now I thankfully acknowledge,
Forced by the gracious providence of Heaven,—
To England I returned,[402] else (though assured   225
That I both was and must be of small weight,
No better than a landsman on the deck
Of a ship struggling with a hideous storm)
Doubtless, I should have then made common cause
With some who perished; haply perished too,   230
A poor mistaken and bewildered offering,—
Should to the breast of Nature have gone back,

---

[401] *crests*: A crest is a heraldic "figure or device (orig. borne by a knight on his helmet) placed on a ... coronet, or chapeau, and borne above the shield and helmet in a coat of arms; also used separately, as a cognizance, upon seals, plate, note-paper" (*Oxford English Dictionary*, s.v. "crest"); plume on a helmet; symbol of pride; elevated ridge (of a mountain, etc.).

[402] *returned*: late November/early December 1792.

With all my resolutions, all my hopes,
A Poet only to myself, to men
Useless, and even, beloved Friend! a soul   235
To thee unknown![403]
               Twice had the trees let fall
Their leaves, as often Winter had put on
His hoary crown, since I had seen the surge
Beat against Albion's[404] shore, since ear of mine
Had caught the accents of my native speech   240
Upon our native country's sacred ground.
A patriot of the world, how could I glide
Into communion with her sylvan shades,
Erewhile my tuneful haunt? It pleased me more
To abide in the great City, where I found   245
The general air still busy with the stir
Of that first memorable onset made
By a strong levy of humanity
Upon the traffickers in Negro blood;[405]
Effort which, though defeated,[406] had recalled   250
To notice old forgotten principles,
And through the nation spread a novel heat
Of virtuous feeling. For myself, I own
That this particular strife had wanted power
To *rivet* my affections; nor did now   255
Its unsuccessful issue much excite
My sorrow; for I brought with me the faith
That, if France prospered, good men would not long
Pay fruitless worship to humanity,
And this most rotten branch of human shame,[407]   260

---

[403] *beloved Friend ... To thee unknown*: Wordsworth first made Coleridge's acquaintance in August 1795.

[404] *Albion's*: Great Britain's; England's.

[405] *that first memorable onset ... Negro blood*: See introductory note to Blake's "The Little Black Boy", p. 25.

[406] *traffickers in Negro blood ... defeated*: Motions to abolish the Slave Trade were narrowly defeated in Parliament on April 2, 1792, and February 26, 1793.

[407] *this most rotten branch of human shame*: i.e., slavery.

Object, so seemed it, of superfluous pains,
Would fall together with its parent tree.
What, then, were my emotions, when in arms
Britain put forth her free-born strength in league,
Oh, pity and shame! with those confederate Powers![408]   265
Not in my single self alone I found,
But in the minds of all ingenuous[409] youth,
Change and subversion from that hour. No shock
Given to my moral nature had I known
Down to that very moment; neither lapse   270
Nor turn of sentiment that might be named
A revolution, save at this one time;
All else was progress on the self-same path
On which, with a diversity of pace,
I had been travelling: this a stride at once   275
Into another region. As a light
And pliant harebell, swinging in the breeze
On some grey rock—its birth-place—so had I
Wantoned,[410] fast rooted on the ancient tower
Of my beloved country, wishing not   280
A happier fortune than to wither there:
Now was I from that pleasant station torn
And tossed about in whirlwind. I rejoiced,
Yea, afterwards—truth most painful to record!—
Exulted, in the triumph of my soul,   285
When Englishmen by thousands were o'erthrown,
Left without glory on the field, or driven,
Brave hearts! to shameful flight. It was a grief,—
Grief call it not, 'twas anything but that,—
A conflict of sensations without name,   290
Of which *he* only, who may love the sight
Of a village steeple, as I do, can judge,

---

[408] *those confederate Powers*: This already included the Holy Roman Empire, Prussia, and the Austrian Netherlands (Belgium). France declared war on Spain on March 7, 1793, and the Vendée rose up on March 11.

[409] *ingenuous*: freeborn; high-minded, magnanimous.

[410] *Wantoned*: frolicked.

When, in the congregation bending all
To their great Father, prayers were offered up,
Or praises for our country's victories;   295
And, 'mid the simple worshippers, perchance
I only, like an uninvited guest
Whom no one owned,[411] sate silent, shall I add,
Fed on the day of vengeance yet to come.

    Oh! much have they to account for, who
        could tear,   300
By violence, at one decisive rent,
From the best youth in England their dear pride,
Their joy, in England; this, too, at a time
In which worst losses easily might wear
The best of names, when patriotic love   305
Did of itself in modesty give way,
Like the Precursor[412] when the Deity
Is come Whose harbinger he was; a time
In which apostasy from ancient faith
Seemed but conversion to a higher creed;   310
Withal[413] a season dangerous and wild,
A time when sage Experience would have snatched
Flowers out of any hedge-row to compose
A chaplet in contempt[414] of his grey locks.

    When the proud fleet that bears the
        red-cross flag[415]   315
In that unworthy service was prepared
To mingle, I beheld the vessels lie,
A brood of gallant creatures, on the deep;

[411] *owned*: knew, claimed to know.

[412] *Precursor*: St. John the Baptist; see John 3:28, where he says, "I am not the Christ, but I have been sent before him."

[413] *Withal*: moreover.

[414] *contempt*: travesty.

[415] *fleet that bears the red-cross flag*: the Royal Navy; the flag is that of England, Argent a cross gules (red cross on white).

I saw them in their rest, a sojourner
Through a whole month of calm and glassy days   320
In that delightful island[416] which protects
Their place of convocation—there I heard,
Each evening, pacing by the still sea-shore,
A monitory[417] sound that never failed,—
The sunset cannon. While the orb went down   325
In the tranquillity of nature, came
That voice, ill requiem![418] seldom heard by me
Without a spirit overcast by dark
Imaginations, sense of woes to come,
Sorrow for human kind, and pain of heart.   330

     In France, the men, who, for their desperate ends,
Had plucked up mercy by the roots, were glad
Of this new enemy. Tyrants, strong before
In wicked pleas, were strong as demons now;
And thus, on every side beset with foes,   335
The goaded land waxed mad; the crimes of few
Spread into madness of the many; blasts
From hell came sanctified like airs from heaven.
The sternness of the just, the faith of those
Who doubted not that Providence had times   340
Of vengeful retribution, theirs who throned
The human Understanding paramount
And made of that their God,[419] the hopes of men
Who were content to barter short-lived pangs[420]
For a paradise of ages, the blind rage   345

[416] *that delightful island*: the Isle of Wight. The Royal Navy was preparing for war off Portsmouth.

[417] *monitory*: warning.

[418] *requiem*: Catholic funeral liturgy; its literal meaning (in context) is "Rest [eternal grant unto them, O Lord]".

[419] *made of that their God*: The actress Mlle Aubry played the Goddess Reason and was enthroned in an imitation Greek temple atop a false "mountain" in the nave Notre Dame (renamed the Temple of Reason) on Sunday, November 10, 1793, amid festivities and "worship".

[420] *pangs*: sharp pains.

Of insolent tempers, the light vanity
Of intermeddlers, steady purposes
Of the suspicious, slips of the indiscreet,
And all the accidents of life were pressed
Into one service, busy with one work.   350
The Senate stood aghast, her prudence quenched,
Her wisdom stifled, and her justice scared,
Her frenzy only active to extol
Past outrages, and shape the way for new,
Which no one dared to oppose or mitigate.   355

    Domestic carnage now filled the whole year
With feast-days;[421] old men from the chimney-nook,
The maiden from the bosom of her love,
The mother from the cradle of her babe,
The warrior from the field—all perished, all—   360
Friends, enemies, of all parties, ages, ranks,
Head after head, and never heads enough
For those that bade them fall.[422] They found their joy,
They made it proudly, eager as a child,
(If like desires of innocent little ones   365

[421] *feast-days:* Feast days (including Name Days) are particularly celebrated in Catholic and Eastern Christian countries. The reference also evokes the new Republican calendar, adopted on October 24, 1793 (during the Terror), and still in use when Wordsworth completed the first version of this book in 1804 (it was abolished in 1806 by Napoleon); it had been Robespierre and Saint-Just's intention to fill it full of new feast days (see Saint-Just's fragmentary *Republican Institutes*: "The first day of the month Germinal the republic shall celebrate the festival of the Divinity, of Nature, and of the People; the first day of the month Floreal, the festival of the Divinity, of love, and of husband and wife"). There is also, possibly, an ironic reference to the Saint Bartholomew's Day Massacre of Protestants by French Catholics in 1572, which had long been a stick to beat the Catholic Church with.

[422] *old men from the chimney-nook . . . those that bade them fall:* The casualties of the Terror rose from the 60s monthly in the early phase to 122 in March 1794; 259 in April; 346 in May; 689 in June; and 966 in July. "Less than nine in a hundred of those guillotined in the Terror were of noble birth; about six per cent were clergy. The rest, eighty-five per cent, came from that class of people known as the Third Estate" (Christopher Hibbert, *The Days of the French Revolution* [London: Penguin, 1989], p. 207).

May with such heinous appetites be compared),
Pleased in some open field to exercise
A toy that mimics with revolving wings
The motion of a wind-mill; though the air
Do of itself blow fresh, and make the vanes   370
Spin in his eyesight, *that* contents him not,
But, with the plaything at arm's length, he sets
His front against the blast, and runs amain,[423]
That it may whirl the faster.

            Amid the depth
Of those enormities, even thinking minds   375
Forgot, at seasons, whence they had their being;
Forgot that such a sound was ever heard
As Liberty upon earth: yet all beneath
Her innocent authority was wrought,
Nor could have been, without her blessed name.   380
The illustrious wife of Roland, in the hour
Of her composure, felt that agony,
And gave it vent in her last words.[424] O Friend!
It was a lamentable time for man,
Whether a hope had e'er been his or not;   385
A woful time for them whose hopes survived
The shock; most woful for those few who still
Were flattered, and had trust in human kind:
They had the deepest feeling of the grief.
Meanwhile the Invaders fared as they deserved: 390
The Herculean Commonwealth had put forth her arms,
And throttled with an infant godhead's might
The snakes about her cradle;[425] that was well,

---

[423] *amain*: at full speed.

[424] *wife of Roland . . . her last words*: Marie-Jeanne Roland de la Platière (known as Madame Rolande; 1754–1793), Girondist activist, wife of Girondist leader Jean-Marie Roland de la Platière. She was arrested during the overthrow of the Girondins; she composed her memoirs during her imprisonment and was guillotined on November 8, 1793. On her way to the scaffold, she famously exclaimed, "O Liberty, what crimes are committed in thy name."

[425] *Herculean . . . snakes about her cradle*: Hercules was the illegitimate son of Zeus and Alcmena. Zeus' jealous wife, Hera, sent two snakes to strangle the newborn demigod in his cot, but the little Hercules, already prodigiously strong,

And as it should be; yet no cure for them
Whose souls were sick with pain of what would be   395
Hereafter brought in charge against mankind.
Most melancholy at that time, O Friend!
Were my day-thoughts,—my nights were miserable;
Through months, through years, long after the last beat
Of those atrocities, the hour of sleep   400
To me came rarely charged with natural gifts,
Such ghastly visions had I of despair
And tyranny, and implements of death;
And innocent victims sinking under fear,
And momentary hope, and worn-out prayer,   405
Each in his separate cell, or penned in crowds
For sacrifice, and struggling with fond mirth
And levity in dungeons, where the dust
Was laid with tears. Then suddenly the scene
Changed, and the unbroken dream entangled me   410
In long orations, which I strove to plead
Before unjust tribunals,—with a voice
Labouring, a brain confounded, and a sense,
Death-like, of treacherous desertion, felt
In the last place of refuge—my own soul.   415

        When I began in youth's delightful prime
To yield myself to Nature, when that strong
And holy passion overcame me first,
Nor day nor night, evening or morn, was free
From its oppression. But, O Power Supreme!   420
Without Whose call this world would cease to breathe,
Who from the fountain of Thy grace dost fill
The veins that branch through every frame of life,
Making man what he is, creature divine,
In single or in social eminence,   425
Above the rest raised infinite ascents

---

strangled them, one in either hand. This was the subject of a celebrated painting
of ca. 1788 by Sir Joshua Reynolds, *The Infant Hercules Strangling Serpents in His
Cradle*.

When reason that enables him to be
Is not sequestered—what a change is here!
How different ritual for this after-worship,
What countenance to promote this second love![426]   430
The first was service paid to things which lie
Guarded within the bosom of Thy will.
Therefore to serve was high beatitude;
Tumult was therefore gladness, and the fear
Ennobling, venerable; sleep secure,   435
And waking thoughts more rich than happiest dreams.

But as the ancient Prophets,[427] borne aloft
In vision, yet constrained by natural laws
With them to take a troubled human heart,
Wanted not consolations,[428] nor a creed   440
Of reconcilement, then when they denounced,
On towns and cities, wallowing in the abyss
Of their offences, punishment to come;

[426] *this second love*: i.e., love of man (his first love being love of nature; see line 417).

[427] *But as the ancient Prophets . . . deluge through the land*: These following lines (437–480) rather unexpectedly bear some resemblance to the thought of Joseph de Maistre (1753–1821):

> The problems that preoccupied him were fundamentally the same as those that confronted Job and Jeremiah—the problem of suffering and evil and the justification of the obscure purposes of God in history. The men of the Enlightenment had lived on the surface of life. They had rejected the very idea of mystery and had done their best to eliminate and ignore everything that was irrational and obscure.... The Revolution was not an event ... it was an epoch in the history of humanity.... De Maistre regarded the Revolution as a cleansing fire in which the forces of evil were employed against their will and without their knowledge as agents of purification and regeneration.... "All our plans ... vanish like dreams.... It seems to me that new workers advance in the profound obscurity of the future and that Her Majesty Providence says, 'Behold I make all things new'." (Christopher Dawson, *The Gods of Revolution* [London: Sidgwick and Jackson, 1972], pp. 134–37). Cf. also Coleridge, "Fears in Solitude", line 125)

[428] *Wanted not consolations*: i.e., were not lacking in consolations.

Or saw, like other men, with bodily eyes,
Before them, in some desolated place,   445
The wrath consummate and the threat fulfilled;
So, with devout humility be it said,
So, did a portion of that spirit fall
On me uplifted from the vantage-ground
Of pity and sorrow to a state of being   450
That through the time's exceeding fierceness saw
Glimpses of retribution, terrible,
And in the order of sublime behests:[429]
But, even if that were not, amid the awe
Of unintelligible chastisement,   455
Not only acquiescences of faith
Survived, but daring sympathies with power,
Motions not treacherous or profane, else why
Within the folds of no ungentle breast
Their dread vibration to this hour prolonged?   460
Wild blasts of music thus could find their way
Into the midst of turbulent events;
So that worst tempests might be listened to.
Then was the truth received into my heart,
That, under heaviest sorrow earth can bring,   465
If from the affliction somewhere do not grow
Honour which could not else have been, a faith,
An elevation and a sanctity,
If new strength be not given nor old restored,
The blame is ours, not Nature's.[430] When a taunt   470
Was taken up by scoffers in their pride,
Saying, "Behold the harvest that we reap
From popular government and equality,"
I clearly saw that neither these nor aught
Of wild belief engrafted on their names   475

---

[429] *behests*: commands; cf. *Paradise Lost*, bk. 8, lines 238–39: "For us he [God] sends upon his high behests / For state".

[430] *blame is ours, not Nature's*: Cf. Shakespeare, *Julius Caesar*, Act 1, scene 2, lines 141–42: "The fault, dear Brutus, is not in our stars, / But in ourselves".

By false philosophy had caused the woe,
But a terrific[431] reservoir of guilt
And ignorance filled up[432] from age to age,
That could no longer hold its loathsome charge,
But burst and spread in deluge through the land.   480

            And as the desert hath green spots, the sea
Small islands scattered amid stormy waves,
So *that* disastrous period did not want
Bright sprinklings of all human excellence,
To which the silver wands[433] of saints in Heaven   485
Might point with rapturous joy. Yet not the less,
For those examples in no age surpassed
Of fortitude and energy and love,
And human nature faithful to herself
Under worst trials, was I driven to think   490
Of the glad times when first I traversed France[434]
A youthful pilgrim; above all reviewed
That eventide, when under windows bright
With happy faces and with garlands hung,
And through a rainbow-arch that spanned the street,   495
Triumphal pomp for liberty confirmed,
I paced, a dear companion at my side,
The town of Arras,[435] whence with promise high
Issued, on delegation to sustain
Humanity and right, *that* Robespierre,   500
He who thereafter, and in how short a time!
Wielded the sceptre of the Atheist crew.[436]

---

[431] *terrific*: of great intensity; terrifying.

[432] *filled up*: gathered from many streams.

[433] *silver wands*: scepters; rods symbolic of office.

[434] *traversed France*: This walking tour, which is described in book 6 of *Prelude*, took place between July 10 and mid-October 1790.

[435] *dear companion ... town of Arras*: The companion is his friend Robert Jones. The town is the city of Robespierre, in the Artois region of northern France.

[436] *Atheist crew*: Milton's description of the fallen angels in *Paradise Lost* (bk. 6, line 370). Demons are not atheists, nor was Robespierre, a kind of ecstatic Deist who instituted the Feast of the Supreme Being, purged the Revolution of the

When the calamity spread far and wide—
And this same city, that did then appear
To outrun the rest in exultation, groaned   505
Under the vengeance of her cruel son,
As Lear reproached the winds[437]—I could almost
Have quarrelled with that blameless spectacle
For lingering yet an image in my mind
To mock me under such a strange reverse.   510

O Friend! few happier moments have
been mine
Than that which told the downfall of this Tribe
So dreaded, so abhorred. The day deserves
A separate record. Over the smooth sands
Of Leven's[438] ample estuary lay   515
My journey, and beneath a genial sun,
With distant prospect among gleams of sky
And clouds, and intermingling mountain tops,
In one inseparable glory[439] clad,
Creatures of one ethereal substance met   520

---

fanatically anti-Christian Hébertists, and associated aristocracy with atheism in his rhetoric (e.g., "atheism is aristocratic" [Speech to the Jacobin Club, November 21, 1793]). The point is that the revolutionaries were at war with God's order and the truths they knew (and, in the case of the revolutionaries, preached), such as the universal brotherhood of man. Cf. 1 John 1:6: "If we say we have fellowship with him while we walk in darkness, we lie", and 1 John 2:9: "He who says he is in the light and hates his brother is in darkness still."

[437] *As Lear reproached the winds*: See Shakespeare, *King Lear*, Act 3, scene 2, lines 14–24: "Rumble thy bellyful; spit, fire; spout, rain./Nor rain, wind, thunder, fire are my daughters./I tax not you, you elements with unkindness./I never gave you kingdom, called you children./You owe me no subscription. Then let fall/Your horrible pleasure. Here I stand you slave,/A poor, infirm, weak and despised old man,/But yet I call you servile ministers,/that will with two pernicious daughters join/Your high-engendered battles 'gainst a head/So old and white as this. O, ho, 'tis foul!"

[438] *Leven's*: The Leven is a river running from Lake Windermere, in the Lake District, to Morecambe Bay, the largest stretch of intertidal mudflats and sand in Britain.

[439] *glory*: halo.

In consistory,[440] like a diadem
Or crown of burning seraphs as they sit[441]
In the empyrean.[442] Underneath that pomp
Celestial, lay unseen the pastoral vales
Among whose happy fields I had grown up   525
From childhood. On the fulgent[443] spectacle,
That neither passed away nor changed, I gazed
Enrapt; but brightest things are wont to draw
Sad opposites out of the inner heart,
As now their pensive influence drew from mine.   530
How could it otherwise? for not in vain
That very morning had I turned aside
To seek the ground where, 'mid a throng of graves,
An honoured teacher of my youth was laid,[444]
And on the stone were graven by his desire   535
Lines from the churchyard elegy of Gray.[445]
This faithful guide, speaking from his death-bed,
Added no farewell to his parting counsel,
But said to me, "My head will soon lie low";
And when I saw the turf that covered him,   540

[440] *consistory*: council; court. Cf. Milton, *Paradise Regained*, bk. 1, lines 40–42: "To council summons all his mighty peers,/Within thick clouds and dark tenfold involved,/A gloomy consistory".

[441] *burning seraphs as they sit*: Cf. Milton, "At a Solemn Music", line 10: "Where the bright Seraphim in burning row".

[442] *empyrean*: highest Heaven. Cf. *Paradise Lost*, bk. 3, lines 56–58: "Now had the Almighty Father from above,/From the pure empyrean where he sits/High throned above all highth".

[443] *fulgent*: resplendent, shining brightly, glittering. Cf. *Paradise Lost*, bk. 10, lines 449–50: "At last as from a cloud his fulgent head/And shape star-bright appeared".

[444] *honoured teacher of my youth was laid*: The Reverend William Taylor (1754–1786), headmaster of Hawkshead Grammar School, was buried in the churchyard of Cartmel Priory, Cumbria.

[445] *Lines from the churchyard elegy of Gray*: Thomas Gray's "Elegy Written in a Country Churchyard", one of the greatest, and most popular, poems of the eighteenth century. Following are the lines (somewhat modified from Gray's last stanza) on Taylor's gravestone: "His merits, stranger, seek not to disclose,/Or draw his frailties from their dread abode/(There they alike in trembling hope repose),/The bosom of his Father and his God."

After the lapse of full eight years, those words,
With sound of voice and countenance of the Man,
Came back upon me, so that some few tears
Fell from me in my own despite. But now
I thought, still traversing that widespread plain, 545
With tender pleasure of the verses graven
Upon his tombstone, whispering to myself:
He loved the Poets, and, if now alive,
Would have loved me, as one not destitute
Of promise, nor belying the kind hope 550
That he had formed, when I, at his command,
Began to spin, with toil, my earliest songs.

As I advanced, all that I saw or felt
Was gentleness and peace. Upon a small
And rocky island near, a fragment stood 555
(Itself like a sea rock) the low remains
(With shells encrusted, dark with briny weeds)
Of a dilapidated structure, once
A Romish[446] chapel, where the vested priest[447]
Said matins[448] at the hour that suited those 560
Who crossed the sands with ebb of morning tide.
Not far from that still ruin all the plain
Lay spotted with a variegated crowd
Of vehicles and travellers, horse and foot,
Wading beneath the conduct of their guide 565
In loose procession through the shallow stream
Of inland waters; the great sea meanwhile
Heaved at safe distance, far retired. I paused,
Longing for skill to paint a scene so bright

[446] *Romish*: Roman Catholic; the term is derogatory, but was very widespread.

[447] *vested priest*: Catholic and quasi-Catholic vestments were not used (and for some time not even legal) in the Church of England until the later nineteenth century.

[448] *Said matins*: See the note to line 45 of book 1 of *Prelude*. Here the reference is to the Catholic liturgy, in which Matins would have been celebrated in the small hours.

And cheerful, but the foremost of the band   570
As he approached, no salutation given,
In the familiar language of the day,
Cried, "Robespierre is dead!"—nor was a doubt,
After strict question, left within my mind
That he and his supporters all were fallen.[449]   575

          Great was my transport, deep my gratitude
To everlasting Justice, by this fiat
Made manifest. "Come now, ye golden times,"
Said I forth-pouring on those open sands
A hymn of triumph: "as the morning comes   580
From out the bosom of the night, come ye:
Thus far our trust is verified; behold!
They who with clumsy desperation brought
A river of Blood, and preached that nothing else
Could cleanse the Augean stable,[450] by the might   585
Of their own helper[451] have been swept away;
Their madness stands declared and visible;
Elsewhere will safety now be sought, and earth
March firmly towards righteousness and peace."—

---

[449] *"Robespierre is dead!" . . . he and his supporters all were fallen*: The tide turned suddenly against Robespierre, who had long overplayed his hand, and suddenly underplayed it, blackly threatening a new purge in his speech of July 26 (8th Thermidor), 1794, but disastrously (for him) failing to name suspects; the combination of accumulated political enmities and renewed fear led, with the brief security afforded by the anonymity of Robespierre's threats, to swift reprisal. He was shouted down and arrested in the Convention the next day, but no prison could be found to take him. In the ensuing power struggle between the forces of the Convention and those of the Robespierrist Commune, Robespierre, who had joined his supporters in Paris' City Hall, was shot in the face in a confrontation with the Convention's troops. Still alive, he was brought before the Revolutionary Tribunal and condemned to death without a trial. He was executed the same day, along with Saint-Just, Couthon, and Hanriot, among others.

[450] *cleanse the Augean stable*: The Fifth Labor of Hercules was to clean the stables of Augeas, king of Elis, in one day; these stables housed enormous herds of cattle and had not been cleaned in thirty years; Hercules washed the accumulated filth away by diverting the river Alpheus.

[451] *their own helper*: either the guillotine or the river of blood released in the Terror.

Then schemes I framed more calmly, when and how   590
The madding[452] factions might be tranquillised,
And how through hardships manifold and long
The glorious renovation would proceed.
Thus interrupted by uneasy bursts
Of exultation, I pursued my way   595
Along that very shore which I had skimmed
In former days, when—spurring from the Vale
Of Nightshade,[453] and St. Mary's[454] mouldering[455] fane,[456]
And the stone abbot,[457] after circuit made
In wantonness of heart, a joyous band   600
Of school-boys hastening to their distant home
Along the margin of the moonlight sea—
We beat with thundering hoofs the level sand.

Book Eleventh (1805)

IMAGINATION, HOW IMPAIRED AND RESTORED

There are in our existence spots of time,[458]
Which with distinct preeminence retain
A renovating virtue, whence, depressed
By false opinion and contentious thought,   260
Or aught of heavier or more deadly weight
In trivial occupations and the round
Of ordinary intercourse, our minds

---

[452] *madding*: frenzied; lunatic. Cf. Gray's "Elegy", lines 73–74: "Far from the madding crowd's ignoble strife,/Their sober wishes never learned to stray".

[453] *Vale/Of Nightshade*: Deadly nightshade once grew so thickly about Furness Abbey (near Barrow-in-Furness, Cumbria) that the area came to be known as the Valley of Nightshade.

[454] *St. Mary's*: the ruins of the former Cistercian abbey, St. Mary of Furness, better known as Furness Abbey.

[455] *mouldering*: crumbling away.

[456] *fane*: temple; church.

[457] *stone abbot*: the stone effigy of a former abbot, now preserved in the site's visitor center.

[458] *spots of time*: He will relate two instances: the first (from line 278), involving the gibbet; the second (from line 344), involving the pitcher-bearing woman.

Are nourished and invisibly repaired—
A virtue by which pleasure is enhanced,   265
That penetrates, enables us to mount
When high, more high, and lifts us up when fallen.
This efficacious spirit chiefly lurks
Among those passages of life in which
We have had deepest feeling that the mind   270
Is lord and master, and that outward sense
Is but the obedient servant of her will.
Such moments, worthy of all gratitude,
Are scattered everywhere, taking their date
From our first childhood—in our childhood even   275
Perhaps are most conspicuous. Life with me,
As far as memory can look back, is full
Of this beneficent influence.

                      At a time
When scarcely (I was then not six years old)
My hand could hold a bridle, with proud hopes   280
I mounted, and we rode towards the hills:
We were a pair of horsemen—honest James
Was with me, my encourager and guide.
We had not travelled long ere some mischance
Disjoined me from my comrade, and, through fear   285
Dismounting, down the rough and stony moor
I led my horse, and stumbling on, at length
Came to a bottom where in former times
A murderer had been hung in iron chains.
The gibbet-mast[459] was mouldered down, the bones   290
And iron case were gone, but on the turf
Hard by, soon after that fell[460] deed was wrought,
Some unknown hand had carved the murderer's name.
The monumental[461] writing was engraven

---

[459] *gibbet-mast*: The gibbet was a gallows-like structure from which criminals
(usually already dead) were suspended in chains, iron bands, or a cage, often to
rot, as a public warning. It was abolished in Britain in 1834.
[460] *fell*: dreadful; cruel.
[461] *monumental*: pertaining to a monument.

In times long past, and still from year to year   295
By superstition of the neighbourhood
The grass is cleared away; and to this hour
The letters are all fresh and visible.
Faltering, and ignorant where I was, at length
I chanced to espy those characters inscribed   300
On the green sod: Forthwith I left the spot
And reascending the bare common saw
A naked pool that lay beneath the hills,
The beacon on the summit, and more near,
A girl who bore a pitcher on her head   305
And seemed with difficult steps to force her way
Against the blowing wind. It was, in truth,
An ordinary sight, but I should need
Colours and words that are unknown to man
To paint the visionary dreariness   310
Which, while I looked all round for my lost guide,
Did at that time invest the naked pool,
The beacon on the lonely eminence,
The woman, and her garments vexed and tossed
By the strong wind. When, in blessèd season,   315
With those two dear ones—to my heart so dear—
When in the blessèd time of early love,
Long afterwards I roamed about
In daily presence of this very scene,
Upon the naked pool and dreary crags,   320
And on the melancholy beacon, fell
The spirit of pleasure and youth's golden gleam[462]—
And think ye not with radiance more divine
From these remembrances, and from the power
They left behind? So feeling comes in aid   325
Of feeling, and diversity of strength
Attends us, if but once we have been strong.

---

[462] *golden gleam*: Cf. "Tintern Abbey", line 148; "Intimations of Immortality",
line 56; *Prelude*, bk. 2, line 368, bk. 11, line 322; "Elegiac Stanzas", line 14;
Tennyson, "Merlin and the Gleam".

Oh mystery of man, from what a depth
Proceed thy honours! I am lost, but see
In simple childhood something of the base 330
On which thy greatness stands—but this I feel,
That from thyself it is that thou must give,
Else never canst receive. The days gone by
Come back upon me from the dawn almost
Of life; the hiding-places of my power 335
Seem open, I approach, and then they close;
I see by glimpses now, when age comes on
May scarcely see at all; and I would give
While yet we may, as far as words can give,
A substance and a life to what I feel: 340
I would enshrine the spirit of the past
For future restoration. Yet another
Of these to me affecting incidents,
With which we will conclude.

               One Christmas-time,
The day before the holidays began, 345
Feverish, and tired, and restless, I went forth
Into the fields, impatient for the sight
Of those two horses which should bear us home,
My brothers[463] and myself. There was a crag,
An eminence, which from the meeting-point 350
Of two highways ascending overlooked
At least a long half-mile of those two roads,
By each of which the expected steeds might come—
The choice uncertain. Thither I repaired
Up to the highest summit. 'Twas a day 355
Stormy, and rough, and wild, and on the grass
I sate half sheltered by a naked wall.
Upon my right hand was a single sheep,
A whistling hawthorn on my left, and there,
With those companions at my side, I watched, 360
Straining my eyes intensely as the mist

---

[463] *My brothers*: Richard (1768–1816) and John (1772–1805).

Gave intermitting prospect of the wood
And plain beneath. Ere I to school returned
That dreary time, ere I had been ten days
A dweller in my father's house, he died,   365
And I and my two brothers orphans then[464]
Followed his body to the grave. The event,
With all the sorrow which it brought, appeared
A chastisement; and when I called to mind
That day so lately past, when from the crag   370
I looked in such anxiety of hope,
With trite[465] reflections of morality,
Yet in the deepest passion, I bowed low
To God who thus corrected my desires.
And afterwards the wind and sleety rain,   375
And all the business of the elements,
The single sheep, and the one blasted tree,
And the bleak music of that old stone wall,
The noise of wood and water, and the mist
Which on the line of each of those two roads   380
Advanced in such indisputable shapes—
All these were spectacles and sounds to which
I often would repair,[466] and thence would drink
As at a fountain. And I do not doubt
That in this later time, when storm and rain   385
Beat on my roof at midnight, or by day
When I am in the woods, unknown to me
The workings of my spirit thence are brought.

Thou wilt not languish here, O friend,[467] for whom
I travel in these dim uncertain ways—   390
Thou wilt assist me as a pilgrim gone
In quest of highest truth. Behold me then

---

[464] *I and my two brothers orphans then*: Wordsworth's mother died in March 1778; his father on December 30, 1783.
[465] *trite*: worn; hackneyed.
[466] *I often would repair*: i.e., betake oneself.
[467] *friend*: Coleridge.

Once more in nature's presence, thus restored
Or otherwise, and strengthened once again
(With memory left of what had been escaped)   395
To habits of devoutest sympathy.

The Solitary Reaper[468]

Behold her, single in the field,
Yon solitary Highland Lass!
Reaping, and singing by herself;
Stop here, or gently pass!
Alone she cuts and binds the grain,   5
And sings a melancholy strain;
O listen! for the Vale profound
Is overflowing with the sound.

No Nightingale[469] did ever chaunt[470]
More welcome notes to weary bands   10
Of Travellers in some shady haunt,
Among Arabian Sands:[471]
A voice so thrilling ne'er was heard
In spring-time from the Cuckoo-bird,
Breaking the silence of the seas[472]   15
Among the farthest Hebrides.

Will no one tell me what she sings?[473]—
Perhaps the plaintive numbers[474] flow

---

[468] Published in *Poems, in Two Volumes*, 1807.

[469] *Nightingale*: Cf. Coleridge, "The Nightingale", lines 12–13.

[470] *chaunt*: chant.

[471] *weary bands . . . Arabian sands*: These lines (cf. also "The Virgin", lines 6–7) reflect the relatively recent influence of Orientalism; Sir William Jones (1746–1794) had translated Hafiz in 1771.

[472] *Breaking the silence of the seas*: Cf. Coleridge, "Ancient Mariner", lines 109–10.

[473] *Will no one tell me what she sings*: She is a Scottish Gaelic speaker.

[474] *plaintive numbers*: verses; poetic harmony or measure; metrics.

For old, unhappy, far-off things,
And battles long ago: 20
Or is it some more humble lay,[475]
Familiar matter of to-day?
Some natural sorrow, loss, or pain,
That has been, and may be again?

Whate'er the theme, the Maiden sang 25
As if her song could have no ending;
I saw her singing at her work,
And o'er the sickle bending;
I listened, motionless and still;
And, as I mounted up the hill, 30
The music in my heart I bore,
Long after it was heard no more.

Elegiac Stanzas[476]

SUGGESTED BY A PICTURE OF PEELE CASTLE, IN A STORM,
PAINTED BY SIR GEORGE BEAUMONT[477]

I was thy Neighbour once, thou rugged Pile![478]
Four summer weeks I dwelt in sight of thee:
I saw thee every day; and all the while
Thy Form was sleeping on a glassy sea.

So pure the sky, so quiet was the air! 5
So like, so very like, was day to day!

---

[475] *lay*: song; narrative song.

[476] Published in *Poems, in Two Volumes*, 1807.

[477] Wordsworth was deeply shaken and permanently affected by the drowning of his younger brother, John, in the shipwreck of *The Earl of Abergavenny* off the coast of Dorset on February 5, 1805. This poem marks a turning point in Wordsworth's confidence in the beneficence of Nature. Peele (Piel) Castle is a largely ruined medieval castle on Piel Island, about one half mile off the Furness Peninsula, Cumbria. Sir John Beaumont (1753–1827) was a painter, patron, and friend of Wordsworth's.

[478] *rugged Pile*: large building.

Whene'er I looked, thy Image still was there;
It trembled, but it never passed away.

How perfect was the calm! It seemed no sleep;
No mood, which season takes away, or brings: 10
I could have fancied that the mighty Deep
Was even the gentlest of all gentle Things.

Ah! THEN, if mine had been the Painter's hand,
To express what then I saw; and add the gleam,[479]
The light that never was, on sea or land,   15
The consecration, and the Poet's dream;

I would have planted thee, thou hoary Pile!
Amid a world how different from this!
Beside a sea that could not cease to smile;
On tranquil land, beneath a sky of bliss: 20

Thou shouldst have seemed a treasure-house, a mine
Of peaceful years; a chronicle of heaven:—
Of all the sunbeams that did ever shine
The very sweetest had to thee been given.

A Picture had it been of lasting ease,   25
Elysian quiet, without toil or strife;
No motion but the moving tide, a breeze,
Or merely silent Nature's breathing life.

Such, in the fond delusion of my heart,
Such Picture would I at that time have made: 30
And seen the soul of truth in every part;
A faith, a trust, that could not be betrayed.

[479] *gleam*: Cf. "Tintern Abbey", line 148; "Intimations of Immortality", line 56; *Prelude*, bk. 2, line 368, bk. 11, line 322; Tennyson, "Merlin and the Gleam".

So once it would have been,—'tis so no more;
I have submitted to a new controul:
A power is gone, which nothing can restore;   35
A deep distress hath humanized my Soul.

Not for a moment could I now behold
A smiling sea and be what I have been:
The feeling of my loss will ne'er be old;
This, which I know, I speak with mind serene.   40

Then, Beaumont, Friend! who would have been the Friend,
If he had lived, of Him whom I deplore,
This Work of thine I blame not, but commend;
This sea in anger, and that dismal shore.

Oh 'tis a passionate Work!—yet wise and well;   45
Well chosen is the spirit that is here;
That Hulk[480] which labours in the deadly swell,
This rueful sky, this pageantry of fear!

And this huge Castle, standing here sublime,
I love to see the look with which it braves,   50
Cased in the unfeeling armour of old time,
The light'ning, the fierce wind, and trampling waves.

Farewell, farewell the Heart that lives alone,
Housed in a dream, at distance from the Kind!
Such happiness, wherever it be known,   55
Is to be pitied; for 'tis surely blind.

But welcome fortitude, and patient cheer,
And frequent sights of what is to be borne!
Such sights, or worse, as are before me here.—
Not without hope we suffer and we mourn.   60

[480] *Hulk*: heavy, unwieldy ship; wreck.

St. Paul's[481]

Pressed with conflicting thoughts of love and fear
I parted from thee, Friend![482] and took my way
Through the great City, pacing with an eye
Downcast, ear sleeping, and feet masterless
That were sufficient guide unto themselves,   5
And step by step went pensively. Now, mark!
Not how my trouble was entirely hushed,
(That might not be) but how by sudden gift,
Gift of Imagination's holy power,
My Soul in her uneasiness received   10
An anchor of stability.—It chanced
That while I thus was pacing, I raised up
My heavy eyes and instantly beheld,
Saw at a glance in that familiar spot
A visionary scene—a length of street   15
Laid open in its morning quietness,
Deep, hollow, unobstructed, vacant, smooth,
And white with winter's purest white, as fair,
As fresh and spotless as he ever sheds
On field or mountain. Moving Form was none   20
Save here and there a shadowy Passenger,[483]
Slow, shadowy, silent, dusky, and beyond
And high above this winding length of street,
This noiseless and unpeopled avenue,
Pure, silent, solemn, beautiful, was seen   25
The huge majestic Temple of St Paul
In awful[484] sequestration, through a veil,
Through its own sacred veil of falling snow.

---

[481] Written in 1808, published posthumously. For St. Paul's Cathedral, see the note to *Prelude*, bk. 7, line 130. The view here is from Fleet Street.

[482] *Friend*: Coleridge.

[483] *Passenger*: pedestrian; passerby.

[484] *awful*: inspiring awe.

"Surprised by joy—impatient as the Wind"[485]

Surprised by joy—impatient as the Wind
   I wished to share the transport[486]—Oh! with whom
   But Thee,[487] long buried in the silent Tomb,
That spot which no vicissitude can find?
Love, faithful love, recall'd thee to my mind—   5
   But how could I forget thee? Through what power,
   Even for the least division of an hour,
Have I been so beguiled as to be blind
To my most grievous loss?—That thought's return
   Was the worst pang that sorrow ever bore,   10
Save one, one only, when I stood forlorn,
   Knowing my heart's best treasure was no more;
That neither present time, nor years unborn
   Could to my sight that heavenly face restore.

[485] Published in *Poems*, 1815. The title of C. S. Lewis' spiritual autobiography
is *Surprised by Joy*.

[486] *transport*: rapture.

[487] *Thee*: Wordsworth's daughter, Catharine, who had died at three-and-a-half
in 1812.

The Virgin[488]

Mother! whose virgin bosom was uncrost
With the least shade of thought to sin allied.
Woman![489] above all women glorified,
Our tainted nature's solitary boast;
Purer than foam on central ocean tost;[490]   5
Brighter than eastern skies at daybreak strewn
With fancied roses, than the unblemished[491] moon[492]
Before her wane begins on heaven's blue[493] coast;
Thy image falls to earth. Yet some, I ween,[494]

[488] Published in *Ecclesiastical Sketches*, 1822. According to Aubrey de Vere (1814–1902), "Wordsworth was a 'high churchman,' and also, in his prose mind, strongly anti-Roman Catholic, partly on political grounds; but that it was otherwise as regards his mind poetic is obvious from many passages in his Christian poetry, especially those which refer to the monastic system, and the Schoolmen, and his sonnet on the Blessed Virgin, whom he addresses as 'Our tainted nature's solitary boast.' He used to say that the idea of one who was both Virgin and Mother had sunk so deep into the heart of Humanity, that there it must ever remain" ("Recollections of Wordsworth", in Grosart, *Prose Works*, vol. 3, pp. 491–92). Wordsworth's treatment of this theme is most unusual for an Anglican, particularly at the time; see Newman, *Apologia*, p. 238: "Such devotional manifestations in honour of our Lady had been my great *crux* as regards Catholicism".

[489] *Woman*: By drawing Mary's motherhood (of Christ) and her epitome of womanhood together, Wordsworth disarms the standard Protestant quotation of "[W]oman, what have you to do with me?" (John 2:4) as a biblical verse supposedly hostile to Catholic Marian doctrine. See the note to line 4 of Blake's "To Tirzah".

[490] *foam on central ocean tost*: Ocean foam is associated with Venus/Aphrodite, with whom Mary is being compared here, as she is (at least latently) in the Litany of Loreto: "Morning star" (Venus is the Morning Star).

[491] *unblemished*: "untainted" and "unblemished" are, of course, synonyms of "immaculate".

[492] *roses . . . moon*: Roses and the moon are associated with the Blessed Virgin and (respectively) Aphrodite and Diana. In Mary's case, see, e.g., the Litany of Loreto: "Mystical rose"; and Revelation 12:1: "And a great sign appeared in heaven, a woman clothed with the sun, with the moon under her feet"; Mary's identification with the moon also derives (among other things) from the parallel with Christ the Son/sun (see the note to line 98 of "The Ancient Mariner").

[493] *her wane begins on heaven's blue*: White and, especially, blue are the colors associated with the Blessed Virgin.

[494] *I ween*: "I believe." The sestet disengages the poet (and, potentially, the reader) from what Protestants would call Mariolatry, but without clearly distancing himself from a Catholic position.

Not unforgiven the suppliant[495] knee might bend, 10
As to a visible Power, in which did blend
All that was mixed and reconciled in thee
Of mother's love with maiden purity,
Of high with low, celestial with terrene![496]

Mutability[497]

From low to high doth dissolution climb,
And sink from high to low, along a scale
Of awful[498] notes, whose concord shall not fail;
A musical but melancholy chime,
Which they can hear who meddle not with crime, 5
Nor avarice, nor over-anxious care.
Truth fails not; but her outward forms that bear
The longest date do melt like frosty rime,
That in the morning whitened hill and plain
And is no more; drop like the tower sublime 10
Of yesterday, which royally did wear
His crown of weeds, but could not even sustain
Some casual shout that broke the silent air,
Or the unimaginable touch of Time.

---

[495] *suppliant*: beseeching.
[496] *terrene*: of this world.
[497] Published in *Ecclesiastical Sketches*, 1822.
[498] *awful*: awe-inspiring.

"Scorn Not the Sonnet"[499]

Scorn not the Sonnet; Critic, you have frowned,
Mindless of its just honours; with this key
Shakespeare[500] unlocked his heart; the melody
Of this small lute gave ease to Petrarch's[501] wound;
A thousand times this pipe did Tasso[502] sound;   5
With it Camöens[503] soothed an exile's grief;
The Sonnet glittered a gay myrtle[504] leaf
Amid the cypress[505] with which Dante[506] crowned
His visionary brow: a glow-worm lamp,

[499] Published in *Poetical Works*, 1827. It was closely imitated by Russia's greatest poet, Alexander Pushkin (1799–1837), in 1830 (Pushkin's sonnet featured Wordsworth among the immortal sonneteers). The sonnet had been virtually abandoned in English poetry since the mid-seventeenth century. Other sonnets on the sonnet form include Wordsworth's own "Nuns fret not at their Convent's narrow room", Keats' "If by dull rhymes our English must be chained", and D.G. Rossetti's "A Sonnet is a moment's monument". Although this sonnet summons an international who's who of sonneteers, the poets of the *Pléiade* are noticeably absent; it has been suggested that this is one of several instances of Wordsworth's low esteem for French literature.

[500] *Shakespeare*: Shakespeare wrote 154 sonnets, many of which appear to afford access to the otherwise enigmatic personality of the dramatist. Cf. Robert Browning (1812–1889), "House": "'Hoity toity! A street to explore,/Your house is the exception!/"With this same key/Shakespeare unlocked his heart," once more'/Did Shakespeare? If so, the less Shakespeare he!"

[501] *Petrarch's*: Francesco Petrarca (Eng. Petrarch; 1304–1374), great Italian poet and important early Renaissance Humanist. He was the most influential sonneteer in history and perfected the form known as the Petrarchan sonnet (of which this poem is an instance, albeit one involving modifications). "Petrarch's wound" is his unrequited love for the woman known in his poems as Laura.

[502] *Tasso*: Torquato Tasso (1544–1595), great Italian lyric and epic poet, author of *Jerusalem Delivered*. A major influence on Spencer and Milton, he was the subject of a drama by Goethe, a poem by Byron, and a symphonic poem by Liszt.

[503] *Camöens*: Luis de Camões (1524–1580), Portugal's greatest poet, as well as author of the epic *Lusiads* and many sonnets. Scholar, soldier, sailor, adventurer, he was briefly exiled in 1548.

[504] *myrtle*: Dante wrote sonnets inspired by his love for Beatrice Portinari. The myrtle is associated with love and was sacred to Aphrodite.

[505] *cypress*: The cypress is associated with death, cemeteries, and (in Graeco-Roman mythology) the Underworld. Dante's epic is set among the souls of the dead.

[506] *Dante*: Dante Alighieri (ca. 1265–1321), the great Florentine epic poet, author of *The Divine Comedy* and the *Vita Nuova*.

It cheered mild Spenser,[507] call'd from Faery-land 10
To struggle through dark ways; and when a damp[508]
Fell round the path of Milton,[509] in his hand
The Thing became a trumpet; whence he blew
Soul-animating strains—alas, too few!

Steamboats, Viaducts, and Railways[510]

Motions and Means, on land and sea at war
With old poetic feeling, not for this,
Shall ye, by Poets even, be judged amiss!
Nor shall your presence, howsoe'er it mar
The loveliness of Nature, prove a bar 5
To the Mind's gaining that prophetic sense
Of future change, that point of vision, whence
May be discovered what in soul ye are.
In spite of all that beauty may disown
In your harsh features, Nature doth embrace 10
Her lawful offspring in Man's art;[511] and Time,
Pleased with your triumphs o'er his brother Space,
Accepts from your bold hands the proffered crown
Of hope, and smiles on you with cheer sublime.

[507] *Spenser*: Edmund Spenser (1552–1599), the author of the epic allegorical fantasy *The Fairie Queene*, was also an innovative and important sonneteer, writing the 89 sonnet cycle *The Amoretti* and developing the Spenserian sonnet form.

[508] *damp*: mist, fog; depression of spirits.

[509] *path of Milton*: Milton wrote eighteen sonnets in English.

[510] Published in *Yarrow Revisited, and Other Poems*, 1835. Cf. J.M.W. Turner (1775–1851), *Rain, Steam and Speed* (1844, National Gallery); also G.K. Chesterton (1874–1936) on Kipling: "He has borne a brilliant part in thus recovering the lost provinces of poetry. He has not been frightened by that brutal materialistic air which clings only to words; he has pierced through to the romantic, imaginative matter of the things themselves. He has perceived the significance and philosophy of steam and of slang. Steam may be, if you like, a dirty by-product of science.... But at least he has been among the few who saw the divine parentage of these things, and knew that where there is smoke there is fire—that is, that wherever there is the foulest of things, there also is the purest" (*Heretics* [London: Bodley Head, 1928]), pp. 35–36).

[511] *Nature doth embrace ... Man's art*: Cf. Edmund Burke (1729–1797), "Letter from the New to the Old Whigs": "Art is man's nature".

SAMUEL TAYLOR COLERIDGE

On Imitation[1]

All are not born to soar—and ah! how few
In tracks where Wisdom leads their paths pursue!
Contagious when to wit or wealth allied,
Folly and Vice diffuse their venom wide.
On Folly every fool his talent tries;   5
It asks some toil to imitate the wise;
Tho' few like Fox[2] can speak—like Pitt[3] can think—
Yet all like Fox can game—like Pitt can drink.

Genevieve[4]

Maid of my Love, sweet GENEVIEVE!
In Beauty's light you glide along:
Your eye is like the star of eve,
And sweet your Voice, as Seraph's song.
Yet not your heavenly Beauty gives   5
This heart with passion soft to glow:
Within your soul a Voice there lives!
It bids you hear the tale of Woe.
When sinking low the Suff'rer wan

---

[1] Published in *Poetical Works*, 1834. The poem dates from the early 1790s.

[2] *Fox*: Charles James Fox (1749–1806), radical Whig politician, great orator, Pitt's arch rival. He was also famous for reckless gambling.

[3] *Pitt*: William Pitt the Younger (1759–1806), perhaps Britain's greatest prime minister (1783–1801, 1804–1806). Until the war with revolutionary France he was a champion of reform; thence he adopted an uncompromisingly Conservative position (he is difficult to classify by party; he is usually called a Tory, but he considered himself an independent Whig). Pitt was also known for his prodigious consumption of port.

[4] Published in *Poems on Various Subjects*, 1796. The poem was originally composed in Coleridge's adolescence; the girl to whom it is addressed seems to have been Jenny Edwards, the daughter of a nurse to one of the wards of Christ's Hospital school, in the City of London, where Coleridge boarded in 1782–1791.

Beholds no hand outstretcht to save,   10
Fair, as the bosom of the Swan
That rises graceful o'er the wave,
I've seen your breast with pity heave,
And *therefore* love I you, sweet GENEVIEVE!

To the River Otter[5]

Dear native brook! wild Streamlet of the West!
    How many various-fated years have passed,[6]
      What happy and what mournful hours, since last
I skimm'd the smooth thin stone along thy breast,
Numbering its light leaps! yet so deep imprest   5
Sink the sweet scenes of childhood, that mine eyes
    I never shut amid the sunny ray,
But straight[7] with all their tints thy waters rise,
    Thy crossing plank, thy marge with willows grey,
And bedded sand that vein'd with various dyes   10
Gleam'd through thy bright transparence! On my way,
    Visions of Childhood! oft have ye beguil'd
Lone manhood's cares, yet waking fondest sighs:
    Ah! that once more I were a careless Child!

[5] Published in *Poems, to Which Are Now Added, Poems by Charles Lamb and Charles Lloyd*, 1797. The river Otter runs from the Blackdown Hills in Somerset, through East Devon and Coleridge's hometown Ottery St. Mary, into the English Channel at Lyme Bay.

[6] *various-fated years have passed*: Cf. Wordsworth, "Tintern Abbey", lines 1–3: "Five years have past; five summers, with the length/Of five long winters! and again I hear/These waters".

[7] *straight*: directly, immediately.

Pantisocracy[8]

No more my Visionary Soul shall dwell
On Joys that were! No more endure to weigh
The Shame and Anguish of the evil Day,
Wisely forgetful! O'er the Ocean swell
Sublime of Hope I seek the cottag'd Dell,   5
Where Virtue calm with careless step may stray,
And dancing to the moonlight Roundelay[9]
The Wizard Passions weave an holy Spell.
Eyes that have ach'd with Sorrow! Ye shall weep
Tears of doubt-mingled Joy, like theirs who start[10]   10
From Precipices of distemper'd[11] Sleep,
On which the fierce-eyed Fiends their Revels keep,
And see the rising Sun, & feel it dart
New Rays of Pleasance[12] trembling to the Heart.

---

[8] Published posthumously. "Pantisocracy" means "government by all". In 1794, Coleridge and the poet Robert Southey (1774–1843) planned to establish a utopian community on the banks of the Susquehanna River in Pennsylvania. In the course of these plans, Coleridge and Southey met the sisters Sara and Edith Fricker, who were initially interested in the pantisocratic idea. Although the scheme broke down in 1795, Coleridge and Southey married, respectively, Sara and Edith, late the same year. Southey's marriage was a success; Coleridge's was not.

[9] *Roundelay*: round dance; a song with a repeated refrain.

[10] *who start*: i.e., who are startled or jump back.

[11] *distemper'd*: profoundly disturbed, disordered.

[12] *Pleasance*: delight, pleasure.

To the Reverend W. L. Bowles[13]

My heart has thank'd thee, BOWLES! for those soft strains,
   That, on the still air floating, tremblingly
   Wak'd in me Fancy, Love, and Sympathy!
For hence, not callous to a Brother's pains

Thro' Youth's gay prime and thornless paths I went   5
   And, when the *darker* day of life began,
   And I did roam, a thought-bewilder'd man
Thy kindred Lays[14] an healing solace lent,

Each lonely pang with dreamy joys combin'd,
   And stole from vain REGRET her scorpion stings;   10
   While shadowy PLEASURE, with mysterious wings,
Brooded the wavy and tumultuous mind,

Like that great Spirit, who with plastic[15] sweep
Mov'd on the darkness of the formless Deep![16]

[13] Published in *Poems on Various Subjects*, 1796. The Reverend William Lisle Bowles (1762–1850) was a minor poet and critic whose influence was considerable. His *Fourteen Sonnets* helped, through its wide popularity and enthusiastic reception and emulation by Coleridge and Wordsworth, to reestablish the sonnet as a major form. His poetry was appreciated for the tenderness and unaffected dignity of its sentiments, its purity of diction, and its feeling for nature. He is also remembered for his 1806 edition of Pope (and subsequent polemics), in which he criticized the master of the Augustan school for the artificiality of his imagery and subject matter, and the incidental and transient inspiration of his sentiments.

[14] *Lays*: songs.

[15] *plastic*: creative, form-bestowing, shaping.

[16] *Spirit . . . formless Deep*: Cf. Milton, *Paradise Lost*, bk. 1, lines 19–22: "[T]hou [the Holy Spirit] from the first / Wast present, and with mighty wings outspread / Dove-like sat'st brooding on the vast abyss / And mad'st it pregnant: what in me is dark / Illumine", and Genesis 1:1–2: "In the beginning God created the heavens and the earth. The earth was without form, and void, and darkness was upon the face of the deep; and the Spirit of God moving over the face of the waters."

To the Author of *The Robbers*[17]

SCHILLER! that hour I would have wish'd to die,[18]
If thro' the shuddering midnight I had sent
From the dark dungeon of the tower time-rent
That fearful voice, a famish'd Father's cry[19]—
Lest in some after moment aught more mean[20]   5
Might stamp[21] me mortal! A triumphant shout
Black HORROR scream'd, and all her *goblin*[22] rout[23]
Diminish'd shrunk from the more with'ring scene!
Ah! Bard tremendous in sublimity!
Could I behold thee in thy loftier mood   10
Wand'ring at eve with finely-frenzied eye
Beneath some vast old tempest-swinging wood!
Awhile with mute awe gazing I would brood:
Then weep aloud in a wild ecstasy!

[17] Published in *Poems on Various Subjects*, 1796. The author of *The Robbers*, Friedrich von Schiller (1759–1805), was a major German poet, and one of Europe's greatest dramatists and critics. Although he came to be a central figure of Weimar classicism, his early work belongs to the proto-Romantic *Sturm und Drang* (Storm and Stress) movement. Coleridge translated most of Schiller's *Wallenstein* trilogy. *The Robbers* (*Die Räuber*, 1781) was Schiller's first play and has remained one of the enduring achievements of *Sturm und Drang*. The violently emotional play revolves around (the evil, calculating younger son) Franz von Moor's plot to ruin his (older, attractive, and initially idealistic) brother Karl, and supplant him in the affections of their (well-meaning, but weak) father, Count Maximilian ("Old Moor"), and Karl's love Amalia. "One night in Winter, on leaving a College-friend's room, with whom I had supped, I carelessly took away with me 'The Robbers' a drama, the very name of which I had never before heard of:—A Winter midnight—the wind high—and 'The Robbers' for the first time!—The readers of Schiller will conceive what I felt. Schiller introduces no supernatural beings; yet his human beings agitate and astonish more than all the goblin rout—even of Shakespeare" (Coleridge's note, *Poems* [London, 1796]).

[18] SCHILLER! *that hour I would have wish'd to die*: Cf. Wordsworth, "London, 1802", line 1: "Milton! thou shouldst be living at this hour".

[19] *famish'd Father's cry*: "The Father of Moor in the Play of 'The Robbers'" (Coleridge's note).

[20] *mean*: small-minded; inferior.

[21] *stamp*: mark; seal; identify.

[22] *goblin*: The premodern use of the word has a more sinister or even demonic flavor than its modern, mischievous impish version.

[23] *rout*: troop, mob.

Sonnet to William Linley While He Sang a Song to Purcell's Music[24]

While my young cheek retains its healthful hues,
   And I have many friends who hold me dear,
     Linley! methinks, I would not often hear
Such melodies as thine, lest I should lose
All memory of the wrongs and sore distress　　　　　　　　5
     For which my miserable brethren weep!
     But should uncomforted misfortunes steep
My daily bread in tears and bitterness;
And if at Death's dread moment I should lie
     With no belovèd face at my bed-side,　　　　　　　　10
To fix the last glance of my closing eye,
     Methinks such strains, breathed by my angel-guide,
Would make me pass the cup of anguish[25] by,
     Mix with the blest, nor know that I had died!

[24] Written in 1797; published in *Sibylline Leaves*, 1817. William Linley (1771–1835) was a member of the British East India Company, a singer, and a minor composer; he was the son of the composer Thomas Linley (1733–1795) and brother-in-law of the playwright and politician Richard Brinsley Sheridan (1751–1816). Henry Purcell (1659–1695) was perhaps the greatest English composer; "I like Beethoven and Mozart—or else some of the aerial compositions of the elder Italians, as Palestrina and Carissimi.—And I love Purcell" (Samuel Taylor Coleridge and Coventry Patmore, *Table Talk and Omniana of S. T. Coleridge* [London: Oxford, 1917], p. 258). "Coleridge shows a greater sensitiveness to music than any English poet except Milton" (Arthur Symons, *The Romantic Movement in English Poetry* [New York: Dutton, 1909], p. 144).

[25] *such strains . . . Would make me pass the cup of anguish*: Cf. Matthew 26:36–43, Jesus' Agony in the Garden, when he said to his disciples, "'My soul is very sorrowful, even to death'. . . . And going a little farther he fell on his face and prayed, 'My Father, if it be possible, let this chalice pass from me; nevertheless, not as I will, but as thou will'" (26:38–39), and Matthew 27:48, 50, when Jesus died on the Cross: "And one of them at once ran and took a sponge, filled it with vinegar, and put it on a reed, and gave it to him to drink. . . . Jesus cried again with a loud voice and yielded up his spirit."

The Eolian Harp[26]

COMPOSED AUGUST 20, 1795 AT CLEVEDON, SOMERSETSHIRE

The Æolian harp is a musical instrument, named after Æolus, god of the winds; it is also known as the wind harp. Often little more than a simple wooden box with a sounding board and strings stretched across two bridges, it produces sounds when exposed to the wind. According to Novalis (1772–1801),

> A fairy-story is like a vision without rational connections [a dream vision], a harmonious whole of miraculous things and events—as, for example, a musical fantasia, the harmonic sequence [anxieties] of Aeolian harp, indeed Nature itself.[27]

Coleridge wrote the first version of the poem shortly before his marriage to Sara Fricker on October 4, 1795. The newly-weds spent several months in Clevedon on the Severn Estuary, near the Bristol Channel. Contrary to widely held opinion, the marriage was initially happy.

This is the first of Coleridge's Conversation Poems, a genre that—in spite of owing much to Cowper's *Task*—Coleridge may legitimately claim to have created and that was very soon to include "Tintern Abbey". These Conversation Poems epit-omized what M. H. Abrams called the Greater Romantic Lyric:

> They present a determinate speaker in a particularized, and usually a localized, outdoor setting, whom we overhear as he carries on, in a fluent vernacular which rises easily to a more formal speech, a sustained colloquy, sometimes with himself or with the outer scene, but more frequently with a silent human auditor, present or absent. The speaker begins with a descrip-tion of the landscape; an aspect or change of aspect in the land-scape evokes a varied but integral process of memory, thought, anticipation, and feeling which remains closely intervolved

[26] Published in *Poems on Various Subjects*, 1796; republished with extensive revisions in *Sibylline Leaves*, 1817.

[27] *Fragment* 1259 (translated by George MacDonald as an epigraph to MacDonald's fantasy novel *Phantastes* [Grand Rapids, Mich.: Eerdmans, 1981], pp. 2–3). Cf. Wordsworth, *Prelude*, bk. 1, lines 95–97.

with the outer scene. In the course of this meditation the lyric
speaker achieves an insight, faces up to a tragic loss, comes to
a moral decision, or resolves an emotional problem. Often the
poem rounds upon itself to end where it began, at the outer
scene, but with an altered mood and deepened understanding
which is the result of the intervening meditation.[28]

This movement proceeding from the poet's heart, out over
a variegated field of observation and returning enriched,
involves a probably conscious imitation of the cardiac cycle on
Coleridge's part.

The Eolian Harp

My pensive SARA![29] thy soft cheek reclin'd
Thus on mine arm, most soothing sweet it is
To sit beside our cot,[30] our cot o'ergrown
With white-flower'd Jasmin, and the broad-leav'd Myrtle,
(Meet[31] emblems they of Innocence and Love!)   5
And watch the clouds, that late[32] were rich with light,
Slow sad'ning round, and mark the star of eve[33]
Serenely brilliant (such should Wisdom be)
Shine opposite! How exquisite the scents
Snatch'd from yon bean-field! and the world *so* hush'd!   10
The stilly[34] murmur of the distant Sea
Tells us of Silence.

---

[28] "Structure and Style in the Greater Romantic Lyric", in *From Sensibility to Romanticism: Essays Presented to Frederick A. Pottle*, ed. Frederick W. Hilles and Harold Bloom (Oxford: Oxford University Press, 1965), pp. 527–28.

[29] *My pensive SARA*: Sara Fricker Coleridge (1770–1845), the poet's wife.

[30] *cot*: cottage.

[31] *Meet*: proper, fitting, appropriate.

[32] *late*: recently.

[33] *star of eve*: Venus.

[34] *stilly*: quiet, calm.

And that simplest Lute,
Plac'd length-ways in the clasping casement,[35] hark!
How by the desultory breeze caress'd,
Like some coy Maid half-yielding to her Lover,   15
It pours such sweet upbraidings, as must needs
Tempt to repeat the wrong! And now, its strings
Boldlier swept, the long sequacious[36] notes
Over delicious surges sink and rise,
Such a soft floating witchery of sound   20
As twilight Elfins[37] make, when they at eve
Voyage on gentle gales from Faery Land,
Where *Melodies* round honey-dropping flowers,
Footless and wild, like birds of Paradise,[38]
Nor pause, nor perch, hovering on untam'd wing!   25
O! the one life within us and abroad,
Which meets all motion and becomes its soul,
A light in sound, a sound-like power in light,[39]
Rhythm in all thought, and joyance[40] every where—
Methinks, it should have been impossible   30
Not to love all things in a world so fill'd;
Where the breeze warbles, and the mute still air
Is Music slumbering on her instrument.

---

[35] *casement*: window hinged at the side.

[36] *sequacious*: "of a person: inclined to follow another, esp. in a servile or unthinking manner ... of a thing: easily moulded ... of musical notes or metrical feet: following one another with consistent and ordered regularity" (*Oxford English Dictionary*, s.v. "sequacious").

[37] *Elfins*: elves.

[38] *birds of Paradise*: striking and exotic Melanesian birds of the family *Paradisaeidae*, but associated in the literary culture of the time with the legendary, legless Persian Huma bird, which was said to spend its entire life on the wing.

[39] *light in sound, a sound-like power in light*: early example of synaesthesia ("the production of a mental sense-impression relating to one sense by the stimulation of another sense ... the use of metaphors in which terms relating to one kind of sense-impression are used to describe sense-impressions of other kinds" [*Oxford English Dictionary*, s.v. "synaesthesia"]). Cf. Baudelaire, "Correspondences" (1857): "Il est des parfums frais comme de chairs d'enfants/Doux comme les hautbois" ("There are scents as cool as children's flesh/As sweet as oboes").

[40] *joyance*: festivity.

And thus, my love! as on the midway slope
Of yonder hill I stretch my limbs at noon,   35
Whilst thro' my half-clos'd eyelids I behold
The sunbeams dance, like diamonds, on the main,[41]
And tranquil muse upon tranquillity;
Full many a thought uncall'd and undetain'd,
And many idle flitting phantasies,   40
Traverse my indolent and passive brain
As wild and various, as the random gales
That swell or flutter on this subject Lute!
And what if all of animated[42] nature
Be but organic Harps diversly fram'd,   45
That tremble into thought, as o'er them sweeps
Plastic[43] and vast, one intellectual[44] Breeze,
At once the Soul of each, and God of All?[45]
But thy more serious eye a mild reproof
Darts, O belovèd Woman! nor such thoughts   50
Dim and unhallowed'd dost thou not reject,
And biddest me walk humbly with my God.

Meek Daughter in the Family of Christ,
Well hast thou said and holily disprais'd

[41] *main*: ocean.

[42] *animated*: perhaps an echo of the Renaissance Neoplatonism of Ficino and Henry More, which involves "a belief that the pictures of nonhuman, yet rational, life presented in the Pagan writers contain a great deal of truth. The universe is full of such life—full of *genii, daemones, aerii homines*. And these are *animals*, animated bodies or incarnate minds" (C. S. Lewis, *A Preface to Paradise Lost* [Oxford: Oxford University Press, 1961], p. 110).

[43] *Plastic*: creative, form-bestowing, shaping.

[44] *intellectual*: "apprehensible or apprehended only by the intellect; nonmaterial, spiritual; ideal" (*Oxford English Dictionary*, s.v. "intellectual").

[45] *all of animated nature ... God of All*: This passage suggests the idealist philosophy of Bishop George Berkeley (1685–1753), in which the objects of perception are indissociable from the mind that perceives them—that they are ideas, in effect, i.e., a unity of sensation, thought, and imagination perceived and identified by a mind, spirit, soul, or self; the source of the being, order, and intelligibility of perceived phenomena is the Supreme Mind/Spirit (God).

These shapings of the unregenerate[46] mind,   55
Bubbles that glitter as they rise and break
On vain Philosophy's aye-babbling[47] spring.
For never guiltless may I speak of Him,
Th' INCOMPREHENSIBLE! save when with awe
I praise him, and with Faith that inly *feels*;   60
Who with his saving mercies healèd me,
A sinful and most miserable man,
Wilder'd[48] and dark, and gave me to possess
PEACE, and this COT, and THEE, heart-honour'd Maid!

On Donne's Poetry[49]

With Donne, whose muse on dromedary trots,
Wreathe iron pokers into true-love knots;
Rhyme's sturdy cripple, fancy's maze and clue,[50]
Wit's forge and fire-blast, meaning's press and screw.[51]

[46] *unregenerate*: not spiritually reborn (through ignorance, indifference, or hostility to Christ the Redeemer), and thus wholly subject to the dark and miserable consequences of the Fall.

[47] *aye-babbling*: forever-chattering.

[48] *Wilder'd*: i.e., bewildered; led astray.

[49] Written in the 1790s, published posthumously. Coleridge and Browning were among the few major figures with a high opinion of John Donne (1573–1631) between the second half of the seventeenth century and the early twentieth century. The imagery of the poem alludes to Donne's dialectical virtuosity with difficult material and his ante/anticlassical aesthetic ruggedness and irregularity (Ben Jonson to Drummond: "Donne, for not keeping of accent, deserved hanging"). Cf. "On Donne's First Poem".

[50] *maze and clue*: the ball of thread with which Theseus (the mythical-founder king of Athens) found his way out of the labyrinth.

[51] *press and screw*: The reference is to a screw press, used to stamp designs and strike coins.

This Lime-Tree Bower My Prison[52]

> In the June of 1797, some long-expected Friends paid a visit
> to the author's cottage; and on the morning of their arrival, he
> met with an accident, which disabled him from walking during
> the whole time of their stay. One evening, when they had left
> him for a few hours, he composed the following lines in the
> garden-bower.

Well, they are gone, and here must I remain,[53]
This lime-tree bower my prison! I have lost
Beauties and feelings, such as would have been
Most sweet to my remembrance even when age
Had dimm'd mine eyes to blindness! They, meanwhile,   5
Friends, whom I never more may meet again,
On springy[54] heath, along the hill-top edge,
Wander in gladness, and wind down, perchance,
To that still roaring dell, of which I told;
The roaring dell, o'erwooded, narrow, deep,   10
And only speckled by the mid-day sun;
Where its slim trunk the ash from rock to rock

---

[52] Published in *Sibylline Leaves*, 1817; a Conversation Poem (see the introductory note to "The Eolian Harp", pp. 275–76). Coleridge has left a more detailed account of the circumstances of its composition: "Charles Lamb has been with me for a week—he left me Friday morning.—The second day after Wordsworth came to me, dear Sara accidentally emptied a skillet of boiling milk on my foot, which confined me during the whole time of C. Lamb's stay & still prevents me from all *walks* longer than a furlong.—while Wordsworth, his Sister, and C. Lamb were out one evening; sitting in the arbour of T. Poole's garden, which communicates with mine, I wrote these lines, with which I am pleased" (Letter to Southey, ca. July 17, 1797). The setting is Nether Stowey, Somerset. Shortly before his death, Coleridge wrote the following marginal note in his copy of the 1834 edition: "Ch. and Mary Lamb—dear to my heart, yea, as it were my Heart. S.T.C. Aet. 63; 1834—1797–1834 = 37 years!" [Samuel T. Coleridge, *The Collected Letters of Samuel Taylor Coleridge*, ed. Earl Leslie Griggs, vol. 1 (Oxford: Oxford University Press, 1992], p. 334.)

[53] *they are gone, and here must I remain*: Cf. Henry Vaughan (1622–1695): "They are all gone into the world of light!/And I alone sit ling'ring here;/Their very memory is fair and bright,/And my sad thoughts doth clear", and T. S. Eliot (1888–1965), *Four Quartets*, "East Coker", 3, lines 1–13: "O dark dark dark. They all go into the dark/... I said to my soul, be still, and let the dark come upon you/Which shall be the darkness of God." See also lines 39–43 of this poem.

[54] *springy*: elastic.

Flings arching like a bridge;—that branchless ash,
Unsunn'd and damp, whose few poor yellow leaves
Ne'er tremble in the gale, yet tremble still,   15
Fann'd by the water-fall! and there my friends
Behold the dark green file of long lank weeds,[55]
That all at once (a most fantastic sight!)
Still nod and drip beneath the dripping edge
Of the blue clay-stone.

      Now, my friends emerge   20
Beneath the wide wide Heaven—and view again
The many-steepled tract magnificent
Of hilly fields and meadows,[56] and the sea,
With some fair bark, perhaps, whose sails light up
The slip of smooth clear blue betwixt two Isles   25
Of purple shadow! Yes! they wander on
In gladness all; but thou, methinks, most glad,
My gentle-hearted Charles![57] for thou hast pined
And hunger'd after Nature, many a year,
In the great City pent,[58] winning thy way   30
With sad yet patient soul, through evil and pain

[55] *dark green file of long lank weeds*: "the Asplenium Scolopendrium, called in some countries the Adder's Tongue, in others the Hart's Tongue; but Withering gives the Adder's Tongue as the trivial name of the Ophioglossum only" (Coleridge's note).

[56] *many-steepled tract . . . fields and meadows*: the beautiful Quantock Hill country in Somerset.

[57] *My gentle-hearted Charles*: Coleridge's great friend from schooldays to the end of his life, the essayist and poet Charles Lamb (1775–1834) was one of the best-loved figures in English literature ("Saint Charles" in the words of Thackeray). Lamb was annoyed by Coleridge's epithet: "For God's sake (I never was more serious), don't make me ridiculous any more by terming me gentle-hearted in print" (Letter to Coleridge, August 6, 1800). He also greatly preferred London to the country; see the note to line 69 of Wordsworth's *Prelude*, bk. 7.

[58] *City pent*: See Milton on Satan's impressions of Eden after Hell: "As one who long in populous city pent,/Where houses thick and sewers annoy the air,/Forth issuing on a summer's morn to breathe/Among the pleasant villages and farms/Adjoined, from each thing met conceives delight,/The smell of grain, or tedded grass, or kine,/Or dairy, each rural sight, each rural sound" (*Paradise Lost*, 9, lines 445–51). Cf. *Prelude*, bk. 1, lines 452–54, "Frost at Midnight", lines 52–54.

And strange calamity![59] Ah! slowly sink
Behind the western ridge, thou glorious Sun!
Shine in the slant beams of the sinking orb,
Ye purple heath-flowers! richlier burn, ye clouds!   35
Live in the yellow light, ye distant groves!
And kindle, thou blue Ocean! So my friend
Struck with deep joy may stand, as I have stood,
Silent with swimming sense; yea, gazing round
On the wide landscape, gaze till all doth seem   40
Less gross[60] than bodily; and of such hues
As veil the Almighty Spirit, when yet he makes
Spirits perceive his presence.[61]

A delight
Comes sudden on my heart, and I am glad
As[62] I myself were there! Nor in this bower,   45
This little lime-tree bower, have I not mark'd[63]
Much that has sooth'd me. Pale beneath the blaze

---

[59] *winning thy way ... strange calamity*: In 1796, Charles Lamb's sister, Mary (1764–1847), stabbed their mother to death in a fit of insanity. Charles Lamb kept her from the madhouse by undertaking her constant supervision at home; and, in spite of subsequent attacks of mental illness, she recovered to the extent that she was able to lead a fairly full and normal life and collaborated with her brother on the children's classic *Tales from Shakespeare*.

[60] *gross*: dense.

[61] *veil the Almighty Spirit ... Spirits perceive his presence*: The ambiguous use of "veil" in this context is reminiscent of the language of "negative theology": "His [pseudo-Dionysus'] writings are usually regarded as the main channel by which a certain kind of theology entered the western tradition. It is the 'negative theology' of those who take in a more rigid sense, and emphasize more persistently than others, the incomprehensibility of God. It is already well rooted in Plato himself, as we see from *Republic* 509 and the Second Epistle (312–13), and central in Plotinus. Its most striking representative in English is *The Cloud of Unknowing*. Some German Protestant Theology of our own time, and some Theistic Existentialism, has perhaps a remote affinity with it" (C.S. Lewis, *The Discarded Image: An Introduction to Medieval and Renaissance Literature* [Cambridge: Cambridge University Press, 1994], p. 70).

[62] *As*: as if.

[63] *mark'd*: taken notice of.

Hung the transparent foliage; and I watch'd
Some broad and sunny leaf, and lov'd to see
The shadow of the leaf and stem above   50
Dappling its sunshine! And that walnut-tree
Was richly ting'd, and a deep radiance lay
Full on the ancient ivy, which usurps
Those fronting elms, and now, with blackest mass
Makes their dark branches gleam a lighter hue   55
Through the late twilight: and though now the bat
Wheels silent by, and not a swallow twitters,
Yet still the solitary humble-bee[64]
Sings in the bean-flower! Henceforth I shall know
That Nature ne'er deserts the wise and pure;   60
No plot so narrow, be but Nature there,
No waste so vacant, but may well employ
Each faculty of sense, and keep the heart
Awake to Love and Beauty! and sometimes
'Tis well to be bereft of promis'd good,   65
That we may lift the Soul, and contemplate
With lively joy the joys we cannot share.
My gentle-hearted Charles! when the last rook
Beat its straight path along the dusky air
Homewards, I blest it! deeming its black wing   70
(Now a dim speck, now vanishing in light)
Had cross'd the mighty Orb's dilated glory,
While thou stood'st gazing; or, when all was still,
Flew creeking o'er thy head,[65] and had a charm
For thee, my gentle-hearted Charles, to whom   75
No sound is dissonant which tells of Life.

---

[64] *humble-bee*: bumble-bee.

[65] *Flew creeking o'er thy head*: "Some months after I had written this line, it gave me pleasure to find that Bartram had observed the same circumstances of the Savanna Crane. 'When these Birds move their wings in flight, their strokes are slow, moderate and regular; and even when at a considerable distance or high above us, we plainly hear the quill-feathers; their shafts and webs upon one another creak as the joints or working of a vessel in a tempestuous sea'" (Coleridge's note).

The Nightingale[66]

A CONVERSATION POEM, APRIL 1798

No cloud, no relique[67] of the sunken day
Distinguishes the West, no long thin slip
Of sullen light, no obscure trembling hues.
Come, we will rest on this old mossy bridge!
You see the glimmer of the stream beneath,   5
But hear no murmuring: it flows silently,
O'er its soft bed of verdure. All is still,
A balmy night! and though the stars be dim,
Yet let us think upon the vernal showers
That gladden the green earth, and we shall find   10
A pleasure in the dimness of the stars.
And hark! the Nightingale begins its song,
"Most musical, most melancholy"[68] bird!
A melancholy bird? Oh! idle thought!
In Nature there is nothing melancholy.   15
But some night-wandering man whose heart was pierced
With the remembrance of a grievous wrong,
Or slow distemper,[69] or neglected love,
(And so, poor wretch! filled all things with himself,
And made all gentle sounds tell back the tale   20
Of his own sorrow) he, and such as he,
First named these notes a melancholy strain.
And many a poet echoes the conceit;[70]

---

[66] Published in *Lyrical Ballads*, 1798. For the Conversation Poems, see the introductory note to "The Eolian Harp", pp. 275–76.

[67] *relique*: i.e., relic.

[68] "*Most musical, most melancholy*": See Milton, "Il Penseroso", line 62. "This passage in Milton possesses an excellence far superior to that of mere description: it is spoken in the character of the melancholy man, and has therefore a *dramatic* propriety. The author makes this remark to rescue himself from the charge of having alluded with levity to a line in Milton: a charge than which none could be more painful to him, except perhaps that of having ridiculed his Bible" (Coleridge's note).

[69] *distemper*: disaffection; emotional derangement.

[70] *conceit*: fanciful notion, poetic image, or expression.

Poet who hath been building up the rhyme[71]
When he had better far have stretched his limbs   25
Beside a brook in mossy forest-dell,
By sun or moon-light, to the influxes
Of shapes and sounds and shifting elements
Surrendering his whole spirit, of his song
And of his fame forgetful! so his fame   30
Should share in Nature's immortality,
A venerable thing! and so his song
Should make all Nature lovelier, and itself
Be loved like Nature! But 'twill not be so;
And youths and maidens most poetical,   35
Who lose the deepening twilights of the spring
In ball-rooms and hot theatres, they still
Full of meek sympathy must heave their sighs
O'er Philomela's[72] pity-pleading strains.

My Friend, and thou, our Sister![73] we have learnt   40
A different lore: we may not thus profane
Nature's sweet voices, always full of love
And joyance![74] 'Tis the merry Nightingale
That crowds, and hurries, and precipitates
With fast thick warble his delicious notes,   45
As he were fearful that an April night
Would be too short for him to utter forth

---

[71] *Poet who hath been building up the rhyme*: Cf. Milton "Lycidas", lines 10–11: "Who would not sing for Lycidas? he knew/Himself to sing, and build the lofty rhyme."

[72] *Philomela's*: i.e., the nightingale's. The etymology of the name is derived from "loving song". In Graeco-Roman mythology, Philomela was raped by her brother-in-law, Tereus, who cut out her tongue to prevent her from telling Procne, her sister and his wife. Philomela nevertheless communicated the outrage in a tapestry she sent to Procne, who killed her son, Itys, and served him up to his father, who ate him. When Tereus learned what had happened he attempted to kill the sisters, when the gods transformed them all into birds: Philomela a nightingale, Procne a swallow, and Tereus a hoopoe (see Ovid, *Metamorphoses* 6.412–674).

[73] *My Friend, and thou, our Sister*: William and Dorothy Wordsworth.

[74] *joyance*: festivity.

His love-chant, and disburthen[75] his full soul
Of all its music!

                And I know a grove
Of large extent, hard by a castle huge,[76]   50
Which the great lord inhabits not; and so
This grove is wild with tangling underwood,
And the trim walks are broken up, and grass,
Thin grass and king-cups[77] grow within the paths.
But never elsewhere in one place I knew   55
So many nightingales; and far and near,
In wood and thicket, over the wide grove,
They answer and provoke each other's song,
With skirmish and capricious passagings,
And murmurs musical and swift jug jug,[78]   60
And one low piping sound more sweet than all—
Stirring the air with such a harmony,
That should you close your eyes, you might almost
Forget it was not day! On moon-light bushes,
Whose dewy leaflets are but half-disclosed,   65
You may perchance behold them on the twigs,
Their bright, bright eyes, their eyes both bright and full,
Glistening, while many a glow-worm in the shade
Lights up her love-torch.

                A most gentle Maid,[79]
Who dwelleth in her hospitable home   70
Hard by the castle, and at latest eve
(Even like a Lady vowed and dedicate

---

[75] *disburthen*: unburden.

[76] *castle huge*: Enmore Castle, seat of the Earl of Egmont—in this case, John Perceval (1738–1822), 3rd Earl, politician, and brother of Spencer Percival (1762–1812), the only British prime minister to be assassinated.

[77] *king-cups*: marsh marigolds (*Caltha palustris*).

[78] *jug jug*: "to utter a sound like 'jug', as a nightingale" (*Oxford English Dictionary*, s.v. "jug jug").

[79] *Maid*: probably Ellen Cruickshank, whose brother was Lord Egmont's agent.

To something more than Nature in the grove)
Glides through the pathways; she knows all their notes,
That gentle Maid! and oft, a moment's space, 75
What time[80] the moon was lost behind a cloud,
Hath heard a pause of silence; till the moon
Emerging, hath awakened earth and sky
With one sensation, and those wakeful birds
Have all burst forth in choral minstrelsy, 80
As if some sudden gale had swept at once
A hundred airy harps! And she hath watched
Many a nightingale perch giddily
On blossomy twig still swinging from the breeze,
And to that motion tune his wanton song 85
Like tipsy Joy[81] that reels with tossing head.

Farewell, O Warbler! till to-morrow eve,
And you, my friends! farewell, a short farewell!
We have been loitering long and pleasantly,
And now for our dear homes.—That strain again! 90
Full fain it would delay me! My dear babe,[82]
Who, capable of no articulate sound,
Mars all things with his imitative lisp,
How he would place his hand beside his ear,
His little hand, the small forefinger up, 95
And bid us listen! And I deem it wise
To make him Nature's play-mate. He knows well
The evening-star; and once, when he awoke
In most distressful mood (some inward pain
Had made up that strange thing, an infant's dream—) 100
I hurried with him to our orchard-plot,
And he beheld the moon, and, hushed at once,

[80] *What time*: i.e., when.
[81] *tipsy Joy*: Cf. Milton, *Comus*, lines 102–4: "Meanwhile welcome joy and feast,/Midnight shout and revelry,/Tipsy dance and jollity."
[82] *My dear babe*: Hartley Coleridge (1796–1849). See the note to line 85 of Wordsworth's "Intimations of Immortality".

Suspends his sobs, and laughs most silently,
While his fair eyes, that swam with undropped tears,
Did glitter in the yellow moon-beam![83] Well!—   105
It is a father's tale: But if that Heaven
Should give me life, his childhood shall grow up
Familiar with these songs, that with the night
He may associate joy.[84] —Once more, farewell,
Sweet Nightingale! once more, my friends! farewell.   110

Kubla Khan: Or, A Vision in a Dream
A FRAGMENT

"Kubla Khan" and the "Ancient Mariner" are Coleridge's most celebrated poems. "Kubla Khan" was published in 1816 at Lord Byron's urging with "Christabel" and "The Pains of Sleep" by John Murray (Byron's publisher) and collected in *Poetical Works* (1828). Until 1834, the prose introduction began: "The following fragment is here published at the request of a poet of great and deserved celebrity, and as far as the Author's own opinions are concerned, rather as a psychological curiosity, than on the ground of any supposed *poetic* merits".

Kublai Khan (1215–1294), the fifth Great Khan (1260–1294) of the Mongol Empire, conqueror and emperor of China (1270s–1294), founder of the Yuan Dynasty, grandson of Genghis Khan, was one of the mightiest rulers in history. He established Peking/Beijing as the capital of China. The wonders of his court were disseminated in Europe through *The Travels* of Marco Polo, who had spent some twenty years there.

---

[83] *eyes . . . glitter in the yellow moon-beam:* "Hartley fell down & hurt himself—I caught him up crying & screaming—& ran out of doors with him.—The Moon caught his eye—he ceased crying immediately—& his eyes & the tears in them, how they glittered in the Moonlight!" (*The Notebooks of Samuel Taylor Coleridge*, ed. Kathleen Coburn, vol. 1 [Princeton, N.J.: Princeton University Press, 1957], p. 219).

[84] *childhood . . . joy:* Cf. "Frost at Midnight", lines 48–64.

In John Beer's persuasive reading,

> *Kubla Khan* ... is a poem with two major themes: genius and the
> lost paradise. In the first stanza the man of commanding genius
> [like Napoleon or Milton's Satan], the fallen but demonic man,
> strives to rebuild the lost paradise in a world which is, like him-
> self, fallen. In the second stanza, the other side of the demonic
> re-asserts itself—the mighty fountain in the savage place, the
> wailing woman beneath the waning moon, the demon-lover.
> The third stanza is a moment of miraculous unity between
> the contending forces—the sunny dome and the caves of ice,
> the fountain and the caves, the dome and the waves all being
> counterpoised and in one harmony. Finally, in the last stanza,
> there is a vision of paradise regained—of man revisited by that
> absolute genius which corresponds to his original, unfallen
> state, of the honey-dew fountain of immortality re-established
> in the garden, of complete harmony between Apollo with his
> lyre and the damsel with the dulcimer, of the established dome,
> and of the multitude, reconciled by the terrible fascination into
> complete harmony.[85]

In the summer of the year 1797, the Author, then in ill health,
had retired to a lonely farm house between Porlock and Linton,
on the Exmoor confines of Somerset and Devonshire. In con-
sequence of a slight indisposition, an anodyne[86] had been
prescribed, from the effect of which he fell asleep in his chair
at the moment that he was reading the following sentence,
or words of the same substance, in "Purchas's Pilgrimage:"[87]

---

[85] *S. T. Coleridge: Poems*, ed. John Beer, Everyman (London: David Campbell
Publishers, 1991), p. 165.

[86] *anodyne*: pain reliever; laudanum, a potentially highly addictive opiate, was
current as a painkiller well into the twentieth century. Coleridge was first pre-
scribed laudanum for medical reasons at school in 1791, and from about 1796
he began to use it as a painkiller and to counteract severe depression. Before the
century was out he had become an addict and would remain one for the rest of his
life, though his condition was improved from 1816 on, when he went to lodge at
Highgate with his physician, James Gillman.

[87] *"Purchas's Pilgrimage"*: Samuel Purchas (1575–1626), Anglican chaplain
and travel writer, was author of *Purchas his Pilgrimage*. Coleridge misquotes the
passage, which actually reads: "In Xamdu did Cublai Can build a stately Palace,

"Here the Khan Kubla commanded a palace to be built, and a stately garden thereunto: and thus ten miles of fertile ground were inclosed with a wall." The Author continued for about three hours in a profound sleep, at least of the external senses, during which time he has the most vivid confidence, that he could not have composed less than from two to three hundred lines; if that indeed can be called composition in which all the images rose up before him as things, with a parallel production of the correspondent expressions, without any sensation or consciousness of effort. On awakening he appeared to himself to have a distinct recollection of the whole, and taking his pen, ink, and paper, instantly and eagerly wrote down the lines that are here preserved. At this moment he was unfortunately called out by a person on business from Porlock, and detained by him above an hour, and on his return to his room, found, to his no small surprise and mortification, that though he still retained some vague and dim recollection of the general purport of the vision, yet, with the exception of some eight or ten scattered lines and images, all the rest had passed away like the images on the surface of a stream into which a stone has been cast, but, alas! without the after restoration of the latter:

> Then all the charm
> Is broken—all that phantom-world so fair
> Vanishes, and a thousand circlets spread,
> And each mis-shape the other. Stay awhile,
> Poor youth! who scarcely dar'st lift up thine eyes—

---

encompassing sixteene miles of plaine ground with a wall, wherein are fertile Meddowes, pleasant springs, delightful Streames, and all sorts of beasts of chase and game, and in the middest thereof a sumptuous house of pleasure, which may be removed from place to place." Some of the imagery also indicates the influence of James Ridley's (1736–1765) *Tales of the Genii*—the meandering river, for instance, and the glittering dome rising to the heavens, can be found in "The Merchant Abuda's Adventure in the Valley of Bocchim" (esp. pp. 39–72), while in the tale of Hassan Assar (p. 122) we find: "but alas! ere the happy couple could meet, the envious earth gave a hideous groan, and the ground, parting under their feet, divided them from each other by a dreadful chasm. While the astonished pair stood on different sides of the gulf, viewing the horrid fissure and the dark abyss, wild notes of strange uncouth warlike music were heard from the bottom of the pit" (London, 1820).

The stream will soon renew its smoothness, soon
The visions will return! And lo! he stays,
And soon the fragments dim of lovely forms
Come trembling back, unite, and now once more
The pool becomes a mirror.[88]

Yet from the still surviving recollections in his mind, the
Author has frequently purposed to finish for himself what had
been originally, as it were, given to him. Αὔριον ἄδιον ἄσω:[89]
but the to-morrow is yet to come.

As a contrast to this vision, I have annexed a fragment[90]
of a very different character, describing with equal fidelity the
dream of pain and disease.

—1816

Kubla Khan: Or, A Vision in a Dream

In Xanadu[91] did Kubla Khan
A stately pleasure-dome decree:
Where Alph,[92] the sacred river, ran

---

[88] From Coleridge's "The Picture".

[89] "I shall sing a sweeter song tomorrow", an inexact reference to Theocritus, *Idylls* 1 (in which Arethusa is addressed—see below), line 145: "In time I shall sing you a sweeter song."

[90] *fragment:* "The Pains of Sleep".

[91] *Xanadu:* Shàngdū (also known as Xandu and Chandu), presently in Inner Mongolia; it is the (now ruined) summer capital of the Chinese Yuan Dynasty established by Kublai Khan in 1271.

[92] *Alph:* There are at least four associations here: (1) the river/god Alpheus, which in Greek mythology ran underground into the well/nymph Arethusa (see Milton, "Lycidas", lines 132–33: "Return, Alpheus, the dread voice is past / That shrunk thy streams"); (2) Revelation 22:1: "Then he showed me the river of the water of life, bright as crystal, flowing from the throne of God and of the Lamb"; (3) the first letter of the Greek (alpha) and Hebrew (aleph) alphabets, which, in turn, has (4) Neoplatonic and Cabalistic significance: "When he was a schoolboy he was already reading the neo-Platonists in Thomas Taylor's translations; and shortly before he wrote *Kubla Khan* in the summer of 1797 he had written to his friend Thelwall, (Nov. 17th 1796) in London, asking him to send him a number of the neo-Platonic texts in the original Greek" (Kathleen Raine, "Traditional Symbolism in *Kubla Khan*", *Studies in Comparative Religion* 1,

Through caverns measureless to man
    Down to a sunless sea.   5
So twice five miles of fertile ground
With walls and towers were girdled round:
And there were gardens bright with sinuous rills,
Where blossomed many an incense-bearing tree;
And here were forests ancient as the hills,   10
Enfolding sunny spots of greenery.

But oh! that deep romantic[93] chasm which slanted
Down the green hill athwart a cedarn cover!
A savage place! as holy and enchanted
As e'er beneath a waning moon was haunted   15
By woman wailing for her demon-lover![94]

---

no. 3 [1967], http://www.studiesincomparativereligion.com/Public/articles/browse
_g.aspx?ID=20). "In Cabalistic lore, Aleph represents the hidden source of
the divine, as distinct from the creative power represented by the letter Beth.
Renaissance Cabalists also drew a distinction between the bright Aleph, the
aspect of the divine essence from which Creation proceeds, and the dark Aleph,
the aspect of the divine essence from which chaos and destruction proceed"
(*The New Encyclopedia of the Occult*, ed. John Michael Greer [St. Paul, Minn.:
Llewellyn, 2004], p. 17). "'Alph, the sacred river' is one such theme, upon which
I can only suggest a few of the associated strands which Coleridge has condensed
into the phrase. The Jewish mystical tradition of the Cabala is based upon the
great symbol of 'the tree of God,' a symbol, like Yggdrasill and other sacred trees,
of the whole of manifested being. The Tree is sometimes also conceived as a river
through which the creative power flows down from the unmanifested source,
the divine origin, symbolized by the letter Aleph, or Alpha; and the river of
life descends perpetually from above down to the lowest plane of manifestation,
matter; the 'sunless sea.' Burnet, whom Coleridge quotes at the beginning of *The
Ancient Mariner*, and Robert Fludd, Christian Cabalists, both give accounts of this
symbol.... Psyche, in Apuleius' legend of Cupid and Psyche, is sent to draw water
from the unapproachable source of the Styx and the Orphic Hymn to the Fates
(Thomas Taylor had translated it) describes those weavers of destiny as dwelling
in a dark cave from whose depths the sacred river flows. Porphyry's *De Antro
Nympharum* (On the Cave of the Nymphs) is a symbolic description of the cave
(Plato's symbol of this world) from whose darkness, 'Through caverns measureless
to man,' issues the river of generation" (Raine, "Traditional Symbolism"). Cf. "A
Tombless Epitaph", line 29.

[93] *romantic*: fantastic, appealing powerfully to the imagination.

[94] *woman wailing for her demon-lover*: Cf. Genesis 6:2, 4: " [T]he sons of God saw
that the daughters of men were fair; and they took to wife such of them as they
chose.... The Nephilim [giants] were on the earth in those days"; also, Fuseli's

And from this chasm, with ceaseless turmoil seething,
As if this earth in fast thick pants were breathing,
A mighty fountain momently[95] was forced:
Amid whose swift half-intermitted burst   20
Huge fragments vaulted like rebounding hail,
Or chaffy grain beneath the thresher's flail:
And 'mid these dancing rocks at once and ever
It flung up momently the sacred river.
Five miles meandering with a mazy motion   25
Through wood and dale the sacred river ran,
Then reached the caverns measureless to man,
And sank in tumult to a lifeless ocean:
And 'mid this tumult Kubla heard from far
Ancestral voices[96] prophesying war!   30

    The shadow of the dome of pleasure[97]
    Floated midway on the waves;
    Where was heard the mingled measure
    From the fountain and the caves.
It was a miracle of rare device,[98]   35
A sunny pleasure-dome with caves of ice!

1781 painting, *The Nightmare*, depicting an incubus squatting upon a sleeping woman sprawled, dishevelled, across a couch.

[95] *momently*: from moment to moment.

[96] *Ancestral voices*: possibly an allusion to Chinese ancestor worship.

[97] *shadow of the dome of pleasure*: "But on the waves of 'the sunless sea' the 'pleasure-dome' is reflected—an image used by Coleridge when he described the fleeting of the idea of the poem itself, 'like the images on the surface of the stream.' Again the symbol is one common to all the Platonic philosophers. Proclus uses the image of a tree reflected in a river; Plotinus and the Hermetica (Milton's Thrice-Great Hermes) abound in images of the temporal world as a reflection, in water, of the eternal forms; and Plato himself in the *Timaeus* calls this world 'a moving image of eternity,' and eternity a sphere, the domed vault of heaven; the same dome which was retained in the symbolic architecture of the Byzantine basilica, itself a product of Platonism" (Raine, "Traditional Symbolism"). See in this connection Shelley, "Adonais", 52 (lines 460–64): "The One remains, the many change and pass;/Heaven's light forever shines, Earth's shadows fly;/Life, like a dome of many-coloured glass,/Stains the white radiance of Eternity,/Until Death tramples it to fragments".

[98] *device*: something devised or contrived as a design.

A damsel with a dulcimer[99]
In a vision once I saw:
It was an Abyssinian[100] maid,
And on her dulcimer she played,   40
Singing of Mount Abora.[101]
Could I revive within me
Her symphony[102] and song,
To such a deep delight 'twould win me,
That with music loud and long,   45
I would build[103] that dome in air,
That sunny dome! those caves of ice!
And all who heard should see them there,
And all should cry, Beware! Beware!
His flashing eyes,[104] his floating hair!   50
Weave a circle round him thrice,

[99] *dulcimer*: It is not entirely clear which instrument Coleridge has in mind here; "dulcimer" generally designates a "musical instrument, having strings of graduated lengths stretched over a sounding board, which are struck with two hammers held in the hands" (*Oxford English Dictionary*, s.v. "dulcimer"), but the word is also sometimes associated with plucked, mandolinlike instruments.

[100] *Abyssinian*: Ethiopian.

[101] *Mount Abora*: Amba Geshen, the mountain in Ethiopia where (succession being potentially available to any male relative of the previous emperor) most of the male heirs to the Abyssinian throne were interned. A description of Amba Geshen (as Mount Amara) features in Purchas' *Pilgrimage*. Cf. also Milton, *Paradise Lost*, bk. 4, lines 280–84: "Nor where Abassin kings their issue guard,/Mount Amara, though this by some supposed/True Paradise, under the Ethiop line/By Nilus' head, enclosed with shining rock,/A whole day's journey high".

[102] *symphony*: harmonious music making.

[103] *with music . . . would build*: In Greek mythology, Amphion, who had been schooled in song by Hermes, sang the walls of Thebes into existence; some legends also credit Apollo with the musical creation of the walls of Troy. This passage also appears to evoke Orpheus, the demigod poet identified with secret knowledge, whose music could move inanimate objects and allow him to pass the Gates of Death and return unscathed.

[104] *flashing eyes*: See the note on eyes to line 151 of "Christabel", the Barfield passage in the introductory note to "Dejection: An Ode" (p. 396), the note on the Book of Nature in the introductory note to "Frost at Midnight" (p. 351), and "Apologia Pro Vita Sua". Cf. "The Ancient Mariner", line 13.

And close your eyes with holy dread,
For he on honey-dew hath fed[105]
And drunk the milk of Paradise.[106]

Fears in Solitude

WRITTEN IN APRIL, 1798, DURING THE ALARM OF AN INVASION

"Fears in Solitude" was published in 1798 with "France: An Ode" and "Frost at Midnight" by Joseph Johnson,[107] and collected in *Sibylline Leaves* (1817). It is one of Coleridge's Conversation Poems (see the introductory note to "The Eolian Harp", pp. 275–76).

There were widespread British fears of a French invasion in 1798. They were not without foundation: "The years 1797–8,

[105] *honey-dew hath fed*: Honey-dew is "an ideally sweet or luscious substance" (*Oxford English Dictionary*, s.v. "honey-dew").

[106] *drunk the milk of Paradise*: Cf. Plato, *Ion* 534a–b:

For all good poets, epic as well as lyric, compose their beautiful poems not by art, but because they are inspired and possessed. And as the Corybantian revellers when they dance are not in their right mind, so the lyric poets are not in their right mind when they are composing their beautiful strains: but when falling under the power of music and metre they are inspired and possessed; like Bacchic maidens who draw milk and honey from the rivers when they are under the influence of Dionysus but not when they are in their right mind. And the soul of the lyric poet does the same, as they themselves say; for they tell us that they bring songs from honeyed fountains, culling them out of the gardens and dells of the Muses; they, like the bees, winging their way from flower to flower. And this is true. For the poet is a light and winged and holy thing, and there is no invention in him until he has been inspired and is out of his senses, and the mind is no longer in him: when he has not attained to this state, he is powerless and is unable to utter his oracles.

Cf. also Exodus 3:7–8: "Then the LORD said, 'I have seen the affliction of my people … and I have come down to deliver them out of the hand of the Egyptians, and to bring them up out of that land into a good and broad land, a land flowing with milk and honey'", and Keats, "La Belle Dame Sans Merci", lines 25–26: "She found me roots of relish sweet, / And honey wild, and manna-dew". See also the note to line 62 of "Dejection: An Ode".

[107] See the note to line 12 of Blake's "London".

the crisis of the first half of the war.... Invasion threatened
us from all the harbours of the Low Countries, France, and
Spain."[108] France had declared war against the Holy Roman
Empire on April 20, 1792; invaded the Austrian Netherlands
(Belgium) in November, 1792; declared war on Great Britain
on February 1, 1793; invaded Italy in April 1796; and invaded
Switzerland in February 1798. French revolutionary troops
entered Rome on February 10, 1798, proclaimed Rome a
republic, and imprisoned Pope Pius VI, who died in captivity
on August 29. A failed French landing (with Irish collusion)
of fifteen thousand troops in Ireland in December 1796 was
followed, on May 23, 1798, by the Irish Rebellion. On August
22, 1798, about one thousand French soldiers arrived in sup-
port, but the rebellion had been put down by October. In the
wake of these developments, Coleridge felt obliged to defend
himself simultaneously as a patriot and as a champion of lib-
erty. Coleridge's position here (like his opinions on the French
Revolutionary Wars) is close to that of G.K. Chesterton:
"'My country, right or wrong,' is a thing that no patriot would
think of saying except in a desperate case. It is like saying, 'My
mother, drunk or sober.'"[109]

Fears in Solitude

A green and silent spot, amid the hills,
A small and silent dell![110] O'er stiller place
No singing sky-lark ever poised himself.
The hills are heathy, save that swelling slope,
Which hath a gay and gorgeous[111] covering on,   5
All golden with the never-bloomless furze,

---

[108] Keith Feiling, *A History of England: From the Coming of the English to 1918*
(London: Book Club Associates, 1973), p. 747.

[109] *The Defendant* (New York: Dodd, Mead, 1902), p. 125.

[110] *green and silent spot . . . small and silent dell*: The scene is set, as in many of his
poems in this period, in the Quantock Hills, Somerset.

[111] *gay and gorgeous*: richly colored.

Which now blooms most profusely: but the dell,
Bathed by the mist, is fresh and delicate
As vernal corn-field,[112] or the unripe flax,
When, through its half-transparent stalks, at eve,   10
The level sunshine glimmers with green light.[113]
Oh! 'tis a quiet spirit-healing nook!
Which all, methinks, would love; but chiefly he,
The humble man, who, in his youthful years,
Knew just so much of folly, as had made   15
His early manhood more securely wise!
Here he might lie on fern or withered heath,
While from the singing-lark (that sings unseen[114]
The minstrelsy that solitude loves best),
And from the sun, and from the breezy air,   20
Sweet influences trembled o'er his frame;
And he, with many feelings, many thoughts,
Made up a meditative joy, and found
Religious meanings in the forms of Nature![115]
And so, his senses gradually wrapt   25
In a half sleep, he dreams of better worlds,
And dreaming hears thee still, O singing-lark,
That singest like an angel[116] in the clouds!

[112] *corn-field*: wheat-field.

[113] *level sunshine glimmers with green light*: See the note to line 29 of "Dejection: An Ode".

[114] *singing-lark (that sings unseen*: Cf. Wordsworth, "To the Cuckoo", lines 15–16.

[115] *from the singing-lark . . . forms of Nature*: See the note on the Book of Nature in the introductory note to "Frost at Midnight", p. 351.

[116] *Religious meanings in the forms of Nature . . . singest like an angel*: Cf. Revelation 19:11, 17: "Then I saw heaven opened, and behold, a white horse! He who sat upon it ... judges and makes war.... [A]nd the name by which he is called is The Word of God.... Then I saw an angel standing in the sun, and with a loud voice he called to all the birds that fly in midheaven, 'Come, gather for the great supper of God'". Cf. J. M. W. Turner's (1775–1851) painting *The Angel Standing in the Sun* (1846). An angel is, literally, a messenger. This angelic bird is an instance of reading the Book of Nature. See the notes to line 63 of "The Ancient Mariner" and line 531 of "Christabel".

My God! it is a melancholy thing
For such a man, who would full fain[117] preserve   30
His soul in calmness, yet perforce must feel
For all his human brethren—O my God!
It weighs upon the heart, that he must think
What uproar and what strife may now be stirring
This way or that way o'er these silent hills—   35
Invasion, and the thunder and the shout,
And all the crash of onset;[118] fear and rage,
And undetermined conflict—even now,
Even now, perchance, and in his native isle:
Carnage and groans beneath this blessed sun!   40
We have offended, Oh! my countrymen!
We have offended very grievously,[119]
And been most tyrannous. From east to west
A groan of accusation pierces Heaven!
The wretched plead against us; multitudes   45
Countless and vehement, the sons of God,
Our brethren! Like a cloud that travels on,
Steamed up from Cairo's swamps of pestilence,[120]
Even so, my countrymen! have we gone forth
And borne to distant tribes slavery and pangs,   50
And, deadlier far, our vices, whose deep taint
With slow perdition murders the whole man,
His body and his soul! Meanwhile, at home,

[117] *fain*: willingly, gladly.

[118] *crash of onset*: attack, assault.

[119] *We have offended ... very grievously*: See the General Confession in the Anglican liturgy: "Almighty and most merciful Father, We have erred and strayed from thy ways like lost sheep, We have followed too much the devices and desires of our own hearts, We have offended against thy holy laws" (The Book of Common Prayer [London: Everyman's Library, 1999], p. 70).

[120] *from Cairo's swamps of pestilence*: In August 1797, Napoleon (with the Directory of the Republic increasingly dependent on their commander of the Interior, who was not to be First Consul till November 9, 1799) proposed an invasion of Egypt to cut off British access to India. The Egyptian campaign began in May 1798, and in spite of success against Ottoman forces, it was effectively ended by Nelson's crushing victory at the Battle of the Nile (August 1–3, 1798). Plague was rife in the Middle East, and the French lost half of their thirty thousand casualties to disease.

All individual dignity and power
Engulfed in Courts, Committees, Institutions,   55
Associations and Societies,
A vain, speech-mouthing, speech-reporting Guild,
One Benefit-Club for mutual flattery,
We have drunk up, demure as at a grace,
Pollutions from the brimming cup of wealth;[121]   60
Contemptuous of all honourable rule,
Yet bartering freedom and the poor man's[122] life
For gold, as at a market! The sweet words
Of Christian promise, words that even yet
Might stem destruction, were they wisely preached,   65
Are muttered o'er by men, whose tones proclaim
How flat and wearisome they feel their trade:
Rank[123] scoffers some, but most too indolent
To deem them falsehoods or to know their truth.
Oh! blasphemous! the Book of Life is made   70
A superstitious instrument, on which
We gabble o'er the oaths we mean to break;
For all must swear[124] —all and in every place,

---

[121] *drunk up . . . Pollutions from the brimming cup of wealth*: Cf. Revelation 17:4:
"The woman was clothed in purple and scarlet, and adorned with gold and jewels
and pearls, holding in her hand a golden cup full of abominations and the impu-
rities of her fornication", and Jeremiah 51:7: "Babylon was a golden cup in the
LORD's hand, making all the earth drunken".

[122] *poor man's*: Jesus Christ is *the* poor man. See Luke 9:58: "And Jesus said to
him, 'Foxes have holes, and birds of the air have nests; but the Son of man has
nowhere to lay his head"; also, St. Augustine: "Fear Christ above; recognise Him
below. Have Christ above bestowing His bounty, recognise Him here in need.
Here He is poor, there He is rich. That Christ is poor here, He tells us Himself for
me, 'I was an hungred, I was thirsty, I was naked, I was a stranger, I was in prison.
And to some He said, You have ministered unto Me, and to some He said, You
have not ministered unto Me'" (Sermon 73).

[123] *Rank*: probable pun—cf. Shakespeare, *As You Like It*, Act 1, scene 2, lines
101–2: Touchstone: "Nay, if I keep not my rank—"; Rosalind: "Thou losest thy
old smell".

[124] *all must swear*: reference to the Test Acts framed against Nonconformists
and Catholics in the two decades following the Restoration of the Monarchy
(1660). They restricted public office to those who would take the Oath of
Supremacy (an oath against any right of resistance to the established govern-
ment), receive Anglican holy communion, and make a declaration against the
dogma of transubstantiation. They were finally repealed in 1828.

College and wharf, council and justice-court;
All, all must swear, the briber and the bribed,   75
Merchant and lawyer, senator and priest,
The rich, the poor, the old man and the young;
All, all make up one scheme of perjury,
That faith doth reel; the very name of God
Sounds like a juggler's charm;[125] and, bold with joy,   80
Forth from his dark and lonely hiding-place,
(Portentous sight!) the owlet[126] Atheism,
Sailing on obscene wings athwart the noon,
Drops his blue-fringèd lids, and holds them close,
And hooting at the glorious sun in Heaven,[127]   85
Cries out, "Where is it?"

                                    Thankless too for peace,
(Peace long preserved by fleets and perilous seas)
Secure from actual warfare, we have loved
To swell the war-whoop, passionate for war!
Alas! for ages ignorant of all   90
Its ghastlier workings, (famine or blue plague,
Battle, or siege, or flight through wintry-snows),
We, this whole people, have been clamorous
For war and bloodshed; animating sports,
The which we pay for as a thing to talk of,   95
Spectators and not combatants![128] No guess

[125] *name of God / Sounds like a juggler's charm*: A juggler is a magician/illusionist; thus "God" or "Jesus Christ" is turned into a political "Abracadabra".

[126] *owlet*: Most owls, of course, are nocturnal, see exceptionally well at night, and were often (wrongly) thought to be hampered or blinded in the daylight. There is also a pagan/Christian comparison implicit (involving jabs at the Enlightenment and classicism), since the owl was sacred to the Graeco-Roman goddess of wisdom, Pallas Athena/Minerva, in a world not yet illuminated by the light of Christ the Son/sun.

[127] *sun in Heaven*: See the note to line 98 of "The Ancient Mariner"; also, vis-à-vis the prominence of the sun in the sky (the sun is often a symbol of Christ): "The fool says in his heart, 'There is no God'" (Psalm 14:1).

[128] *Spectators and not combatants*: Britain was funding Austria's military resistance to France in 1798.

Anticipative of a wrong unfelt,
No speculation[129] on contingency,
However dim and vague, too vague and dim
To yield a justifying cause; and forth,   100
(Stuffed out with big preamble, holy names,
And adjurations of the God in Heaven),
We send our mandates for the certain death
Of thousands and ten thousands! Boys and girls,
And women, that would groan to see a child   105
Pull off an insect's leg, all read of war,
The best amusement for our morning-meal![130]
The poor wretch, who has learnt his only prayers
From curses, who knows scarcely words enough
To ask a blessing from his Heavenly Father,   110
Becomes a fluent phraseman, absolute
And technical in victories and defeats,
And all our dainty[131] terms for fratricide;
Terms which we trundle smoothly o'er our tongues
Like mere abstractions, empty sounds to which   115
We join no feeling and attach no form!
As if the soldier died without a wound;
As if the fibres of this godlike frame
Were gored without a pang; as if the wretch,
Who fell in battle, doing bloody deeds,   120
Passed off to Heaven, translated and not killed;
As though he had no wife to pine for him,
No God to judge him! Therefore, evil days
Are coming on us, O my countrymen!
And what if all-avenging Providence,[132]   125
Strong and retributive, should make us know
The meaning of our words, force us to feel

---

[129] *No guess . . . No speculation:* probably a pun on the extent to which British investments were, supposedly, responsible for Britain's political stance.

[130] *morning-meal:* i.e., over the morning paper.

[131] *dainty:* overdelicate; pleasing to the palate.

[132] *all-avenging Providence:* See the note to Wordsworth, *Prelude,* bk. 10, line 452.

The desolation and the agony
Of our fierce doings?

                 Spare us yet awhile,
Father and God! O! spare us yet awhile![133]   130
Oh! let not English women drag their flight
Fainting beneath the burthen[134] of their babes,
Of the sweet infants, that but yesterday
Laughed at the breast! Sons, brothers, husbands, all
Who ever gazed with fondness on the forms   135
Which grew up with you round the same fire-side,
And all who ever heard the sabbath-bells
Without the infidel's scorn, make yourselves pure!
Stand forth! be men! repel an impious foe,
Impious and false, a light yet cruel race,   140
Who laugh away all virtue, mingling mirth
With deeds of murder; and still promising
Freedom, themselves too sensual to be free,[135]
Poison life's amities, and cheat the heart
Of faith and quiet hope,[136] and all that soothes   145
And all that lifts the spirit! Stand we forth;
Render them back upon the insulted ocean,
And let them toss as idly on its waves[137]
As the vile sea-weed, which some mountain-blast
Swept from our shores! And oh! may we return   150
Not with a drunken triumph, but with fear,
Repenting of the wrongs with which we stung
So fierce a foe to frenzy!

---

[133] *Spare us yet awhile, / Father and God! O! spare us yet awhile!* See the General Confession in the Anglican liturgy: "But thou, O Lord, have mercy upon us miserable offenders; Spare thou them, O God, which confess their faults" (Book of Common Prayer, p. 70).

[134] *burthen*: burden.

[135] *too sensual to be free*: See the note to line 85 of "France: An Ode".

[136] *amities, . . . faith and quiet hope*: love ("amities"), faith, and hope—the three theological virtues.

[137] *toss as idly on its waves*: Cf. "Ancient Mariner", lines 117–18.

I have told,
O Britons! O my brethren! I have told
Most bitter truth, but without bitterness.   155
Nor deem my zeal or factious[138] or[139] mis-timed;
For never can true courage dwell with them,
Who, playing tricks with conscience, dare not look
At their own vices. We have been too long
Dupes of a deep delusion! Some, belike,[140]   160
Groaning with restless enmity, expect
All change from change of constituted power;
As if a Government had been a robe,
On which our vice and wretchedness were tagged
Like fancy-points[141] and fringes, with the robe,   165
Pulled off at pleasure. Fondly[142] these attach
A radical causation to a few
Poor drudges of chastising Providence,
Who borrow all their hues and qualities
From our own folly and rank wickedness,   170
Which gave them birth and nursed them. Others,
    meanwhile,
Dote with a mad idolatry; and all
Who will not fall before their images,
And yield them worship, they are enemies
Even of their country!

                Such have I been deemed—   175
But, O dear Britain! O my Mother Isle!
Needs must thou prove a name most dear and holy
To me, a son, a brother, and a friend,
A husband, and a father! who revere
All bonds of natural love, and find them all   180
Within the limits of thy rocky shores.

[138] *factious*: given to faction; seditious.
[139] *or factious or*: i.e., either factious or.
[140] *belike*: to all appearances.
[141] *fancy-points*: needle-lace.
[142] *Fondly*: foolishly.

O native Britain! O my Mother Isle!
How shouldst thou prove aught else but dear and holy
To me, who from thy lakes and mountain-hills,
Thy clouds, thy quiet dales, thy rocks and seas,   185
Have drunk in all my intellectual life,
All sweet sensations, all ennobling thoughts,
All adoration of the God in nature,
All lovely and all honourable things,
Whatever makes this mortal spirit feel   190
The joy and greatness of its future being?
There lives nor form nor feeling in my soul
Unborrowed from my country! O divine
And beauteous island! thou hast been my sole
And most magnificent temple, in the which   195
I walk with awe, and sing my stately songs,
Loving the God that made me!—[143]

                                May my fears,
My filial fears, be vain! and may the vaunts
And menace of the vengeful enemy
Pass like the gust, that roared and died away   200
In the distant tree: which heard, and only heard
In this low dell, bowed not the delicate grass.

            But now the gentle dew-fall sends abroad
The fruit-like perfume of the golden furze:
The light has left the summit of the hill,   205
Though still a sunny gleam lies beautiful,

---

[143] *O native Britain . . . Loving the God that made me*: Compare these 16 lines
with the following statement by T.S. Eliot: "[The term 'culture'] includes all the
characteristic activities and interests of a people: Derby Day, Henley Regatta,
Cowes, the twelfth of August, a cup final, the dog races, the pin table, the dart
board, Wensleydale cheese, boiled cabbage cut into sections, beetroot in vine-
gar, nineteenth-century Gothic churches and the music of Elgar. The reader can
make his own list. And then we have to face the strange idea that what is part
of our culture is also a part of our *lived* religion" (T.S. Eliot, *Notes towards the
Definition of Culture* [London: Faber, 1979], p. 31).

Aslant the ivied beacon. Now farewell,
Farewell, awhile, O soft and silent spot!
On the green sheep-track, up the heathy hill,
Homeward I wind my way; and lo! Recalled   210
From bodings that have well nigh wearied me,
I find myself upon the brow, and pause
Startled! And after lonely sojourning
In such a quiet and surrounded nook,
This burst of prospect, here the shadowy main,[144]   215
Dim-tinted, there the mighty majesty
Of that huge amphitheatre of rich
And elmy fields, seems like society—
Conversing with the mind, and giving it
A livelier impulse and a dance of thought!   220
And now, belovèd Stowey! I behold
Thy church-tower,[145] and, methinks, the four huge elms
Clustering, which mark the mansion of my friend;[146]
And close behind them, hidden from my view,
Is my own lowly cottage, where my babe   225
And my babe's mother dwell in peace![147] With light
And quickened footsteps thitherward I tend,
Remembering thee, O green and silent dell!
And grateful, that by nature's quietness
And solitary musings, all my heart   230
Is softened, and made worthy to indulge[148]
Love, and the thoughts that yearn for human kind.

---

[144] *shadowy main*: Bristol Channel.

[145] *church-tower*: church tower of St. Mary the Virgin, Nether Stowey.

[146] *my friend*: his neighbor, Thomas Poole; see the introductory note to "This Lime-Tree Bower My Prison" p. 280.

[147] *belovéd Stowey . . . dwell in peace*: Cf. "Frost at Midnight" and "The Eolian Harp".

[148] *made worthy to indulge*: to make room for, as well as to give itself up to.

France: An Ode

"France: An Ode" was first published in the *Morning Post* on April 16, 1798, then in 1798 with "Fears in Solitude" and "Frost at Midnight" by Joseph Johnson,[149] and collected in *Sibylline Leaves* in 1817. (For the political background to this poem, see the introduction to "Fears in Solitude" [pp. 295–96]; it was provoked, above all, by the French invasion of Switzerland in February 1798). Coleridge republished it in the *Morning Post* on October 14, 1802, with the following *argument* or summary:

First Stanza. An invocation to those objects in Nature the contemplation of which had inspired the Poet with a devotional love of Liberty. *Second Stanza.* The exultation of the Poet at the commencement of the French Revolution, and his unqualified abhorrence of the Alliance against the Republic. *Third Stanza.* The blasphemies and horrors during the domination of the Terrorists regarded by the Poet as a transient storm, and as the natural consequence of the former despotism and of the foul superstition of Popery. Reason, indeed, began to suggest many apprehensions; yet still the Poet struggled to retain the hope that France would make conquests by no other means than by presenting to the observation of Europe a people more happy and better instructed than under other forms of Government. *Fourth Stanza.* Switzerland, and the Poet's recantation. *Fifth Stanza.* An address to Liberty, in which the Poet expresses his conviction that those feelings and that grand *ideal* of Freedom which the mind attains by its contemplation of its individual nature, and of the sublime surrounding objects (see Stanza the First) do not belong to men as a society, nor can possibly be either gratified or realized under any form, of human government; but belong to the individual man, so far as he is pure, and inflamed with the love and adoration of God in Nature.

[149] See the note to line 12 of Blake's "London".

France: An Ode

I

Ye Clouds! that far above me float and pause,
Whose pathless march no mortal may controul!
    Ye Ocean-Waves! that, wheresoe'er ye roll,
    Yield homage only to eternal laws!
Ye Woods! that listen to the night-birds singing,   5
    Midway the smooth and perilous slope reclined,
Save when your own imperious branches swinging,
    Have made a solemn music of the wind!
Where, like a man belovèd of God,
Through glooms, which never woodman trod,   10
    How oft, pursuing fancies[150] holy,
My moonlight way o'er flowering weeds I wound,
    Inspired, beyond the guess of folly,
By each rude[151] shape and wild unconquerable sound!
O ye loud Waves! and O ye Forests high!   15
    And O ye Clouds that far above me soared!
Thou rising Sun! thou blue rejoicing Sky!
    Yea, every thing that is and will be free!
    Bear witness for me, wheresoe'er ye be,
    With what deep worship I have still adored   20
        The spirit of divinest Liberty.

II

When France in wrath her giant-limbs upreared,
    And with that oath,[152] which smote air, earth,
        and sea,
    Stamped her strong foot and said she would be free,

[150] *fancies*: mental images; notions.
[151] *rude*: rough, rugged; uncultivated.
[152] *that oath*: the celebrated Tennis Court Oath of June 20, 1789, in which the Third Estate (which had reconstituted itself as the National Assembly on June 17) took a solemn oath, committing themselves unconditionally to solidarity and the creation of a new constitution. Cf. Jacques-Louis David's (1748–1825) painting and sketch of the scene.

Bear witness for me, how I hoped and feared!   25
With what a joy my lofty gratulation[153]
    Unawed I sang, amid a slavish band:
And when to whelm[154] the disenchanted nation,
    Like fiends embattled by a wizard's wand,
      The Monarchs[155] marched in evil day,   30
    And Britain joined the dire array;
Though dear her shores and circling ocean,
Though many friendships, many youthful loves
    Had swoln the patriot emotion
And flung a magic light o'er all her hills and groves;   35
Yet still my voice, unaltered, sang defeat
    To all that braved the tyrant-quelling lance,
And shame too long delayed and vain retreat!
For ne'er, O Liberty! with partial aim
I dimmed thy light or damped thy holy flame;   40
    But blessed the pæans[156] of delivered France,[157]
And hung my head and wept at Britain's name.

III

"And what," I said, "though Blasphemy's loud scream
    With that sweet music of deliverance strove!
    Though all the fierce and drunken passions wove   45
A dance more wild than e'er was maniac's dream!
    Ye storms, that round the dawning East assembled,

---

[153] *gratulation*: exultation; the "expression of pleasure at a person's success, good fortune, or the like" (*Oxford English Dictionary*, s.v. "gratulation").

[154] *whelm*: submerge, bury; overpower.

[155] *Monarchs*: particularly the monarch Francis II of Austria (reigned 1792–1835) and the Prussian kings Frederick William II (reigned 1786–1797) and Frederick William III (reigned 1797–1840).

[156] *pæans*: songs or hymns of thanksgiving or exultation, especially for victory.

[157] *delivered France*: On September 20, 1792, the Allies under Brunswick were unexpectedly halted by the French at the indecisive Battle of Valmy, and withdrew from France. The next day, the National Assembly abolished the monarchy and declared France a Republic. Valmy almost certainly saved the revolution.

The Sun was rising,[158] though ye hid his light!"
  And when, to soothe my soul, that hoped and
    trembled,
The dissonance ceased, and all seemed calm and bright;   50
  When France her front deep-scarr'd and gory
  Concealed with clustering wreaths of glory;
    When, insupportably[159] advancing,
  Her arm made mockery of the warrior's ramp;[160]
    While timid looks of fury glancing,   55
  Domestic treason, crushed beneath her fatal stamp,
Writhed like a wounded dragon[161] in his gore;
  Then I reproached my fears that would not flee;
"And soon," I said, "shall Wisdom teach her lore
In the low huts of them that toil and groan!   60
And, conquering by her happiness alone,
  Shall France compel the nations to be free,
Till Love and Joy look round, and call the Earth
  their own."

IV

Forgive me, Freedom! O forgive those dreams!
  I hear thy voice, I hear thy loud lament,   65
  From bleak Helvetia's[162] icy cavern sent—

---

[158] *East assembled, / The Sun was rising*: For the spiritual symbolism of the east, see the note to line 2 of Blake's "To the Muses"; for the sun, see the note to line 98 of "The Ancient Mariner".

[159] *insupportably*: irresistibly.

[160] *ramp*: furious, threatening posture or behavior. For this and the previous line, see Milton, *Samson Agonistes*, lines 136–39: "When insupportably his foot advanced, / In scorn of their proud arms and warlike tools, / Spurned them to death by troops. The bold Ascalonite / Fled from his iron ramp".

[161] *crushed beneath her fatal stamp, / Writhed like a wounded dragon*: Cf. Revelation 12:1–3, 7–8: "And a great sign appeared in heaven, a woman clothed with the sun.... [S]he was with child and she cried out in her pangs of birth.... And another sign appeared in heaven; behold a great red dragon.... Now war arose in heaven ... and the dragon and his angels fought, but they were defeated".

[162] *Helvetia's*: i.e., Switzerland's.

I hear thy groans upon her blood-stained streams!
   Heroes, that for your peaceful country perished,
And ye that, fleeing, spot[163] your mountain-snows
   With bleeding wounds; forgive me, that I cherished   70
One thought that ever blessed your cruel foes!
     To scatter rage, and traitorous guilt,
     Where Peace her jealous home had built;
       A patriot-race to disinherit
Of all that made their stormy wilds so dear;   75
       And with inexpiable spirit
To taint the bloodless[164] freedom of the mountaineer—
O France, that mockest Heaven, adulterous,[165] blind,
     And patriot only in pernicious toils![166]
Are these thy boasts, Champion of human kind?   80
   To mix with Kings in the low lust of sway,[167]
Yell in the hunt, and share the murderous prey;
To insult the shrine of Liberty with spoils
   From freemen torn; to tempt and to betray?[168]

---

[163] *that, fleeing, spot*: with the added connotation of "taint".

[164] *To taint the bloodless*: i.e., guiltless of others' blood.

[165] *mockest Heaven, adulterous*: Adultery and sexual impurity are characteristic biblical analogues for idolatry and infidelity to God. See Jeremiah 3:1: "If a man divorces his wife and she goes from him and becomes another man's wife, will he return to her? Would not that land be greatly polluted?"; also, St. Augustine: "Thus the soul is guilty of fornication when she turns from You and seeks from any other source what she will nowhere find pure and without taint unless she returns to You" (*Confessions* 2.6 [London: J.M. Dent, 1945], p. 27). The same symbolism is implied in the doctrine of the mystical union of Christ with the Church; see Ephesians 5:23: "[T]he husband is the head of the wife as Christ is the head of the Church".

[166] *toils*: works; nets; traps.

[167] *sway*: power; rule.

[168] *spoils / From freemen torn; to tempt and to betray*: allusions to the destruction of the ancient Republic of Venice; on October 17, 1797, the Treaty of Campo Formio saw Austria cede the Austrian Netherlands (Belgium) to France in exchange for Venice, Istria, and Dalmatia.

V

The Sensual and the Dark[169] rebel in vain,   85
Slaves by their own compulsion! In mad game
They burst their manacles and wear the name
    Of Freedom, graven on a heavier chain![170]
O Liberty! with profitless endeavour
Have I pursued thee, many a weary hour;   90
    But thou nor swell'st the victor's strain,[171] nor ever
Didst breathe thy soul in forms of human power.
    Alike from all, howe'er they praise thee,
    (Nor[172] prayer, nor boastful name delays[173] thee)
        Alike from Priestcraft's[174] harpy[175] minions,   95

---

[169] *Sensual and the Dark*: Christianity views sensuality as a form of bondage. See Matthew 5:8: "Blessed are the pure in heart, for they shall see God"; Titus 1:15: "To the pure all things are pure, but to the corrupt and unbelieving nothing is pure"; Hosea 4:11: "Wine and new wine take away the understanding"; and Aquinas: "[T]he daughters of lust are ... blindness of mind, thoughtlessness, inconstancy, rashness, self-love, hatred of God, love of this world and abhorrence or despair of a future world" (*Summa Theologiae*, II–II, q. 153, art. 5). Cf. "Fears in Solitude", lines 139–46.

[170] *Freedom, graven on a heavier chain*: "At Genoa, the word 'Liberty' is, or used to be, engraved on the chains of the galley-slaves, and the doors of the dungeons" (*Table Talk and Omniana of Samuel Taylor Coleridge* [Oxford University, 1917], p. 151).

[171] *strain*: melody, tune.

[172] *Nor*: neither.

[173] *boastful name delays*: with the added sense of "tempers" "modifies".

[174] *Priestcraft's*: Priestcraft is a standard derogatory term for the (usually Roman Catholic) clergy, its activities, disposition, and influence: "I found him denying or explaining away the existence of that priestcraft which is a notorious fact to every honest student of history" (quoted by Charles Kingsley [1819–1875], in "What, then, does Dr Newman mean?" in Newman, *Apologia* [London: H. Frowde, 1913], p. 33).

[175] *harpy*: In Greek mythology, the harpies (literally "snatchers") were monstrous birds with the faces (and often bare breasts) of women. These cruel and voracious beasts were sent by the gods to steal or defile the food of King Phineas, who had, according to one version, been blinded by the gods for his misuse of his gift of prophecy. The point of the jibe is that, like the harpies, the priests and their hangers-on are robbing the blind (perhaps in Providential retribution for allowing the prophetic office of the Church to be betrayed into Romish degradation); and, the imputation of a monstrous (and implicitly effeminate and dishonest) asexuality to the Catholic clergy (i.e., the celibate priests were not, sexually, as masculine as they looked, just as the harpies were only female to the

And factious[176] Blasphemy's obscener slaves,
　Thou speedest on thy subtle pinions,[177]
The guide of homeless winds, and playmate of the waves!
And there I felt thee!—on that sea-cliff's verge,
　Whose pines, scarce travelled[178] by the breeze above,　100
Had made one murmur with the distant surge!
Yes, while I stood and gazed, my temples bare,
And shot my being through earth, sea and air,
　Possessing all things with intensest love,
　　O Liberty! my spirit felt thee there.　105

waist). Cf. Charles Kingsley: "Truth, for its own sake, had never been a vir-
tue with the Roman clergy. Father Newman informs us that it need not, and
on the whole ought not to be; that cunning is the weapon which Heaven has
given to the saints wherewith to withstand the brute male force of the wicked
world which marries and is given in marriage" (ibid, p. 21).

[176] *factious*: given to faction; seditious.

[177] *pinions*: wings; flight feathers.

[178] *travelled*: worked upon; moved.

Lewti[179]

OR THE CIRCASSIAN[180] LOVE-CHAUNT

At midnight by the stream I roved,
To forget the form I loved.
Image of Lewti! from my mind
Depart; for Lewti is not kind.

The Moon was high, the moonlight gleam   5
    And the shadow of a star
Heaved upon Tamaha's[181] stream;
    But the rock shone brighter far,
The rock half sheltered from my view
By pendent boughs of tressy[182] yew.—   10

---

[179] Published in *Sibylline Leaves*, 1817; originally intended for *Lyrical Ballads*, 1798, but replaced at the last moment with "The Nightingale". "But here, in 'Lewti,' he has his style, his lucid and liquid melody, his imagery of moving light and the faintly veiled transparency of air, his vague, wildly romantic subject matter, coming from no one knows where, meaning one hardly knows what; but already a magic, an incantation.... It ... has all the imagery of a dream" (Symons, *Romantic Movement*, p. 140). The influence of this poem on Edgar Allan Poe (1809–1849) is manifest.

[180] CIRCASSIAN: in the northern Caucasus; Circassian (Adyghe) women were known for their great beauty and refinement, and also for their sorry lot at being often sold or forced into concubinage in the Ottoman Empire. Cf.: Henry Fielding's (1707–1754) *Tom Jones*: "How contemptible would the brightest Circassian beauty, drest in all the jewels of the Indies, appear to my eyes!"; "a Circassian maid richly and elegantly attired for the Grand Signior's seraglio" ([London: Penguin, 1994], p. 239); William Collins' fourth Persian Eclogue, lines 53–58: "In vain *Circassia* boasts her spicy Groves,/For ever fam'd for pure and happy Loves:/In vain she boasts her fairest of the Fair,/Their Eyes' blue languish, and their golden Hair!/Those Eyes in Tears, their fruitless Grief must send,/Those Hairs the *Tartar*'s cruel Hand shall rend"; and Byron, *Don Juan*, canto 4, 114: "[F]ifteen hundred dollars/For one Circassian, a sweet girl, were given,/Warranted virgin. Beauty's brightest colours/Had decked her out in all the hues of heaven./Her sale sent home some disappointed bawlers,/Who bade on till the hundreds reached the eleven,/But when the offer went beyond, they knew/'Twas for the Sultan and at once withdrew."

[181] *Tamaha's*: Tamaha is a fictional river, derived from the Altamaha River in Georgia, U.S.A., via William Bartram's (1739–1823) *Travels*.

[182] *tressy*: like tresses.

So shines my Lewti's forehead fair,
Gleaming through her sable hair.
Image of Lewti! from my mind
Depart; for Lewti is not kind.

I saw a cloud of palest hue,   15
    Onward to the moon it passed;
Still brighter and more bright it grew,
With floating colours not a few,
    Till it reached the moon at last:
Then the cloud was wholly bright,   20
With a rich and amber light![183]
And so with many a hope I seek,
    And with such joy I find my Lewti;
And even so my pale wan cheek
    Drinks in as deep a flush of beauty!   25
Nay, treacherous image! leave my mind,
If Lewti never will be kind.

The little cloud—it floats away,
    Away it goes; away so soon?
Alas! it has no power to stay: 30
Its hues are dim, its hues are grey—
    Away it passes from the moon!
How mournfully it seems to fly,
    Ever fading more and more,
To joyless regions of the sky—   35
    And now 'tis whiter than before!
As white as my poor cheek will be,
    When, Lewti! on my couch I lie,
A dying man for love of thee.
Nay, treacherous image! leave my mind—   40
And yet, thou didst not look unkind.

---

[183] *colours . . . rich and amber light:* On Coleridge and color, see the note on
line 29 of "Dejection: An Ode".

I saw a vapour in the sky,
   Thin, and white, and very high;
I ne'er beheld so thin a cloud:
   Perhaps the breezes that can fly 45
   Now below and now above,
Have snatched aloft the lawny shroud[184]
   Of Lady fair—that died for love.
For maids, as well as youths, have perished
From fruitless love too fondly cherished. 50
Nay, treacherous image! leave my mind—
For Lewti never will be kind.

Hush! my heedless feet from under
   Slip the crumbling banks for ever:
Like echoes to a distant thunder, 55
     They plunge into the gentle river.
The river-swans have heard my tread,
And startle from their reedy bed.
O beauteous birds! methinks ye measure
     Your movements to some heavenly tune! 60
O beauteous birds! 'tis such a pleasure
     To see you move beneath the moon,
I would it were your true delight
To sleep by day and wake all night.

I know the place where Lewti lies, 65
When silent night has closed her eyes:
     It is a breezy jasmine-bower,
The nightingale sings o'er her head:
     Voice of the Night! had I the power
That leafy labyrinth to thread, 70
And creep, like thee, with soundless tread,
I then might view her bosom white
Heaving lovely to my sight,

---

[184] *lawny shroud*: a fine, light, semitransparent linen (from "Lawn").

As these two swans together heave
On the gently swelling wave.   75

Oh! that she saw me in a dream,
    And dreamt that I had died for care;
All pale and wasted I would seem,
    Yet fair withal, as spirits are!
I'd die indeed, if I might see   80
Her bosom heave, and heave for me!
Soothe, gentle image! soothe my mind!
To-morrow Lewti may be kind.

Love[185]

All thoughts, all passions, all delights,
Whatever stirs this mortal frame,
All are but ministers of Love,
    And feed his sacred flame.

Oft in my waking dreams do I   5
Live o'er again that happy hour,
When midway on the mount I lay,
    Beside the ruined tower.

The moonshine, stealing o'er the scene,
Had blended with the lights of eve;   10
And she was there, my hope, my joy,
    My own dear Genevieve![186]

[185] Originally published in the *Morning Post* on December 21, 1799, as an introduction to the (never to be completed) "Ballad of the Dark Ladie", and then, as "Love", in *Lyrical Ballads* (1800). The poem was inspired by Sara Hutchinson; see "Dejection: An Ode" (p. 395). The influence of this poem (particularly from line 57 to the end) on Keats' "La Belle Dame sans Merci" is manifest.

[186] *My own dear Genevieve*: See the introductory note to "Genevieve", p. 269.

She leant against the armèd man,
The statue of the armèd knight;
She stood and listened to my lay,[187]   15
    Amid the lingering light.

Few sorrows hath she of her own,
My hope! my joy! my Genevieve!
She loves me best, whene'er I sing
    The songs that make her grieve.   20

I played a soft and doleful air,
I sang an old and moving story—
An old rude[188] song, that suited well
    That ruin wild and hoary.[189]

She listened with a flitting blush,   25
With downcast eyes and modest grace;
For well she knew, I could not choose
    But gaze upon her face.

I told her of the Knight that wore
Upon his shield a burning brand;[190]   30
And that for ten long years he wooed
    The Lady of the Land.

I told her how he pined: and ah!
The deep, the low, the pleading tone
With which I sang another's love,   35
    Interpreted my own.

She listened with a flitting blush,
With downcast eyes, and modest grace;

---

[187] *lay*: narrative song.
[188] *rude*: simple; unsophisticated; robust.
[189] *hoary*: gray or white with age; ancient.
[190] *burning brand*: i.e., a piece of burning wood, a torch.

And she forgave me, that I gazed
    Too fondly on her face!   40

But when I told the cruel scorn
That crazed that bold and lovely Knight,
And that he crossed the mountain-woods,
    Nor rested day nor night;

That sometimes from the savage den,   45
And sometimes from the darksome shade,
And sometimes starting up at once[191]
    In green and sunny glade,—

There came and looked him in the face
An angel beautiful and bright;   50
And that he knew it was a Fiend,[192]
    This miserable Knight!

And that unknowing what he did,
He leaped amid a murderous band,
And saved from outrage worse than death   55
    The Lady of the Land!

And how she wept, and clasped his knees;
And how she tended him in vain—
And ever strove to expiate
    The scorn that crazed his brain;—   60

And that she nursed him in a cave;
And how his madness went away,
When on the yellow forest-leaves
    A dying man he lay;—

---

[191] *at once:* suddenly.
[192] *angel . . . Fiend:* Cf. 2 Corinthians 11:13–14: "For such men are false apostles, deceitful workmen, disguising themselves as apostles of Christ. And no wonder, for even Satan disguises himself as an angel of light"; also, cf. Geraldine in "Christabel", and "Ancient Mariner", line 450.

His dying words—but when I reached   65
That tenderest strain of all the ditty,[193]
My faltering voice and pausing harp
      Disturbed her soul with pity!

All impulses of soul and sense
Had thrilled my guileless Genevieve;   70
The music and the doleful tale,
      The rich and balmy eve;

And hopes, and fears that kindle hope,
An undistinguishable throng,
And gentle wishes long subdued,   75
      Subdued and cherished long!

She wept with pity and delight,
She blushed with love, and virgin-shame;[194]
And like the murmur of a dream,
      I heard her breathe my name.   80

Her bosom heaved—she stepped aside,
As conscious of my look she stepped—
Then suddenly, with timorous eye
      She fled to me and wept.

She half enclosed me with her arms,   85
She pressed me with a meek embrace;
And bending back her head, looked up,
      And gazed upon my face.

'Twas partly love, and partly fear,
And partly 'twas a bashful art,   90
That I might rather feel, than see,
      The swelling of her heart.

[193] *ditty*: song (not necessarily a short one).
[194] *virgin-shame*: modesty, shyness.

I calmed her fears, and she was calm,
And told her love with virgin pride;
And so I won my Genevieve,   95
    My bright and beauteous Bride.

Christabel

"Christabel" was published in 1816 at Lord Byron's urging
with "Kubla Khan" and "The Pains of Sleep" by John Murray
(Byron's publisher):

> Last spring I saw Wr. Scott. He repeated to me a considerable
> portion of an unpublished poem of yours—the wildest and fin-
> est I ever heard in that kind of composition. The title he did
> not mention, but I think the heroine's name was Geraldine. At
> all events, the "toothless mastiff bitch" and the "witch Lady",
> the description of the hall, the lamp suspended from the image,
> and more particularly of the girl herself as she went forth in
> the evening—all took a hold on my imagination which I never
> shall wish to shake off. I mention this, not for the sake of bor-
> ing you with compliments, but as a prelude to the hope that
> this poem is to be in the volumes you are now about to publish.
> I do not know that even "Love" or the "Antient Mariner" are
> so impressive—and to me there are few things in our tongue
> beyond these two productions.[195]

It was collected in *Poetical Works*, 1828, but remained
incomplete. Coleridge never altogether abandoned the hope
of finishing the poem, but remained thwarted: "The reason of
my not finishing Christabel is not that I don't know how to
do it—for I have, as I always had, the whole plan entire from
beginning to end in my mind; but I fear I could not carry on
with equal success the execution of the idea, an extremely sub-
tle and difficult one" (1833).[196] Gillman has left us a detailed
record of Coleridge's account of the conclusion:

---

[195] Lord Byron, *Selected Letters and Journals* (London: Penguin, 1984), p. 166.
[196] *S.T. Coleridge*, p. 259.

It has been said that "Coleridge never explained the story of Christabel." To his friends he did explain it....

The story of Christabel is partly founded on the notion, that the virtuous of this world save the wicked. The pious and good Christabel suffers and prays for

"The weal of her lover that is far away,"

Exposed to various temptations in a foreign land; and she thus defeats the power of evil represented in the person of Geraldine. This is one main object of the tale....

The following relation was to have occupied a third and fourth canto, and to have closed the tale.

Over the mountains, the Bard, as directed by Sir Leoline, "hastes" with his disciple; but in consequence of one of those inundations supposed to be common to this country, the spot only where the castle once stood is discovered,—the edifice itself being washed away. He determines to return. Geraldine being acquainted with all that is passing, like the Weird Sisters in Macbeth, vanishes. Re-appearing, however, she wait's the return of the Bard, exciting in the mean time, by her wily arts, all the anger she could rouse in the Baron's breast, as well as that jealousy of which he is described to have been susceptible. The old Bard and the youth at length arrive, and therefore she can no longer personate the character of Geraldine, the daughter of Lord Roland de Vaux, but changes her appearance to that of the accepted though absent lover of Christabel. Next ensues a court-ship most distressing to Christabel, who feels—she knows not why—great disgust for her once favoured knight. This coldness is very painful to the Baron, who has no more conception than her-self of the supernatural transformation. She at last yields to her father's entreaties, and consents to approach the altar with this hated suitor. The real lover returning, enters at this moment, and produces the ring which she had once given him in sign of her betrothment. Thus defeated, the supernatural being Geraldine disappears. As predicted, the castle bell tolls, the mother's voice is heard, and to the exceeding great joy of the parties, the right-ful marriage takes place, after which follows a reconciliation and explanation between the father and daughter.[197]

[197] James Gillman, *The Life of Samuel Taylor Coleridge*, vol. 1 (London, 1835), pp. 283, 301–2.

We have a further clue from Derwent Coleridge:

> Talked [with Derwent Coleridge] about the mystery of
> *Christabel.* He considers it to be founded on the Roman
> Catholic notion of expiation for others' sins; that Geraldine
> is a divinely appointed penance imposed on Christabel for the
> redemption of her lover who had committed some crime.[198]

In recent years this poem has attracted much attention
for its supposed portrayal of lesbianism (see, especially, lines
227–331). We know that Coleridge did express himself on this
subject on at least one occasion, in the unpublished "Couplet
on Lesbian Lovers".[199] Nevertheless, there is much evidence
that the lesbian interpretation involves a serious misreading
of the text. Gillman, for one, specifically denies it[200] and con-
strues: "Geraldine ... drew in her breath aloud, and unbound
her cincture. Her silken robe and inner vest then drop to her
feet, and she discovers her hideous form".[201] This is consis-
tent with all the manuscript readings, Coleridge's 1824 gloss,
and with the accounts we have of Byron's and Shelley's inter-
pretation of the poem—the former of whom had discussed it
with the author.[202] Coleridge appears to have left the horrific
deformity of Geraldine's body out of the published text for
aesthetic rather than thematic reasons. This is a poem about
spiritual corruption and evil. Not only Christabel is contam-
inated or perverted by Geraldine, but her father also, who
is turned *unnaturally* against his daughter. Insofar as lesbian
imagery is present, it is used as a symbol of spiritual perver-
sion. Indeed, from what evidence (internal and external) we

[198] R. L. Brett, ed., *Barclay Fox's Journal: 1832–1854* (Cornwall, Eng.: Cornwall
Editions, 2008), p. 118.

[199] See no. 503 in *Collected Works of Samuel Taylor Coleridge: Poetical Works I*
(Princeton: Princeton University Press, 2001), p. 909, and *Notebooks*, vol. 3,
p. 4187.

[200] See *Life*, pp. 293–94.

[201] Ibid., pp. 291–92.

[202] See John Polidori, *Diary* (Cambridge: Cambridge University Press, 2014),
pp. 128–29; Fiona MacCarthy, *Byron: Life and Legend* (New York: Farar, Strauss
and Giroux, 2004), p. 270.

have of Coleridge's intentions, it seems unlikely that the "lesbian" dimension would play a prominent part in its denouement. Equally central—particularly given its prominence as a theme in Romantic and Gothic literature—is the element of vampirism: Geraldine is presented as a seductress, a pervert, a demon, a vampire, a serpent, and a sower of discord within the family—if this *were* a poem about lesbianism, it would be open to the charge of "homophobia". I think it is truer to the poet's purpose to say that, insofar as he is using a sexual metaphor, he is using it to depict spiritual realities—that is, that lesbianism is itself a symbol of spiritual perversion and evil. In this respect it is another instance of reading the Book of Nature (see the introductory note to "Frost at Midnight").

"Christabel"'s impact was immediate and proved deep and wide. Its influence ranged from Scott and Byron, through Keats, to Tennyson, George MacDonald, and the pre-Raphaelites. It remains one of the most highly regarded and popular of Coleridge's works.

> "Christabel," more than anything of Coleridge, is composed like music; you might set at the side of each section, especially of the opening, *largo*, *vivacissimo*, and, as the general expression signature, *tempo rubato*. I know no other verse in which the effects of music are so precisely copied in metre. Shelley, you feel, sings like a bird; Blake, like a child or an angel; but Coleridge certainly writes music.[203]

PREFACE

The first part of the following poem was written in the year 1797, at Stowey, in the county of Somerset. The second part, after my return from Germany, in the year 1800, at Keswick, Cumberland. It is probable that if the poem had been finished at either of the former periods, or if even the first and second part had been published in the year 1800, the impression of its originality would have been much greater than I dare at present

[203] Symons, *Romantic Movement*, p. 145.

expect. But for this, I have only my own indolence to blame. The dates are mentioned for the exclusive purpose of precluding charges of plagiarism or servile imitation from myself. For there is amongst us a set of critics, who seem to hold, that every possible thought and image is traditional; who have no notion that there are such things as fountains in the world, small as well as great; and who would therefore charitably derive every rill they behold flowing, from a perforation made in some other man's tank. I am confident, however, that as far as the present poem is concerned, the celebrated poets whose writings I might be suspected of having imitated, either in particular passages, or in the tone and the spirit of the whole, would be among the first to vindicate me from the charge, and who, on any striking coincidence, would permit me to address them in this doggerel version of two monkish Latin hexameters.

> 'Tis mine and it is likewise yours;
> But an if this will not do;
> Let it be mine, good friend! for I
> Am the poorer of the two.

I have only to add, that the metre of the Christabel is not, properly speaking, irregular, though it may seem so from its being founded on a new principle: namely, that of counting in each line the accents, not the syllables. Though the latter may vary from seven to twelve, yet in each line the accents will be found to be only four. Nevertheless this occasional variation in number of syllables is not introduced wantonly, or for the mere ends of convenience, but in correspondence with some transition, in the nature of the imagery or passion.

Christabel

PART I

'Tis the middle of night by the castle clock,
And the owls have awakened the crowing cock;
Tu—whit!—Tu—whoo!
And hark, again! the crowing cock,
How drowsily it crew.[204]   5

Sir Leoline, the Baron rich,
Hath a toothless mastiff bitch;
From her kennel beneath the rock
She maketh answer to the clock,
Four for the quarters, and twelve for the hour;   10
Ever and aye,[205] by shine and shower,
Sixteen short howls, not over loud;
Some say, she sees my lady's shroud.

Is the night chilly and dark?
The night is chilly, but not dark.   15
The thin grey cloud is spread on high,
It covers but not hides the sky.
The moon is behind, and at the full;
And yet she looks both small and dull.
The night is chill, the cloud is grey: 20
'Tis a month before the month of May,
And the Spring comes slowly up this way.

The lovely lady, Christabel,
Whom her father loves so well,
What makes her in the wood so late,   25
A furlong from the castle gate?[206]

---

[204] *crew*: crowed.

[205] *aye*: on all occasions.

[206] *Is the night chilly . . . castle gate*: "The late Mr. Sotheby informed me, that, at his house in a large party, Sir Walter [Scott] made the following remark: 'I am indebted to Coleridge for the mode of telling a tale by question and answer. This was a new light to me, and I was greatly struck by it'" (Gillman, *Life*, vol. 1, p. 278).

She had dreams all yesternight
Of her own betrothèd knight;
And she in the midnight wood will pray
For the weal[207] of her lover that's far away.   30

She stole along, she nothing spoke,
The sighs she heaved were soft and low,
And naught was green upon the oak,
But moss and rarest mistletoe:
She kneels beneath the huge oak tree,   35
And in silence prayeth she.[208]

The lady sprang up suddenly,
The lovely lady, Christabel!
It moaned as near, as near can be,
But what it is she cannot tell.—   40
On the other side it seems to be,
Of the huge, broad-breasted, old oak tree.

The night is chill; the forest bare;
Is it the wind that moaneth bleak?
There is not wind enough in the air   45
To move away the ringlet curl
From the lovely lady's cheek—
There is not wind enough to twirl
The one red leaf, the last of its clan,
That dances as often as dance it can,[209]   50

---

[207] *weal*: welfare.

[208] *naught was green ... prayeth she*: Note the jarring pagan elements in this otherwise firmly medieval Christian setting. Christabel has dreamt all night of her absent love; her response to what appears to be temptation is to leave the security of the castle, and pray by the oak and mistletoe, where she encounters Geraldine. Cf. Keats' combination of the same elements for different purposes in "The Eve of St. Agnes". In both cases, however, the intrusion of pagan elements into a Christian framework is directly followed by the imagery of sexual transgression.

[209] *one red leaf ... dance it can*: This image was used by John Ruskin (1819–1900) to illustrate his theory of the *pathetic fallacy* (*Modern Painters*, vol. 3, part 4).

Hanging so light, and hanging so high,
On the topmost twig that looks up at the sky.

Hush, beating heart of Christabel!
Jesu,[210] Maria, shield her well!
She folded her arms beneath her cloak,   55
And stole to the other side of the oak.
      What sees she there?

There she sees a damsel bright,
Dressed in a silken robe of white,
That shadowy in the moonlight shone: 60
The neck that made that white robe wan,
Her stately neck, and arms were bare;
Her blue-veined feet unsandal'd were;
And wildly glittered here and there
The gems entangled in her hair.   65
I guess, 'twas frightful there to see
A lady so richly clad as she —
Beautiful exceedingly!

"Mary mother, save me now!"
(Said Christabel,) "And who art thou?"   70

The lady strange made answer meet,[211]
And her voice was faint and sweet:—
"Have pity on my sore distress,
I scarce can speak for weariness:
Stretch forth thy hand, and have no fear!"   75
Said Christabel, "How camest thou here?"
And the lady, whose voice was faint and sweet,
Did thus pursue her answer meet:—

[210] *Jesu*: "Jesu" is pronounced "Jeezu".
[211] *meet*: appropriate, fitting.

"My sire is of a noble line,
And my name is Geraldine: 80
Five warriors seized me yestermorn,
Me, even me, a maid forlorn:
They choked my cries with force and fright,
And tied me on a palfrey[212] white.
The palfrey was as fleet as wind,   85
And they rode furiously behind.
They spurred amain,[213] their steeds were white:
And once we crossed the shade of night.
As sure as Heaven shall rescue me,
I have no thought what men they be;   90
Nor do I know how long it is
(For I have lain entranced, I wis[214])
Since one, the tallest of the five,
Took me from the palfrey's back,
A weary woman, scarce alive.   95
Some muttered words his comrades spoke:
He placed me underneath this oak;
He swore they would return with haste;
Whither they went I cannot tell—
I thought I heard, some minutes past,   100
Sounds as of a castle bell.
Stretch forth thy hand" (thus ended she),
"And help a wretched maid to flee."

Then Christabel stretched forth her hand
And comforted fair Geraldine: 105
"O well, bright dame! may you command
The service of Sir Leoline;
And gladly our stout chivalry

---

[212] *palfrey*: "small saddle horse for a woman" (*Oxford English Dictionary*, s.v. "palfrey"); light horse.

[213] *amain*: vigorously.

[214] *wis*: believe (slightly inaccurate archaism for "I know", "certainly").

Will he send forth and friends withal[215]
To guide and guard you safe and free   110
Home to your noble father's hall."

She rose: and forth with steps they passed[216]
That strove to be, and were not, fast.
Her gracious stars the lady blest,
And thus spake on sweet Christabel: 115
"All our household are at rest,
The hall is silent as the cell;
Sir Leoline is weak in health,
And may not well awakened be,
But we will move as if in stealth,   120
And I beseech your courtesy,
This night, to share your couch[217] with me."

They crossed the moat, and Christabel
Took the key that fitted well;
A little door she opened straight,   125
All in the middle of the gate;
The gate that was ironed within and without,
Where an army in battle array had marched out.
The lady sank, belike through pain,[218]
And Christabel with might and main   130
Lifted her up, a weary weight,

---

[215] *withal*: in addition.

[216] *Christabel stretched forth her hand ... with steps they passed*: "The Strange Lady cannot rise, without the touch of Christabel's Hand: and now she blesses her *Stars*. She will not praise the *Creator* of the Heavens, or name the Saints" (Coleridge's gloss, 1824).

[217] *couch*: bed.

[218] *Christabel / Took the key ... lady sank, belike through pain*: "The strange Lady may not pass the threshold without Christabel's help and will" (Coleridge's gloss, 1824). According to folkloric belief, witches, vampires, and goblins could not freely cross of their own will any threshold; iron was thought to be an effective apotropaic device against the passage of malign supernatural agencies. Cf. the refrain to "The Witch" by Mary Elizabeth Coleridge (1861–1907; Coleridge's great-grandniece): "Oh, lift me over the threshold, and let me in at the door!"

Over the threshold of the gate:
Then the lady rose again,
And moved, as she were not in pain.

So free from danger, free from fear,   135
They crossed the court: right glad they were.
And Christabel devoutly cried
To the Lady by her side;
"Praise we the Virgin all divine,
Who hath rescued thee from thy distress!"   140
"Alas, alas!" said Geraldine,
"I cannot speak for weariness."[219]
So, free from danger, free from fear,
They crossed the court: right glad they were.

Outside her kennel the mastiff old   145
Lay fast asleep, in moonshine cold.
The mastiff old did not awake,
Yet she an angry moan did make!
And what can ail the mastiff bitch?
Never till now she uttered yell   150
Beneath the eye[220] of Christabel.
Perhaps it is the owlet's scritch:[221]
For what can ail the mastiff bitch?[222]

[219] *Praise we the Virgin all divine, . . . I cannot speak for weariness:* "The strange Lady makes an excuse, not to praise the Holy Virgin" (Coleridge's gloss, 1824).

[220] *eye:* The eye in Coleridge is the locus and battleground of spiritual states; of the balance of good and evil; of the ability of a given individual to read the Book of Nature (see the introductory note to "Frost at Midnight", p. 351); and of the drama of the progress of innocence from naïveté to a more holistic experience. See also the Barfield passage in the introductory note to "Dejection: An Ode" (p. 396); "Kubla Khan", line 50; and "Apologia Pro Vita Sua". Cf. "The Ancient Mariner", line 13.

[221] *scritch:* screech, shriek (archaic).

[222] *what can ail the mastiff bitch:* Animals are said to be sensitive to supernatural and preternatural phenomena. See also line 13.

They passed the hall, that echoes still,
Pass as lightly as you will! 155
The brands were flat, the brands were dying,
Amid their own white ashes lying;
But when the lady passed, there came
A tongue of light, a fit of flame;[223]
And Christabel saw the lady's eye, 160
And nothing else saw she thereby,
Save the boss of the shield of Sir Leoline tall,
Which hung in a murky old niche in the wall.
"O softly tread, said Christabel,
My father seldom sleepeth well." 165

Sweet Christabel her feet doth bare,
And, jealous of the listening air,
They steal their way from stair to stair,
Now in glimmer, and now in gloom,
And now they pass the Baron's room, 170
As still as death with stifled breath!
And now have reached her chamber door;
And now doth Geraldine press down
The rushes of the chamber floor.[224]

The moon shines dim in the open air, 175
And not a moonbeam enters here.
But they without its light can see
The chamber carved so curiously,[225]
Carved with figures strange and sweet,
All made out of the carver's brain, 180
For a lady's chamber meet:[226]
The lamp with twofold silver chain

---

[223] *tongue of light, a fit of flame*: another sign of the presence of an evil spirit.

[224] *rushes of the chamber floor*: Rushes (grasslike plants) were commonly used as floor covering in the Middle Ages.

[225] *carved so curiously*: i.e., carved with cunning skill.

[226] *meet*: fitting, proper.

Is fastened to an angel's feet.
The silver lamp burns dead and dim;
But Christabel the lamp will trim.   185
She trimmed the lamp, and made it bright,
And left it swinging to and fro,
While Geraldine, in wretched plight,
Sank down upon the floor below.

"O weary lady, Geraldine,   190
I pray you, drink this cordial wine!
It is a wine of virtuous powers;
My mother made it of wild flowers."

"And will your mother pity me,
Who am a maiden most forlorn?"   195
Christabel answered—"Woe is me!
She died the hour that I was born.
I have heard the grey-haired friar tell,
How on her death-bed she did say,
That she should hear the castle-bell   200
Strike twelve upon my wedding day.
O mother dear! that thou wert here!"
"I would," said Geraldine, "she were!"

But soon, with altered voice, said she—[227]
"Off, wandering mother! Peak and pine![228]   205
I have power to bid thee flee."
Alas! what ails poor Geraldine?
Why stares she with unsettled eye?
Can she the bodiless dead espy?
And why with hollow voice cries she,   210

[227] *with altered voice, said she*: "The Mother of Christabel, who is now her Guardian Spirit, appears to Geraldine, as in answer to her wish. Geraldine fears the Spirit, but yet has power over it for a time" (Coleridge's gloss, 1824).

[228] *Peak and pine*: waste away. Cf. the First Witch in Shakespeare's *Macbeth*, Act 1, scene 3, lines 22–23: "Weary sev'nights nine times nine / Shall he dwindle, peak, and pine".

"Off, woman, off! this hour is mine—[229]
Though thou her guardian spirit be,
Off, woman, off! 'tis given to me."

Then Christabel knelt by the lady's side,
And raised to heaven her eyes so blue—   215
"Alas!" said she, "this ghastly ride—
Dear lady! it hath wildered[230] you!"
The lady wiped her moist cold brow,
And faintly said, "'Tis over now!"

Again the wild-flower wine she drank: 220
Her fair large eyes 'gan glitter bright,
And from the floor whereon she sank,
The lofty lady stood upright;
She was most beautiful to see,
Like a lady of a far countree.[231]   225

And thus the lofty lady spake—
"All they, who live in the upper sky,[232]
Do love you, holy Christabel!
And you love them, and for their sake
And for the good which me befell,   230
Even I in my degree will try,
Fair maiden, to requite you well.
But now unrobe yourself; for I
Must pray, ere yet in bed I lie."

[229] *this hour is mine*: Cf. Christ on his arrest in the Garden of Gethsemane: "[T]his is your hour, and the power of darkness" (Luke 22:53).

[230] *wildered*: bewildered; led astray.

[231] *countree*: (accent on the second syllable).

[232] *All they, who live in the upper sky*: "These 'middle spirits' or dæmons ... naturally inhabit the middle region between Earth and æther; that is, the air—which extends upwards as far as the orbit of the Moon" (Lewis, *Discarded Image*, p. 41). See the note to line 132 of "The Ancient Mariner". Cf. "Ancient Mariner", line 313.

Quoth Christabel, "So let it be!"   235
And as the lady bade, did she.
Her gentle limbs did she undress
And lay down in her loveliness.

But through her brain of weal[233] and woe
So many thoughts moved to and fro,   240
That vain it were her lids to close;
So half-way from the bed she rose,
And on her elbow did recline
To look at the lady Geraldine.

Beneath the lamp the lady bowed,   245
And slowly rolled her eyes around;
Then drawing in her breath aloud
Like one that shuddered, she unbound
The cincture[234] from beneath her breast:
Her silken robe, and inner vest,   250
Dropt to her feet, and full in view,
Behold! her bosom and half her side—[235]

---

[233] *weal*: happiness; welfare.

[234] *cincture*: band, girdle, belt.

[235] All the manuscript versions are followed here by this line: "Are lean and old and foul of Hue". Cf. George MacDonald's (1824–1905) *Phantastes* (Grand Rapids, Mich.: Eerdmans, 1981), pp. 43–46:

I started, and, turning sideways, saw a dim white figure seated beside an intertwining thicket of smaller trees and underwood.... "It is your white lady!" said the sweetest voice.... Yet, if I would have confessed it, there was something either in the sound of the voice, although it seemed sweetness itself ... that did not vibrate harmoniously with the beat of my inward music.... The lady glided round by the wall from behind me, still keeping her face towards me, and seated herself in the furthest corner, with her back to the lamp.... I then saw indeed a form of perfect loveliness before me.... There was one thing in it I did not like; which was, that the white part of the eye was tinged with the same slight roseate hue as the rest of the form.... She began, and told me a strange tale, which ... fixed my eyes and thoughts upon her extreme beauty.... I lay entranced.... I woke as a grey dawn stole into the cave. The damsel had disappeared; but in the shrubbery, at the mouth of the cave, stood a strange horrible object. It looked like an open coffin set up on one end ... a rough representation of

A sight to dream of, not to tell!
O shield her! shield sweet Christabel!

Yet Geraldine nor speaks nor stirs;   255
Ah! what a stricken look was hers!
Deep from within she seems half-way
To lift some weight with sick assay,[236]
And eyes the maid and seeks delay;
Then suddenly as one defied   260
Collects herself in scorn and pride,
And lay down by the maiden's side!—[237]
And in her arms the maid she took,
  Ah well-a-day![238]
And with low voice and doleful[239] look   265
These words did say:
"In the touch of this bosom there worketh a spell,
Which is lord of thy utterance, Christabel!
Thou knowest to-night, and wilt know to-morrow,
This mark of my shame, this seal of my sorrow;   270
  But vainly thou warrest,
   For this is alone in
  Thy power to declare,
   That in the dim forest
  Thou heard'st a low moaning,   275

---

the human frame, only hollow, as if made of decaying bark torn from a tree.... The thing turned round—it had for a face and front those of my enchantress, but now of a pale greenish hue in the light of the morning, and with dead lustreless eyes.... She laughed a low laugh, but now full of scorn and derision; and then she said ... "There he is; you can take him now."

MacDonald was influenced by Coleridge, and refers to "Christabel" in several books, including *The Princess and Curdie*, *The Flight of the Shadow*, and *There and Back*.

[236] *assay*: attempt; trial.

[237] *maiden's side*: "As soon as the wicked Bosom, with the mysterious sign of Evil stamped thereby, touches Christabel, she is deprived of the power of disclosing what has occurred" (Coleridge's gloss, 1824).

[238] *Ah well-a-day!*: alas! (expression of grief).

[239] *doleful*: sorrowful; mournful; grief-stricken; malicious; crafty.

And found'st a bright lady, surpassingly fair:
And didst bring her home with thee in love and in charity,
To shield her and shelter her from the damp air."

THE CONCLUSION TO PART I

It was a lovely sight to see
The lady Christabel, when she   280
Was praying at the old oak tree.
  Amid the jaggèd shadows
  Of mossy leafless boughs,
  Kneeling in the moonlight,
  To make her gentle vows;   285
Her slender palms together prest,
Heaving sometimes on her breast;
Her face resigned to bliss or bale[240]—
Her face, oh call it fair not pale,
And both blue eyes more bright than clear,   290
Each about to have a tear.

With open eyes (ah woe is me!)
Asleep,[241] and dreaming fearfully,
Fearfully dreaming, yet, I wis,
Dreaming that alone, which is—   295
O sorrow and shame! Can this be she,
The lady, who knelt at the old oak tree?
And lo! the worker of these harms,
That holds the maiden in her arms,
Seems to slumber still and mild,   300
As a mother with her child.

A star hath set, a star hath risen,
O Geraldine! since arms of thine

[240] *bale*: evil; woe; harm; pain; death.
[241] *With open eyes (ah woe is me!) / Asleep*: Coleridge was a younger contemporary of Franz Mesmer (1734–1815), and mesmerism and hypnosis feature prominently in Romantic literature from E. T. A. Hoffmann (1776–1822) to Edgar Allan Poe.

Have been the lovely lady's prison.[242]
O Geraldine! one hour was thine— 305
Thou'st had thy will! By tairn[243] and rill,
The night-birds all that hour were still.
But now they are jubilant anew,
From cliff and tower, tu—whoo! tu—whoo!
Tu—whoo! tu—whoo! from wood and fell![244] 310

And see! the lady Christabel
Gathers herself from out her trance;
Her limbs relax, her countenance
Grows sad and soft; the smooth thin lids
Close o'er her eyes; and tears she sheds— 315
Large tears that leave the lashes bright!
And oft the while she seems to smile
As infants at a sudden light!
Yea, she doth smile, and she doth weep,
Like a youthful hermitess, 320
Beauteous in a wilderness,
Who, praying always, prays in sleep.[245]
And, if she move unquietly,
Perchance, 'tis but the blood so free
Comes back and tingles in her feet. 325
No doubt, she hath a vision sweet.
What if her guardian spirit 'twere?
What if she knew her mother near?
But this she knows, in joys and woes,
That saints will aid if men will call: 330
For the blue sky bends over all!

[242] *star hath set ... lady's prison*: Cf. the epigraph to "Dejection: An Ode", p. 396.

[243] *tairn*: small mountain lake. See the note to line 100 of "Dejection: An Ode".

[244] *fell*: moor; hill.

[245] *praying always, prays in sleep*: Cf. St. Augustine, "Exposition on Psalm 38", no. 13: "For it is your heart's desire that is your prayer; and if your desire continues uninterrupted, your prayer continues also. For not without a meaning did the Apostle say, Pray without ceasing [cf. 1 Thessalonians 5:17]."

PART II[246]

"Each matin[247] bell", the Baron saith,
"Knells us back to a world of death."
These words Sir Leoline first said,
When he rose and found his lady dead: 335
These words Sir Leoline will say,
Many a morn to his dying day!

And hence the custom and law began,
That still at dawn the sacristan,
Who duly pulls the heavy bell,   340
Five and forty beads must tell[248]
Between each stroke—a warning knell,
Which not a soul can choose but hear
From Bratha Head [249] to Wyndermere.

---

[246] INTRO TEXT

[Crashaw's] lines on St. Theresa are the finest. Where he does combine
richness of thought and diction nothing can excel, as in the lines you
so much admire—"Since 'tis not to be had at home,/She'l travel to
a martyrdome./No home for her confesses she,/But where she may a
martyr be./She'l to the Moores, and trade with them,/For this invalued
diadem,/She offers them her dearest breath,/With Christ's name in't, in
change for death./She'l bargain with them, and will give/Them God, and
teach them how to live/ In Him, or, if they this deny,/For Him she'l teach
them how to die./So shall she leave amongst them sown,/The Lord's
blood, or, at least, her own./Farewell then, all the world—Adieu,/Teresa
is no more for you:/Farewell all pleasures, sports and joys,/Never till now
esteemed toys—/Farewell what ever dear'st may be,/Mother's arms or
Father's knee;/Farewell house, and farewell home,/She's for the Moores
and martyrdom" ["Hymn to Saint Teresa", lines 43–64]. These verses were
ever present to my mind whilst writing the second part of *Christabel*; if,
indeed, by some subtle process of the mind they did not suggest the first-
thought of the whole poem. (S. T. Coleridge, p. 441)

[247] *matin*: See the note to line 45 of Wordswoth's *Prelude*, bk. 1. Here the ref-
erence is to the Catholic liturgy.

[248] *Five and forty beads must tell*: Though telling one's beads usually means say-
ing the Rosary, it can refer to other prayers.

[249] *Bratha Head*: the source of the Bratha (or, more commonly, Brathay)—a
little river that flows into the northern end of Lake Windermere in Cumbria.

Saith Bracy the bard, "So let it knell!   345
And let the drowsy sacristan
Still count as slowly as he can!
There is no lack of such, I ween,[250]
As well fill up the space between.
In Langdale Pike [251] and Witch's Lair,   350
And Dungeon-ghyll[252] so foully rent,
With ropes of rock and bells of air
Three sinful sextons' ghosts[253] are pent,[254]
Who all give back, one after t'other,
The death-note to their living brother;   355
And oft too, by the knell offended,
Just as their one! two! three! is ended,
The devil mocks the doleful tale[255]
With a merry peal from Borodale."[256]

The air is still! through mist and cloud   360
That merry peal comes ringing loud;
And Geraldine shakes off her dread,
And rises lightly from the bed;
Puts on her silken vestments white,
And tricks[257] her hair in lovely plight,[258]   365
And nothing doubting of her spell
Awakens the lady Christabel.
"Sleep you, sweet lady Christabel?
I trust that you have rested well."

[250] *I ween*: I believe.

[251] *Langdale Pike*: one or all of the peaks on the northern side of Great Langdale—a valley in Cumbria.

[252] *Dungeon-ghyll*: ravine (ghyll) and waterfall in Langdale.

[253] *ghosts*: spirits.

[254] *pent*: imprisoned.

[255] *tale*: tally.

[256] *Borodale*: Borrowdale is a valley in Cumbria; the river Derwent flows through it into Derwent Water.

[257] *tricks*: arranges.

[258] *plight*: "a plait of hair or interwoven mass" (*Oxford English Dictionary*, s.v. "plight").

And Christabel awoke and spied   370
The same who lay down by her side—
O rather say, the same whom she
Raised up beneath the old oak tree!
Nay, fairer yet! and yet more fair!
For she belike[259] hath drunken deep   375
Of all the blessedness of sleep!
And while she spake, her looks, her air
Such gentle thankfulness declare,
That (so it seemed) her girded vests
Grew tight beneath her heaving breasts.   380
"Sure I have sinn'd!" said Christabel,
"Now heaven be praised if all be well!"
And in low faltering tones, yet sweet,[260]
Did she the lofty lady greet
With such perplexity of mind   385
As dreams too lively leave behind.

So quickly she rose, and quickly arrayed
Her maiden[261] limbs, and having prayed
That He, who on the cross did groan,
Might wash away her sins unknown,   390
She forthwith led fair Geraldine
To meet her sire, Sir Leoline.

The lovely maid and the lady tall
Are pacing both into the hall,
And pacing on through page and groom,   395
Enter the Baron's presence room.

[259] *belike*: to appearance.

[260] *faltering tones, yet sweet*: "Christabel is made to believe, that the fearful
Sight had taken place only in a Dream" (Coleridge's gloss, 1824).

[261] maiden: The emphases here on Christabel's virginity and (in the lines that
follow) her failure to identify her "sin" are undoubtedly significant of the com-
plexity of her relationship with Geraldine.

The Baron rose, and while he prest
His gentle daughter to his breast,
With cheerful wonder in his eyes
The lady Geraldine espies,   400
And gave such welcome to the same,
As might beseem so bright a dame!

But when he heard the lady's tale,
And when she told her father's name,
Why waxed Sir Leoline so pale,   405
Murmuring o'er the name again,
Lord Roland de Vaux of Tryermaine?[262]

Alas! they had been friends in youth;
But whispering tongues can poison truth;
And constancy lives in realms above;   410
And life is thorny; and youth is vain;
And to be wroth[263] with one we love,
Doth work like madness in the brain.
And thus it chanced, as I divine,
With Roland and Sir Leoline.   415
Each spake words of high disdain
And insult to his heart's best brother:
They parted—ne'er to meet again!
But never either found another
To free the hollow heart from paining—   420
They stood aloof, the scars remaining,
Like cliffs which had been rent asunder;
A dreary sea now flows between;—
But neither heat, nor frost, nor thunder,
Shall wholly do away, I ween,   425
The marks of that which once hath been.

[262] *Lord Roland de Vaux of Tryermaine*: historical figure of the mid-fourteenth
century, Lord of Triermain Castle, north Cumbria. The castle, which was built
with stone from Hadrian's Wall, was in ruins by the seventeenth century.
[263] *wroth*: incensed.

Sir Leoline, a moment's space,
Stood gazing on the damsel's face:
And the youthful Lord of Tryermaine
Came back upon his heart again.   430

O then the Baron forgot his age,
His noble heart swelled high with rage;
He swore by the wounds in Jesu's side,[264]
He would proclaim it far and wide
With trump[265] and solemn heraldry,   435
That they who thus had wronged the dame,
Were base as spotted[266] infamy!
"And if they dare deny the same,
My herald shall appoint a week,
And let the recreant[267] traitors seek   440
My tourney court[268]—that there and then
I may dislodge their reptile[269] souls
From the bodies and forms of men!"
He spake: his eye in lightning rolls!
For the lady was ruthlessly seized; and he kenned[270]   445
In the beautiful lady the child of his friend!

And now the tears were on his face,
And fondly[271] in his arms he took
Fair Geraldine, who met the embrace,
Prolonging it with joyous look.   450
Which when she viewed, a vision fell[272]

[264] *wounds in Jesu's side*: The interjection "wounds" is derived from an oath on "God's wounds".

[265] *trump*: i.e., trumpet blast; public proclamation.

[266] *spotted*: morally stained.

[267] *recreant*: cowardly; disloyal.

[268] My *tourney court*: reference to Wager of Battle (Trial by Combat).

[269] *reptile*: i.e., like the serpent (satanic); also, cold-blooded.

[270] *kenned*: identified.

[271] *fondly*: affectionately; with foolish tenderness or credulity.

[272] *vision fell*: "Christabel then recollects the whole, and knows that it was not a Dream; but yet cannot disclose the fact, that the strange Lady is a supernatural Being with the stamp of the Evil Ones on her" (Coleridge's gloss, 1824).

Upon the soul of Christabel,
The vision of fear, the touch and pain!
She shrunk and shuddered, and saw again—
(Ah, woe is me! Was it for thee,   455
Thou gentle maid! such sights to see?)
Again she saw that bosom old,
Again she felt that bosom cold,
And drew in her breath with a hissing sound:
Whereat the Knight turned wildly round,   460
And nothing saw, but his own sweet maid
With eyes upraised, as one that prayed.

The touch, the sight, had passed away,[273]
And in its stead that vision blest,
Which comforted her after-rest,   465
While in the lady's arms she lay,
Had put a rapture in her breast,
And on her lips and o'er her eyes
Spread smiles like light!
                          With new surprise,
"What ails then my belovèd child?"   470
The Baron said—His daughter mild[274]
Made answer, "All will yet be well!"[275]
I ween, she had no power to tell
Aught else: so mighty was the spell.

Yet he, who saw this Geraldine,   475
Had deemed her sure a thing divine.

---

[273] *The touch, the sight, had passed away*: "Christabel for a moment sees her Mother's Spirit" (Coleridge's gloss, 1824).

[274] *His daughter mild*: Cf. Julian of Norwich's (1342–ca. 1416) *Revelations of Divine Love*, Sixteenth Revelation, chap. 75: "For the beholding of [God's greatness, works, and sufferings, and our littleness,] maketh the creature marvellously meek and mild."

[275] *Made answer, "All will yet be well!"*: Cf. ibid., Thirteenth Revelation, chap. 27: "Jesus, who in this Vision informed me of all that is needful to me, answered by this word and said: It behoved that there should be sin; but all shall be well, and all shall be well, and all manner of thing shall be well."

Such sorrow with such grace she blended,[276]
As if she feared, she had offended
Sweet Christabel, that gentle maid!
And with such lowly[277] tones she prayed[278]   480
She might be sent without delay
Home to her father's mansion.[279]

                    "Nay!
Nay, by my soul!" said Leoline.
"Ho! Bracy, the bard, the charge be thine!
Go thou, with music sweet and loud,   485
And take two steeds with trappings proud,
And take the youth whom thou lov'st best
To bear thy harp, and learn thy song,
And clothe you both in solemn vest,
And over the mountains haste along,   490

---

[276] *Such sorrow with such grace she blended*: Cf. Isaiah 53:3–5 (the Lord's suffering servant): "He was despised and rejected by men; a man of sorrows, and acquainted with grief.... [H]e was bruised for our iniquities ... and with his stripes we are healed." There follows a whole string of ambiguities in connection with Geraldine, culminating in Sir Bracy's vision of the combat between the snake and the dove, followed straight by Sir Leoline's seeing Geraldine as the dove. As the dove in Bracy's dream represents Christabel, and as Geraldine usurps Christabel's place in Sir Leoline's affections, what we have here is a series of images of impersonation and attempted usurpation whose supreme type is Satan, the ape of God; cf. 2 Corinthians 11:13–14: "For such men are false apostles, deceitful workmen, disguising themselves as apostles of Christ. And no wonder, for Satan disguises himself as an angel of light"; Tertullian, *De Corona*, chap. 15: "Let us take note of the devices of the devil, who is wont to ape some of God's things with no other design than, by the faithfulness of his servants, to put us to shame, and to condemn us"; and St. Augustine, *Confessions* 2.6: "In their perverted way, all humanity imitates you. Yet they put themselves at a distance from you and exalt themselves against you. But even by thus imitating you they acknowledge that you are the creator of all nature and so concede that there is no place where one can entirely escape from you" (Oxford: Clarendon Press, 1992), p. 32.

[277] *lowly*: humble; base. Cf. Genesis 3:14, following the serpent's role in the fall of Adam and Eve: "The LORD God said to the serpent, 'Because you have done this, cursed are you above all cattle, and above all wild animals; upon your belly you shall go, and dust shall you eat all the days of your life.'"

[278] *prayed*: begged; also, prayed.

[279] *Home to her father's mansion*: Cf. the words of Christ in John 14:2: "In my Father's house are many mansions" (KJV).

Lest wandering folk, that are abroad,
Detain you on the valley road.
And when he has crossed the Irthing flood,[280]
My merry bard! he hastes, he hastes
Up Knorren Moor,[281] through Halegarth Wood,   495
And reaches soon that castle good
Which stands and threatens Scotland's wastes.

"Bard Bracy! bard Bracy! your horses are fleet,
Ye must ride up the hall, your music so sweet,
More loud than your horses' echoing feet!   500
And loud and loud to Lord Roland call,
Thy daughter is safe in Langdale hall!
Thy beautiful daughter is safe and free—
Sir Leoline greets thee thus through me.
He bids thee come without delay   505
With all thy numerous array;[282]
And take thy lovely daughter home:
And he will meet thee on the way
With all his numerous array
White with their panting palfreys'[283] foam: 510
And by mine honor! I will say,
That I repent me of the day
When I spake words of fierce disdain
To Roland de Vaux of Tryermaine!—
—For since that evil hour hath flown,   515
Many a summer's sun hath shone;
Yet ne'er found I a friend again
Like Roland de Vaux of Tryermaine."

[280] *Irthing flood*: the river Irthing in Cumbria, along the border of North-umberland; it was once crossed by Hadrian's Wall. "How gladly Sir Leoline repeats the names and shows how familiarly he had once been acquainted with all the spots & paths in the neighbourhood of his former Friend's Castle & Residence" (Coleridge's gloss, 1824).

[281] *Knorren Moor*: or Knorren Fell, near Walton, north Cumbria.

[282] *array*: attendant knights and courtiers.

[283] *palfreys'*: A palfrey is a light horse.

The lady fell, and clasped his knees,
Her face upraised, her eyes o'erflowing;   520
And Bracy replied, with faltering voice,
His gracious hail[284] on all bestowing!—
"Thy words, thou sire of Christabel,
Are sweeter than my harp can tell;
Yet might I gain a boon[285] of thee,   525
This day my journey should not be,
So strange a dream hath come to me;
That I had vowed with music loud
To clear yon wood from thing unblest,
Warned by a vision in my rest!   530
For in my sleep I saw that dove,[286]
That gentle bird, whom thou dost love,
And call'st by thy own daughter's name—
Sir Leoline! I saw the same
Fluttering, and uttering fearful moan,   535
Among the green herbs in the forest alone. [287]
Which when I saw and when I heard,
I wonder'd what might ail the bird;
For nothing near it could I see,
Save the grass and herbs underneath the old tree.   540

"And in my dream methought I went
To search out what might there be found;
And what the sweet bird's trouble meant,
That thus lay fluttering on the ground.
I went and peered, and could descry[288]   545
No cause for her distressful cry;

---

[284] *hail*: well-wishing.

[285] *boon*: favor; blessing.

[286] *dove*: symbol of the Holy Spirit. See the note to line 63 of "The Ancient Mariner" and the note on the Book of Nature in the introductory note to "Frost at Midnight", p. 351. Cf. the note to line 28 of "Fears in Solitude".

[287] *Fluttering . . . alone*: Cf. the note to line 19 of "Inscription: For a Fountain on a Heath".

[288] *descry*: make out.

But yet for her dear lady's sake
I stooped, methought, the dove to take,
When lo! I saw a bright green snake
Coiled around its wings and neck,   550
Green as the herbs on which it couched,
Close by the dove's its head it crouched;
And with the dove it heaves and stirs,
Swelling its neck as she swelled hers!
I woke; it was the midnight hour,   555
The clock was echoing in the tower;
But though my slumber was gone by,
This dream it would not pass away—
It seems to live upon my eye!
And thence I vowed this self-same day,   560
With music strong and saintly song[289]
To wander through the forest bare,
Lest aught unholy loiter there."

Thus Bracy said: the Baron, the while,
Half-listening heard him with a smile;   565
Then turned to Lady Geraldine,
His eyes made up of wonder and love;
And said in courtly accents fine,
"Sweet maid, Lord Roland's beauteous dove,
With arms more strong than harp or song,   570
Thy sire and I will crush the snake!"[290]
He kissed her forehead as he spake,
And Geraldine in maiden wise,[291]
Casting down her large bright eyes,

---

[289] *With music strong and saintly song*: Cf. "Kubla Khan", lines 40ff., on the
power of music.

[290] *Thy sire and I will crush the snake*: In fact, only Christ can crush the serpent:
"And I will put enmity between you [the serpent] and the woman, and between
your seed and her seed [Christ]; he shall bruise your head, and you shall bruise his
heel" (Genesis 3:15).

[291] *wise*: manner.

With blushing cheek and courtesy[292] fine   575
She turned her from Sir Leoline;
Softly gathering up her train,[293]
That o'er her right arm fell again;
And folded her arms across her chest,
And couched her head upon her breast,   580
And looked askance at Christabel—
Jesu, Maria, shield her well!

A snake's small eye blinks dull and shy,
And the lady's eyes they shrunk in her head,
Each shrunk up to a serpent's eye,   585
And with somewhat of malice, and more of dread,
At Christabel she looked askance!—
One moment—and the sight was fled!
But Christabel in dizzy trance
Stumbling on the unsteady ground   590
Shuddered aloud, with a hissing sound;
And Geraldine again turned round,
And like a thing, that sought relief,
Full of wonder and full of grief,
She rolled her large bright eyes divine   595
Wildly on Sir Leoline.[294]

The maid, alas! her thoughts are gone,
She nothing sees—no sight but one!
The maid, devoid of guile and sin,
I know not how, in fearful wise   600
So deeply had she drunken in
That look, those shrunken serpent eyes,
That all her features were resigned

[292] *courtesy*: gracious manner; curtsy.
[293] *her train*: trailing section of her robe.
[294] *eyes divine . . . Sir Leoline*: Geraldine is perceived as a dove by Leoline, and
her eyes appear divine (see line 595); Christabel seems to hiss—the images are
the inverse of their subjects' true spiritual identities; see Luke 6:22, 26: "Blessed
are you when men hate you, and when they exclude you ... and cast out your
name as evil, on account of the Son of man! ... Woe to you, when all men speak
well of you, for so their fathers did to the false prophets."

To this sole image in her mind;
And passively did imitate   605
That look of dull and treacherous hate!
And thus she stood, in dizzy trance,
Still picturing that look askance
With forced unconscious sympathy[295]
Full before her father's view—   610
As far as such a look could be,
In eyes so innocent and blue!
And when the trance was o'er, the maid
Paused awhile, and inly prayed:
Then falling at the Baron's feet,   615
"By my mother's soul do I entreat
That thou this woman send away!"
She said: and more she could not say:
For what she knew she could not tell,
O'er-mastered by the mighty spell.   620

Why is thy cheek so wan and wild,
Sir Leoline? Thy only child
Lies at thy feet, thy joy, thy pride,
So fair, so innocent, so mild;
The same, for whom thy lady died!   625
O by the pangs of her dear mother
Think thou no evil of thy child!
For her, and thee, and for no other,
She prayed the moment ere she died:
Prayed that the babe for whom she died,   630
Might prove her dear lord's joy and pride!
    That prayer her deadly pangs beguiled,
        Sir Leoline!
    And wouldst thou wrong thy only child,
        Her child and thine?   635

---

[295] *unconscious sympathy:* "an affinity or correspondence between particular subjects enabling the same influence to affect each subject similarly or each subject to affect or influence the other, especially in a paranormal way" (*Oxford English Dictionary*, s.v. "unconscious sympathy").

Within the Baron's heart and brain
If thoughts, like these, had any share,
They only swelled his rage and pain,
And did but work confusion there.
His heart was cleft with pain and rage, 640
His cheeks they quivered, his eyes were wild,
Dishonoured thus in his old age;
Dishonoured by his only child,[296]
And all his hospitality
To the wronged daughter of his friend 645
By more than woman's jealousy
Brought thus to a disgraceful end—
He rolled his eye with stern regard
Upon the gentle minstrel bard,
And said in tones abrupt, austere— 650
"Why, Bracy! dost thou loiter here?
I bade thee hence!" The bard obeyed;
And turning from his own sweet maid,
The agèd knight, Sir Leoline,
Led forth the lady Geraldine! 655

THE CONCLUSION TO PART II

A little child, a limber elf,
Singing, dancing to itself,
A fairy thing with red round cheeks,
That always finds, and never seeks,
Makes such a vision to the sight 660
As fills a father's eyes with light;[297]

---

[296] *the Baron, the while [line 564] ... Dishonoured by his own child*: Note the parallel between Satan's separating man from God the Father, and Geraldine's alienating Sir Leoline from Christabel.

[297] *fills a father's eyes with light*: Sir Leoline's morbid retreat from life following his wife's death (lines 118–19, 165, 332–37) and his unfraternal, poisoned relationship with his sometime best friend (lines 408–18) have made him vulnerable to Geraldine's deception. His eyes are darkened and his disposition to his own child (and through her, implicitly, to his wife; see lines 616–17, 621–35) twisted. See Matthew 18:5–6: "Whoever receives one such child in my name receives me;

And pleasures flow in so thick and fast
Upon his heart, that he at last
Must needs express his love's excess
With words of unmeant bitterness.   665
Perhaps 'tis pretty to force together
Thoughts so all unlike each other;
To mutter and mock a broken charm,
To dally with wrong that does no harm.
Perhaps 'tis tender too and pretty   670
At each wild word to feel within
A sweet recoil of love and pity.
And what, if in a world of sin
(O sorrow and shame should this be true!)
Such giddiness of heart and brain   675
Comes seldom save from rage and pain,
So talks as it's most used to do.

Frost at Midnight[298]

This celebrated Conversation Poem (see the introductory note
to "The Eolian Harp", pp. 275–76) contains perhaps the most
explicit reference, in Coleridge's major poems, to the Book of
Nature (see lines 59ff.). The idea that God wrote two books—
nature and the Bible—has featured in Christian thought since
the Patristic period. Saint Augustine refers to "the book of
nature as the production of the Creator of all";[299] again: "We
have a greater book—the world itself. In it I read the accom-
plishment of that of which I read the promise in the Book of

---

but whoever causes one of these little ones who believe in me to sin, it would
be better for him to have a great millstone fastened around his neck and to be
drowned in the depth of the sea." Cf. also "The Nightingale", lines 91–105.

[298] Published in 1798 with "France: An Ode" and "Fears in Solitude" by Joseph
Johnson (see the note to line 12 of Blake's "London"), and collected, with alter-
ations, in Sibylline Leaves (1817).

[299] Contra Faustum 32.20.

God".[300] Saint Bonaventure describes how these two books came into being through the Creation and the Fall:

> It is certain that [in the state of innocence] Man had the knowledge of created things and through their images he was led to God, and to praise, worship and love Him. All creatures were made for this, and in this way are brought back to God. But with the Fall, when this knowledge was lost, there was no one who might lead them back to God. Hence this book, that is, the world, seemed dead and destroyed. And so, another book was necessary, through which the first should be illuminated, that Man might rightly interpret the metaphors in creation. This book is the Bible, which presents similes, qualities, and metaphors of things written in the book of the world. Therefore, the Book of Scriptures restores the whole world to God, knowing, praising, loving.[301]

This relationship between natural and revealed language is particularly well illustrated in the exegesis of Saint Thomas Aquinas—his account of water, for instance:

> In the age of nature, water was a natural sacrament, "suggested in the first production of things, when the Spirit of God hovered over the waters." Indeed, water remains even now a natural sacrament of cleanness, simply because it cleanses.
>
> In the age of law, water afforded "a spiritual regeneration," Thomas says, "but it was imperfect and symbolic." This occurred during the Exodus from Egypt, when the waters parted and the Israelites passed through the Red Sea. "Accordingly," Thomas adds, "they did see the mysteries of the kingdom of God, but only symbolically, 'seeing from afar' (Heb. 11:13)."
>
> In the age of grace, the figure of water receives its "efficacy from the power of the incarnate Word," and, through Baptism, man is born "of water and the Holy Spirit" (Jn. 3:5) into eternal life. With Christ comes the fulfillment of the types in the sacraments of the New Testament. It is only through Christ that we can search the Scriptures, and see the meaning of the types.

[300] *Letters*, 43.
[301] *The Six Days of the Creation*, 13, 12.

... It is when we pass from the final period of history, the state of grace, into the eternal state of glory that man may see divine things as they are, without their sacramental veils. In heaven, Thomas says, "there is perfect regeneration ... because we will be renewed both inwardly and outwardly. And therefore we shall see the kingdom of God in a most perfect way." What will we "see" when God removes the sacramental veils of material water? According to Thomas, water ultimately "signifies the grace of the Holy Spirit ... in the unfailing fountain from whom all gifts of grace flow."[302]

Further elucidations of this theme—central to Coleridge—are in the introduction to "Dejection: An Ode"; the note on eyes to line 151 of "Christabel"; "Kubla Khan", line 50; "Apologia Pro Vita Sua"; and "The Ancient Mariner", line 13. Compare "Fears in Solitude", lines 23–24.

Frost at Midnight

The Frost performs its secret ministry,
Unhelped by any wind. The owlet's cry
Came loud—and hark, again! loud as before.
The inmates of my cottage,[303] all at rest,
Have left me to that solitude, which suits   5
Abstruser musings:[304] save that at my side
My cradled infant[305] slumbers peacefully.
'Tis calm indeed! so calm, that it disturbs
And vexes meditation with its strange
And extreme silentness. Sea, hill, and wood,   10
This populous village! Sea, and hill, and wood,

---

[302] Scott Hahn, *Scripture Matters* (Steubenville, Ohio: Emmaus Road, 2003), pp. 59–61 (the Aquinas passages are from the *Commentary on John*, nos. 433, 188; 443, 185; 443, 188; 443, 185; 577, 239).

[303] *my cottage*: i.e., at Nether Stowey, Somerset.

[304] *Abstruser musings*: surely implying "poetical composition"—the service of the Muse—as well as "reflection".

[305] *My cradled infant*: i.e., Hartley Coleridge, Coleridge's eldest son; cf. "Fears in Solitude", lines 231–32, "Nightingale", lines 91ff.

With all the numberless goings-on of life,
Inaudible as dreams! the thin blue flame
Lies on my low-burnt fire, and quivers not;
Only that film,[306] which fluttered on the grate,   15
Still flutters there, the sole unquiet thing.
Methinks, its motion in this hush of nature
Gives it dim sympathies[307] with me who live,
Making it a companionable form,
Whose puny flaps and freaks[308] the idling Spirit   20
By its own moods interprets, every where
Echo or mirror seeking of itself,
And makes a toy of Thought.

                                         But O! how oft,
How oft, at school,[309] with most believing mind,   25
Presageful, have I gazed upon the bars,[310]
To watch that fluttering *stranger!* and as oft
With unclosed lids, already had I dreamt
Of my sweet birth-place,[311] and the old church-tower,[312]
Whose bells, the poor man's only music, rang   30
From morn to evening, all the hot Fair-day,
So sweetly, that they stirred and haunted me

---

[306] *film:* "In all parts of the kingdom these films are called *strangers* and supposed to portend the arrival of some absent friend" (Coleridge's note).

[307] *motion . . . sympathies:* See the note to line 44 of "The Eolian Harp".

[308] *freaks:* irregular caprices; pranks.

[309] *at school:* Christ's Hospital School was founded by Edward VI in 1552/1553 as one means of addressing the problem of the lack of refuge for the destitute following the closure of the monasteries. It remained at Newgate in the City of London (on the site of Greyfriars, the old Franciscan friary) until 1902, when it moved to its present location in Horsham, West Sussex. Coleridge was a boarder there (1782–1791), and it was at Christ's Hospital School that he met his lifelong friend Charles Lamb.

[310] *bars:* hearth-grate.

[311] *my sweet birth-place:* Ottery St. Mary, Devon.

[312] *church-tower:* St. Mary's, a fourteenth-century Gothic church with a surviving Lady Chapel and a medieval mechanical astronomical clock in the south transept.

With a wild pleasure, falling on mine ear
Most like articulate sounds of things to come!
So gazed I, till the soothing things I dreamt   35
Lulled me to sleep, and sleep prolonged my dreams!
And so I brooded all the following morn,
Awed by the stern preceptor's[313] face, mine eye
Fixed with mock study on my swimming book:
Save if the door half opened, and I snatched   40
A hasty glance, and still my heart leaped up,
For still I hoped to see the *stranger's* face,
Townsman, or aunt, or sister more beloved,[314]
My play-mate when we both were clothed alike![315]

     Dear Babe, that sleepest cradled by my side,   45
Whose gentle breathings, heard in this deep calm,
Fill up the interspersèd vacancies
And momentary pauses of the thought!
My babe so beautiful! it thrills my heart
With tender gladness, thus to look at thee,   50
And think that thou shalt learn far other lore,
And in far other scenes! For I was reared
In the great city, pent 'mid cloisters dim,
And saw nought lovely but the sky and stars.[316]
But *thou*, my babe! shalt wander like a breeze   55
By lakes and sandy shores, beneath the crags
Of ancient mountain, and beneath the clouds,
Which image in their bulk both lakes and shores

[313] *stern preceptor's*: i.e., Rev. James Bowyer (1736–1814), the severe, though able and intelligent, headmaster of Christ's Hospital.

[314] *Townsman, or aunt, or sister more beloved*: Coleridge's older (and only) sister, Ann, who died at the age of twenty-two in 1791. The poet's father, Rev. John Coleridge, had died in 1781.

[315] *My play-mate when we both were clothed alike*: Until after the First World War, it was the custom to clothe the youngest boys in dresses (which were often distinguishable from girls' dresses) until they were at least four years old.

[316] *For I was reared . . . stars*: See the note to line 30 of "This Lime-Tree Bower My Prison"; cf. Wordsworth, *Prelude*, bk. 1, lines 452–54.

And mountain crags: so shalt thou see and hear
The lovely shapes and sounds intelligible   60
Of that eternal language, which thy God
Utters, who from eternity doth teach
Himself in all, and all things in himself.
Great universal Teacher! he shall mould
Thy spirit, and by giving make it ask.[317]   65

      Therefore all seasons shall be sweet to thee,
Whether the summer clothe the general earth
With greenness, or the redbreast[318] sit and sing
Betwixt the tufts of snow on the bare branch
Of mossy apple-tree, while the nigh[319] thatch   70
Smokes in the sun-thaw; whether the eave-drops[320] fall
Heard only in the trances[321] of the blast,
Or if the secret ministry of frost
Shall hang them up in silent icicles,
Quietly shining to the quiet Moon.   75

The Rime of the Ancient Mariner[322]

IN SEVEN PARTS

The "Ancient Mariner" was published in *Lyrical Ballads*, 1798,
and subsequently reprinted several times with substantial

[317] *by giving make it ask*: See the note to line 47 of "Dejection: An Ode"; cf. *Prelude*, bk. 11, lines 331–33.

[318] *redbreast*: the English robin (*Erithacus rubecula melophilus*); cf. Blake, "Auguries of Innocence", line 5.

[319] *nigh*: near, close.

[320] *eave-drops*: i.e., the water dripping from the eaves of the thatched roof.

[321] *trances*: lulls (but perhaps also retaining overtones of enchantment, or near mesmerism).

[322] ARGUMENT [included in 1798 and 1800]: How a Ship having passed the Line [equator] was driven by storms to the cold Country towards the South Pole; and how from thence she made her course to the tropical Latitude of the Great Pacific Ocean; and of the strange things that befell; and in what manner the Ancyent Marinere came back to his own Country.

revisions; the marginal glosses and last important alterations appeared in *Sibylline Leaves*, 1817. The changes introduced by the poet between 1798 and the "definitive" edition of 1834 are so extensive that they have been treated as two distinct poems by some critics (including William Empson, who is unusual in preferring the earlier version).

Coleridge has left us an account of the genesis of the poem:

> During the first year that Mr. Wordsworth and I were neighbours, our conversations turned frequently on the two cardinal points of poetry, the power of exciting the sympathy of the reader by a faithful adherence to the truth of nature, and the power of giving the interest of novelty by the modifying colours of imagination.... The thought suggested itself—(to which of us I do not recollect)—that a series of poems might be composed of two sorts. In the one, the incidents and agents were to be, in part at least, supernatural; and the excellence aimed at was to consist in the interesting of the affections by the dramatic truth of such emotions, as would naturally accompany such situations, supposing them real. And real in this sense they have been to every human being who, from whatever source of delusion, has at any time believed himself under supernatural agency. For the second class, subjects were to be chosen from ordinary life....
>
> In this idea originated the plan of the "Lyrical Ballads;" in which it was agreed, that my endeavours should be directed to persons and characters supernatural, or at least romantic; yet so as to transfer from our inward nature a human interest and a semblance of truth sufficient to procure for these shadows of imagination that willing suspension of disbelief for the moment, which constitutes poetic faith....
>
> With this view I wrote "The Ancient Mariner," and was preparing among other poems, "The Dark Ladie," and the "Christabel".[323]

Wordsworth initially contributed some lines and ideas (most importantly the killing of the albatross and the navigation of

[323] *Biographia Literaria*, 1817, chap. 14.

the ship by reanimated corpses), but soon left the composition entirely to Coleridge.

Other influences on "The Rime of the Ancient Mariner" include *Arcadia* (see particularly book 1, chapter 1) by Sir Philip Sidney (1554–1586); the old ballads, such as those collected in *Reliques* (especially "Sir Cauline") by Thomas Percy; supernatural thriller ballads, like "Lenore", by Gottfried Bürger (1747–1794); and, not least, the dream Coleridge's friend John Cruickshank had of a skeleton ship with figures in it. The travel passages were often indebted to the poet's avid reading of real and semi-fictionalized accounts of such voyages, in particular, Purchas' *Pilgrimage*. Critics have seen similarities between the figure of the Mariner and both Odysseus and the Wandering Jew.

The influence the "Ancient Mariner" has exercised is considerable and extends to foreign literatures, notable instances including the poem "L'Albatros" by Charles Baudelaire (1821–1867) and Edgar Allan Poe's solitary novel, *The Narrative of Arthur Gordon Pym of Nantucket*; among the outstanding translations have been the French of Valery Larbaud (1881–1957), the Russian of Nikolai Gumilev (1886–1921), and the Czech of Josef Palivec (1886–1975), Karel Čapek's brother-in-law.

Initially unsuccessful with critics, it soon came to be, with "Kubla Khan", Coleridge's most famous poem, and is widely regarded as among the greatest achievements in narrative poetry.

Facile credo, plures esse Naturas invisibiles quam visibiles in rerum universitate. Sed horum omnium familiam quis nobis enarrat, et gradus et cognationes et discrimina et singulorum munera? Quid agunt? quæ loca habitant? Harum rerum notitiam semper ambivit ingenium humanum, nunquam attigit. Juvat, interea, non diffiteor, quandoque in animo, tanquam in tabulâ, majoris et melioris mundi imaginem contemplari: ne mens assuefacta hodiernæ vitæ minutiis se contrahat nimis, et tota subsidat in pusillas cogitationes. Sed veritati interea invigilandum est, modusque servandus, ut certa ab incertis, diem a nocte, distinguamus. T. Burnet, *Archæol. Phil.* p. 68[324]

The Rime of the Ancient Mariner

PART I

An ancient Mariner
meeteth three
Gallants bidden to
a wedding-feast, and
detaineth one.

It is an ancient Mariner,
And he stoppeth one of three.
"By thy long grey beard and
      glittering eye,
Now wherefore stopp'st thou me?

The Bridegroom's doors are opened wide,   5
And I am next of kin;
The guests are met, the feast is set:
May'st hear the merry din."

He holds him with his skinny hand,
"There was a ship," quoth he.   10
"Hold off! unhand me, greybeard loon!"
Eftsoons[325] his hand dropt he.

---

[324] I can easily believe there to be more invisible Beings than visible ones in the universe. But who can demonstrate to us their numerous families, their hierarchy and relationships, their distinguishing features and individual gifts? What do they do? Where do they dwell? Since time began the human intellect has striven for knowledge of these things, nor yet achieved it. Meanwhile, I do not deny, it is a delight to contemplate sometimes in the mind, as in a picture, the vision of a greater and better world; so that the brain, accustomed to daily trivia, does not contract too much, and subside utterly into mundane thoughts. But we must be vigilant for truth all the while, and keep all in perspective, so as to distinguish the certain from the uncertain, the day from the night. (Thomas Burnet [1635–1715], *Archaeologiae Philosophicae or the Ancient Doctrine Concerning the Originals of Things*)

[325] *Eftsoons*: forthwith (archaic).

The Wedding-
Guest is spellbound
by the eye of the old
seafaring man, and
constrained to hear
his tale.

He holds him with his glittering eye—[326]
The Wedding-Guest stood still,
And listens like a three years' child: 15
The Mariner hath his will.

The Wedding-Guest sat on a stone:
He cannot choose but hear;
And thus spake on that ancient man,
The bright-eyed Mariner.   20

The ship was cheered, the harbour cleared,
Merrily did we drop
Below the kirk,[327] below the hill,
Below the lighthouse top.

The Mariner tells
how the ship sailed
southward with
a good wind and
fair weather, till it
reached the Line.

The sun came up upon the left,   25
Out of the sea came he!
And he shone bright, and on the right
Went down into the sea.

Higher and higher every day,
Till over the mast at noon—   30
The Wedding-Guest here beat his breast,
For he heard the loud bassoon.

The Wedding-
Guest heareth
the bridal music;
but the Mariner
continueth his tale.

The bride hath paced into the hall,
Red as a rose is she;
Nodding their heads before her goes   35
The merry minstrelsy.

---

[326] *He holds him with his glittering eye*: See the note to line 151 of "Christabel";
also, the note on the Book of Nature in the introductory note to "Frost at
Midnight", and the Barfield passage in the introductory note to "Dejection: An
Ode"; "Kubla Khan", line 50; and "Apologia Pro Vita Sua". Coleridge was a
younger contemporary of Franz Mesmer (1734–1815), and mesmerism and hyp-
nosis feature prominently in Romantic literature from E. T. A. Hoffmann (1776–
1822) to Edgar Allan Poe.

[327] *kirk*: church.

The Wedding-Guest he beat his breast,
Yet he cannot choose but hear;
And thus spake on that ancient man,
The bright-eyed Mariner.   40

The ship drawn by
a storm toward the
south pole.

And now the Storm-Blast came, and he
Was tyrannous and strong:[328]
He struck with his o'ertaking wings,
And chased us south along.

With sloping masts and dipping prow,   45
As who pursued with yell and blow
Still treads the shadow of his foe,
And forward bends his head,
The ship drove fast, loud roared the blast,
And southward aye[329] we fled   50

And now there came both mist and snow,
And it grew wondrous cold:
And ice, mast-high, came floating by,
As green as emerald.

The land of ice, and
of fearful sounds
where no living
thing was to be
seen.

And through the drifts the snowy clifts[330] 55
Did send a dismal sheen:
Nor shapes of men nor beasts we ken—
The ice was all between.

The ice was here, the ice was there,
The ice was all around: 60

---

[328] *he / Was tyrannous and strong*: This personification is not merely poetic. See the note to line 132.
[329] *aye*: continually.
[330] *clifts*: cliffs.

It cracked and growled, and roared and
    howled,
Like noises in a swound![331]

Till a great sea-bird,
called the Albatross,
came through the
snow-fog, and was
received with great
joy and hospitality.

At length did cross an Albatross,[332]
Thorough[333] the fog it came;
As if it had been a Christian soul,   65
We hailed it in God's name.

It ate the food it ne'er had eat,
And round and round it flew.
The ice did split with a thunder-fit;
The helmsman steered us through!   70

And lo! the
Albatross proveth
a bird of good omen,
and followeth the
ship as it returned
northward through
fog and floating ice.

And a good south wind sprung up behind;
The Albatross did follow,
And every day, for food or play,
Came to the mariner's hollo![334]

---

[331] *swound*: swoon.

[332] *At length did cross an Albatross*: See also "Fears in Solitude", lines 27–28,
and "Christabel", lines 531ff. for other examples of a bird representing the Divine
Economy under terrestrial species; see, for this, the note on the Book of Nature in
"Frost at Midnight", introduction. Also, of course, the Holy Spirit is represented
by a dove in the New Testament (e.g., Christ's baptism in the Jordan, Matthew
3:16), just as the ship is a traditional symbol of the Church; cf. Tertullian (ca.
160–ca. 220), *On Baptism*, 12: "That little ship [Jesus and the apostles in the
storm-tossed boat, in Matthew 14:22–34] did present a figure of the Church, in
that she is disquieted in the sea, that is, in the world, by the waves, that is, by
persecutions and temptations; the Lord, through patience, sleeping as it were,
until, roused in their last extremities by the prayers of the saints, He checks the
world, and restores tranquillity to His own."

[333] *Thorough*: through.

[334] *hollo!*: "halloo!", a call.

In mist or cloud, on mast or shroud,[335]   75
It perched for vespers[336] nine;
Whiles all the night, through fog-smoke
    white,
Glimmered the white Moon-shine.

The ancient
Mariner
inhospitably killeth
the pious bird of
good omen.

"God save thee, ancient Mariner!
From the fiends, that plague thee thus!—   80
Why look'st thou so?"—With my cross-bow
I shot the ALBATROSS.

PART II

The Sun now rose upon the right:
Out of the sea came he,
Still hid in mist, and on the left   85
Went down into the sea.

And the good south wind still blew behind,
But no sweet bird did follow,
Nor any day for food or play
Came to the mariners' hollo!   90

His shipmates cry
out against the
ancient Mariner, for
killing the bird of
good luck.

And I had done a hellish thing,
And it would work 'em woe:
For all averred, I had killed the bird
That made the breeze to blow.
Ah wretch! said they, the bird to slay,   95
That made the breeze to blow!

---

[335] *shroud*: "a set of ropes, usually in pairs, forming part of the standing rigging of a ship and supporting the mast or topmast" (*Oxford English Dictionary*, s.v. "shroud").

[336] *vespers*: Evening Prayer/Evensong; here, in what is evidently a pre-Reformation setting. The regenerate Mariner draws particular attention to Vespers at the end of the poem as a manifestation of community in spirit. Here a lack of spiritual harmony among the crew leads to disaster.

But when the fog cleared off, they justify the same, and thus make themselves accomplices in the crime.	Nor dim nor red, like God's own head, The glorious Sun[337] uprist:[338] Then all averred, I had killed the bird That brought the fog and mist. 100 'Twas right, said they, such birds to slay, That bring the fog and mist.
The fair breeze continues; the ship enters the Pacific Ocean, and sails northward, even till it reaches the Line.	The fair breeze blew, the white foam flew, The furrow followed free; We were the first that ever burst 105 Into that silent sea.
The ship hath been suddenly becalmed.	Down dropt the breeze, the sails dropt down, 'Twas sad as sad could be; And we did speak only to break The silence of the sea! 110

[337] *Sun*: The sun is often a symbol of Christ. From ancient times the sun has been a symbol of the Divine because of its fiery domination of the heavens, its royal golden color, and, above all, as the source of light and life. A number of things have linked it more specifically to Christian beliefs. The sun rises, sets, and rises again, echoing the pattern of birth, death, and resurrection. It rises in the east, the direction of the Holy Land for most Christian peoples, and toward which their churches are oriented. Like the sun, Christ is "Light of Light ... by whom all things were made" (Nicene Creed). When the sun goes down, it is often blood-red, like the dying Christ; the Virgin Mary's role, and relationship to Christ, can be seen as analogous to the Moon's in reflecting and distributing her Son's glory. The Gospels identify the sun's extinction with the death of Christ: "It was now about the sixth hour, and there was darkness over all the whole land until the ninth hour, while the sun's light failed; and the curtain of the temple was torn in two. Then Jesus, crying with a loud voice, said, 'Father, into your hands I commit my spirit!' And having said this he breathed his last" (Luke 23:44–46; see also Matthew 27:45; Mark 15:33). One might add Jakob Böhme (1575–1624): "The *stars* being many and several, inexpressible and innumerable, signify the Father: out of the stars the *sun* is come to be; for God hath made it out of *them* and it signifieth the Son of God" (Jakob Böhme, *Aurora the Day-Spring*, Jacob Boehme Online, chap. 3, par. 65, http://www.jacobboehmeonline.com /yahoo_site_admin/assets/docs/AURORAjbo.172115632.pdf). The homophones sun/Son have also proven irresistible to poets writing in English. Cf. "Fears in Solitude", line 85, and Blake's "The Chimney Sweeper", line 16.

[338] *uprist*: uprisen (pseudo-archaic, dating from the late sixteenth century). The change in the sun's orientation indicates that the ship is now traveling northward.

All in a hot and copper sky,
The bloody Sun, at noon,[339]
Right up above the mast did stand,
No bigger than the Moon.

Day after day, day after day,   115
We stuck, nor breath nor motion;
As idle as a painted ship
Upon a painted ocean.[340]

And the Albatross
begins to be
avenged.

Water, water, every where,
And all the boards did shrink;   120
Water, water, every where,
Nor any drop to drink.[341]

The very deep did rot:[342] O Christ!
That ever this should be!

[339] *bloody Sun, at noon*: symbol of the Crucifixion, the bloody Son at noon (see Luke 23:44–45 and note to line 98).

[340] *Day after day ... Upon a painted ocean*: Note the relationship between the Greek πνεῦμα (*pneuma*: the Holy Spirit, spirit, the wind, or movement of the wind), the biblical imagery of wind (Acts 2:1–3: "When the day of Pentecost had come, they were all together in one place. And suddenly a sound came from heaven like the rush of a mighty wind, and it filled all the house where they were sitting. And there appeared to them tongues as of fire"), and the anti-Pelagian character of this imagery (Christ: "[A]part from me you can do nothing" [John 15:5]). The Holy Spirit is symbolized by a *bird* and *wind*, and also *flames*; here we have a crime against an image associated with the Holy Spirit, followed by no wind, and death fires, rather than the flames of the New Life. Cf. "Fears in Solitude", lines 149–50.

[341] *Water, water, every where,/Nor any drop to drink*: The mariners have been alienated from God's grace by the murder of the albatross, and they begin to thirst; cf. John 4:7–10, when Jesus encountered the Samaritan woman at the well: "Jesus said to her, 'Give me a drink.... If you knew the gift of God, and who it is that is saying to you, "Give me a drink," you would have asked him and he would have given you living water.'" Cf. T.S. Eliot, "The Wasteland", lines 331–58: "Here is no water but only rock./... There is not even silence in the mountains/But dry sterile thunder without rain/... If there were water/... But there is no water".

[342] *very deep did rot*: The whole of Creation has been mysteriously afflicted by the Fall: "We know that the whole creation has been groaning with labor pains together until now" (Romans 8:22).

Yea, slimy things did crawl with legs   125
Upon the slimy sea.

About, about, in reel and rout[343]
The death-fires[344] danced at night;
The water, like a witch's oils,
Burnt green, and blue and white.   130

A Spirit had followed   And some in dreams assurèd were
them; one of the
invisible inhabitants   Of the Spirit that plagued us so;[345]
of this planet, neither departed souls nor angels; concerning whom the learned Jew,
Josephus, and the Platonic Constantinopolitan, Michael Psellus, may be consulted.
They are very numerous, and there is no climate or element without one or more.

[343] *rout*: troup; tumultuous crowd.

[344] *death-fires*: corpse-candles, "a thick candle formerly used at lake-wakes ... a
lambent flame seen in a churchyard, and believed to portend a funeral" (*Oxford
English Dictionary*, s.v. "corpse-candles"). Coleridge may have been referring to
St. Elmo's fire, a fiery bluish light (in fact an electrical plasma) sometimes appear-
ing on ships' masts (and elsewhere) in bad weather.

[345] *some in dreams assurèd were / Of the Spirit that plagued us so*: In connection
with this and the gloss' dæmonology, consider the following: Flavius Josephus
(Joseph ben Matthias, A.D. 37–100), Romano-Jewish historian. Coleridge is prob-
ably referring to Josephus' passage on the Essenes' pneumatology: "It is indeed
their unshakeable conviction that bodies are corruptible and the material com-
posing them impermanent, whereas souls remain immortal for ever. Coming
forth from the most rarefied ether they are trapped in the prison-house of the
body as if drawn down by one of nature's spells; but once freed from the bonds
of the flesh, as if released after years of slavery, they rejoice and soar aloft" (*The
Jewish War* [Harmondsworth, Eng.: Penguin, 1959], p. 374). Michael Psellus
(A.D. 1018–1096), Byzantine philosopher, historian, man of letters, and states-
man. Coleridge likely has in mind his *On the Operation of Dæmons* (Peri Energeias
Daimonon—possibly an apocryphal work):

> [The Igneous] order of dæmons haunts the air above us, but the second
> occupies the air contiguous to us, and is called by the proper name Aërial;
> the third is the Earthly, the fourth the Aqueous and Marine, the fifth the
> Subterranean, and the last the Lucifugus, which can scarcely be consid-
> ered sentient beings. But how, said I, or what doing, do they accomplish
> (deception of men's minds, and impulsion to unlawful acts)? Not by lording
> it over us, says Marcus, but by leading us into reminiscences, for when we
> are in an imaginative spirit, approaching by virtue of their spiritual nature,
> they whisper descriptions ... , they insinuate a sort of murmur, that serves
> with them the place of words.... Thus also the dæmons, assuming appear-
> ances and colours, and whatever forms they please, transport them into
> our animal spirit, and occasion us in consequence a vast deal of trouble,

Nine fathom deep[346] he had followed us
From the land of mist and snow.

And every tongue, through utter
    drought,   135
Was withered at the root;
We could not speak, no more than if
We had been choked with soot.

The shipmates, in
their sore distress,
would fain throw the
whole guilt on the
ancient Mariner: in
sign whereof they
hang the dead sea-bird round his neck.

Ah! well a-day![347] what evil looks
Had I from old and young!   140
Instead of the cross, the Albatross
About my neck was hung.[348]

---

suggesting designs, reviving the recollection of pleasures, obtruding representations of sensual delights, both waking and sleeping; ... they create a commotion in men's minds.... Dæmons have not a particle of wit, yet they are dangerous and very terrible, ... agitating men's persons, and injuring their faculties, and obstructing their motions. (trans. Marcus Collisson [Sydney, 1843], pp. 33, 34–35)

See also C. S. Lewis:

The dæmons have bodies of a finer consistency than clouds, which are not normally visible to us.... They are rational "ærial" animals, as we are rational "terrestrial" animals, and the gods proper are rational "ætherial" animals. The idea that even the highest created spirits—the gods, as distinct from God—were, after their own fashion, incarnate, had some sort of material "vehicle", goes back to Plato. He had called the true gods, the deified stars, ζῷα, animals. Scholasticism, in regarding the angels—which is what the gods or ætherial creatures are called in Christian language—as pure or naked spirits, was revolutionary. The Florentine Platonists reverted to the older view. (Lewis, *Discarded Image*, pp. 41–42)

Coleridge was certainly acquainted with the writings on the subject by Florentine Platonist Marsilio Ficino (1433–1499); see, for example, Ficino, *Platonic Theology*, vol. 1 (Cambridge: Harvard University Press, 2001), pp. 267, 287, 295–97.

[346] *Nine fathom deep*: Cf. Shakespeare, *The Tempest*, Act 1, scene 2, lines 399–405: "Full fathom five thy father lies. /... Nothing of him that doth fade / But doth suffer a sea-change / Into something rich and strange. / Sea-nymphs hourly ring his knell".

[347] *well a-day!*: alas!

[348] *I had killed the bird ... That bring the fog and mist.... what evil looks ... hung*: The movement of the poem from the crew's inculpating approval of the Mariner for slaying the bird (lines 99–102), to their attempt to make a scapegoat of him (lines 139–42), culminating in their forcing him to carry the albatross

368

The Romantic Poets

PART III

There passed a weary time. Each throat
Was parched, and glazed each eye.
A weary time! a weary time!   145
How glazed each weary eye,
When looking westward, I beheld
A something in the sky.

At first it seemed a little speck,
And then it seemed a mist;   150
It moved and moved, and took at last
A certain shape, I wist.[349]

A speck, a mist, a shape, I wist!
And still it neared and neared:
As if it dodged a water-sprite,[350]   155
It plunged and tacked and veered.

With throats unslaked, with black lips
   baked,
We could nor laugh nor wail;
Through utter drought all dumb we stood!
I bit my arm, I sucked the blood,   160
And cried, A sail! a sail!

With throats unslaked, with black lips
   baked,
Agape they heard me call:
Gramercy![351] they for joy did grin,
And all at once their breath drew in,   165
As[352] they were drinking all.

The ancient Mariner beholdeth a sign in the element afar off.

At its nearer approach, it seemeth him to be a ship; and at a dear ransom he freeth his speech from the bonds of thirst.

A flash of joy;

---

like a cross, mirrors that of Palm Sunday's "Hosanna" (Matthew 21:9) to Good
Friday's "Let him be crucified.... His blood be on us" (Matthew 27:23, 25).

[349] *wist*: discerned (archaic).

[350] *water-sprite*: spirit, goblin.

[351] *Gramercy!*: "an exclamation of surprise, etc. = 'mercy on us!'" (*Oxford English Dictionary*, s.v. "gramercy").

[352] *As*: as if.

And horror follows. For can it be a ship that comes onward without wind or tide?

See! see! (I cried) she tacks no more!
Hither to work us weal;[353]
Without a breeze, without a tide,
She steadies with upright keel!   170

The western wave was all a-flame.
The day was well nigh done!
Almost upon the western wave
Rested the broad bright Sun;
When that strange shape drove suddenly 175
Betwixt us and the Sun.[354]

It seemeth him but the skeleton of a ship.

And straight the Sun was flecked with
        bars,
(Heaven's Mother send us grace!)
As if through a dungeon-grate he peered
With broad and burning face.   180

Alas! (thought I, and my heart beat loud)
How fast she nears and nears!
Are those her sails that glance in the Sun,
Like restless gossameres?[355]

And its ribs are seen as bars on the face of the setting Sun.

The spectre-woman and her death-mate, and no other on board the skeleton ship.

Are those her ribs through which
        the Sun   185
Did peer, as through a grate?
And is that Woman all her crew?
Is that a DEATH? and are there two?
Is DEATH that woman's mate?

---

[353] *weal*: welfare, good fortune.

[354] *strange shape drove . . . Betwixt us and the Sun*: As through the Fall, man has placed himself in the power of the devil: "Therefore as sin came into the world through one man and death through sin, and so death spread to all men because all men sinned" (Romans 5:12); and 1 John 5:19: "[T]he whole world is in the power of the Evil One" (New Jerusalem version).

[355] *gossameres*: "a fine filmy substance, consisting of cobwebs, spun by small spiders, which is seen floating in the air, especially in autumn" (*Oxford English Dictionary*, s.v. "gossamer").

Like vessel, like
crew!

Her lips were red, her looks were free,   190
Her locks were yellow as gold:
Her skin was as white as leprosy,[356]
The Night-mare LIFE-IN-DEATH[357]
    was she,
Who thicks man's blood with cold.

DEATH AND LIFE-
IN-DEATH have
diced for the ship's
crew, and she (the
latter) winneth the
ancient Mariner.

The naked hulk[358] alongside came,   195
And the twain[359] were casting dice;
"The game is done! I've won! I've won!"
Quoth she, and whistles thrice.

No twilight within
the courts of
the sun.

The Sun's rim dips; the stars rush out:
At one stride comes the dark;   200
With far-heard whisper, o'er the sea,
Off shot the spectre-bark.

At the rising of the
Moon,

We listened and looked sideways up!
Fear at my heart, as at a cup,
My life-blood seemed to sip!   205
The stars were dim, and thick the night,
The steersman's face by his lamp gleamed
    white;
From the sails the dew did drip—

---

[356] *leprosy*: In the Bible, leprosy was sometimes seen as a divine punishment (see 2 Kings 5; Isaiah 53:4); under the Law it meant defilement and exclusion from the community.

[357] *Night-mare* LIFE-IN-DEATH: Cf. St. Augustine, *City of God*: "For that death, which means not the separation of soul from body but the union of both for eternal punishment, is the more grievous death; it is the worst of all evils. There, by contrast, men will not be in the situations of 'before death' and 'after death', but always 'in death', and for this reason they will never be living, never dead, but dying for all eternity. In fact, man will never be 'in death' in a more horrible sense than in that state where death itself will be deathless" (bk. 13, chap. 11). Cf. "Love's Apparition and Evanishment", line 27, and "Epitaph", line 6.

[358] *hulk*: dismantled ship, hull; wreck of a ship.

[359] *twain*: two; pair; twins.

Till clomb[360] above the eastern bar[361]
The hornèd Moon, with one bright star   210
Within the nether tip.[362]

One after another,

One after one, by the star-dogged Moon,
Too quick for groan or sigh,
Each turned his face with a ghastly pang,
And cursed me with his eye.   215

His shipmates drop down dead.

Four times fifty living men,
(And I heard nor sigh nor groan)
With heavy thump, a lifeless lump,
They dropped down one by one.

But Life-in-Death *begins her work on the ancient Mariner.*

The souls did from their bodies fly,—   220
They fled to bliss or woe![363]
And every soul, it passed me by,
Like the whizz of my cross-bow!

PART IV

The wedding-guest feareth that a spirit is talking to him;

"I fear thee, ancient Mariner!
I fear thy skinny hand!   225
And thou art long, and lank, and brown,
As is the ribbed sea-sand.[364]

I fear thee and thy glittering eye,
And thy skinny hand, so brown."—

---

[360] *clomb*: climbed (archaic).

[361] *bar*: horizon.

[362] *hornèd Moon . . . nether tip*: believed to portend disaster.

[363] *fled to bliss or woe*: i.e. to Heaven or Hell, according to the condition of their souls.

[364] *thou art long . . . sea-sand*: "For the last two lines of this stanza, I am indebted to Mr Wordsworth. It was on a delightful walk from Nether Stowey to Dulverton, with him and his sister, in the Autumn of 1797, that this Poem was planned, and in part composed" (Coleridge's note).

But the ancient
Mariner assureth
him of his bodily
life, and proceedeth
to relate his horrible
penance.

Fear not, fear not, thou Wedding-Guest!　230
This body dropt not down.

Alone, alone, all, all alone,
Alone on a wide wide sea!
And never a saint took pity on
My soul in agony.[365]　　　　　　　　　235

He despiseth the
creatures of the
calm,

The many men, so beautiful!
And they all dead did lie:
And a thousand thousand slimy things
Lived on; and so did I.

And envieth that
they should live,
and so many lie
dead.

I looked upon the rotting sea,　　　　　240
And drew my eyes away;
I looked upon the rotting deck,
And there the dead men lay.

I looked to heaven, and tried to pray;
But or[366] ever a prayer had gusht,　　　245
A wicked whisper came, and made
My heart as dry as dust.

I closed my lids, and kept them close,
And the balls like pulses beat;
For the sky and the sea, and the sea and
　　the sky　　　　　　　　　　　　　　250
Lay like a load on my weary eye,
And the dead were at my feet.[367]

[365] *all alone . . . soul in agony*: Cf. the following by Lord Dunsany (1878–1957):
"These sailors seemed to fear loneliness as some people fear being hurt" ("The
Three Sailors' Gambit", in *The Last Book of Wonder* [New York: Cosimo, 2004],
p. 187).

[366] *or*: ere.

[367] *dead were at my feet*: Cf. Psalm 91:7: "A thousand may fall at your side."

But the curse liveth
for him in the eye of
the dead men.

The cold sweat melted from their limbs,
Nor rot nor reek did they:
The look with which they looked on me   255
Had never passed away.

An orphan's curse would drag to hell
A spirit from on high;[368]
But oh! more horrible than that
Is the curse in a dead man's eye!   260
Seven days, seven nights,[369] I saw that curse,
And yet I could not die.

In his loneliness and
fixedness he yearneth
towards the journey-
ing Moon, and the
stars that still sojourn,
yet still move onward;

The moving Moon went up the sky,
And no where did abide:
Softly she was going up,   265
And a star or two beside—

and every where the blue sky belongs to them, and is their appointed rest, and their
native country and their own natural homes, which they enter unannounced, as lords
that are certainly expected and yet there is a silent joy at their arrival.

Her beams bemocked the sultry main,
Like April hoar-frost spread;
But where the ship's huge shadow lay,
The charmèd[370] water burnt alway[371]   270
A still and awful red.

[368] *orphan's curse . . . spirit from on high*: Cf. Mark 9:42: "Whosoever causes one
of these little ones who believe in me to sin, it would be better for him if a great
millstone were hung round his neck and he were thrown into the sea."

[369] *Seven days, seven nights*: This raises the question of whether the Mariner's
sin was forgivable; cf. Matthew 18:21–22: "Then Peter came up and said to him,
'Lord, how often shall my brother sin against me, and I forgive him? As many as
seven times?' Jesus said to him, 'I do not say to you seven times, but seventy times
seven.'"

[370] *charmèd*: enchanted, bewitched.

[371] *alway*: unremittingly.

By the light of the
Moon he beholdeth
God's creatures of
the great calm.

Beyond the shadow of the ship,
I watched the water-snakes:[372]
They moved in tracks of shining white,
And when they reared, the elfish[373] light   275
Fell off in hoary[374] flakes.

Within the shadow of the ship
I watched their rich attire:
Blue, glossy green, and velvet black,
They coiled and swam; and every track   280
Was a flash of golden fire.

Their beauty and
their happiness.

O happy living things! no tongue
Their beauty might declare:
A spring of love gushed from my heart,[375]

He blesseth them in
his heart.

And I blessed them unaware:[376]   285
Sure my kind saint[377] took pity on me,
And I blessed them unaware.

The spell begins to
break.

The self same moment I could pray;
And from my neck so free[378]
The Albatross fell off, and sank   290
Like lead into the sea.

---

[372] *watched the water-snakes*: Cf. Numbers 21:8: "And the Lord said to Moses, 'Make a fiery serpent, and set it up as a sign; and every one who is bitten, when he sees it, shall live.'"

[373] *elfish*: weird, uncanny, enchanted.

[374] *hoary*: grayish-white.

[375] *spring of love gushed from my heart*: See the note to line 122. Cf. Isaiah 35:7: "[A]nd the thirsty ground springs of water".

[376] *blessed them unaware*: Cf. Matthew 25:40: "Truly, I [Jesus] say to you, as you did it to one of the least of these my brethren, you did it to me."

[377] *my kind saint*: patron saint.

[378] *from my neck so free*: Cf. Matthew 11:30: "[M]y yoke is easy, and my burden is light."

PART V

Oh sleep! it is a gentle thing,
Beloved from pole to pole!
To Mary Queen the praise be given![379]
She sent the gentle sleep from Heaven,   295
That slid into my soul.

By grace of the holy
Mother, the ancient
Mariner is refreshed
with rain.

The silly[380] buckets on the deck,
That had so long remained,
I dreamt that they were filled with dew;
And when I awoke, it rained.   300

My lips were wet, my throat was cold,
My garments all were dank;
Sure[381] I had drunken in my dreams,
And still my body drank.

I moved, and could not feel my limbs: 305
I was so light—almost
I thought that I had died in sleep,
And was a blessèd ghost.[382]

He heareth
sounds and seeth
strange sights and
commotions in
the sky and the
element.

And soon I heard a roaring wind:[383]
It did not come anear;[384]   310
But with its sound it shook the sails,
That were so thin and sere.

[379] *To Mary Queen the praise be given*: *Praise* offered to Mary Queen for *interceding*, most unusual reference for an Anglican writer of this period. For Cardinal Newman on the Catholicizing influence of Coleridge, see *Apologia*, pp. 158–59.

[380] *silly*: simple, homely.

[381] *Sure*: surely; certainly.

[382] *blessèd ghost*: spirit.

[383] *heard a roaring wind*: See the note to line 118.

[384] *anear*: near.

The upper air[385] burst into life!
And a hundred fire-flags sheen,[386]
To and fro they were hurried about!   315
And to and fro, and in and out,
The wan stars danced between.

And the coming wind did roar more loud,
And the sails did sigh like sedge;
And the rain poured down from one
    black cloud;   320
The Moon was at its edge.

The thick black cloud was cleft, and still
The Moon was at its side:
Like waters shot from some high crag,
The lightning fell with never a jag,   325
A river steep and wide.

The bodies of the ship's crew are inspirited, and the ship moves on;

The loud wind never reached the ship,
Yet now the ship moved on!
Beneath the lightning and the Moon
The dead men gave a groan.   330

They groaned, they stirred, they all
    uprose,
Nor spake, nor moved their eyes;
It had been strange, even in a dream,
To have seen those dead men rise.

The helmsman steered, the ship
    moved on;   335
Yet never a breeze up blew;
The mariners all 'gan work the ropes,
Where they were wont to do;

---

[385] *upper air*: See the note to line 227 of "Christabel".
[386] *hundred fire-flags sheen*: the phenomena of an aurora.

They raised their limbs like lifeless
    tools—
We were a ghastly crew.   340

The body of my brother's son
Stood by me, knee to knee:
The body and I pulled at one rope,
But he said nought to me.

"I fear thee, ancient Mariner!"   345
Be calm, thou Wedding-Guest!
'Twas not those souls that fled in pain,
Which to their corses[387] came again,
But a troop of spirits blest:

For when it dawned—they dropped their
    arms,   350
And clustered round the mast;
Sweet sounds rose slowly through their
    mouths,
And from their bodies passed.

Around, around, flew each sweet sound,
Then darted to the Sun;[388]   355
Slowly the sounds came back again,
Now mixed, now one by one.[389]

Sometimes a-dropping from the sky
I heard the sky-lark sing;
Sometimes all little birds that are,   360
How they seemed to fill the sea and air
With their sweet jargoning![390]

But not by the souls of the men, nor by dæmons of earth or middle air, but by a blessed troop of angelic spirits, sent down by the invocation of the guardian saint.

[387] *corses*: corpses.

[388] *darted to the Sun*: For celestial harmony, see the note to line 8 of Wordsworth's "The world is too much with us".

[389] *Now mixed, now one by one*: Union with God does not obliterate the individuality of the blessed.

[390] *jargoning*: twittering, chattering.

And now 'twas like all instruments,
Now like a lonely flute;
And now it is an angel's song,   365
That makes the heavens be mute.

It ceased; yet still the sails made on
A pleasant noise till noon,
A noise like of a hidden brook
In the leafy month of June,   370
That to the sleeping woods all night
Singeth a quiet tune.

Till noon we quietly sailed on,
Yet never a breeze did breathe:
Slowly and smoothly went the ship,   375
Moved onward from beneath.

The lonesome spirit
from the south pole
carries on the ship
as far as the Line,
in obedience to
the angelic troop,
but still requireth
vengeance.

Under the keel nine fathom deep,
From the land of mist and snow,
The spirit slid: and it was he
That made the ship to go.   380
The sails at noon left off their tune,
And the ship stood still also.

The Sun, right up above the mast,
Had fixed her to the ocean:
But in a minute she 'gan stir,   385
With a short uneasy motion—
Backwards and forwards half her length
With a short uneasy motion.

Then like a pawing horse let go,
She made a sudden bound: 390
It flung the blood into my head,
And I fell down in a swound.

The Polar Spirit's
fellow-dæmons,
the invisible
inhabitants of the
element, take part
in his wrong; and
two of them relate,
one to the other,
that penance long
and heavy for the
ancient Mariner
hath been accorded
to the Polar Spirit,
who returneth
southward.

How long in that same fit I lay,
I have not to declare;[391]
But ere my living life returned,   395
I heard and in my soul discerned
Two VOICES in the air.

"Is it he?" quoth one, "Is this the man?
By him who died on cross,
With his cruel bow he laid full low   400
The harmless Albatross.

The spirit who bideth by himself
In the land of mist and snow,
He loved the bird that loved the man
Who shot him with his bow."   405

The other was a softer voice,
As soft as honey-dew:[392]
Quoth he, "The man hath penance done,
And penance more will do."

PART VI

First Voice

But tell me, tell me! speak again,   410
Thy soft response renewing—
What makes that ship drive on so fast?
What is the OCEAN doing?

Second Voice

Still as a slave before his lord,[393]
The ocean hath no blast;   415

[391] *I have not to declare*: I am unable to say.

[392] *As soft as honey-dew*: See the notes to the last two lines of "Kubla Khan".

[393] *Still as a slave before his lord*: Cf. Wordsworth, "Intimations of Immortality",
lines 119–21.

His great bright eye[394] most silently
Up to the Moon is cast—

If he may know which way to go;
For she guides him smooth or grim.
See, brother, see! how graciously   420
She looketh down on him.

First Voice

The Mariner hath
been cast into a
trance; for the
angelic power
causeth the vessel
to drive northward
faster than human
life could endure.

But why drives on that ship so fast,
Without or wave or wind?

Second Voice

The air is cut away before,
And closes from behind.   425
Fly, brother, fly! more high, more high!
Or we shall be belated:
For slow and slow that ship will go,
When the Mariner's trance is abated.

The supernatural
motion is retarded;
the Mariner awakes,
and his penance
begins anew.

I woke, and we were sailing on   430
As in a gentle weather:
'Twas night, calm night, the moon was
      high;
The dead men stood together.

All stood together on the deck,
For a charnel-dungeon[395] fitter: 435
All fixed on me their stony eyes,
That in the Moon did glitter.

---

[394] *ocean hath no blast;/His great bright eye*: Cf. Sir John Davies (1569–1626), "Orchestra", stanza 49, lines 1–5: "For lo, the sea that fleets about the land/... his great crystal eye is always cast/Up to the moon and on her fixèd fast".

[395] *charnel-dungeon*: crypt or mausoleum; literally, a secure chamber for dead flesh.

The pang, the curse, with which they died,
Had never passed away:
I could not draw my eyes from theirs,   440
Nor turn them up to pray.

The curse is finally
expiated.

And now this spell was snapt: once more
I viewed the ocean green,
And looked far forth, yet little saw
Of what had else been seen—   445

Like one, that on a lonesome road
Doth walk in fear and dread,
And having once turned round walks on,
And turns no more his head;
Because he knows, a frightful fiend   450
Doth close behind him tread.

But soon there breathed a wind on me,
Nor sound nor motion made:
Its path was not upon the sea,
In ripple or in shade.   455

It raised my hair, it fanned my cheek
Like a meadow-gale[396] of spring—
It mingled strangely with my fears,
Yet it felt like a welcoming.

Swiftly, swiftly flew the ship,   460
Yet she sailed softly too:
Sweetly, sweetly blew the breeze—
On me alone it blew.

And the ancient
Mariner beholdeth
his native country.

Oh! dream of joy! is this indeed
The lighthouse top I see?   465
Is this the hill? is this the kirk?
Is this mine own countree?

[396] meadow-gale: breeze.

We drifted o'er the harbour-bar,[397]
And I with sobs did pray—
O let me be awake, my God!   470
Or let me sleep alway.

The harbour-bay was clear as glass,
So smoothly it was strewn![398]
And on the bay the moonlight lay,
And the shadow of the Moon.   475

The rock shone bright, the kirk no less,
That stands above the rock:[399]
The moonlight steeped in silentness
The steady weathercock.[400]

And the bay was white with silent
          light,[401]
                                              480
Till rising from the same,
The angelic spirits
leave the dead
bodies,
Full many shapes, that shadows were,
In crimson colours came.

[397] *harbour-bar*: sandbank or shoal running across the mouth of a river or harbor, an obstruction to shipping.

[398] *strewn*: calmed (of waves, e.g., after a storm).

[399] *rock*: The rock is a biblical symbol of God: "The LORD is my rock" (2 Samuel 22:2). The rock is also a source of grace under the symbolic form of water: "He cleft rocks in the wilderness, and gave them drink abundantly as from the deep. He made streams come out of the rock, and caused waters to flow down like rivers" (Psalm 78:15–16). Finally, Christ builds his Church on a rock: "And I tell you, you are Peter, and on this rock I will build my Church, and the gates of Hades shall not prevail against it" (Matthew 16:18). For Luther and most subsequent Protestant traditions, the rock refers to Christ, or Peter's confession of faith, rather than to Peter and Catholic Petrine claims.

[400] *weathercock*: weathervane with a rooster, often crowning church steeples as a symbol of spiritual vigilance, and the triumph of light and goodness over darkness and evil.

[401] *bay was white with silent light*: Cf. Matthew 17:2: "[H]e [Jesus] was transfigured … and his face shone like the sun, and his garments became white as the light." The Neoplatonist Plotinus (A.D. 204–270) also refers to "the splendour and white glint of the celestial fire" (*The Enneads*, Second Ennead, First Tractate).

And appear in their
own forms of light.

A little distance from the prow
Those crimson shadows were: 485
I turned my eyes upon the deck—
Oh, Christ! what saw I there!

Each corse lay flat, lifeless and flat,
And, by the holy rood![402]
A man all light, a seraph-man,[403]   490
On every corse there stood.

This seraph-band, each waved his hand:
It was a heavenly sight!
They stood as signals to the land,
Each one a lovely light;   495

This seraph-band, each waved his hand,
No voice did they impart—
No voice; but oh! the silence sank
Like music on my heart.

But soon I heard the dash of oars,   500
I heard the Pilot's cheer;[404]
My head was turned perforce away,
And I saw a boat appear.

The Pilot and the Pilot's boy,
I heard them coming fast: 505
Dear Lord in Heaven! it was a joy
The dead men could not blast.[405]

---

[402] *holy rood*: crucifix. Cf. Shakespeare, *Hamlet*, Act 3, scene 4, line 14: "No, by the rood, not so".

[403] *seraph-man*: The seraphim (literally, "the burning ones") are among the most exalted of the angels.

[404] *cheer*: shout of encouragement.

[405] *blast*: blight, curse.

I saw a third—I heard his voice:
It is the Hermit[406] good!
He singeth loud his godly hymns   510
That he makes in the wood.
He'll shrieve[407] my soul, he'll wash away
The Albatross's blood.

PART VII

The Hermit of the Wood,

This Hermit good lives in that wood
Which slopes down to the sea.   515
How loudly his sweet voice he rears!
He loves to talk with marineres
That come from a far countree.

He kneels at morn, and noon, and eve—
He hath a cushion plump: 520
It is the moss that wholly hides
The rotted old oak-stump.

The skiff-boat neared: I heard them talk,
"Why, this is strange, I trow![408]
Where are those lights so many and fair,   525
That signal made but now?"

Approacheth the ship with wonder.

"Strange, by my faith!" the Hermit said—
"And they answered not our cheer!
The planks looked warped! and see those
    sails,
How thin they are and sere![409]   530
I never saw aught like to them,
Unless perchance it were

[406] *Hermit*: See the note to line 27 of Blake's "The Grey Monk".
[407] *He'll shrieve*: He'll hear my confession and give me absolution (archaic).
[408] *trow*: think; feel sure.
[409] *sere*: thin, worn; dried up, withered.

Brown skeletons of leaves that lag
My forest-brook along;
When the ivy-tod[410] is heavy with snow, 535
And the owlet whoops to the wolf below,
That eats the she-wolf's young."

"Dear Lord! it hath a fiendish look—
(The Pilot made reply)
I am a-feared"—"Push on, push on!" 540
Said the Hermit cheerily.

The boat came closer to the ship,
But I nor spake nor stirred;
The boat came close beneath the ship,
And straight a sound was heard. 545

The ship suddenly sinketh.

Under the water it rumbled on,
Still louder and more dread:
It reached the ship, it split the bay;
The ship went down like lead.

The ancient Mariner is saved in the Pilot's boat.

Stunned by that loud and dreadful sound, 550
Which sky and ocean smote,
Like one that hath been seven days
drowned[411]
My body lay afloat;
But swift as dreams, myself I found
Within the Pilot's boat. 555

Upon the whirl, where sank the ship,
The boat spun round and round;

---

[410] *ivy-tod*: ivy-bush.

[411] *seven days drowned*: In the Genesis account, God created the heavens and the Earth in six days and rested on the seventh. Thus seven days is an image both of perfect completion and spiritual rest. Equally, the restoration of the ostensibly drowned prophet is depicted in Jonah and is adverted to by Christ in connection with his death and Resurrection.

And all was still, save that the hill
Was telling[412] of the sound.

I moved my lips—the Pilot shrieked   560
And fell down in a fit;
The holy Hermit raised his eyes,
And prayed where he did sit.

I took the oars: the Pilot's boy,
Who now doth crazy[413] go,   565
Laughed loud and long, and all the while
His eyes went to and fro.
"Ha! Ha!" quoth he, "full plain I see,
The Devil knows how to row."

And now, all in my own countree,   570
I stood on the firm land!
The Hermit stepped forth from the boat,
And scarcely he could stand.

The ancient
Mariner earnestly
entreateth the
Hermit to shrieve
him; and the
penance of life falls
on him.

"O shrieve me, shrieve me, holy man!"
The Hermit crossed his brow.   575
"Say quick," quoth he, "I bid thee say—
What manner of man art thou?"

Forthwith this frame of mine was wrenched
With a woful agony,
Which forced me to begin my tale;   580
And then it left me free.

And ever and anon
throughout his
future life an agony
constraineth him
to travel from land
to land,

Since then, at an uncertain hour,
That agony returns:
And till my ghastly tale is told,
This heart within me burns.   585

---

[412] *telling*: reverberating with.
[413] *crazy*: "full of cracks or flaws; impaired; liable to fall to pieces ... of unsound mind" (*Oxford English Dictionary*, s.v. "crazy").

I pass, like night, from land to land;
I have strange power of speech;
That moment that his face I see,
I know the man that must hear me:
To him my tale I teach.   590

What loud uproar bursts from that door!
The wedding-guests are there:
But in the garden-bower the bride
And bride-maids singing are:
And hark the little vesper[414] bell,   595
Which biddeth me to prayer!

O Wedding-Guest! this soul hath been
Alone on a wide wide sea:
So lonely 'twas, that God himself
Scarce seemèd there to be.   600

O sweeter than the marriage-feast,
'Tis sweeter far to me,
To walk together to the kirk
With a goodly company!—

To walk together to the kirk,   605
And all together pray,
While each to his great Father bends,
Old men, and babes, and loving friends,
And youths and maidens gay!

And to teach, by his
own example, love
and reverence to
all things that God
made and loveth.

Farewell, farewell! but this I tell   610
To thee, thou Wedding-Guest!
He prayeth well, who loveth well[415]
Both man and bird and beast.

414 *vesper*: See the note to line 76.

415 *He prayeth well, who loveth well*: Cf. 1 Corinthians 13:2: "And if I have pro-
phetic powers, and understand all mysteries and all knowledge, and if I have all
faith, so as to remove mountains, but have not love, I am nothing."

He prayeth best, who loveth best
All things both great and small;   615
For the dear God who loveth us,
He made and loveth all.[416]

The Mariner, whose eye is bright,
Whose beard with age is hoar,
Is gone: and now the Wedding-Guest   620
Turned from the bridegroom's door.

He went like one that hath been
     stunned,
And is of sense forlorn:
A sadder and a wiser man,
He rose the morrow morn.   625

Apologia Pro Vita Sua[417]

The poet in his lone yet genial hour
Gives to his eyes a magnifying power:[418]
Or rather he emancipates his eyes

---

[416] *the little vesper bell . . . loveth all*: This last passage, from Vespers to the end of the Mariner's narrative, can be summed up in three central biblical statements: "In the beginning God created the heavens and the earth.... And God saw that it was good" (Genesis 1:1, 18); "He who does not love does not know God; for God is love" (1 John 4:8); "You shall love the Lord your God with all your heart, and with all your soul, and with all your mind. This is the great and first commandment. And the second is like it, You shall love your neighbor as yourself" (Matthew 22:37–39).

[417] Published in *Blackwood's Magazine*, January 1822, but only collected posthumously. The Latin title means "A defence of his life". Cf. Newman's spiritual autobiography *Apologia Pro Vita Sua* (1864).

[418] *eyes a magnifying power*: See the note on eyes to line 151 of "Christabel", the Barfield passage in the introductory note to "Dejection: An Ode", the note on the Book of Nature in the introductory note to "Frost at Midnight", and "Kubla Khan", line 50. Cf. "The Ancient Mariner", line 13.

From the black shapeless accidents of size[419]—
In unctuous[420] cones of kindling coal,[421]   5
Or smoke upwreathing from the pipe's trim bole,[422]
    His gifted ken[423] can see
    Phantoms of sublimity.

Inscription

FOR A FOUNTAIN ON A HEATH[424]

This Sycamore, oft musical with bees,—
Such tents the Patriarchs[425] loved! O long unharmed
May all its agèd boughs o'er-canopy
The small round basin, which this jutting stone
Keeps pure from falling leaves! Long may the Spring,   5
Quietly as a sleeping infant's breath,
Send up cold waters to the traveller
With soft and even pulse! Nor ever cease
Yon tiny cone of sand its soundless dance,
Which at the bottom, like a Fairy's Page,   10
As merry and no taller, dances still,
Nor wrinkles the smooth surface of the Fount.
Here Twilight is and Coolness: here is moss,
A soft seat, and a deep and ample shade.
Thou may'st toil far and find no second tree.   15

---

[419] *accidents of size*: Coleridge is echoing the language of transubstantiation in which the *accidents* (i.e., the physical characteristics) of bread and wine remain after consecration though their *substance* is changed into the Body and Blood of Christ.

[420] *unctuous*: oily.

[421] *kindling coal*: i.e., in the stove or fireplace.

[422] *bole*: bowl.

[423] *ken*: vision; mental perception.

[424] Published in the *Morning Post*, September 24, 1801, and collected in *Sibylline Leaves*, 1817.

[425] *Patriarchs*: the great leaders and saints of the Old Testament, such as Noah, Abraham, Isaac, Jacob, and David.

Drink, Pilgrim, here; Here rest! and if thy heart
Be innocent, here too shalt thou refresh
Thy spirit,[426] listening to some gentle sound,
Or passing gale or hum of murmuring bees![427]

The Knight's Tomb[428]

Where is the grave of Sir Arthur O'Kellyn?
Where may the grave of that good man be?—
By the side of a spring, on the breast of Helvellyn,[429]
Under the twigs of a young birch tree!
The oak that in summer was sweet to hear,   5
And rustled its leaves in the fall of the year,
And whistled and roared in the winter alone,
Is gone,—and the birch in its stead is grown.—

---

[426] *heart/Be innocent . . . Thy spirit*: Cf. Matthew 5:8: "Blessed are the pure in
heart, for they shall see God."

[427] *listening to some gentle sound . . . hum of murmuring bees*: Cf. Virgil, *Eclogues* 1,
lines 51–56: "Happy old man! You will stay here, between the rivers that you
know so well, by springs that have their Nymphs, and find some cool spot under-
neath the trees. . . . The hedge there . . . will have its willow-blossom rifled by
Hyblaean bees and coax you with the gentle humming through the gates of sleep.
On the other side, at the foot of the high rock, you will have the vine-dresser
singing to the breezes"; and Tennyson, "Come down, O maid", lines 29–31:
"Myriads of rivulets hurrying thro' the lawn,/The moan of doves in immemorial
elms,/And murmuring of innumerable bees."

[428] Published in *Poetical Works*, 1834, though it is thought to have been com-
posed, in some form at least, as early as 1802.

> Sir Walter Scott always spoke in high praise of the Christabel, and more
> than once of his obligations to Coleridge; of this we have proof in his
> Ivanhoe, in which the lines by Coleridge, entitled "The Knight's Tomb,"
> were quoted by Scott before they were published, from which circum-
> stance, Coleridge was convinced that Sir Walter was the author of the
> Waverly [sic] Novels. The lines were composed as an experiment for a
> metre, and repeated by him to a mutual friend—this gentleman the fol-
> lowing day dined in company with Sir Walter Scott, and spoke of his
> visit to Highgate, repeating Coleridge's lines to Scott, and observing at
> the same time, that they might be acceptable to the author of Waverley.
> (Gillman, *Life*, vol. 1, p. 277)

[429] *Helvellyn*: mountain in the Lake District, the third highest in England.

The Knight's bones are dust,
And his good sword rust;— 10
His soul is with the saints, I trust.

Hymn

BEFORE SUN-RISE, IN THE VALE OF CHAMOUNI[430]

> Besides the Rivers, Arve[431] and Arveiron,[432] which have their
> sources in the foot of Mont Blanc,[433] five conspicuous torrents
> rush down its sides; and within a few paces of the Glaciers, the
> Gentiana Major grows in immense numbers, with its "flowers
> of loveliest blue."

Hast thou a charm[434] to stay[435] the morning-star[436]
In his steep course? So long he seems to pause
On thy bald[437] awful[438] head, O sovran[439] BLANC!
The Arve and Arveiron at thy base
Rave[440] ceaselessly; but thou, most awful Form! 5
Risest from forth thy silent sea of pines,
How silently! Around thee and above

[430] Published in the *Morning Post*, September 11, 1802, and, much revised, in
Sibylline Leaves, 1817. It was adapted and expanded from an original poem by
Friederike Brun (1765–1835). Cf. Wordsworth, *Prelude*, bk. 6, lines 528ff. The
poem had a marked influence upon Percy Bysshe Shelley's "Mont Blanc" and
Mary Shelley's (1797–1851) *Frankenstein* (esp. vol. 2, chaps. 1–2).

[431] *Arve*: A tributary of the Rhône, the river Arve is fed by many of the glaciers
of the Chamonix Valley.

[432] *Arveiron*: the Arveyron, a tributary of the Arve, flowing into it at Chamonix.

[433] *Mont Blanc*: highest mountain in the Alps (15,782 feet above sea level); on
the French-Italian border.

[434] *charm*: magical power; spell.

[435] *stay*: delay, arrest the progress of.

[436] *morning-star*: the planet Venus.

[437] *bald*: undisguised; marked with white: Mont Blanc's summit is a thick,
perennial dome formed of ice and snow.

[438] *awful*: sublimely majestic; inspiring dread and awe.

[439] *sovran*: sovereign; supreme.

[440] *Rave*: anagram of "Arve". Cf. Poe, "Ulalaume", lines 6–7: "It was hard by
the *dim* lake of Auber, / In the misty *mid* region of Weir" (italics mine).

Deep is the air and dark, substantial, black,[441]
An ebon mass: methinks thou piercest it,
As with a wedge! But when I look again,   10
It is thine own calm home, thy crystal shrine,
Thy habitation from eternity!
O dread and silent Mount! I gazed upon thee,
Till thou, still present to the bodily sense,
Didst vanish from my thought: entranced in prayer   15
I worshipped the Invisible alone.

Yet, like some sweet beguiling melody,
So sweet, we know not we are listening to it,
Thou, the meanwhile, wast blending with my Thought,
Yea, with my Life and Life's own secret joy: 20
Till the dilating Soul, enrapt,[442] transfused,
Into the mighty vision passing—there
As in her natural form, swelled vast to Heaven!

Awake, my soul! not only passive praise
Thou owest! not alone these swelling tears,   25
Mute thanks and secret ecstasy! Awake,
Voice of sweet song! Awake, my Heart, awake!
Green vales and icy cliffs, all join my Hymn.

Thou first and chief, sole sovran of the Vale!
O struggling with the darkness all the night,   30
And visited all night by troops of stars,
Or when they climb the sky or[443] when they sink:
Companion of the morning-star at dawn,

---

[441] *Deep . . . black:* Cf. *Paradise Lost,* bk. 1, lines 59–63: "At once as far as angels
ken he views/The dismal situation waste and wild:/A dungeon horrible, on all
sides round/As one great furnace flamed, yet from those flames/No light, but
rather darkness visible".

[442] *enrapt:* "carried away in an ecstasy; hence, absorbed in contemplation,
enraptured" (*Oxford English Dictionary,* s.v. "enrapt").

[443] *Or...or:* Either...or.

Thyself Earth's rosy star,[444] and of the dawn
Co-herald: wake, O wake, and utter praise! 35
Who sank thy sunless pillars deep in Earth?[445]
Who filled thy countenance with rosy light?
Who made thee parent of perpetual streams?

And you, ye five wild torrents[446] fiercely glad!
Who called you forth from night and utter death, 40
From dark and icy caverns[447] called you forth,
Down those precipitous, black, jaggèd rocks,
For ever shattered and the same for ever?
Who gave you your invulnerable life,[448]
Your strength, your speed, your fury, and your joy, 45
Unceasing thunder and eternal foam?
And who commanded (and the silence came),
Here let the billows stiffen, and have rest?

Ye Ice-falls! ye that from the mountain's brow
Adown enormous ravines slope amain[449]— 50
Torrents, methinks, that heard a mighty voice,
And stopped at once amid their maddest plunge!
Motionless torrents! silent cataracts!
Who made you glorious as the Gates of Heaven
Beneath the keen full moon? Who bade the sun 55
Clothe you with rainbows? Who, with living flowers

[444] *Earth's rosy star*: the effects of sunrise on the snowy peak.

[445] *Who sank thy sunless pillars deep in Earth?*: Cf. Job 38:4: "Where were you when I laid the foundation of the earth?"

[446] *And you, ye five wild torrents*: the glaciers descending into the Chamonix Valley.

[447] *five wild torrents . . . dark and icy caverns*: This is a classical allusion; in Graeco-Roman mythology, the Underworld had five rivers (Acheron, Cocytus, Phlegethon, Lethe, and Styx) and was sometimes reached by way of a cave— Avernus (which recalls the rivers Arve and Arveiron), Taenarum.

[448] *wild torrents . . . Who gave you your invulnerable life*: another classical echo; Achilles (renowned for his strength, speed, and fury) was dipped at birth in the Styx by his mother and made invulnerable apart from his heel.

[449] *amain*: vehemently; at full speed.

Of loveliest blue, spread garlands at your feet?—
GOD! let the torrents, like a shout of nations,[450]
Answer! and let the ice-plains echo, GOD!
GOD! sing ye meadow-streams with gladsome voice!　　　60
Ye pine-groves, with your soft and soul-like sounds!
And they too have a voice, yon piles of snow,
And in their perilous fall shall thunder, GOD!

　　　Ye living flowers that skirt the eternal frost!
Ye wild goats sporting round the eagle's nest!　　　65
Ye eagles, play-mates of the mountain-storm!
Ye lightnings, the dread arrows of the clouds!
Ye signs and wonders of the element!
Utter forth GOD, and fill the hills with praise!

　　　Thou too, hoar Mount! with thy sky-pointing
　　　　　peaks,　　　70
Oft from whose feet the avalanche, unheard,
Shoots downward, glittering through the pure serene[451]
Into the depth of clouds, that veil thy breast—
Thou too again, stupendous Mountain! thou
That as I raise my head, awhile bowed low　　　75
In adoration, upward from thy base
Slow travelling with dim eyes suffused with tears,
Solemnly seemest, like a vapoury cloud,
To rise before me—Rise, O ever rise,
Rise like a cloud of incense, from the Earth!　　　80
Thou kingly Spirit throned among the hills,
Thou dread ambassador from Earth to Heaven,
Great Hierarch![452] tell thou the silent sky,

---

[450]*Who made you glorious ... GOD! let the torrents, like a shout of nations*: Cf.
Psalm 19:1–3: "The heavens are telling the glory of God" (19:1), and Job 38:4,
6–7: "Where were you when I [God] laid the foundation of the earth? ... On what
were its bases sunk, ... when the morning stars sang together, and all the sons of
God shouted for joy?"

[451]*pure serene*: calm brightness; clear sky.

[452]*Great Hierarch*: high priest; archangel.

And tell the stars, and tell yon rising sun,
Earth, with her thousand voices, praises GOD.   85

Dejection: An Ode

"Dejection: An Ode" was first published in the *Morning Post* as
"A Letter to—" on October 4, 1802, the day of Wordsworth's
marriage to Mary Hutchinson, the sister of Sara Hutchinson
(the original addressee) with whom Coleridge was unhap-
pily in love, as also the anniversary of Coleridge's marriage
to Sara Fricker in 1795. It was republished with substantial
revisions in *Sibylline Leaves* (1817). It is usually classed among
the Conversation Poems (see introductory note to Coleridge's
"The Eolian Harp").

Central to the concerns of "Dejection: An Ode" is the
theme of man's participation through creative exchange with
the natural world:

> For we are told by the Romantic theory that we must no longer
> look for the nature-spirits—for the Goddess Natura—on the
> farther side of the appearances; we must look for them *within
> ourselves* ... or, in the well-known words of Coleridge: "We
> receive but what we give / And in our life alone does Nature
> live."...
>
> If nature is indeed "dis-godded", and yet we again begin
> to experience her, as Wordsworth did—and as millions have
> done since his time—no longer as dead but as alive; if there
> is no "represented" on the far side of the appearances, and yet
> we begin to experience them once more *as* appearances, as
> representations—the question arises, of *what* are they represen-
> tations? It was no doubt the difficulty of answering this ques-
> tion which led Wordsworth to relapse occasionally into that
> nostalgic hankering after *original* participation, which is called
> pantheism—and from which Coleridge was rendered immune
> by his acquaintance with Kantian philosophy....
>
> Henceforth, if nature is to be experienced as representation,
> she will be experienced as representation of—Man. But what
> is Man? Herein lies the direst possibility inherent in idolatry.

... We have learned that art can represent nothing but Man himself, and we have interpreted that as meaning that art exists for the purpose of enabling Mr. Smith to "express his personality". And all because we have not learnt—though our very physics shouts it at us—that nature herself is the representation of Man.

... If I know that nature herself is the system of my representations, I cannot do otherwise than adopt a humbler and more responsible attitude to the representations of art and the metaphors of poetry.... What is meant, when I say she is my representation, is, that I stand, whether I like it or not, in— ... a "directionally creator" relation to her. But I know also that what so stands is not my poor temporal personality, but the Divine Name in the unfathomable depths behind it. And if I strive to produce a work of art, I cannot then do otherwise than strive humbly to create more nearly as *that* creates, and not as my idiosyncrasy wills.[453]

Further elucidations of this theme—central to Coleridge—are in the introduction to "Frost at Midnight" (on the Book of Nature); the note on eyes to line 151 of "Christabel"; "Kubla Khan", line 50; "Apologia Pro Vita Sua"; and "The Ancient Mariner", line 13. Cf. "Fears in Solitude", lines 23–24.

> Late, late yestreen I saw the new Moon,
> With the old Moon in her arms;
> And I fear, I fear, My Master dear!
> We shall have a deadly storm.
> *Ballad of Sir Patrick Spence*[454]

---

[453] Owen Barfield, *Saving the Appearances: A Study in Idolatry* (Middletown, Conn.: Wesleyan University Press, 1988), pp. 129–32.

[454] The Scottish ballad "Sir Patrick Spens", collected in Thomas Percy's *Reliques of Ancient English Poetry* (1765). See also the introductory note to "The Rime of the Ancient Mariner".

Dejection: An Ode

I

Well! If the Bard was weather-wise, who made
    The grand old ballad of Sir Patrick Spence,
    This night, so tranquil now, will not go hence
Unroused by winds, that ply a busier trade
Than those which mould yon cloud in lazy flakes,   5
Or the dull sobbing draft, that moans and rakes,
    Upon the strings of this Æolian lute,[455]
      Which better far were mute.
    For lo! the New-moon winter-bright!
    And overspread with phantom light,   10
    (With swimming phantom light o'erspread
    But rimmed and circled by a silver thread)
I see the old Moon in her lap, foretelling
    The coming on of rain and squally blast.[456]
And oh! that even now the gust were swelling,   15
    And the slant night-shower driving loud and fast!
Those sounds which oft have raised me, whilst they awed,
      And sent my soul abroad,
Might now perhaps their wonted impulse give,
Might startle this dull pain, and make it move and live!   20

II

A grief without a pang, void, dark, and drear,
    A stifled, drowsy, unimpassioned grief,
    Which finds no natural outlet, no relief,
      In word, or sigh, or tear—

---

   [455]*Æolian lute:* Æolian harp; see introductory note to Coleridge's "The Eolian Harp".

   [456]*Moon in her lap, foretelling . . . rain and squally blast:* "If a circle forms round the moon, /Twill rain soon"—often-accurate proverb; the "halo" is a refraction of light through high cirrus clouds, usually the vanguard of a low-pressure system bringing bad weather.

O Lady!⁴⁵⁷ in this wan and heartless mood,   25
To other thoughts by yonder throstle⁴⁵⁸ woo'd,
    All this long eve, so balmy and serene,
Have I been gazing on the western sky,
    And its peculiar tint of yellow green:⁴⁵⁹
And still I gaze—and with how blank an eye!⁴⁶⁰   30
And those thin clouds above, in flakes and bars,
That give away their motion to the stars;
Those stars, that glide behind them or between,
Now sparkling, now bedimmed, but always seen:
Yon crescent Moon, as fixed as if it grew   35
In its own cloudless, starless lake of blue;
I see them all so excellently fair,
I see, not feel, how beautiful they are!

III

    My genial spirits fail;
    And what can these avail   40
To lift the smoth'ring weight from off my breast?
    It were a vain endeavour,
    Though I should gaze for ever
On that green light that lingers in the west:
I may not hope from outward forms to win   45
The passion and the life, whose fountains are within.

⁴⁵⁷ *Lady*: Sara Hutchinson.

⁴⁵⁸ *throstle*: song thrush or blackbird.

⁴⁵⁹ *tint of yellow green*: "The first personal merit which appears in his ... early work is a sense of colour. In a poem written at twenty-one he sees Fancy 'Bathed in rich amber-glowing floods of light,' and next year the same colour reappears, more expressively, in a cloud, 'wholly bright,/With a rich and amber light.' The two women in 'The Two Graves,' during a momentous pause, are found discussing whether the rays of the sun are green or amber; a valley is 'Tinged yellow with the rich departing light'; seen through corn at evening, 'The level sunshine glimmers with green light'; and there is the carefully observed 'western sky/And its peculiar tint of yellow green'" (Symons, *Romantic Movement*, pp. 143–44).

⁴⁶⁰ *gaze—and with how blank an eye*: See the note to line 151 of "Christabel".

IV

O Lady! we receive but what we give,[461]
And in our life alone does Nature live:
Ours is her wedding-garment, ours her shroud!
    And would we aught behold, of higher worth,   50
Than that inanimate[462] cold world allowed
To the poor loveless[463] ever-anxious crowd,[464]
    Ah! from the soul itself must issue forth
A light, a glory,[465] a fair luminous cloud[466]
    Enveloping the Earth—   55
And from the soul itself must there be sent[467]
    A sweet and potent voice, of its own birth,
Of all sweet sounds the life and element![468]

---

[461] *we receive but what we give*: See Acts 20:35: "[H]e [Jesus] said, 'It is more blessed to give than to receive'", and Matthew 7:12: "So whatever you wish that men would do to you, do so to them". Cf. *Prelude*, bk. 11, lines 331–33, and "Frost at Midnight", lines 64–65.

[462] *inanimate*: literally, "soulless".

[463] *To the poor loveless*: Cf. 1 John 4:7: "Beloved, let us love one another; for love is of God".

[464] *ever-anxious crowd*: This "crowd" would appear to involve a knot of echoes: the modern urban multitude, and two of Jesus' statements in the Gospel of St. Matthew: "[T]he gate is narrow and the way is hard, that leads to life, and those who find it are few" (7:14), and, "For many are called, but few are chosen" (22:14). See also the "*massa damnata*" of St. Augustine (*Ad Simplicianum* 1, 2, 16: "Therefore all men are ... one condemned mass of sin").

[465] *glory*: Beyond the usual senses of the word, a "glory" means a halo, including the halo of light seen about one's shadow cast onto clouds or mist before oneself when walking high in the mountains with sunlight behind. Cf. John 1:14: "And the Word became flesh and dwelt among us.... [W]e have beheld his glory".

[466] *fair luminous cloud*: Cf. Exodus 13:21: "And the LORD went before them by day in a pillar of cloud".

[467] *from the soul itself must there be sent*: Cf. the words of Christ to the apostles: "Behold, I send you out as sheep in the midst of wolves" (Matthew 10:16), and "the Counselor, the Holy Spirit, whom the Father will send in my name,... will teach you all things" (John 14:26).

[468] *from the soul ... life and element*: Coleridge is anchoring his thought in biblical imagery, particularly the Gospel and First Epistle of St. John: God is love (John 4:8); Jesus, the Word made flesh (John 1:14), is the Light of the World (John 8:12), through whom all things were made (John 1:3; Nicene Creed); man is created in the image and likeness of God (Genesis 1:26–27), who lives in him

V

O pure of heart![469] thou need'st not ask of me
What this strong music in the soul may be!   60
What, and wherein it doth exist,
This light, this glory,[470] this fair luminous mist,
This beautiful and beauty-making power.

     Joy,[471] virtuous Lady! Joy that ne'er was given,
Save to the pure, and in their purest hour,   65
Life,[472] and Life's effluence,[473] cloud at once and shower,
Joy, Lady! is the spirit and the power,
Which wedding Nature to us gives in dower,
     A new Earth and new Heaven,[474]

---

who loves God (John 15:5; 1 John 4:7–8; Galatians 2:20); and it is only those who love from whom the inner Jesus can proceed to clothe the created world with life: the creative, priestly, and poetic vocation of man. See also "Jesus the Imagination" and the *poet as maker* in the introductory note to Blake's *Songs of Innocence and of Experience* (pp. 20–21).

[469] *pure of heart*: Cf. Matthew 5:8: "Blessed are the pure in heart, for they shall see God"; Titus 1:15: "To the pure all things are pure".

[470] *need'st not ask of me . . . this glory*: The poet's power is analogous to that of the saint: "Neither the person of the artist nor his life discloses to us the world and essence of his works but the works themselves, which, in the case of a great artist, usually far surpass what he amounted to as a human being. Apart from their own artistic content, the works reveal what was highest and deepest within the artist and for which he at least had a yearning. To actualize as a human being the spirit embodied by his work, Mozart would have had to have been a saint— and that he was not" (Dietrich von Hildebrand, "Mozart", trans. John Henry Crosby, in *Saint Austin Review* 6, no. 4, p. 6). Something similar is evoked in the last stanza of "Kubla Khan".

[471] *This light, this glory . . . Joy*: Cf. Luke 2:8–10: "[T]here were shepherds out in the field. . . . And an angel of the Lord appeared to them, and the glory of the Lord shone around them. . . . And the angel said to them, 'Be not afraid. . . . I bring you good news of a great joy'", and John 15:11: "These things I have spoken to you, that my joy may be in you, and that your joy may be full." Cf. also Wordsworth's "Surprised by Joy".

[472] *Life*: Cf. John 10:10: "I came that they may have life, and have it abundantly."

[473] *effluence*: that which flows forth; emanation.

[474] *new Earth and new Heaven*: Cf. 2 Peter 3:13: "[W]e wait for new heavens and a new earth"; Revelation 21:1: "Then I saw a new heaven and a new earth".

Undreamt of by the sensual and the proud—[475]   70
Joy is the sweet voice, Joy the luminous cloud—
    We in ourselves rejoice!
And thence flows all that charms or ear or[476] sight,
    All melodies the echoes of that voice,
All colours a suffusion[477] from that light.   75

VI

There was a time when, though my path was rough,
    This joy within me dallied with distress,
And all misfortunes were but as the stuff
    Whence Fancy[478] made me dreams of happiness:
For hope grew round me, like the twining vine,[479]   80
And fruits, and foliage, not my own, seemed mine.
But now afflictions bow me down to earth:
Nor care I that they rob me of my mirth,
    But oh! each visitation
Suspends what nature gave me at my birth,   85
    My shaping spirit of Imagination.[480]

[475] *sensual and the proud*: For the spiritual darkening Christianity attributes to sensuality, see the note to line 85 of "France: An Ode"; the same applies to pride, the queen of vices— and as spiritual pride, the worst of sins.

[476] *or ear or*: either ear or.

[477] *suffusion*: the spreading of colors over a surface.

[478] *Fancy*: For Coleridge's view of fancy, see the introductory note to "Fancy in Nubibus".

[479] *This joy ... vine*: This passage draws on the previous stanza's echoes of John 15.

[480] *My shaping spirit of Imagination*: Coleridge stated,

> The Imagination then I consider either as primary, or secondary. The primary Imagination [which is not subject to the conscious human will] I hold to be the living Power and prime Agent of all human Perception, and as a repetition in the finite mind of the eternal act of creation of the infinite I AM. The secondary [poetic Imagination] I consider as an echo of the former, co-existing with the conscious will, yet still as identical with the primary in the *kind* of its agency, and differing only in *degree*, and in the *mode* of its operation. It dissolves, diffuses, dissipates, in order to re-create; or where this process is rendered impossible, yet still at all events it struggles to idealize and to unify. It is essentially *vital*, even as all objects (*as objects*) are essentially fixed and dead. (Coleridge, *Biographia Literaria*, chap. 13)

For not to think of what I needs must feel,
    But to be still and patient, all I can;
And haply[481] by abstruse research to steal
    From my own nature all the natural man—   90
    This was my sole resource, my only plan:
Till that which suits a part infects the whole,
And now is almost grown the habit of my soul.

VII

Hence, viper thoughts, that coil around my mind,
    Reality's dark dream!   95
I turn from you, and listen to the wind,
    Which long has raved unnoticed. What a scream
Of agony by torture lengthened out
That lute sent forth! Thou Wind, that ravest without,[482]
    Bare crag, or mountain-tairn,[483] or blasted tree,   100
Or pine-grove whither woodman never clomb,[484]
Or lonely house, long held the witches' home,
    Methinks were fitter instruments for thee,
Mad Lutanist![485] who in this month of showers,
Of dark-brown gardens, and of peeping flowers,   105
Mak'st Devils' yule,[486] with worse than wintry song,
The blossoms, buds, and timorous leaves among.
    Thou Actor, perfect in all tragic sounds!
Thou mighty Poet, e'en to frenzy bold!
    What tell'st thou now about?   110
    'Tis of the rushing of an host[487] in rout,

---

[481] *haply*: perchance; with fortune.

[482] *without*: outside.

[483] *mountain-tairn*: "Tairn is a small lake, generally if not always applied to the lakes up in the mountains, and which are the feeders of those in the vallies. This address to the Storm-wind will not appear extravagant to those who have heard it at night, in a mountainous country" (Coleridge's note).

[484] *clomb*: climbed.

[485] *Lutanist*: i.e., the wind.

[486] *yule*: Christmas festivities (the word originally referred to a pagan winter festival).

[487] *host*: armed multitude.

With groans of trampled men, with smarting
     wounds—
At once they groan with pain, and shudder with the cold!
But hush! there is a pause of deepest silence!
     And all that noise, as of a rushing crowd,   115
With groans, and tremulous shudderings—all is over—
     It tells another tale, with sounds less deep and loud!
          A tale of less affright,
          And tempered with delight,
As Otway's[488] self had framed the tender lay,[489]—   120
          'Tis of a little child
          Upon a lonesome wild,
Not far from home, but she hath lost her way:[490]
And now moans low in bitter grief and fear,
And now screams loud, and hopes to make her mother
     hear.   125

VIII

'Tis midnight, but small thoughts have I of sleep:
Full seldom may my friend such vigils keep!
Visit her, gentle Sleep! with wings of healing,
     And may this storm be but a mountain-birth,[491]
May all the stars hang bright above her dwelling,   130
     Silent as though they watched the sleeping Earth!
          With light heart may she rise,
          Gay fancy, cheerful eyes,
Joy lift her spirit, joy attune her voice;

[488] *Otway's*: Thomas Otway (1651–1685) was the most important writer of verse tragedies of the Restoration period, in particular *The Orphan* and *Venice Preserved*. Although these are plays of considerable power and pathos, they have been largely neglected since the end of Otway's brief life. He died in want. His name carried a similar resonance to Chatterton's (see Wordsworth, "Resolution and Independence", line 43, and Coleridge's "Monody on the Death of Chatterton").

[489] *lay*: narrative song.

[490] *little child . . . lost her way*: This is reminiscent of Wordsworth's "Lucy Gray".

[491] *mountain-birth*: Cf. Horace's "The Art of Poetry", line 139: "The mountains will give birth, a ridiculous mouse will be born."

To her may all things live,[492] from pole to pole,   135
Their life the eddying of her living soul!
  O simple[493] spirit, guided from above,
Dear Lady! friend devoutest of my choice,
Thus may'st thou ever, evermore rejoice.[494]

The Good Great Man[495]

"How seldom, friend! a good great man inherits
      Honour or wealth with all his worth and pains!
It sounds like stories from the land of spirits
If any man obtain that which he merits
      Or any merit that which he obtains."   5

REPLY TO THE ABOVE

For shame, dear friend, renounce this canting[496] strain!
What would'st thou have a good great man obtain?
Place?[497] titles? salary? a gilded chain?[498]
Or throne of corses[499] which his sword had slain?
Greatness and goodness are not *means*, but *ends*!   10
Hath he not always treasures, always friends,
The good great man? *three* treasures, LOVE, and LIGHT,
    And CALM THOUGHTS, regular as infant's breath:
And three firm friends, more sure than day and night,
    HIMSELF, his MAKER, and the ANGEL DEATH!   15

---

[492] *Joy lift . . . may all things live*: See the notes to stanza 4.

[493] *simple*: free from pride; unspoiled; ingenuous.

[494] *Thus may'st thou ever, evermore rejoice*: Cf. Philippians 4:4: "Rejoice in the Lord always; again I will say, Rejoice."

[495] First published in the *Morning Post*, September 23, 1802, but only collected posthumously.

[496] *canting*: whining manner; use of stock phrases.

[497] *Place*: position, rank.

[498] *gilded chain*: symbol of political office—the lord chancellor's for example, which another good, great man, St. Thomas More, famously resigned.

[499] *corses*: corpses.

The Pains of Sleep[500]

Ere on my bed my limbs I lay,[501]
It hath not been my use to pray
With moving lips or bended knees;
But silently, by slow degrees,
My spirit I to Love compose, 5
In humble trust mine eye-lids close,
With reverential resignation,
No wish conceived, no thought exprest,
Only a sense of supplication;
A sense o'er all my soul imprest 10
That I am weak, yet not unblest,
Since in me, round me, every where
Eternal Strength and Wisdom are.

But yester-night I prayed aloud
In anguish and in agony, 15
Up-starting from the fiendish crowd
Of shapes and thoughts that tortured me:
A lurid light, a trampling throng,
Sense of intolerable wrong,
And whom I scorned, those only strong! 20
Thirst of revenge, the powerless will
Still baffled,[502] and yet burning still!

---

[500] Published in 1816 with "Kubla Khan" and "Christabel" by John Murray (Byron's publisher) and collected in *Poetical Works*, 1828. Coleridge had attempted to do without opium and was suffering from what would now be called withdrawal symptoms: "My spirits are dreadful, owing entirely to the Horrors of every night—I truly dread to sleep/it is no shadow with me, but substantial Misery foot-thick, that makes me sit by my bedside of a morning, & cry—. I have abandoned all opiates ... but still I can not get quiet rest.... I do not know how I came to scribble down these verses to you—my heart was aching, my head all confused—but they are, doggrels as they may be, a true portrait of my nights" (Letter to Southey, September 10, 1803). For Coleridge's opium addiction, see the note to his introduction to "Kubla Khan".

[501] *Ere on my bed my limbs I lay*: Cf. "A Child's Evening Prayer", lines 1–2: "Ere on my bed my limbs I lay,/God grant me grace my prayers to say".

[502] *baffled*: foiled, defeated in its efforts; confounded.

Desire with loathing strangely mixed
On wild or hateful objects fixed.
Fantastic[503] passions! maddening brawl!   25
And shame and terror over all!
Deeds to be hid which were not hid,
Which all confused I could not know,
Whether I suffered, or I did:
For all seemed guilt, remorse or woe,   30
My own or others still the same
Life-stifling fear, soul-stifling shame.
So two nights passed: the night's dismay
Saddened and stunned the coming day.
Sleep, the wide blessing,[504] seemed to me   35
Distemper's[505] worst calamity.
The third night, when my own loud scream
Had waked me from the fiendish dream,
O'ercome with sufferings strange and wild,
I wept as[506] I had been a child;   40
And having thus by tears subdued
My anguish to a milder mood,
Such punishments, I said, were due
To natures deepliest stained with sin,—
For aye[507] entempesting anew   45
The unfathomable[508] hell within,
The horror of their deeds to view,
To know and loathe, yet wish and do!
Such griefs with such men well agree,

[503] *Fantastic*: "perversely or irrationally imagined" (*Oxford English Dictionary*, s.v. "fantastic"); inspired by phantasms; grotesque.

[504] *wide blessing*: I.e., the blessing is comprehensive and generous.

[505] *Distemper's*: Distemper is an illness or a derangement.

[506] *as*: as if.

[507] *aye*: ever.

[508] *unfathomable*: bottomless (too deep to be fathomed by a sounding line); incomprehensible.

But wherefore,[509] wherefore fall on me?   50
To be beloved is all I need,
And whom I love, I love indeed.

What Is Life?[510]

Resembles Life what once was deem'd of Light,
Too simple in itself for human Sight?
An absolute Self—an Element ungrounded[511]—
All, that we see, all colours of all shade
    By encroach[512] of Darkness made?—   5
Is *very* life by consciousness unbounded?[513]
And all the Thoughts, Pains, Joys of mortal Breath,
A War-embrace of wrestling Life and Death?

Reason for Love's Blindness[514]

I have heard of reasons manifold
    Why Love must needs be blind,
But this the best of all I hold—
    His eyes are in his mind.

What outward form and feature are   5
    He guesseth but in part;
But that within is good and fair
    He seeth with the heart.

---

    [509] *wherefore*: why; for what end?
    [510] First published in Alaric Alexander Watts's *Literary Souvenir*, 1829; collected posthumously.
    [511] *ungrounded*: unsupported, independent.
    [512] *encroach*: gradual approach.
    [513] *Is very life by consciousness unbounded?*: I.e., Is life itself unbounded by consciousness?
    [514] Published in *Poetical Works*, 1828.

Metrical Feet[515]

LESSON FOR A BOY

Trŏchĕe trīps[516] frŏm lōng tŏ shŏrt;
From long to long in solemn sort[517]
Slow Spōndēe stālks; strōng fōōt! yet ill able
Ēvĕr tŏ cōme ŭp wĭth Dāctl trĭsyllăblĕ.
Īāmbĭcs mārch frŏm shōrt tŏ lōng;—   5
Wĭth ă lēā.
p ănd ă bōŭnd thĕ swĭft Ānăpæsts thrōng;
One syllable long, with one short at each side,
Ămphībrăchs hāstes wĭth ă stātely stride;—
Fĭrst ănd lāst bēĭng lōng, mīddlĕ shŏrt, Aphĭmācer
Strīkes hĭs thūndērĭng hōōfs līke ă prōŭd hīgh-brĕd
    Rācer.   10
If Derwent be innocent, steady and wise,
And delight in the things of earth, water, and skies;
Tender warmth[518] at his heart, with these metres to
    show it,
With sound[519] sense in his brains, may make Derwent
    a poet,—
May crown him with fame, and must win him the love   15
Of his father on earth and his Father above.
        My dear, dear child!
Could you stand upon Skiddaw,[520] you would not from
    its whole ridge
See a man who so loves you as your fond S. T. COLERIDGE.

---

[515] Written as a verse letter to the poet's son Derwent (1800–1883) in 1807 and published in *Poetical Works*, 1834. (Derwent was to be a distinguished scholar and remarkable linguist.)

[516] *trips*: steps nimbly, skips.

[517] *sort*: manner.

[518] *earth, water, and skies;/Tender warmth*: The use of "warmth" following "earth, water, and skies" appears to complete the reference to the four elements.

[519] *sound*: free from error; here, a pun.

[520] *Skiddaw*: mountain in Cumbria, the fourth highest in England. Cf. *Prelude*, bk. 1, line 295.

Recollections of Love[521]

I

How warm this woodland wild Recess!
    Love surely hath been breathing here;
    And this sweet bed of heath, my dear!
Swells up, then sinks with faint caress,
    As if to have you yet more near.   5

II

Eight springs have flown, since last I lay
    On sea-ward Quantock's heathy hills,[522]
    Where quiet sounds from hidden rills
Float here and there, like things astray,
    And high o'er head the sky-lark shrills.   10

III

No voice as yet had made the air
    Be music with your name; yet why
    That asking look? that yearning sigh?
That sense of promise every where?
    Belovéd! flew your spirit by?   15

IV

As when a mother doth explore
    The rose-mark on her long-lost child,
    I met, I loved you, maiden mild!
As whom I long had loved before—
    So deeply had I been beguiled.   20

[521] Published in *Sibylline Leaves*, 1817, for Sara Hutchinson, to whom the poem is addressed; see the introductory note to "Dejection: An Ode".

[522] *sea-ward Quantock's heathy hills*: See "This Lime-Tree Bower My Prison", lines 22–26.

V

You stood before me like a thought,
    A dream remembered in a dream.
    But when those meek eyes first did seem
To tell me, Love within you wrought—
    O Greta,[523] dear domestic stream!   25

VI

Has not, since then, Love's prompture deep,
    Has not Love's whisper evermore
    Been ceaseless, as thy gentle roar?
Sole voice, when other voices sleep,
    Dear under-song in clamor's hour.   30

The Visionary Hope[524]

Sad lot, to have no Hope! Though lowly kneeling
He fain[525] would frame a prayer within his breast,
Would fain entreat for some sweet breath of healing,
That his sick body might have ease and rest;
He strove in vain! the dull sighs from his chest   5
Against his will the stifling load revealing,
Though Nature forced; though like some captive guest,
Some royal prisoner at his conqueror's feast,
An alien's restless mood but half concealing,
The sternness on his gentle brow confessed   10
Sickness within and miserable feeling:
Though obscure pangs made curses of his dreams,
And dreaded sleep, each night repelled in vain,
Each night was scattered by its own loud screams:[526]

---

[523] *Greta*: river in Cumbria that flows through Keswick, where Coleridge lived (at Greta Hall), 1800–1803.

[524] Published in *Sibylline Leaves*, 1817.

[525] *fain*: Willingly, gladly.

[526] *Sickness within . . . night was scattered by its own loud screams* : Cf. "The Pains of Sleep" and its introductory note.

Yet never could his heart command, though fain,   15
One deep full wish to be no more in pain.

   That Hope, which was his inward bliss and boast,
Which waned and died, yet ever near him stood,
Though changed in nature, wander where he would—
For Love's Despair is but Hope's pining Ghost!   20
For this one hope he makes his hourly moan,
He wishes and can wish for this alone!
Pierced, as with light from Heaven, before its gleams
(So the love-stricken visionary deems)
Disease would vanish, like a summer shower,   25
Whose dews fling sunshine from the noon-tide bower!
Or let it stay! yet this one Hope should give
Such strength that he would bless his pains and live.

Constancy to an Ideal Object[527]

Since all that beat about in Nature's range,
Or veer or[528] vanish; why should'st thou remain
The only constant in a world of change,
O yearning Thought! that liv'st but in the brain?
Call to the Hours, that in the distance play,   5
The faery people of the future day—
Fond[529] Thought! not one of all that shining swarm
Will breathe on thee with life-enkindling breath,
Till when, like strangers shelt'ring from a storm,
Hope and Despair[530] meet in the porch of Death!   10
Yet still thou haunt'st me;[531] and though well I see,

527 Published in *Poetical Works*, 1828.
528 *Or veer or*: either veer or.
529 *Fond*: foolish.
530 *Hope and Despair*: Hope is—with faith and charity—one of the three theo-
logical virtues: "And now abideth faith, hope, charity, these three" (1 Corinthians
13:13; KJV); despair is its opposing sin.
531 *thou haunt'st me*: It is likely that Coleridge has Sara Hutchinson in mind.
See the introductory note to "Dejection: An Ode".

She is not thou, and only thou art she,
Still, still as though some dear embodied Good,
Some living Love before my eyes there stood
With answering look a ready ear to lend,   15
I mourn to thee and say—"Ah! loveliest friend!
That this the meed[532] of all my toils might be,
To have a home, an English home, and thee!"
Vain repetition! Home and Thou are one.

The peacefull'st cot,[533] the moon shall shine upon,   20
Lulled by the thrush and wakened by the lark,
Without thee were but a becalmèd bark,
Whose Helmsman on an ocean waste and wide
Sits mute and pale his mouldering helm beside.

And art thou nothing? Such thou art, as when   25
The woodman winding westward up the glen
At wintry dawn, where o'er the sheep-track's maze
The viewless snow-mist weaves a glist'ning haze,[534]
Sees full before him, gliding without tread,
An image with a glory round its head;[535]   30
The enamoured rustic worships its fair hues,
Nor knows he makes the shadow he pursues!

---

[532] *meed*: reward.

[533] *cot*: cottage.

[534] *At wintry dawn . . . haze*: Cf. Wordsworth, "Resolution and Independence",
lines 8–14.

[535] *image with a glory round its head*: "This phenomenon, which the Author has
himself experienced, and of which the reader may find a description in one of the
earlier volumes of the *Manchester Philosophical Transactions*, is applied figuratively
in the following passage of the *Aids to Reflection*: 'Pindar's fine remark respect-
ing the different effects of music, on different characters, holds equally true of
Genius: as many as are not delighted by it are disturbed, perplexed, irritated. The
beholder either recognizes it *as a projected form of his own Being, that moves before
him with a Glory round its head*, or recoils from it as a spectre.'—*Aids to Reflection*,
p. 220" (Coleridge's note, *Poems* [London: 1796]). See the note to line 54 of
"Dejection: An Ode".

Time, Real and Imaginary[536]

AN ALLEGORY

On the wide level of a mountain's head,
(I knew not where, but 'twas some faery[537] place)
Their pinions, ostrich-like, for sails outspread,
Two lovely children run an endless race,
      A sister and a brother!   5
      That far outstripp'd the other;
Yet ever runs she with reverted face,
And looks and listens for the boy behind:
      For he, alas! is blind!
O'er rough and smooth with even step he passed,   10
And knows not whether he be first or last.

A Tombless Epitaph[538]

'Tis true, Idoloclastes Satyrane![539]
(So call him, for so mingling blame with praise,
And smiles with anxious looks, his earliest friends,
Masking his birth-name, wont to character
His wild-wood fancy[540] and impetuous zeal),   5

---

[536] Published in *Sibylline Leaves*, 1817. "By imaginary Time, I meant the state of a school boy's mind when on his return to school he projects his being in his day dreams, and lives in his next holidays, six months hence: and this I contrasted with real Time" (Coleridge's note, *Poems*).

[537] *faery*: enchanted; uncanny.

[538] First published in *The Friend*, no. 14 (November 23, 1809); collected in *Sibylline Leaves*, 1817. "Imitated, though in the movements rather than the thoughts, from the viith of *Gli Epitafi* of [Gabriello] Chiabrera [1552–1638]" (Coleridge's note). This is a self-portrait.

[539] *Idoloclastes Satyrane*: Idoloclastes, breaker of idols; Sir Satyrane, "in Spenser's *Faerie Queene* (I. vi), a knight 'Plaine, faithfull, true, and enimy of shame', son of a satyr and the nymph Thyamis. He rescues Una from the satyrs, perhaps symbolizing the liberation of the true religion by Luther" (*Concise Oxford Dictionary of English Literature* [Oxford: Oxford University Press, 1986], p. 511). Coleridge had been making notes for an attack on superstitions for the better part of a decade.

[540] *wild-wood fancy*: Cf. Milton, "L'Allegro", lines 133–34: "Or sweetest Shakespeare, Fancy's child,/Warble his native wood-notes wild."

'Tis true that, passionate for ancient truths,
And honouring with religious love the Great
Of elder times, he hated to excess,
With an unquiet and intolerant scorn,
The hollow Puppets of a hollow Age,　　　　　　　　10
Ever idolatrous, and changing ever
Its worthless Idols! Learning, Power, and Time,
(Too much of all) thus wasting in vain war
Of fervid colloquy. Sickness, 'tis true,
Whole years of weary days, besieged him close,　　　15
Even to the gates and inlets of his life!
But it is true, no less, that strenuous, firm,
And with a natural gladness, he maintained
The citadel unconquered, and in joy
Was strong to follow the delightful Muse.　　　　　20
For not a hidden path, that to the shades
Of the beloved Parnassian[541] forest leads,
Lurked undiscovered by him; not a rill
There issues from the fount of Hippocrene,[542]
But he had traced it upward to its source,　　　　　25
Through open glade, dark glen, and secret dell,
Knew the gay wild flowers on its banks, and culled
Its med'cinable herbs. Yea, oft alone,
Piercing the long-neglected holy cave,[543]
The haunt obscure of old Philosophy,　　　　　　　30
He bade with lifted torch its starry walls
Sparkle, as erst[544] they sparkled to the flame

[541] *Parnassian*: mountain in Greece, sacred to Apollo; it is the home of the Muses.

[542] *fount of Hippocrene*: fountain on Mount Helicon, sacred to the Muses; its waters, when drunk, were thought to be a source of poetic inspiration. Cf. Keats, "Ode to a Nightingale", lines 15–19: "O for a beaker full of the warm South/Full of the true, the blushful Hippocrene,/With beaded bubbles winking at the brim,/And purple-stainèd mouth,/That I might drink".

[543] *long-neglected holy cave*: See the note to line 3 of "Kubla Khan" for the relationship between Plato's cave, Porphyry's *De Antro Nympharum*, and Coleridge's "caverns measureless to man".

[544] *erst*: of old.

Of odorous lamps tended by Saint and Sage.
O framed for calmer times and nobler hearts!
O studious Poet, eloquent for truth!   35
Philosopher! contemning wealth and death,
Yet docile, childlike, full of Life and Love!
Here, rather than on monumental stone,
This record of thy worth thy Friend inscribes,
Thoughtful, with quiet tears upon his cheek.   40

The Virgin's Cradle-Hymn[545]

COPIED FROM A PRINT OF THE VIRGIN, IN A ROMAN CATHOLIC
VILLAGE IN GERMANY

Dormi, Jesu! Mater ridet
Quæ tam dulcem somnum videt,
  Dormi, Jesu! blandule!
Si non dormis, Mater plorat,
Inter fila cantans orat,
  Blande, veni, somnule.

ENGLISH

Sleep, sweet babe! my cares beguiling:
Mother sits beside thee smiling;
  Sleep, my darling, tenderly!
If thou sleep not, mother mourneth,
Singing as her wheel she turneth: 5
  Come, soft slumber, balmily!

[545] First published in *The Courier*, August 30, 1811; collected in *Sibylline Leaves*, 1817. In a manuscript version, Coleridge specified that the village was located in the Electorate of Mainz (corresponding roughly with the Rhineland and Hesse).

The Limbo Poems[546]

[On Donne's First Poem[547]]

Be proud, as Spaniards! and Leap for Pride, ye Fleas
Henceforth in Nature's *Minim*[548] World Grandees,[549]
In Phœbus' Archives[550] registered are ye—
And this[551] your Patent of Nobility.
No Skip-Jacks[552] now, nor civiller Skip-Johns,   5
Dread Anthropophagi![553] Specks of living Bronze,
I hail you one & all, sans[554] Pros or Cons,
Descendants from a noble Race of *Dons*.[555]

What tho' that great ancestral Flea be gone
Immortal with immortalizing Donne—   10
His earthly Spots bleach'd off as Papists gloze,[556]
In purgatory fire on Bardolph's Nose,[557]

---

[546] A sequence from *Notebooks*, vol. 3, pp. 4073–74. "Limbo" and "Ne Plus Ultra" were first published by Coleridge in *Poetical Works*, 1834. Fragments of "On Donne's First Poem" were published posthumously. It is evident from the sequence's publishing history that Coleridge was never thoroughly satisfied with the lines on Donne's Flea, which remain difficult to follow.

[547] Coleridge had been reading and annotating Donne, in the early editions of whose poems "The Flea" was placed first among the "Songs and Sonnets". The unacknowledged partner in Coleridge's poem is Goethe's *Faust, Part I*—specifically the scene in Auerbach's Tavern where Mephistopheles sings the song of the Spanish king's flea and the swarm of relations who quickly occupy positions of importance at the Spanish court.

[548] Minim: littlest.

[549] *Grandees*: high-ranking Spanish noblemen.

[550] *Phœbus' Archives*: Phoebus Apollo is the patron of the Muses; thus the fleas are taking their place among the sources of poetic inspiration.

[551] *this*: probably Donne's "The Flea".

[552] *Skip-Jacks*: "a foolish conceited person; a fop, a dandy" (*Oxford English Dictionary*, s.v. "skip-jack"); something skipping or nimble.

[553] *Anthropophagi*: man-eaters.

[554] *sans*: without.

[555] Dons: Spanish noblemen; pun on "Donne", as also on the Oxford/Cambridge "don" (head fellow or tutor of a college).

[556] *gloze*: interpret (i.e., in the un-Protestant dogma of Purgatory).

[557] *In purgatory fire on Bardolph's Nose*: See Shakespeare, *Henry V*, Act 2, scene 3, lines 41–43: "Do you not remember 'a saw a flea stick upon Bardolph's nose, and 'a said it was a black soul burning in hell?"

Or else starved out, his aery tread defied
By the dry Potticary's[558] bladdery Hide,[559]
Which cross'd unchang'd[560] and still keeps in ghost-Light   15
Of lank Half-nothings his, the thinnest Sprite[561]
The sole true *Something*[562] this in Limbo Den
It frightens Ghosts as Ghosts here frighten men—
For skimming in the wake, it mock'd the care
Of the Old Boat-God[563] for his Farthing Fare,   20
Tho' Irus'[564] Ghost itself he ne'er frown'd blacker on,
The skin and skin-pent[565] Druggist crost the Acheron,
Styx and with Puriphlegethon Cocytus:[566]
The very names, methinks, might thither fright us—
Unchang'd it cross'd & shall some fated Hour,   25
Be pulverized[567] by Demogorgon's[568] Power
And given as poison, to annihilate Souls—
Even now it shrinks them! they shrink in, as Moles

---

[558] *Potticary's*: i.e., apothecary's. An apothecary is someone who prepared and sold drugs (and poisons) for medicinal purposes. Apothecaries' weights facilitated the measurement of very small quantities.

[559] *bladdery Hide*: The apothecary has got hold of the flea's carcases. For the dead to rest, according to the Ancient Greeks, the body had to be buried and Charon paid (Charon ferries the dead across the rivers Styx and Acheron to the Underworld).

[560] *cross'd unchang'd*: crossed the Acheron without paying Charon his fare.

[561] *Sprite*: spirit.

[562] *sole true* Something: Half of something is still so much more than the insubstantial shades that inhabit the Underworld.

[563] *Old Boat-God*: i.e., Charon.

[564] *Irus*: the hulking, insolent, drunken, and ravenous beggar who is beaten by Odysseus in the boxing match; the former provokes him to fight (see Homer, *Odyssey*, bk. 18).

[565] *skin-pent*: skin-enclosed; skin-imprisoned.

[566] *Acheron / Styx . . . Cocytus*: the rivers of Hades. Cf. *Paradise Lost*, bk. 2, lines 575–81: "Of four infernal rivers that disgorge / Into the burning lake their baleful streams: / Abhorrèd Styx, the flood of deadly hate; / Sad Acheron of sorrow, black and deep; / Cocytus, named of lamentation loud / Hear on the rueful stream; / Fierce Phlegethon, / Whose waves of torrent fire inflame with rage."

[567] *pulverized*: reduced to dust.

[568] *Demogorgon's*: Demogorgon is the name of a mysterious and terrible infernal deity, originally identified with Statius' "supreme being of the threefold world" (*Thebaid*, bk. 4, line 516).

(Nature's mute Monks, live Mandrakes[569] of the ground)
Creep back from Light, then listen for its Sound—   30
See but to dread, and dread they know not why
The natural Alien of their negative Eye.

[Limbo]

'Tis a strange place, this Limbo! not a Place,
Yet name it so;—where Time and weary Space
Fettered from flight, with night-mare sense of Fleeing,
Strive for their last crepuscular Half-being—
Lank Space, and scytheless Time[570] with branny[571] Hands   5
Barren and soundless as the measuring Sands,[572]
Not mark'd by Flit of Shades—unmeaning they
As Moonlight on the Dial[573] of the Day—
But that is lovely—looks like Human Time,
An old Man with a steady Look sublime   10
That stops his earthly Task to watch the skies;
But he is blind—a statue hath such Eyes;—
Yet having moon-ward turn'd his face by chance,
Gazes[574] the orb with moon-like Countenance,
With scant white hairs, with foretop bald & high,   15
He gazes still,—his eyeless Face all Eye;—
As 'twere an Organ full of silent Sight,
His whole Face seemeth to rejoice in Light!—
Lip touching Lip, all moveless, Bust and Limb,
He seems to gaze at that which seems to gaze on Him!   20

[569] *Mandrakes: Mandragora officinarum*, a poisonous, human-shaped plant containing hallucinogens. It was fabled to shriek (and sometimes to kill all who heard it) when drawn from the ground.

[570] *Lank Space, and scytheless Time*: I.e., there is nothing to kill or destroy here.

[571] *branny*: dry and flaky, like husks of cereal grain.

[572] *measuring Sands*: of an hourglass.

[573] *Dial*: sundial.

[574] *Gazes*: gazes at.

No such sweet Sights doth Limbo Den immure,[575]
Wall'd round, and made a Spirit-jail secure
By the mere Horror of blank Naught-at-all,
Whose circumambience[576] doth these Ghosts enthral.
A lurid Thought is growthless dull Privation,   25
Yet that is but a Purgatory Curse;
Hell knows a fear far worse,
A fear—a future state;—'tis *positive Negation!*

[Ne Plus Ultra[577]]

      Sole Positive of Night!
      Antipathist[578] of Light!
Fate's only essence! primal scorpion rod—
The one permitted opposite of God!—
Condensèd blackness[579] and abysmal[580] storm   5
      Compacted to one sceptre
      Arms the Grasp enorm—
      The Intercepter—
The Substance that still casts the shadow Death!—
      The Dragon[581] foul and fell[582]—   10
      The unrevealable,
And hidden one, whose breath

---

[575] *immure*: wall in.

[576] *circumambience*: going round.

[577] *Ne Plus Ultra*: Nothing further.

[578] *Antipathist*: "one possessed by an antipathy: a natural enemy" (*Oxford English Dictionary*, s.v. "antipathist").

[579] *one permitted opposite of God!—/Condensèd blackness*: Cf. *Paradise Lost*, bk. 1, lines 59–63: "At once as far as angels ken he [Satan] views/The dismal situation waste and wild:/A dungeon horrible, on all sides round/As one great furnace flamed, yet from those flames/No light, but rather darkness visible".

[580] *abysmal*: abyss-like or related. Cf. Shakespeare, *The Tempest*, Act 1, scene 2, lines 49–50: "What seest thou else/In the dark backward and abysm of time?"

[581] *Dragon*: See the note to line 57 of "France: An Ode".

[582] *fell*: fierce; ruthless; terrible.

Gives wind and fuel to the fires of Hell!—
        Ah! sole despair
    Of both th'eternities[583] in Heaven!   15
Sole interdict[584] of all-bedewing prayer,
        The all-compassionate!
        Save to the Lampads Seven[585]
Reveal'd to none of all th' angelic state,
        Save to the Lampads Seven,
        That watch the throne of Heaven!   20

Human Life

ON THE DENIAL OF IMMORTALITY[586]

If dead, we cease to be; if total gloom
    Swallow up life's brief flash for aye,[587] we fare
As summer-gusts, of sudden birth and doom,
    Whose sound and motion not alone declare,
But are their whole of being! If the breath   5
    Be Life itself, and not its task and tent,
If even a soul like Milton's can know death;
    O Man! thou vessel purposeless, unmeant,
Yet drone-hive[588] strange of phantom purposes!
    Surplus of Nature's dread activity,   10
Which, as she gazed on some nigh-finished vase,
Retreating slow, with meditative pause,
    She formed with restless hands unconsciously.

---

[583] *both th'eternities*: Harold Bloom has plausibly suggested "Divine Love and Divine Knowledge"; see Harold Bloom, *The Oxford Anthology of English Literature*, vol. 4, *Romantic Poetry and Prose* (Oxford University Press, 1973), p. 284.

[584] *interdict*: authoritative prohibition.

[585] *Save to the Lampads Seven*: See Revelation 4:5: "From the throne issues flashes of lightning, and voices and peals of thunder, and before the throne burn seven torches of fire, which are the seven spirits of God."

[586] Published in *Sibylline Leaves*, 1817.

[587] *aye*: ever.

[588] *drone-hive*: Drone bees produce no honey, do no building; their primary function is sexual intercourse.

Blank accident! nothing's anomaly!
    If rootless thus, thus substanceless thy state,   15
Go, weigh thy dreams, and be thy hopes, thy fears,
The counter-weights!—Thy laughter and thy tears
    Mean but themselves, each fittest to create
And to repay the other! Why rejoices
    Thy heart with hollow joy for hollow good?   20
    Why cowl thy face beneath the mourner's hood?
Why waste thy sighs, and thy lamenting voices,
    Image of Image, Ghost of Ghostly Elf,[589]
That such a thing as thou feel'st warm or cold?
Yet what and whence thy gain, if thou withhold   25
    These costless shadows of thy shadowy self?
Be sad! be glad! be neither! seek, or shun!
Thou hast no reason why! Thou canst have none;
Thy being's being is contradiction.

Song

FROM *ZAPOLYA*[590]

A sunny shaft did I behold,
    From sky to earth it slanted:
And poised therein a bird so bold—
    Sweet bird, thou wert enchanted!

He sank, he rose, he twinkled, he trolled   5
    Within that shaft of sunny mist;
His eyes of fire, his beak of gold,
    All else of amethyst!

---

[589] *Ghostly Elf*: spectral being.

[590] Coleridge's play, *Zapolya: A Christmas Tale*, published in 1817. The song features in Act 2, scene 1, lines 65–80. It was collected apart from the play posthumously. "Glycine's song in 'Zapolya' is the most glittering poem in our language, with a soft glitter like that of light seen through water. And he is continually endeavouring, as later poets have done on a more deliberate theory, to suffuse sound with colour or make colours literally a form of music" (Symons, *Romantic Movement*, p. 144).

And thus he sang: "Adieu! adieu!
Love's dreams prove seldom true.   10
The blossoms they make no delay:
The sparkling dew-drops will not stay.
   Sweet month of May,
    We must away;
      Far, far away!   15
       To-day! to-day!"

Fancy in Nubibus[591]

OR THE POET IN THE CLOUDS

O! it is pleasant, with a heart at ease,
   Just after sunset, or by moonlight skies,
To make the shifting clouds be what you please,
   Or let the easily persuaded eyes
Own each quaint likeness issuing from the mould   5
   Of a friend's fancy; or with head bent low
And cheek aslant see rivers flow of gold
   'Twixt crimson banks; and then, a traveller, go
From mount to mount through Cloudland, gorgeous land!
   Or list'ning to the tide, with closèd sight,   10
Be that blind bard, who on the Chian strand[592]
   By those deep sounds possessed with inward light,
Beheld the Iliad and the Odyssee
   Rise to the swelling of the voiceful sea.[593]

[591] First published in *The Courier*, January 30, 1818, and collected in *Poetical Works*, 1828. The title means "Fancy in the Clouds". The distinction between Fancy and Imagination was important to Coleridge; his admirer and interpreter Owen Barfield describes Fancy as "that which is responsible for, that which produces, the kind of imagery, or combinations of images, that come into the mind ready-made and almost unbidden simply out of the impressions of the senses which the memory has stored and retained" (*The Rediscovery of Meaning* [San Rafael, Calif.: Barfield Press, 2006], p. 88).

[592] *that blind bard, who on the Chian strand*: Homer (ca. eighth century B.C.), to whom the *Iliad* and the *Odyssey* are traditionally attributed. According to the Greeks, he was a blind native of the island of Chios.

[593] *voiceful sea*: Cf. Jeremiah 50:42: "[T]heir voice shall roar like the sea" (KJV); and Shakespeare, *The Tempest*, Act 3, scene 2, lines 138–46: "Be not

To Nature[594]

It may indeed be phantasy, when I
    Essay[595] to draw from all created things
    Deep, heartfelt, inward joy that closely clings;
And trace in leaves and flowers that round me lie
Lessons of love and earnest piety.[596]   5
    So let it be; and if the wide world rings
    In mock of this belief, it brings
Nor fear, nor grief, nor vain perplexity.
So will I build my altar in the fields,
    And the blue sky my fretted dome shall be,   10
And the sweet fragrance that the wild flower yields
    Shall be the incense I will yield to Thee,
Thee only God! and thou shalt not despise
Even me, the priest of this poor sacrifice.

Work Without Hope[597]

LINES COMPOSED 21ST FEBRUARY, 1827

All Nature seems at work. Slugs leave their lair—
The bees are stirring—birds are on the wing—
And Winter slumbering in the open air,
Wears on his smiling face a dream of Spring!
And I, the while, the sole unbusy thing,   5
Nor honey make, nor pair, nor build, nor sing.

---

afeard. The isle is full of noises, / Sounds, and sweet airs, that give delight and hurt not. / Sometimes a thousand twangling instruments / Will hum about mine ears, and sometime voices / That, if I then had waked after long sleep, / Will make me sleep again; and then in dreaming / The clouds methought would open and show riches / Ready to drop upon me, that when I waked / I cried to dream again."

[594] Published posthumously. See the note on the Book of Nature in the introductory note to "Frost at Midnight".

[595] *Essay*: attempt.

[596] *Lessons of love and earnest piety*: Cf. Wordsworth, "My heart leaps up when I behold", lines 8–9.

[597] First published in *The Bijou, or Annual of Literature and the Arts*, 1828; collected in *Poetical Works*, 1828.

Yet well I ken the banks where amaranths[598] blow,[599]
Have traced the fount whence streams of nectar flow.[600]
Bloom, O ye amaranths! bloom for whom ye may,
For me ye bloom not! Glide, rich streams, away!   10
With lips unbrightened, wreathless brow, I stroll:
And would you learn the spells that drowse my soul?
Work without Hope draws nectar in a sieve,
And Hope without an object cannot live.

Duty Surviving Self-Love[601]

THE ONLY SURE FRIEND OF DECLINING LIFE.
A SOLILOQUY

Unchanged within, to see all changed without,
Is a blank[602] lot and hard to bear, no doubt.
Yet why at others' wanings should'st thou fret?
Then only might'st thou feel a just regret,
Hadst thou withheld thy love or hid thy light   5
In selfish forethought of neglect and slight.
O wiselier then, from feeble yearnings freed,
While, and on whom, thou may'st—shine on! nor heed
Whether the object by reflected light
Return thy radiance or absorb it quite: 10
And though thou notest from thy safe recess

---

[598] *amaranths*: Because of its meaning in Greek ("unfading"), the amaranth has long been associated with immortality. Cf. *Paradise Lost*, bk. 3, lines 353–61: "Immortal amarant, a flower which once/In Paradise, fast by the Tree of Life/Began to bloom, but soon for man's offence/To Heaven removed where first it grew, there grows/And flowers aloft shading the fount of life,/And where the river of bliss through midst of Heaven/Rolls o'er Elysian flowers her amber stream;/With these that never fade the spirits elect/Bind their resplendent locks inwreathed with beams".

[599] *blow*: bloom.

[600] *fount . . . flow*: Cf. "Kubla Khan".

[601] Published in *Poetical Works*, 1828.

[602] *blank*: i.e., of emotions: prostrating to the faculties; empty.

Old Friends burn dim, like lamps in noisome⁶⁰³ air,
Love them for what they are; nor love them less,
Because to thee they are not what they were.

Youth and Age⁶⁰⁴

Verse, a breeze mid blossoms straying,
Where Hope clung feeding, like a bee—
Both were mine! Life went a maying⁶⁰⁵
    With Nature, Hope, and Poesy,
        When I was young!   5
When I was young?—Ah, woful When!
Ah! for the change 'twixt Now and Then!
This breathing house not built with hands,⁶⁰⁶
This body that does me grievous wrong,
O'er aery cliffs and glittering sands,   10
How lightly then it flashed along:—
Like those trim skiffs,⁶⁰⁷ unknown of yore,
On winding lakes and rivers wide,
That ask no aid of sail or oar,
That fear no spite of wind or tide!   15
Nought cared this body for wind or weather
When Youth and I lived in't together.

Flowers are lovely; Love is flower-like;
Friendship is a sheltering tree;
O! the joys, that came down shower-like,   20

---

⁶⁰³ *noisome*: noxious. Cf. Milton, "Arcades", lines 48–49: "And all my plants I save from nightly ill/Of noisome winds and blasting vapors chill".

⁶⁰⁴ Published in *Poetical Works*, 1834.

⁶⁰⁵ *went a maying*: gathering flowers, dancing around the Maypole, etc., in celebration of May Day; similar merriment.

⁶⁰⁶ *breathing house not built with hands*: Cf. 2 Corinthians 5:1: "For we know that if the earthly tent we live in is destroyed, we have a building from God, a house not made with hands, eternal in the heavens."

⁶⁰⁷ *skiffs*: "small light rowing- or sculling-boat for a single rower" (*Oxford English Dictionary*, s.v. "skiff").

Of Friendship, Love, and Liberty,
        Ere I was old!
Ere I was old? Ah, woful Ere,
Which tells me, Youth's no longer here!
O Youth! for years so many and sweet,   25
'Tis known that Thou and I were one,
I'll think it but a fond conceit—
It cannot be that Thou art gone!
Thy vesper-bell[608] hath not yet toll'd:—
And thou wert aye a masker[609] bold!   30
What strange disguise hast now put on,
To make believe that thou art gone?
I see these locks in silvery slips,
This drooping gait, this alter'd size:
But Spring-tide blossoms on thy lips,   35
And tears take sunshine from thine eyes!
Life is but thought: so think I will
That Youth and I are house-mates still.

Dew-drops are the gems of morning,
But the tears of mournful eve!   40
Where no hope is, life's a warning
That only serves to make us grieve,
        When we are old:
That only serves to make us grieve
With oft and tedious taking-leave,   45
Like some poor nigh-related guest,
That may not rudely[610] be dismist;
Yet hath outstay'd his welcome while,
And tells the jest without the smile.

---

[608] *vesper-bell*: the bell for Vespers/Evening Prayer. See the note to line 76 of the "Ancient Mariner".

[609] *masker*: masquerader.

[610] *rudely*: discourteously; abruptly.

The Pang More Sharp Than All[611]

AN ALLEGORY

I

He too has flitted from his secret nest,
Hope's last and dearest child without a name!—
Has flitted from me, like the warmthless flame,
That makes false promise of a place of rest
To the tired Pilgrim's still believing mind;— 5
Or like some Elfin Knight in kingly court,
Who having won all guerdons[612] in his sport,
Glides out of view, and whither none can find!

II

Yes! he hath flitted from me—with what aim,
Or why, I know not! 'Twas a home of bliss, 10
And he was innocent, as the pretty shame
Of babe, that tempts and shuns the menaced kiss,
From its twy-cluster'd[613] hiding place of snow!
Pure as the babe, I ween,[614] and all aglow
As the dear hopes, that swell the mother's breast— 15
Her eyes down gazing o'er her claspèd charge;—
Yet gay as that twice happy father's kiss,
That well might glance aside, yet never miss,
Where the sweet mark emboss'd so sweet a targe[615]—
Twice wretched he who hath been doubly blest! 20

---

[611] Published in *Poetical Works*, 1834.
[612] *guerdons*: rewards.
[613] *twy-cluster'd*: a pair together; i.e., nestling between its mother's snowy breasts.
[614] *I ween*: I believe.
[615] *targe*: light shield. A target is, literally, a small targe.

III

Like a loose blossom on a gusty night
He flitted from me—and has left behind
(As if to them his faith he ne'er did plight)
Of either sex and answerable mind
Two playmates, twin-births of his foster-dame:—   25
The one a steady lad (Esteem he hight[616])
And Kindness is the gentler sister's name.
Dim likeness now, though fair she be and good,
Of that bright Boy who hath us all forsook;—
But in his full-eyed aspect when she stood,   30
And while her face reflected every look,
And in reflection kindled—she became
So like Him, that almost she seem'd the same!

IV

Ah! he is gone, and yet will not depart!—
Is with me still, yet I from Him exiled!   35
For still there lives within my secret heart
The magic image of the magic Child,
Which there he made up-grow by his strong art,
As in that crystal orb—wise Merlin's feat,—
The wondrous "World of Glass,"[617] wherein inisled   40
All long'd for things their beings did repeat;—
And there he left it, like a Sylph[618] beguiled,
To live and yearn and languish incomplete!

[616] *hight*: is called.

[617] *Merlin's feat . . . "World of Glass,"*: See Spenser, *Faerie Queene*, bk. 3, canto 2, lines 18–19: "The great Magitian *Merlin* had deuiz'd,/By his deepe science, and Hell-dreaded might,/A looking glasse, right wondrously aguiz'd,/Whose vertues through the wyde world soone were solemniz'd./It verue had, to shew imperfect sight, what euer thing was in the world contained,/Betwixt the lowest earth and heauens hight,/So that it to the looker appertayn'd;/What euer foe had wrought, or frend had faynd,/Therein discouered was, ne ought mote pas,/Ne ought in secret from the same remaynd;/For thy it round and hollow shaped was,/Like to the world it selfe, and seem'd a world of glas."

[618] *Sylph*: an elemental of the air.

V

Can wit[619] of man a heavier grief reveal?
Can sharper pang from hate or scorn arise?—   45
Yes! one more sharp there is that deeper lies,
Which fond[620] Esteem but mocks when he would heal.
Yet neither scorn nor hate did it devise,
But sad compassion and atoning zeal!
One pang more blighting-keen than hope betray'd!   50
And this it is my woful hap[621] to feel,
When, at her Brother's hest,[622] the twin-born Maid
With face averted and unsteady eyes,
Her truant playmate's faded robe puts on;
And inly shrinking from her own disguise   55
Enacts the faery Boy that's lost and gone.
O worse than all! O pang all pangs above
Is Kindness counterfeiting absent Love!

Lines[623]

SUGGESTED BY THE LAST WORDS OF BERENGARIUS
(OB.[624] ANNO DOM. 1088)

Berengarius is seen as a hero and forerunner by many Protestants
both for his opposition to Catholic Eucharistic theology and
his friction with the popes; nevertheless, the Berengarian con-
troversies also contributed decisively to the development of
orthodox Catholic Eucharistic theology.

Berengarius (or Berengar) of Tours (ca. 1000–1088) was a
theologian who contested the orthodox Catholic doctrine of

---

[619] *wit*: mental apprehension and resourcefulness.

[620] *fond*: affectionate; foolish.

[621] *hap*: fortune.

[622] *hest*: bidding, behest.

[623] First published in Alaric Alexander Watts's *Literary Souvenir*, 1827; col-
lected in *Poetical Works*, 1828.

[624] OB.: obiit, i.e., he died (in the year of Our Lord 1088).

the Eucharist. Imprisoned by Henry I of France in 1050, he was condemned in 1059 by a Roman synod, Pope Nicholas II presiding. Berengarius signed a profession of faith and returned to France, then attacked the pope and synod, defending his own position. Roman synods followed in 1078 and 1079, presided over by Saint Gregory VII. In 1078 Berengarius submitted an equivocal profession of faith. In 1079 an orthodox confession was submitted to him; he signed it and promised to teach his own views no more, then retired to lead a hermit's life.

> Lanfranc and most other contemporaries—as well as [Jean de] Montclos' study [*Lanfranc et Bérenger: La controverse eucharistique du XIe siècle*]—hold that Berengarius defended a purely symbolic Presence. In fact, if one may find a parallel in later history, it is possible that Berengarius' own thought fluctuated between the "Presence in symbol" of a Zwingli and the "Presence in power or virtue" of a Calvin.... What all agree upon is that Berengarius taught the continued existence of the full reality of the bread and wine after the Consecration and denied that Christ was received bodily; he was rather received only according to faith and understanding.[625]

Lines

No more 'twixt conscience staggering and the Pope
Soon shall I now before my God appear,
By him to be acquitted, as I hope;
By him to be condemnèd, as I fear.—

REFLECTION ON THE ABOVE

Lynx amid moles! had I stood by thy bed,
Be of good cheer, meek soul! I would have said:
I see a hope spring from that humble fear.[626]

---

[625] James T. O'Connor, *The Hidden Manna: A Theology of the Eucharist* (San Francisco: Ignatius Press, 1988), p. 105.

[626] *humble fear*: Humility is of central importance in Christianity. See James 4:6: "God opposes the proud, but gives grace to the humble." For fear in this context, see Proverbs 9:10: "The fear of the LORD is the beginning of wisdom, and the knowledge of the Holy One is insight."

All are not strong alike through storms to steer
Right onward. What? Though dread of threaten'd death
And dungeon torture made thy hand and breath   10
Inconstant to the truth within thy heart?
That truth, from which, through fear, thou twice didst start,
FEAR haply[627] told thee, was a learnèd strife,
Or not so vital as to claim thy life:
And myriads had reached Heaven, who never knew
Where lay the difference 'twixt the false and true!   15

Ye, who secure 'mid trophies not your own,[628]
Judge him who won them when he stood alone,
And proudly talk of recreant[629] BERENGARE—
O first the age, and then the man compare!
That age how dark![630] congenial minds how rare!   20
No host of friends with kindred zeal did burn!
No throbbing hearts awaited his return!
Prostrate alike when prince and peasant fell,
He only disenchanted from the spell,
Like the weak worm that gems the starless night,[631]   25
Moved in the scanty circlet of his light:
And was it strange if he withdrew the ray
That did but guide the night-birds to their prey?

The ascending day-star[632] with a bolder eye
Hath lit each dew-drop on our trimmer lawn!   30
Yet not for this, if wise, shall we decry
The spots[633] and struggles of the timid DAWN;

---

[627] *haply*: perhaps.

[628] *trophies not your own*: i.e., Anglican/Protestant disbelief in the Catholic doctrine of the Eucharist and the pope's authority, and freedom from popish persecution of heresy.

[629] *recreant*: cowardly; disloyal.

[630] *That age how dark*: It was only in the twentieth century that the Middle Ages began to emerge from the realm of ignorant caricature, even among the intelligentsia. The very term "Dark Ages" has been largely abandoned by scholars.

[631] *worm that gems the starless night*: the glow-worm (*Lampyris noctiluca*).

[632] *ascending day-star*: Venus.

[633] *spots*: small marks of color.

Lest so we tempt th' approaching Noon to scorn
The mists and painted vapours of our MORN.

Cologne[634]

In Köhln, a town of monks[635] and bones,
And pavements[636] fang'd with murderous stones,
And rags, and hags, and hideous wenches;
I counted two and seventy stenches,
All well defined, and several stinks!　　　　　　　5
Ye Nymphs that reign o'er sewers and sinks,
The river Rhine, it is well known,
Doth wash your city of Cologne;[637]
But tell me, Nymphs, what power divine
Shall henceforth wash the river Rhine?　　　　　　10

---

[634] First published in H.D. Inglis' *Friendship's Offering*, 1834; collected in
Poetical Works, 1834. Coleridge had been on a tour of the Rhine with Wordsworth
in 1828.

[635] *town of monks*: a reference to the Catholic heritage of the city; cf. Joseph
Lins, *The Catholic Encyclopaedia* (1908): "The ecclesiastical importance of the city
[in the twelfth and thirteenth centuries] was equally great; no city north of the
Alps was so rich in great churches, sanctuaries, relics, and religious communities.
It was known as the 'German Rome,' and was annually visited by pilgrims, espe-
cially after Rainald of Dassel, Archbishop of Cologne (1159–67), brought thither
the remains of the Three Magi from Milan. Learning was zealously cultivated in
the cathedral school, in the collegiate chapters, and the cloisters; famous philos-
ophers taught here, among them [Benedictine] Rupert of Deutz [ca. 1075–1139],
[Cistercian] Caesarius of Heisterbach [ca. 1180–ca. 1240]". The Dominicans St.
Thomas Aquinas (1225–1274) and St. Albert the Great (ca. 1200–1280) and the
Franciscan Bl. John Duns Scotus (ca. 1265–1308) all taught at the University of
Cologne, and the latter two are buried in the city. "[Coleridge] quite failed to
recognise the enormous value which monastic orders can and should have in the
community" (T.S. Eliot, *The Idea of a Christian Society* [London: Faber and Faber,
1942], p. 35).

[636] *pavements*: sidewalks; paved public areas.

[637] *Doth wash your city of Cologne*: a pun on the perfume *Eau de Cologne*, man-
ufactured in the city.

The Garden of Boccaccio[638]

Of late, in one of those most weary hours,
When life seems emptied of all genial powers,
A dreary mood, which he who ne'er has known
May bless his happy lot, I sate alone;
And, from the numbing spell to win relief,　　　　5
Call'd on the past for thought of glee or grief.
In vain! bereft alike of grief and glee,
I sate and cow'r'd o'er my own vacancy!
And as I watch'd the dull continuous ache,
Which, all else slum'bring, seem'd alone to wake;　　10
O Friend![639] long wont to notice yet conceal,
And soothe by silence what words cannot heal,
I but half saw that quiet hand of thine
Place on my desk this exquisite design.
Boccaccio's Garden and its faery,[640]　　　　15
The love, the joyaunce, and the gallantry!
An Idyll, with Boccaccio's spirit warm,
Framed in the silent poesy of form.

　　Like flocks adown a newly-bathèd steep
　　　　Emerging from a mist; or like a stream　　20
Of music soft that not dispels the sleep,
　　　　But casts in happier moulds the slumberer's dream,
Gazed by an idle eye with silent might
The picture stole upon my inward sight.
A tremulous warmth crept gradual o'er my chest,　　25
As though an infant's finger touch'd my breast.

---

638 First published in F. M. Reynolds' *The Keepsake*, 1829; collected in *Poetical Works*, 1829. The poem was partly inspired by one of the illustrations by Thomas Stothard (1755–1834), an illustration to Boccaccio's *Decameron*, depicting the setting of the third day's stories, an exquisite walled garden within a palace.

639 *Friend*: Mrs. Gillman. See the note to Coleridge's introduction to "Kubla Khan".

640 *Boccaccio's Garden and its faery*: here acting as the presiding genius of poetry and enchantment.

And one by one (I know not whence) were brought
All spirits of power that most had stirr'd my thought
In selfless boyhood, on a new world tost
Of wonder, and in its own fancies lost;   30
Or charm'd my youth, that, kindled from above,
Loved ere it loved, and sought a form for love;
Or lent a lustre to the earnest scan
Of manhood, musing what and whence is man!
Wild strain of Scalds,[641] that in the sea-worn caves   35
Rehearsed[642] their war-spell to the winds and waves;
Or fateful hymn of those prophetic maids,
That call'd on Hertha[643] in deep forest glades;
Or minstrel lay,[644] that cheer'd the baron's feast;
Or rhyme of city pomp, of monk and priest,   40
Judge, mayor, and many a guild in long array,
To high-church pacing on the great saint's day.[645]
And many a verse which to myself I sang,
That woke the tear yet stole away the pang,
Of hopes which in lamenting I renew'd.   45
And last, a matron now, of sober mien,
Yet radiant still and with no earthly sheen,
Whom as a faery child my childhood woo'd
Even in my dawn of thought—Philosophy;
Though then unconscious of herself, pardie,[646]   50
She bore no other name than Poesy;
And, like a gift from heaven, in lifeful glee,
That had but newly left a mother's knee,
Prattled and play'd with bird and flower, and stone,
As if with elfin playfellows well known,   55
And life reveal'd to innocence alone.

---

[641] *Scalds*: Scandinavian bards.
[642] *Rehearsed*: declaimed.
[643] *Hertha*: (Nerthus) Germanic/Scandinavian fertility goddess.
[644] *lay*: narrative song.
[645] *high-church pacing on the great saint's day*: Saint's day celebrations are a major feature of public and private life in Catholic and Orthodox countries.
[646] *pardie*: indeed.

Thanks, gentle artist! now I can descry
Thy fair creation with a mastering eye,
And all awake! And now in fix'd gaze stand,
Now wander through the Eden of thy hand;   60
Praise the green arches, on the fountain clear
See fragment shadows of the crossing deer;
And with that serviceable[647] nymph I stoop
The crystal from its restless pool to scoop.
I see no longer! I myself am there,   65
Sit on the ground-sward, and the banquet share.
'Tis I, that sweep that lute's love-echoing strings,
And gaze upon the maid who gazing sings:
Or pause and listen to the tinkling bells
From the high tower, and think that there she dwells.   70
With old Boccaccio's soul I stand possest,
And breathe an air like life, that swells my chest.

The brightness of the world, O thou once free,
And always fair, rare land of courtesy!
O Florence! with the Tuscan fields and hills,   75
And famous Arno, fed with all their rills;
Thou brightest star of star-bright Italy!
Rich, ornate, populous,—all treasures thine,
The golden corn,[648] the olive, and the vine.
Fair cities, gallant mansions, castles old,   80
And forests, where beside his leafy hold
The sullen boar hath heard the distant horn,
And whets his tusks against the gnarlèd thorn;
Palladian[649] palace with its storied[650] halls;
Fountains, where Love lies listening to their falls;   85

[647] *serviceable*: willing to be of service. Cf. Shakespeare, *King Lear*, Act 4, scene 6, lines 256–58: "I know thee well: a serviceable villain,/As duteous to the vices of thy mistress/As badness would desire."

[648] *golden corn*: wheat.

[649] *Palladian*: in the neo-classical style of Andrea Palladio (1508–1580).

[650] *storied*: storeyed, divided into storeys.

Gardens, where flings the bridge its airy span,
And Nature makes her happy home with man;
Where many a gorgeous[651] flower is duly fed
With its own rill, on its own spangled bed,
And wreathes the marble urn, or leans its head,   90
A mimic mourner, that with veil withdrawn
Weeps liquid gems, the presents of the dawn;—
Thine all delights, and every muse is thine;
And more than all, the embrace and intertwine
Of all with all in gay and twinkling dance!   95
Mid gods of Greece and warriors of romance,
See! Boccace sits, unfolding on his knees
The new-found roll of old Maeonides;[652]
But from his mantle's fold, and near the heart,
Peers Ovid's Holy Book of Love's sweet smart![653]   100

    O all-enjoying and all-blending sage,
Long be it mine to con[654] thy mazy page,
Where, half conceal'd, the eye of fancy views
Fauns, nymphs, and wingèd saints, all gracious to thy muse!

Still in thy garden let me watch their pranks,[655]   105
And see in Dian's vest[656] between the ranks

[651] *gorgeous*: richly colored.

[652] *old Maeonides*: Homer—he was thought to have been a native of Maeonia (Lydia). "Boccaccio claimed for himself the glory of having first introduced the works of Homer to his countrymen" (Coleridge's note).

[653] *Ovid's Holy Book of Love's sweet smart*: "I know few more striking or more interesting proofs of the overwhelming influence which the study of the Greek and Roman classics exercised on the judgments, feelings, and imaginations of the literati of Europe at the commencements of the restoration of literature, than the passage in the Filocopo of Boccaccio: where the sage instructor, Racheo, as soon as the young prince and the beautiful girl Biancofiore had learned their letters, sets them to study the Holy Book, Ovid's Art of Love" (Coleridge's note).

[654] *to con*: to pore over; to learn.

[655] *pranks*: frolics.

[656] *Dian's vest*: symbol of commitment to chastity (worn by the nymphs in the virgin goddess' train) or purity; here evoking the nuns (with their habits), maidens, and wives who often take lovers in the *Decameron*.

Of the trim vines, some maid that half believes
The vestal fires,[657] of which her lover grieves,
With that sly satyr peeping through the leaves!

Phantom or Fact?[658]

A DIALOGUE IN VERSE

Author

A lovely form there sate beside my bed,
And such a feeding calm its presence shed,
A tender love so pure from earthly leaven,
That I unnethe[659] the fancy[660] might control,
'Twas my own spirit newly come from heaven,   5
Wooing its gentle way into my soul!
But ah! the change—It had not stirr'd, and yet—
Alas! that change how fain would I forget!
That shrinking back, like one that had mistook!
That weary, wandering, disavowing look!   10
'Twas all another, feature, look, and frame,
And still, methought, I knew, it was the same!

Friend

This riddling tale, to what does it belong?
Is't history? vision? or an idle song?
Or rather say at once, within what space   15
Of time this wild disastrous change took place?

Author

Call it a moment's work (and such it seems)
This tale's a fragment from the life of dreams;

---

[657] *vestal fires*: vows of chastity.
[658] Published in *Poetical Works*, 1828.
[659] *unnethe*: barely; with difficulty.
[660] *fancy*: See the introductory note to "Fancy in Nubibus".

But say, that years matur'd the silent strife,
And 'tis a record from the dream of life.   20

Phantom[661]

All Look and Likeness caught from Earth,
All accident of Kin and Birth,
Had pass'd Away: there was no Trace
Of Aught on that illumin'd Face
Uprais'd beneath the rifted Stone,   5
But of one Spirit all her own;—
She, she herself, and only she
Shone thro' her body visibly.

Love's Apparition and Evanishment[662]

AN ALLEGORIC ROMANCE

Like a lone Arab, old and blind,
Some caravan had left behind,
Who sits beside a ruin'd well,
Where the shy sand-asps[663] bask and swell;
And now he hangs his agèd head aslant,   5
And listens for a human sound—in vain!

[661] Published in *Poetical Works*, 1834, but written before 1805. "These lines,
without title or heading, are quoted ('vide ... my lines') in an entry in one of
Coleridge's Malta Notebooks, dated Feb. 8, 1805, to illustrate the idea that the
love-sense can be abstracted from the accidents of form or person (see *Anima
Poetae*, 1895, p. 120). It follows that they were written before that date. *Phantom*
was first published in 1834, immediately following (ii. 71) *Phantom or Fact. A
dialogue in Verse*, which was first published in 1828, and was probably written
about that time. Both poems are 'fragments from the life of dreams'; but it was
the reality which lay behind both 'phantom' and 'fact' of which the poet dreamt,
having his eyes open" (E. H. Coleridge, in *The Complete Poetical Works of Samuel
Taylor Coleridge*, vol. 1 [Oxford: Clarendon Press, 1912], p. 393).

[662] First published in H. D. Inglis' *Friendship's Offering*, 1834; collected in
Poetical Works, 1834. "Evanishment" means "disappearance".

[663] *sand-asps*: probably *Cerastes vipera* (also known as the Sahara sand viper,
Cleopatra's asp, etc.). Cf. "Dejection: An Ode", line 94.

And now the aid, which Heaven alone can grant,
Upturns his eyeless face from Heaven to gain;—[664]
Even thus, in vacant mood, one sultry hour,
Resting my eye upon a drooping plant,   10
With brow low-bent, within my garden-bower,
I sate upon the couch of camomile;
And—whether 'twas a transient sleep, perchance,
Flitted across the idle brain, the while
I watch'd the sickly calm with aimless scope,   15
In my own heart; or that, indeed a trance,
Turn'd my eye inward—thee, O genial Hope,
Love's elder sister! thee did I behold,
Drest as a bridesmaid, but all pale and cold,
With roseless cheek, all pale and cold and dim,   20
    Lie lifeless at my feet!
And then came Love, a sylph in bridal trim,
    And stood beside my seat;
She bent, and kiss'd her sister's lips,
    As she was wont to do;—   25
Alas! 'twas but a chilling breath
Woke just enough of life in death[665]
    To make Hope die anew.

Know Thyself[666]

—E cœlo descendit γνῶθι σεαυτόν.—Juvenal[667]
Γνῶθι σεαυτόν!—and is this the prime
And heaven-sprung adage of the olden time!—
Say, canst thou make thyself?—Learn first that trade;—
Haply[668] thou mayst know what thyself had made.

---

[664] *from Heaven to gain*: i.e., to gain this aid from Heaven.
[665] *life in death*: Cf. "The Ancient Mariner", line 193, and "Epitaph", line 6.
[666] Published in *Poetical Works*, 1834.
[667] Juvenal (A.D. ca. 50–138), *Satires*, 11, line 27: "It came down from heaven: *gnôthi seautón* [Know thyself]." Attributed to many different Greek sages, *gnôthi seautón* was inscribed in the temple of Apollo at Delphi.
[668] *Haply*: perhaps.

What hast thou, Man, that thou dar'st call thine own?—   5
What is there in thee, Man, that can be known?—
Dark fluxion,[669] all unfixable by thought,
A phantom dim of past and future wrought,
Vain sister of the worm,—life, death, soul, clod—
Ignore thyself, and strive to know thy God!   10

My Baptismal Birth-Day[670]

God's child in Christ adopted,—Christ my all,—
What that earth boasts were not lost cheaply, rather
Than forfeit that blest name, by which I call
The Holy One, the Almighty God, my Father?—[671]
Father! in Christ we live, and Christ in Thee—[672]   5
Eternal Thou, and everlasting we.[673]
The heir of heaven, henceforth I fear not death:[674]
In Christ I live! in Christ I draw the breath

---

[669] *fluxion*: flowing forth; flux; "the (real or supposed) outflow of material particles too subtle to be perceived by the senses; ... a stream of such particles" (*Oxford English Dictionary*, s.v. "fluxion").

[670] First published in H.D. Inglis' *Friendship's Offering*, 1834; collected in *Poetical Works*, 1834. Originally published under the title "Lines composed on a sick-bed, under severe bodily suffering, on my spiritual birthday, October 28th".

[671] *forfeit that blest name ... Almighty God, my Father*: Cf. Matthew 16:26: "For what will it profit a man, if he gains the whole world and forfeits his soul?"; Galatians 4:6: "And because you are sons, God has sent the Spirit of his Son into our hearts, crying, 'Abba! Father!'"; and Matthew 6:9: "Pray then like this: Our Father who art in heaven, Hallowed be thy name."

[672] *Father! in Christ we live, and Christ in Thee*: See Galatians 2:20: "[I]t is no longer I who live, but Christ who lives in me", and John 14:9–10: "Jesus said to him, 'Have I been with you so long, and yet you do not know me, Philip? ... Do you not believe that I am in the Father and the Father is in me?'"

[673] *Eternal Thou, and everlasting we*: Perhaps this is an essentially nonpantheistic statement about the infinite distance between the creature and the creator. Also, it asserts the eternally dynamic relationship between God and mankind—one in which priority and initiative are always God's.

[674] *heir of heaven, henceforth I fear not death*: Cf. 1 Corinthians 15:54–55: "When ... the mortal puts on immortality, then shall come to pass the saying that is written, 'Death is swallowed up in victory.... O death, where is your sting?'"

Of the true life![675]—Let then earth, sea, and sky
Make war against me! On my front I show   10
Their mighty master's seal.[676] In vain they try
To end my life, that can but end its woe.—
Is that a death-bed where a Christian lies?—
Yes! but not his—'tis Death itself there dies.[677]

Epitaph[678]

Stop, Christian passer-by!—Stop, child of God,
And read with gentle breast. Beneath this sod
A poet lies, or that which once seem'd he.—
O, lift one thought in prayer for S. T. C.;
That he who many a year with toil of breath   5
Found death in life,[679] may here find life in death!
Mercy for praise—to be forgiven for fame
He ask'd, and hoped, through Christ. Do thou the same!

[675] *In Christ I live . . . Of the true life*: Cf. John 10:10: "I came that they may have life, and have it abundantly."

[676] *Their mighty master's seal*: Cf. Revelation 7:2: "I saw another angel ascend from the rising of the sun, with the seal of the living God".

[677] *death-bed where a Christian lies . . . Death itself there dies*: Cf. 1 Corinthians 15:20: "Christ has been raised from the dead, the first fruits of those who have fallen asleep"; and Donne, "Death, be not proud": "One short sleep past, we wake eternally, / And death shall be no more; Death, thou shalt die" (lines 13–14).

[678] Published in *Poetical Works*, 1834. This poem is inscribed on Coleridge's tombstone in St. Michael's Church, Highgate, though there is conflicting evidence as to whether such was the poet's intention.

[679] *many a year . . . death in life*: For Coleridge's physical, marital, and drug problems, see the note to his introduction to "Kubla Khan" and the introductory note to "The Pains of Sleep". For "death in life", cf. the note to line 193 of "The Ancient Mariner"; here, of course, Coleridge hopes death will be the beginning of eternal life.

Contemporary Criticisms

"A Still More Naked and Simple Style"—the English Romantic Poets and the Ballad

Raimund Borgmeier
University of Giessen

In their endeavor to renew English poetry fundamentally, the Romantic poets did not only look for new themes and subject matter; they also sought new, or at least different, models than those favored by the era before them. William Wordsworth in his Preface to *Lyrical Ballads*—a collection of poems by Wordsworth and Samuel Taylor Coleridge, which is the most significant manifesto of the English Romantic movement—defends and explains his poetic principles. Referring to exemplary models, he points out:

> It might, perhaps, as far as relates to these Volumes, have been almost sufficient to observe, that poems are extant, written upon more humble subjects, and in a still more naked and simple style, which have continued to give pleasure from generation to generation.[1]

In spite of Wordsworth's extremely cautious mode of expression, it is perfectly clear that he is referring to the genre of the ballad, and it does not come as a surprise when, a little later, he quotes from a well-known ballad, "one of the most justly-admired stanzas of the '*Babes in the Wood*'" (see p. 108), and contrasts it favorably with a passage from a parody by the classicist Dr. Johnson (the byname of the eighteenth-century poet Samuel Johnson), which he finds "trivial and simple" (see p. 108) in a negative sense.

---

[1] William Wordsworth, Preface to the third edition of *Lyrical Ballads*, in *The Romantic Poets*, ed. Joseph Pearce and Robert Asch, vol. 1, Ignatius Critical Editions (San Francisco: Ignatius Press, 2014), p. 103. Subsequent quotations from this edition will be cited in the text.

For Wordsworth and the Romantic poets in general, the ballad was one of the most important generic models. When they thought of good poetry, they very often had the ballad in mind, and this is probably the reason why Wordsworth and Coleridge chose to give their seminal first collection the title *Lyrical Ballads* (1798). Almost all the English Romantic poets experimented with the genre and used it for their own purposes.

In this essay, I will first attempt to clarify what characterizes the ballad as a literary form and distinguish between different kinds of it. This will lead to the question why the Romantics were so much attracted to the ballad. Then we will look at the context of literary history and consider how the Romantic poets came into contact with the genre. In the main part of the essay, I will discuss some outstanding examples of Romantic ballad-writing—poems by Coleridge, Wordsworth, and Keats—and will examine in what way these poets continue the ballad tradition, and in what aspects, on the other hand, they may possibly be viewed as different.

Defined simply, a ballad is "a song or poem that tells a story in short stanzas and simple words, with repetition, refrain etc."[2] But this definition is not sufficient to grasp the essential nature of the genre, and with good reason the dictionary entry I have quoted here continues, "most old ballads are anonymous and have been handed down orally in more than one version." In this sense, the ballad means the traditional or popular or folk ballad, or the Child ballad, as it is nowadays also called, after the American scholar Francis James Child, who edited the canonical collection *The English and Scottish Popular Ballads* (1882–1898) in five volumes with 305 ballads and their numerous variants.

The traditional ballad constitutes a completely different species of poetry from the usual poetical texts. It is not the work of an individual author but is essentially shaped by the process

---

[2] *Webster's New World Dictionary of the American Language*, 2nd ed. (New York: Prentice Hall, 1986), s.v. "ballad".

of being handed down orally from one singer to the next, as Cecil Sharp, a leading expert on folk art, explained as early as 1907: "The method of oral transmission is not merely one by which the folksong lives; it is a process by which it grows and by which it is created."[3]

Ballads of tradition, as we find them in Child's collection, tell moving stories of life and death, vices and virtues, and powerful emotions. They concentrate on a central situation, a critical phase of the story, and relate it in terms of dramatic action, with a great deal of dialogue (some ballads, like the famous "Edward" or "Lord Randal", consist exclusively of dialogue). As a rule, the action is presented in an impersonal style, without any emotional comment, but with a specific rhetoric that is characterized by formulaic language, repetition, and hyperbole.[4] Nobody knows exactly about the origins of the ballad, yet the earliest examples date back to the late Middle Ages.

In the second half of the sixteenth century, the traditional ballad was joined by a younger, perhaps less reputable, cousin: the street ballad or broadside. As the ballad-monger Autolycus in Shakespeare's *The Winter's Tale* illustrates, street ballads were texts printed for a semiliterate reading public with a sensational content (frequently dealing with a topical event) and a decidedly commercial interest. The slightly dubious reputation that they achieved, which surfaced occasionally as a definite contempt for ballad-mongers and their wares, continued right into modern times, when, for example, in a letter dated August 25, 1872, Child referred to broadside ballads as "veritable dung-hills, in which, only after a great deal of sickening grubbing, one finds a very moderate jewel".[5]

At any rate, the two forms were related and could not be clearly distinguished, since quite a few versions of popular

---

[3] Quoted in Gordon Hall Gerould, *The Ballad of Tradition* (1932; repr., New York: Oxford University Press, 1957), p. 167.

[4] A very good introduction is to be found in ibid., particularly chap. 5, "Ballad Characteristics", pp. 84–130.

[5] Quoted in Roy Palmer, "'Veritable Dunghills': Professor Child and the Broadside", *Folk Music Journal* 7, no. 2 (1996): 155.

ballads, brought together by diligent collectors, came from printed texts and not from actual singers. The most important difference between the two forms, however, is the personal style of presentation in the street ballad, where the ballad singer expressly addresses his audience and finally makes an ostensible effort to underline the moral lesson of the poem. Yet when one looks, for instance, at Wordsworth's comments on the ballad, one gains the impression that he did not see much of a difference between the two kinds of ballads, since he quotes, as we saw, "Babes in the Wood", a street ballad, as a positive example of ballad poetry. Nevertheless, it was certainly, above all, the traditional ballad that engaged the Romantics' interest and esteem.

The Romantic poets admired the ballad mainly for three reasons: it was folk art, it was old, and it dealt with strong emotions. And as we could see from Wordsworth's argument, the first reason is probably the most important one.

Since the ballad was folk literature, it could be regarded by the Romantics as the antithesis to the poetic ideal of the previous period; it was something genuine instead of artificial. Of the two basic directions envisaged by classical rhetoric, *monstrare artem* (artfulness) versus *celare artem* (artlessness), the Romantics decidedly favored the latter. They wanted their poetry to be unobtrusive and "natural". And this is what the ballad stood for. The ballad, being folk poetry, was seen as genuine both as far as its subject matter and its style were concerned. It is true that ballads often tell about heroes and aristocratic leaders, but still they are generally sung by common people and represent essential human fates and problems, so they can be considered as fulfilling Wordsworth's claim of having to do with "incidents and situations from common life." At the same time, the style of the ballads is not stilted but simple (exactly the opposite of the poetic diction Wordsworth and his fellow poets disapproved of so much). One would be justified in maintaining then, in Wordsworth's words, that ballads are written (or sung) "in a selection of language really used by men" (see p. 87).

Even if we cannot say exactly how old the ballad is, it is a genre that is known to be ancient and is very much associated with the past and bygone ages. Therefore it was bound to hold a strong appeal in an era that more or less discovered history and highly esteemed things reminiscent of old times. In this sense, Wordsworth is probably referring to the ballad when, in his famous poem "The Solitary Reaper", the speaker ponders what the young woman he has encountered in the highlands might be singing:

> Perhaps the plaintive numbers flow
> For old, unhappy, far-off things,
> And battles long ago: (See pp. 258–59, lines 18–20.)

With this quotation, the third aspect that distinguishes the ballad in the eyes of the Romantics is referred to. According to Wordsworth, "all good poetry" has to do with "powerful feelings" (see p. 90). And in a different context, Wordsworth explains that "passion … is derived from a word which signifies *suffering*; but the connection which suffering has with effort, with exertion, and *action*, is immediate and inseparable."[6] This pertains to a high degree to the traditional ballad, where, as we have seen, critical situations connected with fatal suffering and dramatic action are invariably related.

Just as the Romantic movement did not happen overnight, the contact of the Romantics with the genre of the ballad has a history. An important starting point can be found already in the early eighteenth century when Joseph Addison dedicated a number of editions of his influential *Spectator* to "[t]he old song of *Chevy-Chase* [that] is the favourite Ballad of the common people of *England*" and "professed [himself, like Sir Philip Sidney and Ben Jonson before him,] an Admirer of this antiquated Song."[7] Addison continues this positive

---

[6] "Essay, Supplementary to the Preface", *Poetical Works*, ed. Thomas Hutchinson, rev. Ernest de Selincourt (London: Oxford University Press, 1936), p. 750.

[7] Joseph Addison, *Spectator*, no. 70 (May 21, 1711), quoted in *The Spectator*, ed. Gregory Smith, Everyman's Library, 4 vols. (New York: Dutton, 1945), 1:215–16.

appreciation shortly afterward in another issue of the *Spectator* where he endeavours to "shew that the Sentiments in that Ballad are extreamly Natural and Poetical, and full of the majestick Simplicity which we admire in the greatest of the ancient Poets".[8] Two weeks later, Addison again turns to the genre when he relates "a most exquisite Pleasure" he has received from reading a certain poem, and the way he announces this shows the surprising nature of his assessment:

> My Reader will think I am not serious, when I acquaint him that the Piece I am going to speak of was the old Ballad of the *Two Children in the Wood* [or *Babes in the Wood*], which is one of the Darling Songs of the Common People, and has been the Delight of most *Englishmen* in some Part of their Age.[9]

To support his position, Addison, toward the end of his essay, calls in an authority and says:

> I have heard that the late Lord DORSET [Charles Sackville], who had the greatest Wit tempered with the greatest Candour, and was one of the finest Criticks as well as the best Poets of his Age, had a numerous Collection of old *English* Ballads, and took a particular Pleasure in the Reading of them.[10]

Ballad collectors of this kind and their collections became even more influential in changing the prevailing attitude toward ballads and poetry in general in the further course of the eighteenth century. Easily the most important landmark in this process was Dr. (or Bishop) (Thomas) Percy's *Reliques of Ancient English Poetry* (1765). Wordsworth considers Percy's *Reliques* an absolute turning point in the history of English poetry and states the following about its unique importance for the Romantic poets and himself:

> For our own country, its poetry has been absolutely redeemed by it. I do not think that there is an able writer in verse of the

---

[8] *Spectator*, no. 74 (May 25, 1711), quoted in ibid., p. 228.
[9] *Spectator*, no. 85 (June 7, 1711), quoted in ibid., p. 265.
[10] Ibid., p. 266.

present day who would not be proud to acknowledge his obligations to the "Reliques"; I know that is so with my friends; and for myself, I am happy in this occasion to make a public avowal of my own.[11]

Yet, according to Wordsworth, the literary climate, at the time of the publication of the *Reliques*, was not favourable, and a detour was needed for the full impact to reach English poetry:

> [The ballad] models sank, in this country, into temporary neglect; while Bürger, and other writers of Germany, were translating or imitating these Reliques, and composing, with the aid of inspiration thence derived, poems which are the delight of the German nation.[12]

Gottfried August Bürger was, indeed, received also in Britain, with enormous enthusiasm. In particular, his ballad "Lenore" (1774), based on the popular Scottish ballad "Sweet William's Ghost" (Child 77), translated into English by William Taylor as "Lenora" and published in the new *Monthly Magazine* in 1796, was a huge success and, among other things, inspired Scott, as he later confessed, to be a poet.[13] The ballad had been recognized as an outstanding generic model for the Romantic movement in Britain, and the poets felt challenged to compose ballads of their own.

"The Rime of the Ancient Mariner" by Samuel Taylor Coleridge is undoubtedly the most famous ballad in English Romantic poetry. Both Wordsworth and Coleridge were aware of the eminent quality and poetic potential of this poem, and they put it at the beginning of their collection *Lyrical Ballads* (1798) to function as a kind of pilot piece.

It is plain that "The Ancient Mariner" was essentially inspired by the popular ballad. Like many ballads of tradition,

---

[11] "Essay, Supplementary", p. 749.

[12] Ibid., p. 748.

[13] See Stephen Maxfield Parrish, *The Art of the Lyrical Ballads* (Cambridge, Mass.: Harvard University Press, 1973), p. 87.

such as, for example "Thomas Rymer" (Child 37) or "The Wife of Usher's Well" (Child 79), it tells a story with central supernatural elements. The eponymous main character narrates how his ship was drawn toward the South Pole by a storm, but then appears to be saved miraculously when an albatross comes through the snow-fog and is received with joy and hospitality. The sailor, however, kills the bird. A curse falls on the ship, and all the crew die of thirst, with only the old sailor surviving, so as to be punished for his crime. Yet, after some time, he experiences an awakening; the spell breaks and the ship can return to England. As atonement for his sin, the sailor has to go around and tell people his story.

As usual in the traditional ballad, there is an immediate, dramatic beginning:

> It is an ancient Mariner,
> And he stoppeth one of three.
> "By thy long grey beard and glittering eye,
> Now wherefore stopp'st thou me?" (See p. 359, lines 1–4.)

The direct speech is not introduced by a special introductory phrase, an *inquit* formula, and we only subsequently learn who the speaker is.

The language and style are archaic and powerful, reminiscent of oral literature:

> The fair breeze blew, the white foam flew,
> The furrow followed free;
> We were the first that ever burst
> Into that silent sea. (See p. 364, lines 103–6.)

The alliterations and internal rhymes create impressive sound effects. At the same time, this is also the familiar stanza (with the rhyme scheme *abcb*, and iambic lines with four and three stresses alternating) that can be found in more than half the ballads in Child's collection.[14] Formulaic repetition and its

---

[14] That Coleridge occasionally expands the stanza by adding another pair of lines (or, more rarely, a single line) is a phenomenon also to be found in popular ballads.

special form of incremental repetition, characteristic of the ballad genre, occurs in salient passages, such as the following:

> Water, water, every where,
> And all the boards did shrink;
> Water, water, every where,
> Nor any drop to drink. (See p. 365, lines 119–22.)

The story the old man tells leads the readers into the typical archaic ballad world, where things are not unrelated and events do not occur by chance, but where one finds an ordered universe with secret power lines connecting everything. Statements about time are often made in a premodern manner: "It perched for vespers nine" (see p. 363, line 76), and mystical numbers play an important role: "Seven days, seven nights, I saw that curse" (see p. 373, line 261). The ancient mariner belongs to the old faith; he prays to the Virgin Mary: "Heaven's Mother send us grace!" (see p. 369, line 178), and "To Mary Queen the praise be given!" (see p. 375, line 294). People reaffirm their utterances with Christian formulae: "By him who died on cross" (see p. 379, line 399), or "by the holy rood!" (see p. 383, line 489). In a later edition of the poem, in 1817, Coleridge even enhances the medieval touch of the poem by adding glosses in the margin to explain the plot in an archaic language; for example, a gloss appears at the end of the first part: "The ancient Mariner inhospitably killeth the pious bird of good omen" (see p. 363).

So, in most respects, "The Ancient Mariner" reads like a traditional ballad. With its 625 lines, it is true, it is much longer than most ballads in Child's collection, but, on the other hand, "A Gest of Robyn Hode" (Child 117), which consists of eight parts, is more than three times the length of Coleridge's poem. Nevertheless, "The Ancient Mariner" is also more than a traditional ballad. It does not merely tell a thrilling story of life and death, but it has a definitive message, which must be understood in both Christian and Romantic terms.

In his killing of the albatross, the ancient mariner commits a crime against God and nature. In this there is a link to original sin. We are never given a reason for this deed and have to view it as purely evil. The mariner's confession, which concludes the first part, comes as a hammer blow: "With my cross-bow/I shot the ALBATROSS" (see p. 363, lines 81–82).

The crisis the mariner then undergoes is like Saint Paul's experience on the road to Damascus. Suddenly, he comes to see how fundamentally wrong he was and repents. In this case, he sees the beauty of the created universe, the beauty of nature, which the Romantics esteemed so highly. Before, he had despised the lower life forms in the sea as "a thousand thousand slimy things" (see p. 372, line 238), and now he becomes aware of their beauty, as he narrates, in typical ballad language with formulaic repetitions and a wealth of adjectives of color:

> Beyond the shadow of the ship,
> I watched the water-snakes:
> They moved in tracks of shining white,
> And when they reared, the elfish light
> Fell off in hoary flakes.
>
> Within the shadow of the ship
> I watched their rich attire:
> Blue, glossy green, and velvet black,
> They coiled and swam; and every track
> Was a flash of golden fire.
>
> O happy living things! no tongue
> Their beauty might declare:
> A spring of love gushed from my heart,
> And I blessed them unaware:
> Sure my kind saint took pity on me,
> And I blessed them unaware.
>
> The self same moment I could pray;
> (See p. 374, lines 272–88.)

In keeping with the medieval, Catholic world, there is a hermit who hears the mariner's confession after he has returned to England. As an act of penance, the mariner has to go around and tell his story, which he brings to an end with the moral lesson:

> Farewell, farewell! but this I tell
> To thee, thou Wedding-Guest!
> He prayeth well, who loveth well
> Both man and bird and beast.
>
> He prayeth best, who loveth best
> All things both great and small;
> For the dear God who loveth us,
> He made and loveth all. (See pp. 387–88, lines 610–17.)

The frame story, to which the wedding guest belongs, is another central aspect that distinguishes Coleridge's poem from the ballad of tradition. The wedding guest functions as a kind of proto-audience: he shows the powerful impact of the mariner's tale. After he has heard it he can no longer enjoy the pleasures of life, in this case the wedding festivities, as if nothing had happened, but the tale and its lesson have made him (as the poet wishes his reader to be) "[a] sadder and wiser man" (see p. 388, line 624). The frame story helps the poet to achieve what, in his *Biographia Literaria*, he calls "that willing suspension of disbelief for the moment, which constitutes poetic faith",[15] since the wedding guest, to some extent, represents the world of the reader, the world of everyday experiences as opposed to the supernatural experiences of the mariner.

There is no space here to discuss the archetypical symbolism represented in the recurrent antagonism of the sun and the moon, which one would certainly not look for in a proper ballad. It has become clear, however, that Coleridge in "The Ancient Mariner" realizes the potential of the folk ballad in a masterful manner and, at the same time, transcends the limitations of the genre and uses it for poetic purposes of his own.

---

[15] See *English Literary Criticism: Romantic and Victorian*, ed. Daniel G. Hoffman and Samuel Hynes (London: Peter Owen, 1966), p. 44.

In a comparable though different way, William Wordsworth made use of the ballad, as can be seen in the poem "Lucy Gray", which was composed in Germany in the winter of 1798–1799 and published in 1800. Wordsworth was far more productive as a poet than Coleridge, and there are as many as seven poems by him in the first edition of *Lyrical Ballads* (1798) that can be regarded as ballads.[16] As Coleridge reports in *Biographia Literaria*, the two poets had made an agreement: while Coleridge himself was to specialize in the supernatural (as we saw in "The Ancient Mariner"),

> Mr. Wordsworth, on the other hand, was to propose to himself as his object, to give the charm of novelty to things of every day, and to excite a feeling analogous to the supernatural, by awakening the mind's attention from the lethargy of custom, and directing it to the loveliness and the wonders of the world before us.[17]

Modern critics would describe such an objective as alienation or estrangement. It could be one explanation why Wordsworth, as mentioned above, was more drawn to the street ballad, which, as we have seen, is closer to everyday life than the ballad of tradition and often deals with a topical event. The story of "Lucy Gray" was, as Wordsworth explained in a later note,

> Founded on a circumstance told me by my Sister, of a little girl who, not far from Halifax in Yorkshire, was bewildered in a snow-storm. Her footsteps were traced by her parents to the middle of the lock of a canal, and no other vestige of her, backward or forward, could be traced. The body however was found in the canal.[18]

---

[16] They are "Goody Blake and Harry Gill", "The Thorn", "The Idiot Boy", "The Female Vagrant", "We Are Seven", "Simon Lee", and "The Last of the Flock". See Patrick Campbell, *Wordsworth and Coleridge: Lyrical Ballads*, Critical Perspectives (London: Macmillan, 1991), p. 44.

[17] Hoffman and Hynes, *English Literary Criticism*, p. 44.

[18] Quoted in William Wordsworth, *Selected Poems and Prefaces*, ed. Jack Stillinger (Boston: Houghton Mifflin, 1965), p. 519.

In the poem, Wordsworth tells his story with the poetical equipment of the ballad. The customary ballad stanza is only slightly changed by adding a new rhyme (*abab* instead of *abcb*). After a short introduction of three stanzas, the focus is immediately on the dramatic crisis, which is told by means of direct speech in a dialogue without *inquit* formulae using a simple style:

> "To-night will be a stormy night,
> You to the Town must go,
> And take a lantern, Child, to light
> Your Mother thro' the snow."
>
> "That, Father! will I gladly do;
> 'Tis scarcely afternoon—
> The Minster-clock has just struck two,
> And yonder is the Moon." (See pp. 138–39, lines 13–20.)

In the middle of the poem, the point of view turns from Lucy to the parents, who search in vain for the lost child. Here Wordsworth, for reasons to be discussed below, changes the story—the body of the child is never found.

That Wordsworth follows the model of the street ballad (and its rhyme scheme) is quite obvious from the fact that he is imitating here the very stanza from the "Babes in the Wood" [or "The Children in the Wood"] that he quotes in his Preface as an example of a simple style in the positive sense:

> "These pretty Babes with hand in hand
> Went wandering up and down;
> But never more they saw the Man
> Approaching from the Town." (See p. 108.)

The corresponding stanza in "Lucy Gray" reads:

> The storm came on before its time,
> She wandered up and down,
> And many a hill did Lucy climb
> But never reached the Town. (See p. 139, lines 29–32.)

Yet while "The Children in the Wood", as Dr. Percy published it in his *Reliques*, was merely a cautionary tale, warning greedy and unscrupulous guardians,[19] Wordsworth has no interest in writing a similar warning to parents to be careful not to send their children on a hazardous mission in bad weather and in dangerous territory. Instead, Wordsworth uses the ballad for his own poetical concept.

It is significant that the protagonist of the poem is both a country dweller and a child. "Humble and rustic life" is, as Wordsworth explains in his Preface, his favorite subject matter "because, in that condition, the essential passions of the heart find a better soil in which they can attain their maturity, are less under restraint, and speak a plainer and more emphatic language" (see pp. 88–89). Lucy's closeness to nature is underlined by three comparisons with wildlife: "the Fawn at play" (see p. 138, line 9), "[t]he Hare upon the Green" (see p. 138, line 10), and "the mountain roe" (see p. 139, line 25).

Wordsworth, like other Romantics, has a very high opinion of children because they are special beings naturally in touch with the essential core of life. This is evident in many poems, especially in "Ode: Intimations of Immortality from Recollections of Early Childhood", where he addresses the child as "Mighty prophet! Seer blest!" (see p. 174, line 114). So Lucy is a special person in that respect, too. Her specialness gets particularly emphasized by the alternative subtitle Wordsworth gives the poem: "Or, Solitude". To the Romantic

---

[19] In the final stanza, the moral lesson is clearly expressed:

> You that executors be made,
>   And overseers eke
> Of children that be fatherless,
>   And infants mild and meek;
> Take you example by this thing,
>   And yield to each his right,
> Lest God with such like miserye
>   Your wicked minds requite.

Thomas Percy, ed., *Reliques of Ancient English Poetry* (Edinburgh: Wm. Nimmo, 1881), p. 239.

poets, solitude is a desirable condition since it represents a particular closeness to nature and makes communion with nature possible. First and foremost, the subtitle refers to the poem's protagonist. In the final line of stanza 1, Lucy is called "the solitary Child", and this is intensified in the next line by the statement: "No Mate, no comrade Lucy knew;/She dwelt on a wide Moor" (see p. 138, lines 5–6). Lucy's solitariness and closeness to nature are a precondition for her final transformation. As we saw, Wordsworth deviates from the authentic state of events. Instead of having the corpse of the child found by the miserable parents, in the two concluding stanzas, he reports Lucy's (potential) transfiguration—her becoming one with nature:

> Yet some maintain that to this day
> She is a living Child,
> That you may see sweet Lucy Gray
> Upon the lonesome Wild.
>
> O'er rough and smooth she trips along,
> And never looks behind;
> And sings a solitary song
> That whistles in the wind. (See p. 140, lines 57–64.)

In order to be able to report this, it is necessary for the poet to be solitary himself. So, in a secondary sense, the subtitle also refers to the poet, who is on his own and therefore open to receive nature's message, as we learn in the opening stanza ("when I crossed the Wild,/I chanced to see at break of day" [see p. 138]). Thus, "Lucy Gray" must be viewed as both a ballad and a Romantic poem in the full sense of the words.

The Architecture of English Romanticism: Constructions of Wordsworth and Coleridge

Crystal Downing
Messiah College

When did the Romantic era begin? Such a question is comparable to asking, in what year did your grandfather grow old? Though there are clear differences between his youth and old age, the transition was gradual, with characteristics of his personality overlapping his early and later years. Selecting a date for the onset of old age—perhaps the birth of a grandchild or the year of retirement—is therefore usually symbolic.

Identifying when the Romantic age began in England is also largely symbolic. Many scholars select 1798, the year William Wordsworth and Samuel Taylor Coleridge published *Lyrical Ballads*. Others reverse the "98" to situate beginnings in 1789, the year that William Blake first published *Songs of Innocence* and, more dramatically, the year that marks the start of the French Revolution.

Both 1789 and 1798 have something in common: they signal a rupture from the past. This is significant because, as Peter Gay notes in *Pleasure Wars*, Romantic artists were the first to self-consciously define themselves in opposition to society, believing their work ruptured extant cultural expectations.[1] Wordsworth and Coleridge, for example, defied the artistic sensibilities of their contemporaries by the very name they gave their anthology: *Lyrical Ballads*. Most eighteenth-century writers did not regard lyric poetry and folk ballads as ennobling literary forms. True art, for them, followed the canons of classical Greece, which placed epic, tragedy, ode, and elegy as the highest genres of literature. Appropriately described as "neo-classical", these eighteenth-century authors assumed that the Greek genres

---

[1] Peter Gay, *Pleasure Wars* (New York: Norton, 1998), p. 24.

reinforced cultural ideals through their focus on noble characters' relationship with society. In contrast, lyric poetry wallowed in the personal, while ballads reflected the interests of the common people. Even the language of the vernacular was considered indecorous to neo-classical poets, who eschewed words such as "big", "elbow", "sneeze", and "cheese". To avoid using the lowbrow word "rats" in a poem, one neo-classical writer substituted the phrase "the whiskered vermin race".[2]

In reaction to neo-classical proprieties about poetic diction, Wordsworth self-consciously employed the language of common people in *Lyrical Ballads*, focusing especially on "humble and rustic life".[3] In an "Advertisement" appended to the first edition, Wordsworth describes its contents as "experiments",[4] and in his famous Prefaces to subsequent editions (1800 and 1802), he explicitly delineates how the poems break with the "modern" poetic diction of his time, warning that "they who have been accustomed to the gaudiness and inane phraseology of many modern writers, if they persist in reading this book to its conclusion, will, no doubt, frequently have to struggle with feelings of strangeness and awkwardness" (see p. 87). *Lyrical Ballads* would seem strange and awkward to advocates of literary elitism.

Not surprisingly, Wordsworth and Coleridge supported the French Revolution. Like their *Lyrical Ballads* a decade later, the revolution demonstrated the rupture of privilege. Significantly, the French Revolution is memorialized, to this day, through a concrete, literal rupture: the storming of the Bastille on July 14, 1789. Though the fortress was not politically

---

[2] X. J. Kennedy and Dana Gioia, *An Introduction to Poetry*, 10th ed. (New York: Longman, 2002), pp. 65–66.

[3] William Wordsworth, Preface to the third edition of *Lyrical Ballads* (1802), in *The Romantic Poets*, ed. Joseph Pearce and Robert Asch, vol. 1, Ignatius Critical Editions (San Francisco: Ignatius Press, 2014), p. 88. Subsequent quotations from this edition will be cited in the text.

[4] William Wordsworth, "Advertisement to *Lyrical Ballads* (1798)", in *William Wordsworth: Selected Poems and Prefaces*, ed. Jack Stillinger (Boston: Houghton Mifflin, 1965), p. 443.

significant, containing only a handful of prisoners at the time, breaking it open—rupturing its architecture—has come to symbolize the destruction of seemingly insurmountable barriers between upper and lower classes.

As with the Bastille, architecture provides a helpful way to think of the rupture between neo-classical and Romantic sensibilities, as well as between Wordsworth and Coleridge. For, in the same year that Wordsworth published the amplified version of his Preface to *Lyrical Ballads* (1802), outlining his revolt against "what is usually called poetic diction" (see pp. 92, 102), Coleridge wrote a friend that he and Wordsworth "begin to suspect that there is some where or other a radical Difference in our opinions".[5] In the remainder of this essay I will demonstrate how architecture can help us understand these various ruptures of English Romanticism.

I

A phrase from Alexander Pope's 559-line poem "An Essay on Criticism" (1711) famously summarizes the neo-classical commitment to proper poetic diction: "*True wit* is *Nature* to Advantage dressed,/What oft was *Thought*, but ne'er so well *Exprest*."[6] Pope implies that poetry should reinforce the "often thought" of cultural norms. Poetry, then, does not celebrate nature so much as improve it. Pope commends "*Nature Methodiz'd*",[7] a concept reinforced a year later by Joseph Addison, in an issue of the *Spectator*: "The poet seems to get the better of nature: he takes, indeed, the landskip after her, but gives it more vigorous touches, heightens its beauty, and so enlivens the whole piece."[8]

[5] Ernest Hartley Coleridge, ed., *Letters of Samuel Taylor Coleridge*, 2 vols. (Boston: Houghton, 1895), 1:375.

[6] Alexander Pope, "An Essay on Criticism", in *Eighteenth-Century English Literature*, ed. Geoffrey Tillotson et al. (New York: Harcourt, Brace and World, 1969), p. 558, lines 297–98.

[7] Ibid., p. 556, line 89.

[8] Joseph Addison, *Spectator* 166 (June 27, 1712), quoted in *Critical Theory since Plato*, ed. Hazard Adams (New York: Harcourt Brace Jovanovich, 1971), p. 290.

As with neo-classical poetry, so with neo-classical architecture, which appropriated the ordered symmetry of Greek pediments, Roman rotundas, and Palladian windows. Pope makes the parallel explicit in "An Essay on Criticism", comparing an effective work of literature with a "well-proportion'd Dome".[9] Even neo-classical gardens were well-proportioned with nature methodized into geometrical parterres, like those at the Palace of Versailles, where King Louis and Marie Antoinette maintained the sumptuous lifestyle that helped incite the French Revolution.

For most neo-classicals, a woeful lack of proportion, order, and control was illustrated by Gothic architecture, the style arising during the medieval period. For this reason, Pope, when adapting Chaucer's unfinished "House of Fame" (ca. 1380), superimposed neo-classical styles onto Chaucer's Gothic edifice. Each façade in Pope's adaptation, as Jean Hagstrum points out, is presented as "a work of meaning and majesty"[10]—except for one Gothic portion, which Pope describes as "o'er wrought with Ornaments of barb'rous Pride".[11]

By later in the century, however, the overwrought and barbarous elements of Gothicism became all the rage. A new genre called "the Gothic novel"—most famously Horace Walpole's *The Castle of Otranto* (1764), Ann Radcliffe's *The Mysteries of Udolfo* (1794), and Matthew Lewis' *The Monk* (1796)—employed hoary Gothic settings to intensify terrors in texts that repudiated the "oft' was thought but ne'er so well expressed." Gothic architecture thus contributed to the rupture between neo-classical proprieties and Romantic emotion.

Ironically, it was the neo-classical impulse that led to the Romantic fascination with the Gothic. Eighteenth-century antiquarians studied the ruins of the Greek and Roman cultures to learn as much as they could about the eras their own

---

[9] Pope, "An Essay on Criticism", p. 558, line 247.

[10] Jean H. Hagstrum, *The Sister Arts: The Tradition of Literary Pictorialism and English Poetry from Dryden to Gray* (Chicago: University of Chicago Press, 1958), p. 224.

[11] Quoted in ibid.

times emulated. Wealthy landowners often built sham classical ruins, called "follies", in their gardens as emblems of more sophisticated times. In 1730, for example, a ruined "Temple of Modern Virtue" was constructed at Stowe to symbolize "the diminished role of virtue in modern British life".[12] The ruin, which in previous generations had represented the ineluctable forces of nature, became a prefabricated object "to get the better of nature"[13] by allegorizing it.

At first the "proper" ruins were classical, but as the century advanced, Gothic styles became more fashionable. Kenneth Clark explains why: "Authentic ruins were often as effective as sham ones and cost nothing to erect; and in England practically all the authentic ruins are medieval."[14] Soon supplanting the eighteenth-century's blessed rage for order was a "ruin rhapsody", which Rose Macaulay allies with Romanticism.[15] And, of course, nothing visualizes rupture better than a ruin.

II

The "ruin rhapsody" of eighteenth-century Gothicism provides a suitable analogue for the work of Samuel Taylor Coleridge, who left many of his poems unfinished. Thomas McFarland spends the majority of *Romanticism and the Forms of Ruin* discussing "modalities of fragmentation", not only in Coleridge's philosophy and writings, but also in his daily existence.[16] Timothy Bahti states that Coleridge's work "stands as *the* fragmentary poetry of English romanticism.... [H]is writings lie there like a field of ruins and fragments."[17]

[12] John Archer, "The Beginnings of Association in British Architectural Esthetics", *Eighteenth-Century Studies* 16 (1983): 252.

[13] Joseph Addison, *Spectator* 166, quoted in *Critical Theory since Plato*, p. 290.

[14] Kenneth Clark, *The Gothic Revival: An Essay in the History of Taste* (New York: Harper, 1962), pp. 47–48.

[15] Rose Macaulay, *Pleasure of Ruins* (New York: Walker, 1953), p. 16.

[16] Thomas McFarland, *Romanticism and the Forms of Ruin: Wordsworth, Coleridge, and Modalities of Fragmentation* (Princeton: Princeton University Press, 1981).

[17] Timothy Bahti, "Coleridge's 'Kubla Khan' and the Fragment of Romanticism", *Modern Language Notes* 96 (1981): 1036.

This, however, was not Coleridge's intent. In actuality, as Edward Bostetter wryly comments, Coleridge

> believed that given the proper conditions he had the power to write great philosophical epics in which from a position of detached omniscience he could erect the imaginative structures whereby all philosophical mysteries were revealed and all human problems resolved.[18]

Indeed, Coleridge employs architectural tropes to elucidate his sense of ideal imaginative structures. In chapter 1 of his famous work of literary criticism, *Biographia Literaria* (1817), he praises some of his favorite poets by saying

> it would be scarcely more difficult to push a stone out from the pyramids with the bare hand, than to alter a word, or the position of a word, in Milton or Shakespeare ... without making the author say something else, or something worse, than he does say.[19]

The pyramid, which elsewhere Coleridge describes as "that base of stedfastness [sic] that rises yet never deserts itself", seems to be his metaphoric archetype for "the language of poetry", by which he means "the formal construction, or architecture of the words and phrases".[20]

Coleridge's architectural idealization of poetic language, I would like to suggest, resulted from his disappointment in the French Revolution. When the revolutionary call for "Liberty, Fraternity, and Equality" turned into a Reign of Terror, he and his friend Robert Southey developed a plan to build their own utopian community in America—along the shore of the Susquehanna River in Pennsylvania, where a group of married couples might exercise liberty, fraternity, and equality in peace. Calling the experimental society "Pantisocracy", Coleridge wrote a sonnet in 1794 ("Pantisocracy") to describe it:

[18] Edward Bostetter, *The Romantic Ventriloquists: Wordsworth, Coleridge, Keats, Shelley, Byron* (Seattle: University of Washington Press, 1963), p. 94.

[19] Coleridge, *Biographia Literaria*, ed. J. Shawcross, 2 vols. (Oxford: Oxford University Press, 1907), 1:15.

[20] Coleridge, *Notebooks*, ed. Kathleen Coburn, Bollingen Series L, 2 vols. (New York: Pantheon, 1957–1961), 2:2342; Coleridge, *Biographia Literaria*, 2:48.

> O'er the ocean swell
> Sublime of Hope, I seek the cottag'd Dell
> Where Virtue calm with careless step may stray,
> And dancing to the moonlight Roundelay,
> The Wizard Passions weave an holy Spell.
>
> (See p. 271, lines 4–8.)

Pantisocracy, meaning "ruled by all", would provide an escape from the "Shame and Anguish" of the revolution's terror (see p. 271, line 3) through the safety of a "cottag'd Dell". Pantisocracy never materialized, largely due to lack of funding. However, "Pantisocracy", the poem, is still with us, signaling where Coleridge next placed his revolutionary hopes: in poetry that might weave holy spells. The perfect citizen of an ideal society was replaced by the poet of "ideal perfection", who can invoke the wizardry of imagination. In chapter 14 of the *Biographia*, Coleridge famously writes,

> The poet, described in *ideal* perfection, brings the whole soul of man into activity, with the subordination of its faculties to each other, according to their relative worth and dignity. He diffuses a tone and spirit of unity, that blends, and (as it were) *fuses*, each into each, by that synthetic and magical power, to which we have exclusively appropriated the name of imagination.[21]

The desire for "magical power" that can "weave an holy spell" is manifest in Coleridge's most famous architectural poem, "Kubla Khan", which describes the poet of ideal perfection:

> I would build that dome in air,
> That sunny dome! those caves of ice!
> And all who heard should see them there,
> And all should cry, Beware! Beware!
> His flashing eyes, his floating hair!
> Weave a circle round him thrice,
> And close your eyes with holy dread,
> For he on honey-dew hath fed,
> And drunk the milk of Paradise.
>
> (See pp. 294–95, lines 46–54.)

---

[21] Coleridge, *Biographia Literaria*, 2:12; emphasis in original.

The poet's construction, emulating the "stately pleasure-dome" decreed by Kubla Khan (see p. 291, lines 1–2), is "in air" because poetry is made with the breath of words, just as the "symphony and song" of the "Abyssinian maid" is made with the intangibles of sound (see p. 294, lines 39, 43).

With the failure of the French Revolution and Pantisocracy to establish paradise on earth, Coleridge seems to sublimate his hopes onto the wizardry of words, words that might create the paradisal space of a poem. Significantly, the lines indented above are preceded with a conditional tense phrase: "*Could* I revive within me/[The Abyssinian maid's] symphony and song, [then]/To such a deep delight 'twould win me,/That with music loud and long,/I would build that dome in air" (see p. 294, lines 42–46; emphasis mine). Readers cannot help questioning whether he *did* revive within himself the symphony and song in order to create a poetic "miracle of rare device,/A sunny pleasure-dome with caves of ice" (see p. 293, lines 35–36). A Preface explaining the origins of "Kubla Khan" answers that he did not. Coleridge explains that, after falling asleep over a book about Xanadu, "all the images [of the poem] rose up before him" (see p. 290) in a dream—until a visitor interrupted the dream. In consequence, most of the poem "had passed away like the images on the surface of a stream into which a stone has been cast" (see p. 290). Thus, the "Huge fragments" that "vaulted" out of Xanadu's "mighty fountain" in his dream (see p. 293, lines 19–21) anticipate the state of the poem that contains them: it is only a fragment. Along with the "Huge fragments" a "sacred river" was "flung up" (see p. 293, line 24), only to sink "in tumult to a lifeless ocean" (see p. 293, line 28), like the poem that sinks—due to tumult—in the poet's imagination.

As though in memory of his "Kubla Khan" experience, Coleridge later writes in the *Biographia* that "men of commanding genius"—like builders of domes (in air or otherwise)—can "exhibit a perfect poem in palace, or temple, or landscape-garden.... But alas! in times of *tumult* they are the men destined to come forth as the shaping spirit of Ruin."[22] Times of

---

[22] Coleridge, *Biographia Literaria*, 1:20–21; emphasis mine.

tumult increasingly seemed to overpower Coleridge, who felt inadequate to produce poetic miracles of rare device.

Ironically, much of Coleridge's tumult resulted from the failure of Pantisocracy. For, in order to establish paradise along the Susquehanna, the planners needed wives for the propagation of their community. Coleridge therefore married a woman he hardly knew (Sara Fricker), simply because her sister was quite conveniently the fiancée of fellow planner Robert Southey. The incompatibility between Coleridge and Sara, along with a debilitating dependence upon laudanum (opium dissolved in water, which doctors had prescribed to ease Coleridge's mounting medical ailments), led to intense dejection about his ability to function as a "poet of ideal perfection". As early as 1800 he writes to John Thelwall, "As to Poetry, I have altogether abandoned it, being convinced that I never had the essentials of poetic Genius, & that I mistook a strong desire for original power."[23] Coleridge's idealized "dome in air", which had replaced his idealized Pantisocratic "cottage", which had replaced the idealized Bastille, was in ruin.

Coleridge gives expression to his ruined hopes in a famous 1802 poem: "Dejection: An Ode". The third stanza reads,

> My genial spirits fail;
> And what can these avail
> To lift the smoth'ring weight from off my breast?
> It were a vain endeavour,
> Though I should gaze for ever
> On that green light that lingers in the west:
> I may not hope from outward forms to win
> The passion and the life, whose fountains are within.
>
> (See p. 398, lines 39–46.)

Fountains, for him, just produce "Huge fragments", like the unfinished "Kubla Khan" and "Christabel". He explains in *Table Talk*,

---

[23] Earl Leslie Griggs, ed., *Collected Letters of Samuel Taylor Coleridge*, 6 vols. (Oxford: Clarendon, 1956–1971), 1:656.

The reason of my not finishing *Christabel* is not, that I don't know how to do it—for I have, as I always had, the whole plan entire from beginning to end in my mind; but I fear I could not carry on with equal success the execution of the idea, an extremely subtle and difficult one.[24]

The problem is not that he has lost his ideals; the problem is that he feels inadequate to fulfill his ideals. As he recounts in "Dejection: An Ode", "afflictions bow me down to earth:/.../Suspend[ing] what nature gave me at my birth,/My shaping spirit of Imagination" (see p. 401, lines 82, 85–86).

Coleridge wrote "Dejection: An Ode" after having been stunned with the beauty of Wordsworth's recently composed "Ode: Intimations of Immortality" (1802). Wordsworth seemed to have the "shaping spirit of Imagination" that Coleridge lacked. In fact, it was "Coleridge's awareness of Wordsworth's greatness as a poet", argues McFarland, that "constituted part of the reason for his virtual abandonment of his poetic ambitions."[25]

In contrast to Coleridge, Wordsworth's ability to keep writing poetry landed him the honor of England's poet laureate. Ironically, the poet laureate before him was Robert Southey, Coleridge's friend who gave up on Pantisocracy—only to write reams of mediocre verse. Perhaps Wordsworth and Southey maintained their poetic output because, unlike Coleridge, they did not idealize "domes in air" as "miracle[s] of rare device".

III

In *The Starlit Dome*, G. Wilson Knight remarks that the contrast between Wordsworth's unfinished sheepfold in "Michael" (1800) and the "flashing dome in 'Kubla Khan' almost distinguishes the two poets". Knight does not follow through on the implications of this statement, because "Wordsworth is too full of surprises for that."[26] But we can see an interesting irony in his

---

[24] Coleridge, *Table Talk*, 4th ed. (London: Routledge, 1884), p. 223.

[25] McFarland, *Romanticism and the Forms of Ruin*, p. 344.

[26] G. Wilson Knight, *The Starlit Dome: Studies in the Poetry of Vision* (London: Oxford University Press, 1941), p. 37.

distinction: Wordsworth's incomplete circle of stones occurs in a finished poem, while Coleridge's circular dome is part of a fragment. Like those of Coleridge, Wordsworth's descriptions of architecture illuminate his attitude toward poetry: an attitude markedly different from that of his friend's.

Throughout Wordsworth's work appear architectural forms that are either in ruin or remain incomplete, like Michael's sheepfold. Take, for example, his 1800 inscription poem entitled "Lines Written With a Slate Pencil upon a Stone, the Largest of a Heap Lying Near a Deserted Quarry, upon One of the Islands at Rydal". In contrast to Coleridge's desire to "build" a poem like the "stately pleasure-dome" of Kubla Khan, Wordsworth describes "a little Dome / Or Pleasure-house, once destined to be built", which is intentionally "unfinished" (see p. 141, lines 5–6, 13). Unlike Kubla Khan, the dome-builder in Wordsworth's poem, a Gothic knight named Sir William, "Desisted" from his task, leaving behind a "hillock of misshapen stones" (see p. 141, lines 1, 5–6, 12–13). Wordsworth ends the poem with advice for all purveyors of idealistic conceptions:

> [I]f disturbed
> By beautiful conceptions, thou hast hewn
> Out of the quiet rock the elements
> Of thy trim Mansion destined soon to blaze
> In snow-white splendour,—think again, and taught
> By old Sir William and his quarry, leave
> Thy fragments to the bramble and the rose:
> There let the vernal slow-worm sun himself,
> And let the redbreast hop from stone to stone.
>
> (See p. 142, lines 27–35.)

Not coincidentally, perhaps, the man described by these lines on a stone—Sir William—bears the same name as the one who inscribed the lines of this poem. The maker of a poem is aligned with the maker of a mound—who is praised for leaving the "rude embryo of a little Dome" unfinished (see p. 141, line 5). In fact, both quarry and mound "Are *monuments* of his unfinished task" (see p. 141, line 13; emphasis mine), seeming to monumentalize the crudeness of the building materials rather than the "splendour" of a finished product.

Wordsworth's poem implies that, rather than "miracle[s] of rare device" woven by wizard spells, domes (in air and otherwise) are made from stoney lumps of language; no matter how "snow-white" a splendid mansion might appear, it is still composed of common everyday things. While Coleridge believes that the poetic imagination can be nearly God-like—"a repetition in the finite mind of the eternal act of creation in the infinite I AM",[27] Wordsworth seems to accept that poetic creations, like the bramble and the rose, are subject to the Fall. Just as the fallen stones of nature's quarry cannot be seen from within the rarified enclosure of a "little Dome" or "trim Mansion", the limits of language cannot be seen within Coleridge's philosophy of "ideal perfection".

Wordworth's "stress on the inadequacy of words" is discussed by David Perkins in his book *The Quest for Permanence*:

> There is, in Wordsworth, a comparative absence of the mixed pain and hope with which romantic and contemporary poets have tended to regard creative achievements. They have tended, that is, to see in the edifices of human thought, usually symbolized in architectural structures or some form of sculpture—Keats' Grecian urn, Yeats' bird of "hammered gold" or "moonlit dome"—a form of immortality which stands in sharp, often ironic contrast to flesh and blood. This is seldom the case in Wordsworth. Instead he insists that even the "consecrated works of Bard and Sage," what seem to be "adamantine holds of truth," will vanish.[28]

Seeming to contradict Perkins' assertion, Wordsworth does employ architectural terms to describe his greatest poetic achievement: "the poem on the growth of my own mind", a

---

[27] Coleridge, *Biographia Literaria*, 1:202.

[28] David Perkins, *The Quest for Permanence: The Symbolism of Wordsworth, Shelley and Keats* (Cambridge, Mass.: Harvard University Press, 1965), pp. 25, 35. Perkins quotes from Wordsworth's *Prelude*, bk. 5, lines 15–42.

fourteen-book work posthumously named *The Prelude*. In a letter to Thomas De Quincey, he describes the poem "as a sort of portico to *The Recluse*, part of the same building", [29] and elsewhere as similar to "the ante-chapel" of "a gothic church".[30] Like most poets, Wordsworth wants to give "Substance and life to what I feel, *enshrining*", as in a gothic church, "the spirit of the past/For future restoration."[31] However, Wordsworth nevertheless recognizes, even if sadly, that language can only provide a fragile shrine:

> Oh! why hath not the Mind
> Some element to stamp her image on
> In nature somewhat nearer to her own?
> Why, gifted with such powers to send abroad
> Her spirit, must it lodge in *shrines* so frail?[32]

IV

In a book entitled *Enlarging the Temple*, Charles Altieri distinguishes Wordsworth from Coleridge by engaging metaphors of enclosure:

> Coleridge's meditations on poetic structure and on the mind's dialectical pursuit of an ideal unity represent an essentially symbolist model.... I call the alternative logical model represented by early Wordsworth an essentially immanentist vision of the role of poetry. Here poetic creation is conceived more as the discovery and the disclosure of numinous relationships within nature than as the creation of containing and structuring forms.[33]

---

[29] Quoted in M. H. Abrams, *Natural Supernaturalism: Tradition and Revolution in Romantic Literature* (New York: Norton, 1971), p. 73.

[30] William Wordsworth, "Preface to *The Excursion* (1814)", in Stillinger, *Selected Poems and Prefaces*, p. 469.

[31] William Wordsworth, *The Prelude, or Growth of a Poet's Mind: An Autobiographical Poem*, in Stillinger, *Selected Poems and Prefaces*, p. 347, bk. 12, lines 284–86; emphasis mine.

[32] Ibid., p. 242, bk. 5, lines 45–49; emphasis mine.

[33] Charles Altieri, *Enlarging the Temple: New Directions in American Poetry During the 1960s* (London: Associated University Presses, 1979), p. 17.

Altieri implies that, just as neo-classical and Gothic architecture coexisted throughout the eighteenth century and into our own, so also do two very different attitudes about poetry. While the Coleridgean vision of poetry reflects a desire for the perfection of a prelapsarian "dome in air" that transcends the discursive limits of language, the Wordsworthian vision recognizes that a "little Dome", like the quarry of components from which it is built, is always already as fallen as the humans who construct it. This distinction, then, might explain the difference in number and content of the two poets' poems. Acknowledging the limits of language, Wordsworth has no illusions about his ability to weave holy spells of linguistic wizardry and hence is able to continue doing the best he can. Coleridge, however, due to his "willing suspension of disbelief" in poetic miracles,[34] ends up suspending belief in his own miraculous abilities. The "quest for permanence" eschewed by Wordsworth thus becomes, for Coleridge, an inquest into his failure.

[34] Coleridge, *Biographia Literaria*, 2:6.

The Romantic Sonnet in England

Michael Hanke
University of Giessen

The Romantics inaugurated the second great era of the English sonnet, the first having been the Elizabethan Age, with Shakespeare as the dominant figure. The genre had fallen into disfavor during the age of classicism and underwent a revival among poets of whom the most prominent was Wordsworth, who wrote hundreds of sonnets.[1]

The "father of the English sonnet" was Sir Thomas Wyatt.[2] A cultural ambassador of Henry VIII in the early sixteenth century, he came across the sonnet in Italy, where Dante and Petrarch had given it a formal perfection and a spiritual refinement, never to be surpassed by their successors. Wyatt relished the form's elegance and divined its potential for a country whose poets, since the death of Chaucer, had failed to keep up with the achievements of their Continental counterparts. In line with the Humanist principle of rivalry through imitation, he began to write Petrarchan sonnets at the English court. But the awkward eloquence of his imitations of the Italian master falls far short of the original. Without the technical means and the abundance of rhyme words at the disposal of the Italians, he was bound to fail.

Wyatt's younger friend Henry Howard, Earl of Surrey, threw off the constraints of the Italian (or Petrarchan) sonnet by devising what is now known as the English (or Shakespearean)

---

[1] See Michael Hanke, ed., introduction to *Fourteen English Sonnets: Critical Essays* (Trier: Wissenschaftlicher Verlag Trier, 2007), pp. 7–18.

[2] See J.W. Lever, *The Elizabethan Love Sonnet*, rev. ed. (1956; repr., London: Methuen, 1966), pp. 14–36, and Michael R.G. Spiller, *The Development of the Sonnet: An Introduction* (London: Routledge, 1992), pp. 83–101, 208–13 (on Wyatt and Surrey).

sonnet.[3] He broke down the original contours of the Italian octave-sestet division with its corresponding rhyme scheme (*abba abba—cde cde*, or some other variant for the sestet) into three cross-rhymed quatrains (*abab cdcd efef*) and the concluding couplet (*gg*), which Wyatt had introduced. He also disposed of the volta, the turn in thought required by the Italian form between the octave and the sestet, which Wyatt had struggled to maintain. With three quatrains now followed by an epigram, the English sonnet may be said to have its sting in its tail, as in Shakespeare's Sonnet 30 or in Michael Drayton's "Since there's no help, come let us kiss and part". Surrey's more adaptable English form has, since Elizabethan times, been favored by writers of sequences (Shakespeare, Drayton, Auden), while writers of individual sonnets (Milton, Wordsworth, Hopkins, Campbell) have retained the Italian form.

In Italy the sonnet had been a vehicle for virtually all subjects and sentiments, from the religious and devout to the heroic, sentimental, and lascivious. But in Elizabethan England most sonnets were, in the tradition of Petrarch, devoted to love. Of course, there had been a religious component in Petrarch's sonnets. His homage to Laura would have been pointless and devoid of emotional depth had he not believed in an afterlife and reunion with his beloved. Wyatt and Surrey, however, eliminated the religious element. Only with the arrival of John Donne did the English religious sonnet become established. The Romantics, with the exception of Wordsworth and Coleridge, avoided religious themes altogether or used the sonnet—as did Keats in his feeble "Written in Disgust of Vulgar Superstitions"—to attack Christianity.

Milton, in the seventeenth century, reacted to the lusciousness and prolixity of the Elizabethans and Jacobeans by advocating austerity. He no longer divides his sonnets into meaning units as dictated by both the English and the Italian sonnet. While following the Italian rhyme scheme, he eschews closure or change between lines 8 and 9, resulting in what Wordsworth

---

[3] See John Fuller's introduction to his anthology *The Oxford Book of Sonnets* (Oxford: Oxford University Press, 2000), pp. xxx–xxxii.

admiringly called a "pervading sense of intense Unity".[4] He uses enjambment to good effect, dissociating syntax and meter. More than any English poet before him, Milton treats personal themes in his sonnets (his blindness, the death of his wife, his religious convictions), but he also uses the sonnet, in Michael Spiller's phrase, as "an instrument in the moral ordering of the commonwealth".[5] His syntax is more involved than that of his predecessors, which earned him a rebuke from Dr. Johnson. Asked how the author of *Paradise Lost* could have got stuck in the lowlands of sonneteering, the great man answered that "Milton was a genius that could cut a colossus from a rock, but he could not carve heads upon cherry-stones."[6]

We recall that in *A Dictionary of the English Language* (1755) Dr. Johnson had defined a "sonneteer" as a "small poet". And he was by no means the only authority to hold the sonnet in low esteem. Pope too had passed severe judgment in his *Essay on Criticism*: "What woeful stuff this madrigal would be/In some starv'd hackney sonneteer, or me?"[7] Not even Shakespeare's sonnets escaped a thrashing, today regarded as paragons of the form and accorded more space in anthologies than those of any other English poet. As late as 1793, George Steevens justified the exclusion of the sonnets from his edition of Shakespeare's works: "We have not reprinted the Sonnets, &c. of Shakespeare, because the strongest act of Parliament that could be framed would fail to compel readers into their service.... Had Shakespeare produced no other works than these, his name would have reached us with as little celebrity as time has conferred on that of Thomas Watson, an older and much more elegant sonneteer."[8]

[4] *The Letters of William and Dorothy Wordsworth: The Later Years, Part 2, 1829–1834*, ed. Alan G. Hill (Oxford: Clarendon Press, 1979), p. 603.

[5] Spiller, *Development of the Sonnet*, p. 23.

[6] See James Boswell, *Life of Johnson*, ed. George Birkbeck Hill, vol. 4 (Oxford: Clarendon Press, 1971), p. 305.

[7] Alexander Pope, *Poetical Works*, ed. Herbert Davis (Oxford: Oxford University Press, 1978), p. 76, part 2, lines 418–19.

[8] George Steevens, "From the Preface of the Plays of William Shakespeare" (1793), quoted in *Shakespeare: The Critical Heritage*, vol. 6, *1774–1801*, ed. Brian Vickers (London: Routledge and Kegan Paul, 1981), p. 577.

In the second half of the eighteenth century, a number of minor poets, many of them women (Anna Seward, Charlotte Smith, Mary Robinson),[9] tried more or less successfully to infuse new life into a form that had fallen into disrepute. So inimical to the sonnet had the cultural climate become that even Wordsworth, the most prolific of the great English sonneteers, with more than five hundred sonnets to his credit, initially took a condescending view of the form, though his first published poem had in fact been a sonnet. He liked some of them, Charlotte Smith's in particular, but was not moved to direct his poetic potentialities toward that form. Not until 1802, after having forged a distinctive style of his own marked by a combination of dramatic and lyric powers, did he become a convert to the art of the sonnet.

On May 21, 1802, Wordsworth's sister, Dorothy, read him some of Milton's sonnets. He "took fire" and wrote three sonnets that same afternoon.[10] His biographer Stephen Gill is certain that Wordsworth's desire "to align himself with Milton" was not just an older man's "fiction about the conjunction of genius".[11] Had it been no more than that, how would he have been able to produce, within a few months, several of his finest sonnets? Among these are "Composed upon Westminster Bridge", "It is a beauteous evening, calm and free", "To Toussaint L'Ouverture", and "London, 1802" ("Milton! thou should'st be living at this hour").[12] This last sonnet is his deepfelt homage to Milton, "the only figure he was prepared to acknowledge as having fired his ambition to excel in the sonnet form and as having swayed his practice".[13] It is motivated by

---

[9] See Daniel Robinson, "Reviving the Sonnet: Women Romantic Poets and the Sonnet Claim", *European Romantic Review* 6 (1995): 98–127.

[10] See Raymond Dexter Havens, *The Influence of Milton on English Poetry* (1922; repr., New York: Russell and Russell, 1961), p. 529.

[11] Stephen Gill, "William Wordsworth: 'Composed upon Westminster Bridge, September 3, 1802'", in Hanke, *Fourteen English Sonnets*, p. 55.

[12] William Wordsworth, "London, 1802", in *The Romantic Poets*, ed. Joseph Pearce and Robert Asch, vol. 1, Ignatius Critical Editions (San Francisco: Ignatius Press, 2014), p. 159, line 1. Subsequent quotations from this edition will be cited in the text.

[13] Gill, "Wordsworth: 'Composed upon Westminster Bridge'", p. 54.

nostalgia and admiration for past poetic grandeur, a monument to the poet in the service of liberty (as Milton and Wordsworth understood it). It also marks a new beginning. It is the first in the English tradition of eulogies in sonnet form to great poets and artists, among which are Coleridge's "To the Author of *The Robbers*", Shelley's "To Wordsworth" (a wittily critical tribute), Keats' "On First Looking into Chapman's Homer", Hopkins' "Henry Purcell", and Campbell's "Luis de Camões".

Several motives animated the Romantics to take up the sonnet. For one thing, they felt an understandable need to throw off what they considered the tyranny of the heroic couplet and the polished but stilted and artificial diction of the followers of Dryden and Pope. They were also reacting against the arrogance and didacticism of classical literature and criticism, and they rejected wit, satire, and moral reflection at the expense of a more personal and intimate tone. Their conception of poetry—with the exception of Byron—was diametrically opposed to the classicists who had believed that even the greatest of English poets, Chaucer, Spenser, and Shakespeare, were but detours on the path leading to the golden age of English poetry in the eighteenth century.

Pope, the arch poet and apex of classicism, had defined poetic wit as "what oft was thought but ne'er so well expressed", while Wordsworth set against this concept originality, individuality, and "the spontaneous overflow of powerful feelings".[14] In rehabilitating the sonnet, the Romantics cleared the air for a new kind of poetry in harmony with their search for a natural, expressive poetic diction that should, according to Wordsworth, be the language of "a man speaking to men".[15] Milton's capacity for combining in his sonnets the intricate rhyme scheme of the "legitimate" (Italian) form with daring technical innovations, his passionate intensity, and subjectivity proved to be precisely what the Romantics needed to demonstrate the viability of a form that the classicists had held

---

[14] Wordsworth and Coleridge, *Lyrical Ballads*, ed. R.L. Brett and A.R. Jones (London: Routledge and Kegan Paul, 1971), p. 246.
[15] Ibid., p. 255.

in the same contempt as the ballad, which Wordsworth and Coleridge had already triumphantly resurrected in their *Lyrical Ballads*.

Wordsworth introduced his poetry collection of 1807 with the sonnet "Nuns fret not at their Convent's narrow room", in which he defends the form and rejects the notion then still in vogue of the limitations of the sonnet:

> In truth, the prison unto which we doom
> Ourselves, no prison is: and hence for me,
> In sundry moods, 'twas pastime to be bound
> Within the Sonnet's scanty plot of ground:
> Pleased if some Souls (for such there needs must be)
> Who have felt the weight of too much liberty,
> Should find brief solace there, as I have found.
>
> (See p. 153.)

The sonnet's supposedly "scanty plot of ground" turns out to be no less than "a sanctuary in which the mind can reflect upon the vast vistas of thought or experience".[16] The allegedly restrictive space of the sonnet is paradoxically redefined as a liberating challenge to poets willing—and able—to submit to the dialectics of nature and art. One is reminded of Goethe's final statement in his sonnet on the pain and pleasure of sonnetizing: "Wer Großes will, muß sich zusammenraffen:/In der Beschränkung erst zeigt sich der Meister,/Und das Gesetz nur kann uns Freiheit geben"[17] (Who desires greatness must concentrate powers:/Mastery's measured in minutes, not hours,/And the law alone makes us free).

In a later sonnet, "Scorn Not the Sonnet", Wordsworth asserts that the form is particularly suited for expressing the poet's deepest personal feelings and implicitly recommends the autobiographical approach to Shakespeare's sonnets, which was to dominate critical readings for more than a century:

---

[16] Frederick Burwick, "'Narrow Rooms' or 'Wide Expanse'? The Construction of Space in the Romantic Sonnet", *Studien zur englischen Romantik* 14 (2001): 52.

[17] Johann Wolfgang Goethe, "Natur und Kunst, sie scheinen sich zu fliehen" (1800), in Goethe, *Gedichte*, ed. Erich Trunz (Munich: Beck, 1999), p. 245.

Scorn not the Sonnet; Critic, you have frowned,
Mindless of its just honours; with this key
Shakespeare unlocked his heart; the melody
Of this small lute gave ease to Petrarch's wound;
A thousand times this pipe did Tasso sound;
With it Camöens soothed an exile's grief;
The Sonnet glittered a gay myrtle leaf
Amid the cypress with which Dante crowned
His visionary brow: a glow-worm lamp,
It cheered mild Spenser, call'd from Faery-Land
To struggle through the dark ways; and when a damp
Fell round the path of Milton, in his hand
The Thing became a trumpet; whence he blew
Soul-animating strains—alas, too few! (See pp. 266–67.)

One of the best and certainly the best loved of Wordsworth's sonnets is "Composed upon Westminster Bridge, September 3, 1802":

Earth has not anything to shew more fair:
Dull would he be of soul who could pass by
A sight so touching in its majesty:
The City now doth like a garment wear
The beauty of the morning; silent, bare,
Ships, towers, domes, theatres, and temples lie
Open unto the fields, and to the sky;
All bright and glittering in the smokeless air.
Never did sun more beautifully steep
In his first splendor valley, rock, or hill;
Ne'er saw I, never felt, a calm so deep!
The river glideth at his own sweet will:
Dear God! The very houses seem asleep;
And all that mighty heart is lying still! (See p. 154.)[18]

---

[18] Also, see Hermann J. Weiand, "William Wordsworth: 'Composed upon Westminster Bridge, September 3, 1802'", in *Insight III: Analyses of English and American Poetry*, ed. Reinhold Schiffer and Hermann J. Weiand (Frankfurt am Main: Hirschgraben, 1969), pp. 338–44; and Gill, "Wordsworth: 'Composed upon Westminster Bridge'", pp. 53–65. For Wordsworth's sonnets in general see Lee M. Johnson, *Wordsworth and the Sonnet* (Copenhagen: Rosenkilde and Bagger, 1973).

The date of composition given in the title is not correct. It is likely that the sonnet was begun on July 31, 1802, when Wordsworth and his sister were on their way to France. Thirteen years after the French Revolution, which he had warmly welcomed until shocked out by the Terror, and after ten years of war, Wordsworth was hoping to meet his former love Annette Vallon and their daughter, Caroline, and to settle financial matters with her before marrying Mary Hutchinson in October 1802. Stephen Gill points out that by crossing the English Channel, "Wordsworth would have felt that he was leaving security and delivering himself into the hands of the enemy".[19] Wordsworth had represented England as a nation in decline ("a fen/Of stagnant waters") but, compared to France, as free (see "London, 1802", p. 159, lines 2–3). "From the coach crossing Westminster Bridge passengers could take in at a glance symbols of their nation's history", so that the exclamatory first line "carries its own charge of national pride".[20]

Wordsworth chooses the one moment when the majesty of the metropolis is most apparent, the moment after dawn, before the ugly aspects of urban civilization begin to obliterate it, before "that mighty heart" makes itself heard and the splendour is replaced by smoke and dirt. Wordsworth seems to be subliminally aware that the sonnet is—as Dante Gabriel Rossetti put it—"a moment's monument",[21] a monument far removed from the one presented by Blake in his poem "London", that admirably chilling piece of social criticism to which Wordsworth, as several other of his poems testify, was by no means averse.

The sonnet certainly fits Wordsworth's own conception of poetry as "a man speaking to men", with careful avoidance of archaic diction (the word "temples" indicates his classicizing of the city, with domes and theatres, a kind of utopian

---

[19] Gill, "Wordsworth: 'Composed upon Westminster Bridge'", p. 61.

[20] Ibid., p. 63.

[21] Dante Gabriel Rossetti, "The Sonnet", in *British and American Classical Poems*, ed. Horst Meller and Rudolf Sühnel (Braunschweig: Westermann, 1966), p. 149.

vision of Athens or Rome or Florence) and with a convincing blend of breathless enthusiasm and detailed description, of feeling and seeing. The city is seen in a majestic personification, embodying the beauties otherwise associated with nature. And we have in this sonnet, alongside Keats' sonnet on Chapman's Homer and Shelley's "Ozymandias", the most convincing proof that Wordsworth was right in extolling the "sonnet's scanty plot of ground". Wordsworth was quite happy, in "Composed upon Westminster Bridge" and in most of his sonnets, to make use of the Miltonic precedent. For him, Milton was a master in legitimizing his search for a sonnet form adaptable to his own emotional and mental states, without forcing him to abandon the traditional verse form of fourteen prescriptively rhymed iambic pentameters. The best of his sonnets show "that pervading sense of intense Unity in which the excellence of the Sonnet has always seemed to me mainly to consist".[22]

John Keats' relationship with the sonnet was, by contrast, an on-again, off-again affair. He began by using the original Italian form, reinstating Petrarch's demanding rhyme scheme and sometimes even showing a marked turn in the line of thought between the octave and the sestet, but after having written about two-thirds of his sonnets (not counting a few experimental ones) he resorted to the Shakespearean form with its final couplet. He expresses his doubts as to whether either of the two traditional types was really adaptable to his own poetic intentions in one of his "deviant" sonnets:

> If by dull rhymes our English must be chained,
> And, like Andromeda, the Sonnet sweet
> Fettered, in spite of painèd loveliness,
> Let us find out, if we must be constrained,
> Sandals more interwoven and complete
> To fit the naked foot of Poesy:
> Let us inspect the lyre, and weigh the stress
> Of every chord, and see what may be gained

---

[22] *Letters: Later Years*, Part 2, p. 604.

> By ear industrious, and attention meet;
> Misers of sound and syllable, no less
> Than Midas of his coinage, let us be
> Jealous of dead leaves in the bay wreath crown;
> So, if we may not let the Muse be free,
> She will be bound with garlands of her own.[23]

Keats is bent on endowing the sonnet with the capacity to mutate into whatever shape its momentary occasion requires, and the intricate rhyme scheme (*abcabd cab cdede*) is certainly more "interwoven" than in his other sonnets. Paradoxically, however, the verses seem to be cringing under the overpowering shadow of the old masters. It is hard, in fact, not to discern an undertone of resentment in his somewhat tentative demand for artistic independence. The Elizabethans were unbound by convention. Even in Shakespeare's day there were poets favoring sixteen-line sonnets or unrhymed sonnets.

Keats is much more at ease in the earliest of his famous sonnets, "On First Looking into Chapman's Homer", written at the age of twenty, in October 1816.[24] After having been worried by a long period of writer's block and hoping in vain to find some inspiration on the coast at Margate, he returned disconsolately to London, where his friend Charles Cowden Clarke showed him George Chapman's translation of Homer's epics. The story of Keats' response has become famous. Keats was so carried away by Chapman's rugged vernacular that on his way home he managed to express his excitement in a sonnet that has lost none of its force:

[23] John Keats, "If by dull rhymes our English must be chained", in *The Complete Poems*, ed. John Barnard, 3rd ed. (1973; repr., Harmondsworth: Penguin, 1988), p. 340.

[24] For the biographical background see Robert Gittings, *John Keats* (1968; repr., Harmondsworth: Penguin, 1979), pp. 127–31. The most recent of many interpretations is Rudolf Sühnel, "John Keats: 'On First Looking into Chapman's Homer'" (1998), in Hanke, *Fourteen English Sonnets*, pp. 77–83. On Keats' sonnets in general, see Lawrence J. Zillman, *John Keats and the Sonnet Tradition: A Critical and Comparative Study* (1939; repr., New York: Octagon, 1966).

Much have I travelled in the realms of gold,
And many goodly states and kingdoms seen;
Round many western islands have I been
Which bards in fealty to Apollo hold.
Oft of one wide expanse had I been told
That deep-browed Homer rules as his demesne;
Yet did I never breathe its pure serene
Till I heard Chapman speak out loud and bold:
Then felt I like some watcher of the skies
When a new planet swims into his ken;
Or like stout Cortez when with eagle eyes
He stared at the Pacific—and all his men
Looked at each other with a wild surmise—
Silent, upon a peak in Darien.[25]

Pedants have been pointing out that Keats had confused two passages in William Robertson's *History of America* (it was Balboa, not Cortez, who first caught sight of the Pacific) and faulting the slightly awkward fourth verse as no less serious a blemish than the two or three ink-horn terms necessitated by Keats' use of the demanding Italian rhyme scheme ("demesne" for "dominion", "serene" for "air", and "ken" for "awareness").[26] But apart from the fact that Keats may have been evoking a kind of medieval aura ("fealty", for instance), as if Homer were a writer of romances, no other English sonnet offers in such a pleasurable way the basic principles of the Petrarchan form with its two units. The subject matter dovetails neatly with the two-part structure of the Italian sonnet. Keats had been fleetingly acquainted with Alexander Pope's elegant neo-classical translation of Homer, but it had failed to evince more than mild admiration for Homer's stupendous genius. This biographical background, metaphorically referred to in the octet, where the poet speaks in the role of the Homeric Ulysses ("Much have I

---

[25] John Keats, "On First Looking into Chapman's Homer", in *Complete Poems*, p. 72.
[26] See Cedric Watts, *A Preface to Keats* (London: Longman, 1985), p. 107.

travelled ..."), is followed by the volta, the turn between octet and sestet. Keats' rejuvenating shock at coming upon Homer viva voce in Chapman's exuberantly vital Elizabethan version leaves the young Romantic breathless, but, as the sestet proves, by no means speechless ("Then felt I ...").

The cleavage between present and past, the Augustan Pope and the Elizabethan Chapman, between dutifully expressed admiration from various *points de vue* in the octet, and involvement in the real thing in the sestet, is given sense and shape by Keats' brilliant handling of the form that, like Wordsworth's Westminster sonnet, seems to encompass an ever-widening vista. The two-part structure also shines through, not only in the choice of rhyme words but also in the subtle modulation from fairly conventional images in the octet to striking similes in the sestet. Keats' predilection for sharp contours, finely chiselled periods, and metrical elegance—not as far from Pope as he might have wished—enables him to put the Italian form at the service of his personal designs and makes one wonder why he should ever have doubted the suitability of the form for English poets.

Keats followed, as we have seen, first the Petrarchan, then, after a period of wavering, the Shakespearean scheme. Wordsworth, Miltonist that he was, preferred the Petrarchan form throughout, while it was left to Shelley to compose, with "Ozymandias", one of only a handful of irregularly rhymed sonnets that are perfect in their formal complexity.[27] This was the result of a competition with his friend Horace Smith in late December 1817. The two poets had set themselves the task of writing a sonnet on the subject of Ozymandias, and both poems were published, as Keats' Chapman's Homer sonnet had been, a few weeks later in the journal *The Examiner*. There have been heated discussions among source hunters as to where Shelley drew the material for the following desolate scene:

[27] See Anne Janowitz, "Shelley's Monument to Ozymandias", *Philological Quarterly* 63 (1984): 477–91; William Freedman, "Postponement and Perspectives in Shelley's 'Ozymandias'", *Studies in Romanticism* 25 (1986): 63–73; and Michael Ferber, "Percy Bysshe Shelley: 'Ozymandias'", in Hanke, *Fourteen English Sonnets*, pp. 67–75.

I met a traveller from an antique land,
Who said—"Two vast and trunkless legs of stone
Stand in the desert ... near them, on the sand,
Half sunk a shattered visage lies, whose frown,
And wrinkled lip, and sneer of cold command,
Tell that its sculptor well those passions read
Which yet survive, stamped on these lifeless things,
The hand that mocked them, and the heart that fed;
And on the pedestal these words appear:
My name is Ozymandias, King of Kings,
Look on my Works ye Mighty, and despair!
Nothing beside remains. Round the decay
Of that colossal Wreck, boundless and bare
The lone and level sands stretch far away."[28]

Critics agree that Shelley must have known Booth's trans-
lation of Diodorus Siculus' account of the statue and its
inscription in his *Biblioteca historica*: "This piece is not only
commendable for its greatness, but admirable for its cut and
workmanship, and the excellency of the stone. In so great a
work there is not to be discerned the least flaw, or any other
blemish. Upon it there is this inscription: 'I am Osymandias,
king of kings; if any would know how great I am, and where I
lie, let him excel me in any of my works.'"[29]

This description is in striking contrast to the features of
Shelley's tyrant, since the inscription quoted by Diodorus
describes an intact, not time-worn, weather-beaten figure. The
poem's statue is the poet's, and its wreckage constitutes an ima-
ginative procedure of the highest order, given Shelley's aver-
sion to all forms of tyranny. The poem is soaked through with
irony. Ozymandias' arrogant claim of being "King of Kings",
with its biblical (and thus blasphemous) ring, has long been
turned against him, and no "willing suspension of disbelief"[30]

[28] Percy Bysshe Shelley, "Ozymandias", in *The Poems of Shelley*, ed. Kevin
Everest and Geoffrey Matthews, vol. 2 (Harlow: Longman, 2000), pp. 310–11.
[29] Quoted in Janowitz, "Shelley's Monument to Ozymandias", p. 481.
[30] Samuel Taylor Coleridge, *Biographia Literaria*, 1817, chap. 14.

would enable even the most sympathetic spectator to imagine the "shattered visage" repeating the preposterous claim. It is the paradoxical confrontation of a seemingly timeless statement cut in stone accompanied by its implicit denial symbolized by the strewn blocks and the vast lifeless desert surroundings. The moral is quite clear: tyrants are ugly (*vide* Ozymandias' face so faithfully reproduced by the sculptor) and in the long run bound to fall. It is not wide of the mark to suspect Milton to be not so much a dominating as an inspiring force behind Shelley's pronouncement of his political credo.

And yet it would be wrong to mistake the poem as optimistic. It is, like the tyrant's visage, Janus-faced. Few readers can have failed to wonder at the fact that the sculptor should have given a lifelike, that is, repelling, portrait of his patron. Did he smile this work to see? It is unlikely. But it is even less likely that Shelley would not have noticed the implication that the consequences of offering too uncomplimentary a portrait might have serious consequences for the artist. Shelley, like Milton, had some experience in such matters—having been relegated from Oxford for his atheism. Suffice it to say that the reader is right to feel slightly uneasy about the artist's fate. Ozymandias may well have outlived him, and we may even doubt whether he would have been seriously troubled by the state of his monument after he had made his way out. The poem ends in a suspended and rather disquieting harmony that calls to mind Auden's belief—in contrast to the view of the classicists—that poetry "is not concerned with telling people what to do, but with extending our knowledge of good and evil, perhaps making the necessity for action more urgent and its nature more clear, but only leading us to the point where it is possible for us to make a rational and moral choice.... Poetry may illuminate but it will not dictate."[31]

The Romantics, Keats and Shelley in particular, have often been castigated—not least by their contemporary Byron—for their blurred emotionalism, for the supposed inaccuracy of their

---

[31] W. H. Auden, ed., *The Poet's Tongue* (London: Bell, 1935), p. ix.

images, and for their slovenly attitude toward form. Despite these attacks, the Romantic masterpieces have refused to cave in. Instead they offer a vital and viable alternative to the older classical concept of the poet as *arbiter literarum et literatorum* (judge of literature and men of letters). Chesterton must be given credit for having drawn attention to the fact that the Romantics brought about a new conception of poetry and its function, a conception that called into question some of the basic principles of European aesthetics. He called it "one vast revolution in the poetical manner of looking at things" and "a vital change in the conception of the functions of the poet".[32] He refers to poems by Goldsmith and Burns—representatives of classicism and Romanticism, respectively—in order to show that the poet as *vates* sitting in judgment as "supreme and absolute critic of human existence"[33] gives way to a "cry out of the very heart of the situation itself, which tells us things which would have been quite left out of account by the poet of the general rule".[34] The sonnets of Wordsworth, Keats, and Shelley document a belief in this permanent value of expressive and creative art.[35]

[32] G. K. Chesterton, *Robert Browning* (1903; repr., London: Macmillan, 1967), pp. 168, 169.

[33] Ibid., p. 169.

[34] Ibid., p. 170.

[35] This essay does not take into account Michael Ferber's recently published *Cambridge Introduction to British Romantic Poetry* (Cambridge: Cambridge University Press, 2013), which devotes an excellent chapter to the sonnet.

The Externalization of the Internal:
Perception in Blake's *Songs of Innocence and of Experience**

Louis Markos
Houston Baptist University

On July 14, 1789, a revolutionary mob seized control of a notorious state prison known as the Bastille. The French Revolution had begun.

On the other side of the English Channel, nineteen-year-old British poet William Wordsworth had just completed his second year at Cambridge. A decade later, Wordsworth would begin work on a poetic autobiography (*The Prelude*) that would eventually swell to epic proportions. In book 11 of *The Prelude*, he would capture, in two immortal lines, what it was like to be a college student in the shadow of the storming of the Bastille:

> Bliss was it in that dawn to be alive,
> But to be young was very Heaven! (lines 108–9)

The Age of Aquarius had dawned over France, and it would only be a matter of time before liberty, equality, and fraternity spread their warming rays over all Europe. To those entrenched in the old power structures of Europe, this might not have seemed like good news, but to the young it seemed to promise nothing less than a return to Eden.

In the famous—or, perhaps, infamous—opening sentence of his *Social Contract* (1762), Jean Jacques Rousseau had boldly proclaimed that man was born free but was everywhere in chains. The year 1789 held out the hope that that insidious process could be reversed, that man could throw off his chains and return to his original state of freedom and innocence.

This essay has been adapted from chapter 1 of his The Eye of the Beholder: How to See the World Like a Romantic Poet *(Hamden, Conn.: Winged Lion Press, 2011).*

To a certain extent city-dwelling Westerners—from fifth century B.C. Athenians, to Renaissance Florentines, to twenty-first-century New Yorkers—have always cast an eye of longing upon the primitive inhabitants of Tahiti or Tibet or the Kalahari. When compared to their own hectic, jaded, inhibited lives, the lives of these noble savages seemed simple, peaceful, and natural. However, while most pre-eighteenth-century writers had treated the myth of the noble savage as a species of nostalgia or wishful thinking, Rousseau turned it into a rallying cry for political action against the corruption of modern civilization. We could be "noble" again, Rousseau promised, if the social-political-religious slate could be wiped clean. The French Revolution seemed to offer up this possibility, not as an idyllic dream of Arcadia or El Dorado or Utopia, but as a historical reality.

Indeed, it held out an even greater possibility: that our internal dreams, hopes, and desires could reshape the external world around us—that we could, quite literally, will ourselves to be free. There would be no need to climb an ice-capped mountain or sail on a black ship over the wine dark sea to find our way to Shangri-La or the fabled land of the Hyperboreans. Here and now, we could transform our *own* world into a utopia of peace and plenty.

In its early stages, the French Revolution had been relatively bloodless, and it seemed to many in Europe that just such a utopia was forming before their very eyes in the charmed city of Paris. In the glow of that hope-filled expectation, British poet William Blake (1757–1827) published a series of deceptively simple poems that celebrate a world in which man and nature are reunited and all division is healed. He titled his collection *Songs of Innocence* (1789), and he peopled it with rich pastoral imagery that fuses into one the Judeo-Christian longing for the Garden of Eden with the Graeco-Roman yearning for the lost Golden Age.

Alas, the new dawn promised by the French Revolution and embodied in Blake's pastoral effusions was never to reach its zenith. The revolution grew increasingly violent and intolerant, culminating in 1793 with the executions of Louis XVI and Marie Antoinette. The shedding of royal blood begat, in its turn, the spilling of rivers of blood, and the would-be Age of Aquarius morphed into the Reign of Terror. Under the tyrannical rule of Robespierre, thousands of aristocrats and out-of-favor revolutionaries lost their heads to the guillotine, a year-long orgy of guilt, fear, and cruelty that only ended when Robespierre himself was beheaded. There was to be no return to Eden, only the forging of a new and heavier chain of oppression. Out of the crucible of the revolution would arise not utopia but Napoleon.

During the height of the Terror, Blake republished his *Songs* in conjunction with a new set of poems, *Songs of Experience* (1794). This time, Blake conjured for his readers a dark, brooding world of angst, dread, and isolation, one in which joy and hope have turned against themselves and sickened into despair. He titled his combined collection *Songs of Innocence and of Experience* and then, that his readers—at least those with eyes to see and ears to hear—might grasp the full meaning and import of his work, he added to it a subtitle: "Shewing [showing] the Two Contrary States of the Human Soul".

Those who would rightly understand Blake's great work and its centrality to the themes and perspectives of the Romantic Age must pay close attention to the wording of the subtitle. For if we overlook it, we are apt to conclude that by "innocence" and "experience" Blake means two different socio-political states: the first of peace and equality, the second of injustice and exploitation. But such was not his intent. By innocence and experience, Blake did not intend to refer to external realities but to internal perceptions.

For Blake, the central question is not whether the world itself is one of innocence or experience; what really matters is how we perceive that world—through eyes of innocence or eyes of experience. On one level, Blake's decision to privilege the way things are perceived over the way they are may be seen as a legacy of the French Revolution. Perhaps if true freedom could not be realized in the social or political realm, it could be cultivated within. Certainly, as the French Revolution—not to mention the later Russian and Chinese Revolutions—demonstrated, if a people who are still enslaved in their minds throw off an oppressor, they will inevitably end up enslaving themselves to a new and harsher taskmaster.

However, Blake's privileging of internal perception over external reality also reflects a general change in the philosophical atmosphere of eighteenth-century Europe, one that shifted the focus from the world around us to the world within us.

From Ontology to Epistemology

Traditionally, philosophy, theology, and aesthetics concerned themselves with the essence of things, whether those things were natural or metaphysical, poems or political systems, the idea of Beauty or the attributes of God. This form of philosophy is known as ontology (Greek for "the study of being"); it attempts to determine the thingness of things by exploring their true and original nature, essence, and purpose. As an ontologist, Aristotle wrote a treatise on every field of study known to his age: politics, ethics, physics, rhetoric, poetics, and so forth. In each of his works, Aristotle sought to define all facets of the field under study, to categorize each of those facets in accordance with a classification system, and to rank the importance of each facet against a scale of functionality and/or value.

Ontology, in its varied and sundry forms, continued to dominate philosophy throughout the classical, medieval, and early Renaissance periods; however, by the time of the French Revolution, it was quickly being supplanted by a competing branch of philosophy that, though practiced by thinkers from Aristotle to Augustine to Aquinas, had previously played a relatively minor role. I speak of epistemology ("the study of knowing"), a branch of the philosophical tree that seeks to know not what things are but how are they perceived. Thus, whereas the ontological Aristotle wrote a treatise on every field of knowledge, the epistemological Kant (1724–1804) wrote a separate treatise on each of the mental faculties (or modes of thought) by which we perceive and interact with the world around us.

In his three great *Critiques* (of *Pure Reason*, *Practical Reason*, and *Judgment*), Kant explored the various ways in which our thoughts and perceptions of physical reality give shape, form, and meaning to those realities. In the *Critique of Judgment* (1790), Kant employed a vital distinction between the subject and the object, a distinction much used by epistemologists, especially Edmund Burke, whose *Philosophical Inquiry into the Origin of Our Ideas of the Sublime and the Beautiful* (1756) exerted a strong influence on Kant. Philosophically speaking, a subject is a conscious self that perceives, while an object is an unconscious thing that does not perceive but is, rather, perceived by a subject. Whereas ontologists focus their attention on the object, epistemologists focus theirs on the subject. Indeed, epistemologists go so far as to claim that when people speak of the beauty of a poem, they are not ultimately referring to the beauty of the object (the poem), but to the impact that object exerts on the eye and the consciousness of the subject (the one who reads or recites the poem).

When my daughter (the subject) looks at a flower (the object) and exclaims, "How beautiful!", she is not—according to both Burke and Kant—making an objective statement about the flower itself, but a subjective statement about the mental response that is occurring in her mind. Beauty, that is, resides not in the flower itself (the object), but in the perceiving mind of my daughter (the subject). Or, to say the same thing in common parlance, beauty is in the eye of the beholder.

I would hasten to add here that when Burke and Kant defined our response to art (or nature) as a purely subjective one, they were not thereby advocating a wholesale relativism that would reduce all statements of beauty to mere expressions of personal taste. Still, their carrying of epistemology into the aesthetic realm did, one could argue, open a Pandora's box that would pave the way for a radically interiorized and personalized view of the arts and the artist. In any case, the modern notion that the arts are first and foremost a form of self-expression, rather than an imitation of external truths and realities (whether they be natural or supernatural), does begin here with the philosophical/aesthetic shift from object to subject. Thus, in the same way that the Impressionists captured on their canvases not nature per se but the "impression" that nature made on their senses, so Blake and his Romantic heirs were less interested in faithfully recording the world around them than in projecting their own inner moods onto the surrounding world.

Picture, if you will, two female college seniors returning to their dorm rooms on the same rainy evening. The first, Mary, has just come from the most expensive restaurant in town where her boyfriend of three years has finally overcome his fears of commitment and proposed to her in a devastatingly romantic fashion. The second, Mona, has just come back from a disastrous date during which *her* boyfriend of three years has broken up with her in a devastatingly cruel and insensitive manner. When they log on to the Internet to check their e-mails, they discover that they have both received an assignment from their English professor asking them to study the storm raging outside their windows and write a poem about it. Mary studies the rain and then composes a flowing, joyous paean in which she compares the storm to a universal baptism washing clean all the dirt and sorrow of the world. Mona, after gazing long on the same rain, dashes off a bitter, angry jeremiad fueled by images of fiery darts that fall from the sky and scorch the earth with their fury. Both ladies believe that they are describing the storm, when, in fact, they are describing their own inner mood, a mood which they have projected onto the rain. Mary, buoyed up by a spirit of love, joy, and harmony, discovers that same spirit in the rain. Mona, dragged down by feelings of angst, sorrow, and betrayal, equally discovers her own inner (subjective) feelings in the same (objective) rain.

Could William Blake have read their poems, he would have said that Mary was viewing the world through eyes of innocence, while Mona was viewing the (same external) world through eyes of experience. And could he have placed their two rain poems side by side, he would have found in them a succinct representation of the "two contrary states of the human soul". Mary embodies the mood of Rousseau; Mona that of the Reign of Terror. Nevertheless, though their inner moods of innocence and experience are at variance, they both give birth to their rain poems by the same aesthetic/perceptual process—a process I like to call the externalization of the internal.

The Mind Is Its Own Place

Thus far I have argued that Blake's *Songs of Innocence and of Experience*, which center around speakers who externalize their inner, subjective states, embody the dual legacy of the French Revolution and aesthetic epistemology. But they also betray the influence of two English poets who left a deep and lasting mark on all the British Romantics: William Shakespeare and John Milton.

Shakespeare's *Hamlet* was never far from the minds of the Romantics. Indeed, they saw in the play's central character a young man who shared their own angst and overself-consciousness. When Hamlet tells his treacherous friends, Rosencrantz and Guildenstern, that "there is nothing either good or bad, but thinking makes it so" (Act 2, scene 2, lines 250–51),[1] he voices the very thesis of the *Songs of Innocence and of Experience*. It is our thoughts, whether they be sanguine or melancholy, that shape and affect the world, and not vice versa. In the same conversation, Hamlet complains that Denmark's a prison, and, when Rosencrantz and Guildenstern counter that if it be a prison, it certainly is a large and spacious one, the moody young Prince explains that size has nothing to do with it: "O God, I could be bounded in a nutshell and count myself a king of infinite space, were it not that I have bad dreams" (Act 2, scene 2, lines 253–55). The imprisonment Hamlet complains of resides in his mind, not in the thick walls

---

[1] All quotations from *Hamlet* are from William Shakespeare, *Hamlet, Prince of Denmark*, ed. Joseph Pearce (San Francisco: Ignatius, 2008).

of the castle of Elsinore. As long as his inner state remains dark and constricting, the castle will appear equally claustrophobic.

A generation later, Milton would explore more fully the relationship between inner mood and outer world in two exquisite companion poems titled "L'Allegro" ("the happy one") and "Il Penseroso" ("the pensive one"). Both take place against the same natural landscape, but in the poems, that landscape is perceived from the point of view, first of a sanguine and then of a melancholy speaker. The first, a lover of the day, rejoices in the life, freshness, and spontaneity that surround him; the second, a creature of the night, broods on images of death, horror, and decay. The two speakers prefigure powerfully the inhabitants of Blake's twin states of innocence and experience. Blake surely cast his eye back on these two lyrical, and quite experimental, poems, but even they exerted less of an influence than did two pregnant lines from Milton's *Paradise Lost*: "The mind is its own place, and in itself/Can make a Heaven of Hell, a Hell of Heaven" (lines 254–55).

Blake, as both a thinker and a poet, took seriously the idea that the mind is its own place and used it as the framework upon which he built his *Songs of Innocence and of Experience*. Those who read these unforgettable poems will remember "innocence" and "experience" as places, but those places exist less in the real world of history than in the happy or tormented mind of their speakers. Rather than attempt to survey the many poems that make up Blake's *Songs*, I shall consider briefly three representative poems that help define the overall shape and import of the collection.

The first, "The Clod and the Pebble", appears in *Songs of Experience*, but Blake could equally well have used it as the frontispiece for the entire work. For, in this single poem, Blake allows us to study side by side the contrary states of innocence and experience.

> "Love seeketh not Itself to please,
> Nor for itself hath any care;
> But for another gives its ease,
> And builds a Heaven in Hell's despair."

So sang a little Clod of Clay
Trodden with the cattle's feet:
But a Pebble of the brook,
Warbled out these metres meet:

"Love seeketh only Self to please,
To bind another to its delight;
Joys in another's loss of ease,
And builds a Hell in Heaven's despite."[2]

If we were to judge the lives of the Clod and the Pebble solely on the basis of their physical situation, we would clearly prefer the life of the latter. While the soft Clod lives in filth, unable to maintain even its own shape and integrity, the hard Pebble is washed clean by the cool, flowing brook. Just as most people, to paraphrase an old song, would rather be a hammer than a nail, so would most, if forced to choose, select the protected existence of the Pebble over the utter vulnerability of the Clod. Surely, the reader concludes, the Pebble lives in the world of innocence, and the Clod lives in the world of experience.

But the conclusion is too hasty. Though their external, bodily circumstances seem to suggest this categorization, the internal state of their mind/soul (psyche in Greek) reveals just the reverse. The Clod dwells in innocence, for it perceives and interacts with the world around it through "eyes" of love, mercy, and generosity. It gives of itself in the most radical way, and, because it does so, it is able to transform its hellish existence into a heaven of contentment and joyous surrender. The Pebble, on the other hand, is grasping, manipulative, and self-centered. It is incapable of moving out of itself or of taking joy in the ease of others. Blinded by selfishness, it is locked firmly in the world of experience, and thus transforms its heavenly surroundings into a hell of spite and envy.

---

[2] William Blake, "The Clod and the Pebble", in *The Romantic Poets*, ed. Joseph Pearce and Robert Asch, vol. 1, Ignatius Critical Editions (San Francisco: Ignatius Press, 2014), p. 34. Subsequent quotations from this edition will be cited in the text.

In the contrasting psyches of the Clod and the Pebble is made manifest the truth of the passage from *Paradise Lost*: "The mind is its own place, and in itself/Can make a Heaven of Hell, a Hell of Heaven." Of course, we need neither Milton nor Blake to "prove" this truth to us. Have we not all known Clods and Pebbles? Have we not met at least one quiet, unassuming woman who, though she has suffered terrible sexual and emotional abuse, continues not only to trust in goodness but to shower compassion upon those who have suffered far less than she? Have we not met at least one privileged son of a rich father who yet looks upon the world with weariness, thanklessness, and cynicism?

The message of the poem both echoes and embodies the four blessings and woes that Jesus pronounces in the Gospel of Luke (see 6:20–26). Like those whom Jesus proclaims blessed in their poverty, hunger, weeping, and rejection, the Clod will laugh and be satisfied and leap for joy. And not just in the heaven to come, Blake suggests, but here, now, in the midst of its woe and oppression. The Pebble, in contrast, is like those who Jesus says are rich and well fed, who laugh and are spoken well of by men. A time will come when they shall hunger and weep, and that time, Blake again suggests, is even now. No, Blake reveals to us, it is not the Clod but the Pebble that we should pity—both in this life and the next.

I do not mean to imply that Blake is adding a new dimension to the words of Jesus. What Blake "adds" is already implicit in Jesus' teachings. Blake significantly structures his first and third stanzas around the Clod and Pebble's differing definitions of love. What the Pebble calls love is not love at all but a justification for narcissism and self-righteousness. But the Clod's true understanding of love captures fully the Christian understanding of God's unconditional and sacrificial love (*agape* in Greek; *caritas* in Latin; charity in English).

In two companion poems—one printed in *Songs of Innocence*, the other in *Songs of Experience*—that bear the same title ("The Nurse's Song"), Blake explores further the contrasting ways that love is defined by a self-giving psyche who views the world through eyes of innocence, and a self-centered psyche who views the same world through eyes of experience. Let us consider first the one from *Innocence*:

> When the voices of children are heard on the green
> And laughing is heard on the hill,
> My heart is at rest within my breast
> And everything else is still.
>
> "Then come home my children, the sun is gone down
> And the dews of night arise;
> Come, come, leave off play, and let us away
> Till the morning appears in the skies."
>
> "No, no, let us play, for it is yet day
> And we cannot go to sleep;
> Besides, in the sky, the little birds fly
> And the hills are all cover'd with sheep."
>
> "Well, well, go & play till the light fades away
> And then go home to bed."
> The little ones leaped & shouted & laugh'd
> And all the hills echoèd.[3]

Blake's nurse (or nanny, as we would call her in America) perceives the world through a heart that is as innocent and carefree as those of the children she watches. She feels no envy toward them but takes delight in their simple play. Her entire being rests calmly and trustingly in a state of peace and harmony.

Suddenly, the nurse notices that twilight is beginning to fall and that it will soon be unsafe for the children. She beckons them to leave the playground and return with her to their homes, promising that they will resume their play when the sun rises anew. But the children are too excited to leave yet,

[3] William Blake, "The Nurse's Song", in *English Romantic Poetry and Prose*, ed. Russell Noyes (New York: Oxford, 1956), p. 203.

and so, like countless children throughout time and culture, they beg their kind nurse for five more minutes … and she acquiesces.

Some mothers who read this poem might scold the nurse for her indulgence, but she neither harms nor endangers the children by giving in to their request. Rather, she shows herself capable of entering in to the joy and laughter of the children, of seeing the world through their eyes. Rather than impose her own adult worries—and *fatigue*—upon the innocent children, she allows herself to be rejuvenated by their youthful joy and energy.

Not so the nurse of experience who crushes their joy and energy, rather than allowing it to bubble up within her:

> When the voices of children are heard on the green
> And whisp'rings are in the dale,
> The days of my youth rise fresh in my mind,
> My face turns green and pale.
>
> Then come home, my children, the sun is gone down
> And the dews of night arise;
> Your spring & your day are wasted in play,
> And your winter and night in disguise.[4]

The first thing a reader should notice when taking up this poem is that its opening line is identical to that of the previous poem. Only in the second line does the wording change—and what a sad change it is. Whereas the former nurse hears "laughing", the latter hears only "whisperings". Paranoid and mistrustful of the intentions of the children, the nurse of experience shields herself behind an "adult-versus-child" mentality that prevents her from participating in the innocent play of the children.

Indeed, their innocent play, far from rejuvenating her, inspires deeper envy and jealousy. In response, her face turns "green", a color which in the grass signifies life and health, but which in the human face signifies sickness and dis-ease.

---

[4] Ibid., p. 205.

And that sickness spreads its dis-ease over the whole poem. Not only is this poem half the length of the former one, but the voices of the children are completely erased, squelched, it seems, by the bitter and warped psyche of the narcissistic governess.

There is little chance that this nanny will grant the children extra playtime. Rather, she attempts to indoctrinate her innocent charges with her own spiteful view of the world. All is falseness, she teaches them; all is disguise. Play is a useless pastime that will do them no good. Her world is one of division and hypocrisy that keeps her perennially separated from the very children she claims to care for.

Neither of Blake's nurses has visited Paris, but they do not need to. The first embodies the naïve hope for liberty, equality, and fraternity that the French Revolution promised to bestow on all of Europe. The second, imprisoned by hate and bitterness, carries the Reign of Terror within herself. She is like the demon Mephastophilis of Christopher Marlowe's *Doctor Faustus*, who, when asked by Faust why it is that he is not confined to Hell, replies simply: "Why this is hell, nor am I out of it" (Act 1, scene 3, line 76).

CONTRIBUTORS

Robert Asch is an English critic, specializing in the nineteenth and early twentieth centuries. Educated in London and Toronto, he spent most of the 1990s in Central Europe and presently lives in France with his wife and children. He is a cofounder and coeditor of the *Saint Austin Review*, and editor of the Saint Austin Press. He is currently translating Léon Bloy and preparing an annotated edition of Lionel Johnson's writings.

Raimund Borgmeier is professor emeritus of English Literature at the University of Giessen, Germany. He has been visiting professor of English at the University of Wisconsin in both Madison and Milwaukee. His research fields are Shakespeare, eighteenth-century and Romantic poetry and culture, special genres (science fiction and crime fiction), nineteenth-century fiction, and contemporary literature. In 2000, he was honored with the Festschrift *Lineages of the Novel: Essays in Honour of R. B.*, ed. B. Reitz and E. Voigts-Virchow.

Crystal Downing received her Ph.D. from the University of California, Santa Barbara, and is a distinguished professor of English and Film Studies at Messiah College in Pennsylvania, where she teaches British Romantic Literature. Her three books explore the relationship between Christianity and post-structuralism: *Writing Performances* (2004); *How Postmodernism Serves (My) Faith* (2006); and *Changing Signs of Truth* (2012).

Michael Hanke obtained his Ph.D. and his habilitation at German universities. He taught English Literature at the universities of Hamburg, Duisburg, and Gießen; has published books on John Crowe Ransom, Roy Campbell, and German Expressionist poetry; has written many articles on English literature; and has edited several collections of critical essays.

Louis Markos is a professor in English and scholar in residence at Houston Baptist University and holds the Robert H. Ray Chair in Humanities; he is author of *From Achilles to Christ*, *Pressing Forward: Tennyson and the Victorian Age*, *Apologetics for the 21st Century*, and *Eye of the Beholder: How to See the World Like a Romantic Poet*.

Joseph Pearce is writer in residence and director of the Center for Faith and Culture at Aquinas College in Nashville, Tennessee. He is the editor of the *Saint Austin Review* and editor of the Ignatius Critical Editions of *Romeo and Juliet*, *Julius Caesar*, *The Merchant of Venice*, *Hamlet*, *Macbeth*, and *King Lear*. He is the author of three books on Shakespeare, published by Ignatius Press: *The Quest for Shakespeare: The Bard of Avon and the Church of Rome* (2008), *Through Shakespeare's Eyes: Seeing the Catholic Presence in the Plays* (2010), and *Shakespeare on Love: Seeing the Catholic Presence in Romeo and Juliet* (2013). He has also published books on a number of modern literary figures, including Oscar Wilde, G. K. Chesterton, Hilaire Belloc, Roy Campbell, J. R. R. Tolkien, C. S. Lewis, and Alexander Solzhenitsyn.